A PATRISTIC TREASURY

Early Church Wisdom for Today

Readings from the Church Fathers
Selected, and with an introduction, by

James R. Payton, Jr.

The Ancient Christian Faith for the Modern World

CHESTERTON, INDIANA

A Patristic Treasury: Early Church Wisdom for Today
Copyright © 2013 James R. Payton, Jr.

All Rights Reserved

Published by:
    Ancient Faith Publishing
    A division of Ancient Faith Ministries
    P.O. Box 748
    Chesterton, IN 46304

Printed in the United States of America

Except where publishers prohibited any change to the quoted material, quotations and citations from the Bible are taken from the New King James Version, © 1979, 1980, 1982 by Thomas Nelson, Inc. Used by permission.

ISBN: 978-1-936270-44-6

to Chris,
my youngest son,
from whom I have learned so much

Contents

Acknowledgments	7
Abbreviations	9
Preface	11
Getting into the Church Fathers	14

PART I: THE ANTE-NICENE FATHERS

Clement of Rome	33
"2 Clement"	36
Ignatius of Antioch	39
Polycarp	44
The Didache	47
The Letter of Barnabas	50
The Shepherd of Hermas	52
The Letter to Diognetus	55
Papias	58
Justin Martyr	59
Athenagoras	69
Theophilus of Antioch	73
Melito of Sardis	76
Irenaeus	85
Hippolytus	107
Novatian	113
Minucius Felix	116
Clement of Alexandria	118
Origen	125
Tertullian	133
Cyprian	148
Lactantius	154

PART II: THE NICENE AND POST-NICENE FATHERS

Eusebius of Caesarea	163
The Desert Fathers and Mothers	169
Pseudo-Macarius	193
Athanasius	214
Cyril of Jerusalem	226
Basil of Caesarea	239
Gregory Nazianzen	246
Gregory of Nyssa	266
John Chrysostom	298
Cyril of Alexandria	323
Hilary of Poitiers	331
Ambrose	337
Rufinus	345
Jerome	350
Augustine of Hippo	356
John Cassian	387
Vincent of Lérins	391
Prosper of Aquitaine	398
Leo the Great	404
Julianus Pomerius	411
Gregory the Great	419
Pseudo-Dionysius	429
Maximus the Confessor	437
John of Damascus	450
Permissions	466

∽ Acknowledgments

I am indebted to many people for their help and encouragement as I have worked on this project. First, I express my gratitude to Daniel Savage, formerly head librarian at Redeemer University College. About twenty-five years ago, he generously gave me the numerous third copies of volumes in the Ancient Christian Writers series which had come to the library with the rest of the collection purchased from a Franciscan institution. This inaugurated the lengthy project of reading the Church Fathers that has led to this volume.

I also want to thank colleagues at Redeemer University College who have shared my interest in the Church Fathers: David Benner (now Distinguished Professor of Psychology at the Psychological Studies Institute in Atlanta, Georgia), Jacob Ellens, David Koyzis, and Wayne Norman (now Professor of Psychology at Simpson University, in Redding, California) have all contributed to this project by the discussions I have enjoyed with them on patristic topics over the years.

Redeemer University College awarded me a sabbatical for the winter term of 2012, which allowed me to work on this material and bring it into publishable form, and a grant to help defray the costs of obtaining permissions to republish excerpts not in the public domain. For this assistance and for the privilege of teaching upper-level church history courses in which I have been able to explore Christian antiquity with my students over the last quarter-century, I am truly thankful to this institution, where I have spent most of my scholarly career.

To other institutions that afforded me the opportunity to carry my work in patristics further by teaching seminary-level and graduate courses in the field, I also express my gratitude: St. Stephen's College of the University of Alberta (in Edmonton, Alberta), as Adjunct Professor of Orthodox Doctrine and Spirituality; McMaster Divinity College (in Hamilton, Ontario), as Adjunct Professor of Christian History; Evangelical Theological Seminary (in Osijek, Croatia), as Guest Professor in Ecumenics; and Matthias Flacius Illyricus Faculty of Theology (in Zagreb, Croatia), as Guest Professor in Patristics. These interdenominational and international experiences underlined and enriched my appreciation for what the Church Fathers offer the contemporary Church.

I am deeply grateful to the various publishers and authors who granted me permission to republish excerpts from their patristic works. While these are listed at the end of the book under "Permissions," I want to highlight their willingness to cooperate in this project: literally (and legally), I could not have done it without them. In that regard, I express gratitude also to the staff of Copyright Clearance Center for facilitating permissions for several patristic publications.

I express my gratitude to Conciliar Press for their interest in and encouragement of this venture. To the late Fr. Peter Gillquist, a former member of the publications board and someone who became a revered friend, I express appreciation for inviting me to submit the manuscript of this work for consideration. I also want to thank Katherine Hyde and her colleagues, who have been cooperative and helpful in producing the proofs and working with me to bring this project to publication. I appreciate their patience, support, and understanding through the entire process.

Finally, I want to thank my wife and our four children for their patience with me while I was "reading those old books from the early Church again." Over the years, my family put up with my frequent distraction as I worked on this project, they patiently endured my attempts to pass on to them some of what I found exciting in the Church Fathers, and they even managed to become interested in the work themselves. For all that, I cannot thank them enough. This volume is dedicated to my youngest son, Chris, who has always shown special delight in pithy, insightful statements that help us navigate the shoals of life—the kind of fare the Church Fathers so regularly spread before us in their writings.

∽ *Abbreviations*

ACW Walter J. Burghardt, S.J., et al., ed. *Ancient Christian Writers*, 66 vols. Mahwah, New Jersey: Paulist Press, 1946– (originally published by Newman Press, Westminster, Maryland).

ANF Alexander Roberts and James Donaldson, *Ante-Nicene Fathers*, 10 vols., 1885–1896. Peabody, Massachusetts: Hendrickson Publishers, 2004 (4th reprint ed.).

AposFrs Michael W. Holmes, ed. and rev., *The Apostolic Fathers: Greek Texts and English Translations of Their Writings*, 2d ed. Grand Rapids, Michigan: Baker Book House, 1992.

FC *The Fathers of the Church: English Translations of Early Christian Texts*, 124 vols. Washington, D.C.: Catholic University of America Press, 1948–.

LXX The Septuagint.

NPNF (1st) Alexander Roberts and James Donaldson, *Nicene and Post-Nicene Fathers*, First Series (Augustine and Chrysostom), 14 vols., 1886–1900. Peabody, Massachusetts: Hendrickson Publishers, 2004 (4th reprint ed.).

NPNF (2ⁿᵈ) Alexander Roberts and James Donaldson, *Nicene and Post-Nicene Fathers*, Second Series, 14 vols., 1886–1900. Peabody, Massachusetts: Hendrickson Publishers, 2004 (4ᵗʰ reprint ed.).

In the readings that follow, selections from these works will be indicated with the series abbreviation, the number of the volume (except for *AposFrs*, which is a single volume), and the pages on which the patristic document appears. The full text of bibliographical data appears under "Permissions."

∼ *Preface*

Orthodox, Roman Catholics, and Anglicans have long held the Church Fathers in high esteem and looked to them as guides for appropriating and practicing the Christian faith. For most of evangelicalism and other segments of Protestantism, though, reference (and certainly deference) to the Church Fathers has been notable mostly by its absence. Over the last few years, however, that has begun to change.

As the second millennium ended and the third began, a remarkable development has been taking place: among Protestants of all stripes, interest in the works of the Church Fathers has arisen. A considerable number of Protestants have become patristic specialists over the past two decades, and publishing houses that serve a largely Protestant market are bringing out series of volumes offering the exegetical, doctrinal, and devotional insights of the Church Fathers.[1] This is quite a change from what has been the Protestant pattern for centuries.

While the Protestant Reformers of the sixteenth century had shown respect for and deference to the Church Fathers, Protestants of more recent vintage have shown patristic literature scant regard.[2] By and large,

---

1 While other Protestant publishers have recently ventured into this field (such as Wm. B. Eerdmans Publishing Company), the leader in such initiatives is InterVarsity Press, which has produced three series of patristic resources: *The Ancient Christian Commentary on Scripture, Ancient Christian Doctrine,* and *Ancient Christian Texts.*

2 For comment on this, see my *Getting the Reformation Wrong: Correcting Some Misunderstandings* (Downers Grove, IL: IVP Academic, 2010), pp. 236–245; as background, see the treatment of religious authority and the role of the ancient Church for the Protestant Reformers, pp. 132–160.

they have long been content to search for wisdom little further than their own contemporaries or those in their particular denominational tradition. However, in a variety of ways and for various reasons, interest in the Church Fathers has resurfaced in the last few years.

This development can only be welcomed by all those who profess the Christian faith. It has brought Protestants into conversation with Orthodox, Roman Catholics, and Anglicans in a common recognition of the riches of the Church Fathers' writings as the conduit through which the apostolic message has been passed down through the early centuries of the Church's history. Without diminishing the notable differences among these Christian traditions, it is bracing to sense a deeper, shared awareness of and appreciation for the apostolic Tradition upheld, expounded, and defended by the Church Fathers.

The Church Fathers have much to offer contemporary Christianity. The patristic period shows us the Church as it emerged from apostolic labors, the ways it subsequently developed, how it presented and defended the Christian faith, and what the early leaders of the Church thought essential to faith and life. During the patristic period, the Church shared a consensus in the faith, in the face of divergent cultures and languages. At the beginning of the third millennium, multiplied thousands of denominations claimed a place in the ecclesiastical landscape. Shared interests in the Church Fathers might help contemporary Christians find each other again: in the patristic era, we who live in the Church so many centuries later find our roots.

Over the past three decades, I have been engaged in occasional reading of the works of the Church Fathers. My impetus for doing so was not this new Protestant fascination with patristic literature; indeed, I embarked on this venture before I knew anyone else in the contemporary Protestant world had turned in this direction. I began this reading project because of my interest in church history; I simply wanted to get to know this formative period of the Church more immediately.

I found the journey intriguing and enriching. Along the way, I highlighted statements or sections I found stimulating in the patristic works I was reading; in due course, I collated these for my own reflection and use. Students with whom I used this collection in upper-level undergraduate and in graduate church history courses responded with keen interest and expressed appreciation for the exposure it offered them to patristic wisdom and insight. This volume offers this selection of readings as an aid to those who would like to become more familiar with the Church Fathers.

Preface

To assist readers, I should explain how the "locations" of these patristic excerpts can be understood. Some Church Fathers wrote their works in a series of "books"; in that case, references are to the book, followed by the section (or, in some cases, by a chapter and one of its sections), distinguished by appropriate punctuation differences. Others of the Church Fathers organized some of their works by chapters (indicated by "ch." and number). Still others have been divided up by scholars into sections or paragraphs (indicated in this volume by § and the respective number). With some other Church Fathers, the organization flows from the way the original material was delivered (e.g., "Sermon," followed by the number of the sermon). To enable ready comparison with other versions of the Church Fathers' works, I have not indicated the page number(s) where the excerpt is found in the English translations I have used, except where a patristic work is without any such divisions, whether by the Church Father or the scholars who have published the translation; in that case, the page number is given within curled brackets (i.e., {}).

James R. Payton, Jr.
Hamilton, Ontario
May 11, 2012
The Feast Day of Ss. Cyril and Methodius

~ *Getting into the Church Fathers*

The Church Fathers deserve to be better known than they are among contemporary Christians. Patristic[1] works are the "classics" of Christian theology; as with other classics, though, they are regularly lauded but rarely read. Admittedly, working through the whole of patristic literature would be a daunting task: J. P. Migne's *Patrology* runs to some four hundred volumes, with more than a hundred thousand pages of dense Greek and Latin text. However, one can manage a solid acquaintance with the Church Fathers without navigating the seven seas of Migne: some good series have made works of the major (and some of the minor) Church Fathers available in English translation. Working through them is challenging but far from impossible; over the past twenty-five years, I have read through much of the literature from the entire patristic period, from the Apostolic Fathers (beginning in the late first century) through John of Damascus (in the mid-eighth century). The selection of patristic readings that follows in this volume is one of the fruits of that reading.

This collection can serve as a first introduction for those—such as university students and most members of Christian churches—who have not previously been exposed to patristic works. It can also serve as a resource for those—such as clergy, seminary graduates, and others who are not patristic scholars—who may have already studied the Church Fathers and want a handy compendium of patristic readings. I trust that this volume

---

1 *Patristic* is the adjective taken from the Latin *patres* ("fathers"). *Patristics* is the academic designation for the study of the Church Fathers.

will help to increase familiarity with the Church Fathers and be of benefit to Christians living in the early third millennium.

By way of introduction to the readings, we will consider what the designation "Church Father" means, why it can be beneficial to read their writings, the historical sequence that helps us better understand and appreciate what they have to say, and how to approach the readings that follow. Those interested in further reading in the works of the Church Fathers should consult the works and series listed in the appendix ("Permissions"); additional resources are available via numerous websites.

The Designation "Church Father"

Those who have come to be known as "Church Fathers" led Christianity during the first centuries of its existence after the apostles. Not everyone who lived and wrote during that period qualified as a Church Father, though. The designation is an honorific, bestowed at some point subsequent to the author's death. One only qualified as a "Church Father" if he met four tests: antiquity, holiness of life, orthodox teaching, and ecclesiastical approval. These tests distinguished those ancient Christian writers who had been and could be trusted as faithful witnesses to genuine Christian life and teaching. Being accorded the designation "Church Father" was a stamp of approval; it assured that the author's works could be read with confidence and profit.

Why Read the Church Fathers?

Some contemporary Christians might question the value of reading the works of Christian authors from so long ago, but reading the Church Fathers offers many benefits to Christians today. For one thing, the works of the Church Fathers give us access to the Christianity that emerged fresh from the apostles' lives and labors. Patristic literature thus offers us a window on what the early Church had learned from the apostles. For the many today who naively believe that their particular denomination or congregation practices New Testament Christianity, pure and simple, patristic literature can be at once humbling and enlightening.

In addition, whether we today recognize it or not, the patristic era was a critical period for Christianity. We trust it for the delimitation of the New Testament canon. The doctrine of the Trinity we profess was articulated by the Church Fathers, as against several heresies. In embracing the teaching that Jesus Christ had two natures—one divine and one human—in one Person, we take terminology refined by the Church Fathers to confess faith in the Savior. If we follow the architectural metaphor of St. Paul, according to which the apostles and prophets are the foundation of the Church, with Jesus Christ the cornerstone (Eph 2:20), then the patristic period erected the first story of the building—that ecclesiastical edifice in which Christians still live.

The Church Fathers long ago unfolded what it means to think and live as Christians; as the third millennium begins, we can still learn much from them about Christian thought and life. Their times were, of course, much different from the present day; even so, the Church Fathers lived in periods of great social and cultural dislocation, in which momentous changes were afoot—similar enough to our contemporary postmodern (and even post-Christian) situation to make it worthwhile to give them a hearing. Their valiant endeavor to understand their situation, to speak to it responsibly, and thus to navigate the Church through those turbulent waters potentially has much to offer to thoughtful Christians trying to find their way in the early twenty-first century. So getting to know the Church Fathers is not just an exercise in antiquarianism; it has the potential for significant practical benefits for contemporary Christians.

Beyond this, becoming familiar with the great works of the early Church may help contemporary Christians deal with the problem of amnesia that afflicts so much Christian thought and practice today. Especially in North America, we are impressed with the most recent gadgets, latest improvements, and newest technology; that fascination has not served us well in approaching the teaching and practice of Christianity, however. While much contemporary Christian writing calls us to be abreast of new worship and outreach options, and while it is important to know and relate to the issues of contemporary culture, it does not serve us well to remain ignorant of the past that has shaped the Church and the faith we profess. Not to know where we have come from is not a form of freedom; without a past, wisdom is not possible, for wisdom builds on what has been learned through experience. Amnesia of any kind is pitiful; ecclesiastical amnesia can be deadly. The way to develop firsthand acquaintance with the early history of the Church is to read patristic works.

Another good reason for reading the works of the Church Fathers is that their writings are not esoteric pieces intended only for those professionally initiated in theology—quite the contrary, in fact! The Church Fathers wrote for the faithful, not for scholars. They addressed the needs of the Church in their days for instruction, edification, and exhortation. Consequently, much of patristic literature comes to us in sermons or catechetical instruction; apart from references to specific cultural settings that have changed in the meanwhile, such material usually remains accessible to contemporary readers.

To be sure, the Church Fathers also wrote to defend the Christian faith against pagan opponents or heretics; in both cases, though, they sought a clarity that would guide readers to truth, rather than a scholarly profundity that might enlighten only an academic few. Even so, the needs of argument in such conflicts sometimes forced the Church Fathers to wrestle over terminology or to articulate careful responses to complicated alternative positions; these patristic works admittedly make special demands on readers. Given the difficulties inherent in such writings, I have avoided excerpting from their more technical and complicated segments in the selections that appear in this volume. On the whole, though, and in almost all particulars, patristic literature is rarely difficult to understand—but it is almost always challenging to ponder.

Further, patristic literature is not dry and detached; rather, the Church Fathers' works show authors passionately involved with important questions. In patristic literature, a reader can hear the heartbeat in every sentence; in some theological literature in later centuries (e.g., in medieval scholasticism and Protestant scholasticism—but not only there!), it is at times difficult even to detect a pulse. The Christian faith matters profoundly and obviously to the Church Fathers; of that, no reader will have any question.

In that regard, another facet of patristic literature is worth highlighting. Most of the Church Fathers received a thorough training in rhetoric, the area of study that stood as the culmination of ancient education in both the Greek-speaking and the Latin-speaking cultures. In antiquity, communication was an art form, as well as a means of passing on information. Studying rhetoric prepared students to present their opinions in engaging fashion—with well-honed logic, to be sure, but as fitted out with abundant allusions, metaphors, maxims, epigrams, and the whole host of literary artifices that enlivened and beautified both spoken and written communication. Those who mastered the art—and many of the Church Fathers were marvelously proficient in it—could express their views in memorable, pithy, aphoristic ways that conjured up pictures for the mind or offered tasty delights for the discerning palates of their readers. Patristic literature is richly spiced with allusions and axiomatic statements that demand to be savored. The following selections include an abundance of these delicacies.

Moreover, for those impatient with the fragmentation of theological discussions today, when works focus on one or another element of doctrine without particularly indicating how that element relates to the whole, the Church Fathers offer welcome relief. Their writings manifest a doctrinal integrity that offers a wider view onto the significance of any issue they discuss. In this way, they remind us that every element of the Christian faith is related to and bound up with other elements, in a wondrous pattern of complex simplicity.

That leads to another, and very significant, strength of patristic literature. For all the Church Fathers, doctrine is to be experienced, not just talked about. They had no room for the dichotomy between the "head" (i.e., intellectual understanding of doctrine) and the "heart" (i.e., personal, existential appropriation of truth) to which so many Christians have become accustomed in the subsequent history of the Church. For the Church Fathers, doctrine affects and changes life, or it is not true doctrine. For them, not only is all truth interrelated, it also inevitably affects life. Patristic literature is always engaged with the reader, seeking to lead him or her into more faithful Christian discipleship.

More pointedly, in the Church Fathers, all this integrated and compelling truth is related to salvation. All the controversies in which they engaged, all the disputes about the Trinity and Christology, all the concerns regarding lifestyle and discipleship, arose from and were dealt with in relationship to the Christian message of salvation in Christ by the love of God the Father, as applied by the working of the Holy Spirit. In seeking to give voice to the Church's experience of grace and to defend it from misrepresentation, the Church Fathers focused on the core of the Christian message. In so doing, they remind contemporary readers of the one thing that is important in the face of all the other emphases clamoring for attention.

Beyond all this, the Church Fathers are constantly engaged with Scripture. Their works abound in citations of and allusions to it, and they regularly expound it in their writings. Of course, they did not utilize the exegetical approaches that developed only hundreds of years later and often are taken for granted in contemporary biblical scholarship. Patristic exegesis has a robust hermeneutical approach of its own, shaped by a Christ-centered reading of the Old Testament and a confidence that God's Word was packed with allusion and significance. The Church Fathers interpreted Scripture in ways that deserve careful attention and are worth pondering.

The Church Fathers also approached Scripture differently than readers in later centuries have become accustomed to do. One especially intriguing feature of the patristic approach is that it comes to Scripture without the hesitation with which Christians have so often learned to come to it in subsequent periods. Because of the numerous controversies that have bedeviled the history of Christian thought, many Christians commonly come to Scripture with a host of cautions and reactions, which we use to keep us from stumbling into error as we read the Word of God. A reflective Christian may sometimes wonder what it would be like to read Scripture without these blinders in place; the Church Fathers can show the way in that regard. They lived and wrote before most of these controversies; they show no particular unease as they encounter, for example, passages that treat of both faith and works, or grace and human effort, or solid assurance and warning against apostasy. The readiness with which the Church Fathers embrace together emphases that many Christian readers so readily contrast can serve as a reminder of the coherence of scriptural teaching—which many of us stand all too ready to dissect, label, and store in sealed containers. Thus, reading patristic literature can be a wistful exercise, one in which we learn to read the Word of God afresh and allow it to confront us with its full power.

Reading patristic works can also be an exercise in nostalgia. The Church Fathers all lived and wrote in a Church that was one, united in a shared consensus of the faith. While the Church was spread out into different cultural settings, which led to some variations in practice, and although it faced challenges from divergent teachings, the Church during the patristic period maintained its unity.[2] It was not fractured into rival denominations: it managed to remain one.

As the third millennium dawned, the number of denominations had already crested 26,000. In this situation, the only way to embrace the unity of the Church is to vaporize it into an invisible realm or to restrict it to a particular denomination or tradition; neither of these approaches, however, begins to do justice to either biblical teaching or our Lord's own prayer

---

2   I recognize that much recent patristic scholarship has stressed the divergences within Christian antiquity. In my estimation, though, while this has served as a healthy corrective to naive claims about patristic unity, it overstates the case. By comparison with any later period in the history of the Church, what is striking about the patristic era is the wide-ranging consensus among the Church Fathers—which served to maintain ecclesiastical unity in the face of cultural, linguistic, and liturgical differences.

(John 17:17–21). In the present day, we can hardly imagine what it would be like for the entirety of Christ's followers to "be one"; for the Church Fathers, though, that was their reality. Just pondering that tremendous difference between them back then and ourselves today will give us reason to plunge into reading the Church Fathers, to see how they managed to avoid splitting up the Body of Christ.

In this regard, the Church Fathers may be able to help us find each other again in the Church early in the third millennium. The patristic period lasted for seven centuries,[3] and during that time passed through numerous struggles; not surprisingly, this led to differing emphases and concerns in various times and situations. With all this, patristic literature could hardly be blandly uniform or monolithic—and it was not. Even so, the Church Fathers recognized a commonality in faith and life that united them, and that consensus is discernible in the works they wrote. They agreed on the rudiments of Christianity—rudiments Christians today affirm with them. Perhaps patristic literature can guide contemporary Christians, centuries later, in distinguishing the incidental from what is essential, since the Church Fathers keep coming back to what is fundamental to Christianity.

For all these reasons, reading the Church Fathers can be a feast. In what follows in this volume, I have tried to spread the table. From my extensive reading in patristic literature, I have culled out selections I found to be devotionally stimulating, doctrinally thought-provoking, or epigrammatically striking. I recognize that others might well have included some passages that do not appear in this collection, and that some readers may find certain of the following selections less than personally enriching. I can say, though, that I have tasted and seen that these are good; I hope that many readers will enjoy what is set before them. The selections that follow in this volume offer insights, teachings, and perspectives on the Christian faith that open up how to live faithfully before God in the hurly-burly of everyday life—not only for the patristic period, but for the third millennium as well.

---

3 Since Orthodoxy stands firmly on patristic bases, it is common among Orthodox to assert that patristic *teaching* still continues; in common usage, though, the patristic *period* is seen as coming to a close with the last of the universally recognized Church Fathers, John of Damascus, who died in the mid-eighth century.

Differentiating Among the Church Fathers

Given that the patristic period lasted for some seven centuries, it is not surprising to find differences of emphasis and orientation within the large corpus of patristic literature. Even so, the Church Fathers were conscious of their responsibility to their forebears, and more ultimately to the apostles and Christ, to maintain the Christian faith unchanged and undefiled. That common commitment did not preclude variations in experience, outlook, background, or emphasis, though, as the Church passed through the centuries. Because of all this, the most helpful way to distinguish among the Church Fathers is to do so chronologically.

Within the sweep of the patristic period, the most dramatic difference is the one between the experience of the Church before and after the conversion of Constantine. Until Constantine, Christianity was an illegal religion, periodically exposed to persecution and without any sure rights before the government. At a critical juncture in Constantine's life, he came to favor Christianity; with his eventual elevation to the imperial throne in 312, his positive orientation toward Christianity resulted in a dramatic change in the fortunes of the Church. From his time onward, the Christian Church enjoyed privileged status. The most common way of distinguishing these different periods is with reference to the Council of Nicea in 325, which Constantine convened to deal with some issues within the Church. The two periods have come to be known as the "ante-Nicene" period and the "Nicene and post-Nicene" period.

Beyond that, another distinction became evident within the Church, already before the Council of Nicea, but especially after it—that between the Greek-speaking and the Latin-speaking segments of the Church. The Roman Empire, within which the Church had grown, had long known two distinct major cultures. One was the Latin culture, which stemmed from Rome, the capital and the most important city in the western half of the empire; the other was the Greek culture, which had arisen during the Hellenistic period inaugurated by the conquests of Alexander the Great in the fourth century BC, through which Greek cultural attitudes and practices permeated what would later become the eastern half of the Roman Empire. These two cultures were unmistakably different, even within the confines of the single Roman Empire. As the Church had spread throughout that empire, it had responded to and developed within each of those cultures. This occasioned no differences in basic Christian faith, to be sure, but the teaching and practice of Christianity in each segment had taken on the distinctive hues of that culture. This began to become evident only in the late ante-Nicene period; it became much more pronounced in the Nicene and post-Nicene period.

Thus, the following selections will be divided between the ante-Nicene Fathers and the Nicene and post-Nicene Fathers, with the latter group also being distinguished by whether they were Latin or Greek Church Fathers. Beyond that, we will distinguish the Nicene and post-Nicene Fathers according to whether they lived and wrote in the fourth and fifth centuries (an age of great productivity and controversy for the whole Church) or the sixth through eighth centuries (the last segment of the patristic period).

Ante-Nicene Fathers

The Church Fathers who lived before the Council of Nicea include those immediately after the apostles (some of whom had known the apostles) through those who lived during the incredible change inaugurated by the conversion of Constantine. Throughout this period, the Church was exposed to pressure and persecution from the government, owing to the Church's status as an illegal religion in the Roman Empire. Beyond this external pressure, the Church experienced growing pains as it proclaimed the Christian message and showed what difference it must make to those who embrace it. Doing so required instructing Christ's disciples in faithfulness and opposing those whose teaching and practice fell short of that mark.

In addition, during this period several Christian authors endeavored to respond to their culture's suspicions about this upstart religious group. These writings advised those outside the faith of what Christians actually believed and practiced, challenged the views and conduct of non-Christians, and sought to deflect unjust and unwarranted opposition to Christianity. During the whole period, though, the Church was under threat by a potentially hostile government; that situation influenced how the Church lived, taught, and viewed its milieu, and what the Church Fathers of the period emphasized in their works.

The selections in this volume are drawn from all of the major and most of the minor ante-Nicene Church Fathers. (A complete list of the ante-Nicene Fathers whose works are excerpted in this volume can be found in the Table of Contents. Not all of them are mentioned in the following paragraphs.)

THE APOSTOLIC FATHERS

The earliest extant collection of Christian writings outside the works eventually accepted as the New Testament canon is the one known as "the Apostolic Fathers." This group of works is a prime source for information about the teachings, practices, and concerns of the Church in the period immediately after the apostles (c. 60–160). Some of the Apostolic Fathers knew one or another of the apostles: Clement of Rome (c. 30–101) was a coworker with the Apostle Paul (Phil 4:3), and Ignatius of Antioch (c. 30–110) was trained by the Apostle John, as were Polycarp of Smyrna (c. 69–155) and Papias of Hierapolis (c. 70–c. 155). Their writings, thus, afford insight into what the apostles had taught. So highly prized were some of the Apostolic Fathers' works that, until well into the fourth century, some Christians looked on one or more of these writings as canonical Scripture: Clement of Rome's *Letter of the Romans to the Corinthians* (c. 95) was thus viewed, as were *The Didache* (written between 50 and 80) and *The Shepherd of Hermas* (c. 95–100).

The Apostolic Fathers always show great deference to the apostles: they are conscious of having received the Christian faith from the apostles and of the necessity of preserving that faith inviolate. There is never a hint that any of the Apostolic Fathers considered modifying what they had received—quite the opposite, in fact! They see themselves, by the mercy of God, as faithfully passing on what they had received, so that others after them can pass it on faithfully as well—in fulfillment of apostolic injunction (2 Tim 1:13–14; 2:2).

The Apostolic Fathers also show responsible pastoral engagement with changing pressures facing the infant Church. They address issues that had not arisen during the apostles' times, they deal with questions about practical daily life for the early Church, and they protect and proclaim the Christian message. Reading the Apostolic Fathers offers insight into what the earliest Church saw as essential to faith and practice. As well, these works indicate what the Church had learned from the apostles and saw as basic Christianity.

The Apostolic Fathers had considerable influence in the early Church. By around the fifth century, though, they had largely been forgotten in favor of subsequent patristic writings. While a few of their writings remained known in intervening centuries, it was not until the seventeenth century that the larger corpus began to be rediscovered and published. Only in the nineteenth century, with the discovery and 1873 publication of *The Didache*, did the whole corpus of the Apostolic Fathers become accessible. Since then, the Apostolic Fathers have had significant influence, not only on the study of early church history, but also for the contextualized understanding of the New Testament.

THE APOLOGISTS

The Christian authors of the later second century have come to be known as "the Apologists" (from the Greek ἀπολογέω ["apologeo"], "I offer a defense"). Their contributions partially overlapped with, but for the most part followed after, those of the Apostolic Fathers. The most prolific of the Apologists was Justin Martyr (c. 100–165), but both Athenagoras (second half of the second century) and Theophilus of Antioch (?–183) also produced powerful defenses of the Christian faith.

The Apologists had a different focus from the Apostolic Fathers (with the exception of *The Letter to Diognetus*). The difference did not concern the message proclaimed; it lay in the audiences the two groups addressed. The Apostolic Fathers had sent their letters to churches to offer instruction in the Christian faith and how to live it out, but the Apologists addressed their writings to opponents of the Christian faith. The works of the Apologists show that Christianity was making a significant impact on the world in that day and indicate how Christian leaders responded to the demand to give an account of the movement to a surrounding, largely skeptical world. Thus, they show how Christianity saw itself in contrast to the surrounding intellectual milieu and contemporary religious practices. In their endeavor to defend the Christian faith against calumny and to relate that faith to the world of their day, the Apologists raised issues subsequent Church Fathers dealt with in contrasting ways in Rome, Alexandria, and North Africa.

THE ROMANS

During the ante-Nicene period, Rome continued to be the capital. Given the city's prominence, its influence was preponderant in the western half of the Roman Empire. As the site of the apostolic labors and martyrdoms of St. Peter and St. Paul, Rome enjoyed considerable prestige as well. With all this, it is not surprising that the Church in the western half of the empire accorded the Roman church's leaders significant status and looked to them for guidance. Moreover, the church in Rome attracted the attention and, too often, the hostility of its surrounding culture.

From records preserved in the ancient Church, we know who the successive leaders of the church in Rome were throughout the entire ante-Nicene period. Even so, after the Apostolic Father Clement, the church in Rome was not blessed with leaders whose written works have been preserved; the only exceptions in this regard are Hippolytus (c. 170–235), Novatian (c. 200–c. 258), and the layman Minucius Felix (from the third century). While respect for Rome remained undiminished for a variety of reasons, the North Africans (see below) proved to be more influential teachers in the Latin-speaking Christian churches during the period.

THE ALEXANDRIANS

Long the intellectual center of the Roman Empire and the site of a great library, Alexandria was home to many schools of philosophy and literature. With the wide acceptance of Christianity throughout much of the Roman Empire by the late second century, it is not surprising that Christians also set up a school in Alexandria. Its instructors made use of the approaches to education, thought, and argument that were the common currency of Alexandrian intellectual culture. The leaders of this school of Christian thought tried to set forth the Christian message in ways that could answer the suspicions held against the faith by many intellectuals, on the one hand, and to present that faith with all the polish that could be borrowed from the high achievements of Hellenic and Hellenistic philosophy and literature, on the other. In doing so, these leaders pursued some of the ideas earlier set forth by the Apologists.

The first great figure of this school was Clement of Alexandria (c. 150–c. 215). He set the tone for the Alexandrian school with his wide scholarship and respectful approach to debate. His most famous student, Origen (c. 185–254), became his successor. Origen's genius was so overwhelming that, although gentle like his teacher, he eclipsed the influence of his instructor. Reputedly the author of more than two thousand works, Origen fell under suspicion in later Christian antiquity for some of his teaching, and a great number of his works have not been preserved.

With a renewal of persecution during the third century, the Alexandrian school closed down. However, its legacy continued, and Alexandria remained one of the main centers of intellectual culture and ecclesiastical leadership.

THE NORTH AFRICANS

During the ante-Nicene period, the North Africans made a much greater contribution to Christian literature and doctrine in the Latin half of the empire than their contemporaries in Rome. In Tertullian (c. 155–c. 220), the North African church bestowed on Latin Christianity its most original thinker of the ante-Nicene period; his trenchant challenge, "What has Jerusalem to do with Athens?" (*Prescriptions Against the Heretics* §7), has echoed down through the centuries against an uncritical accommodation of Christian teaching to non-Christian intellectual perspectives. In Cyprian (195–258), North African Christianity offered a gifted, compassionate pastor-martyr who stood firm against heresy and schism but inclined gently toward the repentant. In Lactantius (c. 250–c. 320), the North Africans gave Latin Christianity a solid (although not deeply insightful) defense of the faith against the surrounding world as the ante-Nicene period came to an end—and a tutor to one of Emperor Constantine's sons.

The North African church kept in close touch with Rome and carefully watched all that went on in the church there. The North Africans may have faced greater pressures from heresies and schisms than the church in Rome did; at the least, the pressures were more intense in North Africa. This may be reflected in what several scholars have noted about North African Christianity at this time: it was somehow harder and harsher in orientation, more demanding and rigid than was common in Rome and elsewhere.

Together with Rome, North Africa shaped Latin Christianity. The North African Christian authors clearly come at issues from another direction and with a different expectation than their contemporaries in Alexandria, although without severing the Church's unity in the apostolic message. With the writings of these North African Christians, one sees the clearest early manifestations of that Latin/Greek distinction which only becomes more pronounced in the Nicene and post-Nicene period.

Nicene and Post-Nicene Fathers

The Church experienced an unanticipated and nearly incredible transition with the conversion of Constantine (r. 312–337): persecution ended, Christianity was given freedom, and under Theodosius (r. 379–395), it became the official religion of the empire. This all brought tremendous changes for the Church in its wake. Much had to be adjusted, and the

Church had to wrestle with issues it had not dealt with in the ante-Nicene period.

Not surprisingly, this resulted in shifts in emphasis in patristic writings. The Nicene and post-Nicene Church Fathers no longer had to deal with the opposition of a hostile state or a suspicious culture. They could and did settle into the welcome task of setting forth the Christian message in ways that could shape life and practice in the dramatically different situation inaugurated by Constantine's conversion.

With the exception of the twenty-month reign of Emperor Julian the Apostate (r. 361–363), throughout this period the empire favored Christianity, and the Church Fathers of the era wrote for a wide audience of interested readers throughout the empire. The selections in this volume are drawn from all of the major and most of the minor Nicene and post-Nicene Church Fathers. (A complete list of the Nicene and post-Nicene Fathers whose works are excerpted appears in the Table of Contents. Not all of them are mentioned in the following paragraphs.)

THE GREEK FATHERS OF THE FOURTH AND FIFTH CENTURIES

During the fourth and fifth centuries, Christianity went through extended controversies over the doctrines of the Trinity and of Christology. Much of the Church Fathers' focus during this period was on these questions. In the course of these disputes, the Greek Church Fathers played the leading roles. Consequently, their works are especially important for understanding these controversies, as well as for seeing how faith and life were held together in a time of argument and tension. Among them, Athanasius (296–372) and the Cappadocian Fathers—Basil of Caesarea (329–379), Gregory Nazianzen (330–390), and Gregory of Nyssa (c. 330–395)—defended the faith valiantly while serving diligently as pastors; Cyril of Jerusalem (c. 315–387) and John Chrysostom (347–407) were exceptional preachers; and Cyril of Alexandria (376–444) was a gifted exegete and controversialist.

THE LATIN FATHERS OF THE FOURTH AND FIFTH CENTURIES

During the fourth and early fifth centuries, the Church in the western half of the empire had some great leaders, but only a couple of them—Hilary of Poitiers (315–368) and Leo the Great (?–461)—contributed significantly to the controversies about the Trinity and Christology; other issues occupied most of their attention. Ambrose (333–397) was an outstanding orator whose sermons attracted large crowds, including a young man converted to Christianity under his influence, Augustine (354–430)—who would become the most influential theologian in the history of Western Christianity. Jerome (345–420) labored to produce the *Vulgate*, an improved Latin version of the Scriptures, translated from the original Hebrew and Greek; Jerome's Latin version influenced Western Christianity for many centuries. To mention no others, Vincent of Lérins (?–c. 450) wrestled with the challenge of distinguishing the essential Christian faith from other viewpoints that had been articulated by his day.

Almost all these Latin Church Fathers wrote during the fourth century or the early part of the fifth. For most of the fifth century, the Church in the Latin-speaking half of the empire was exposed to the invasions of the Germanic tribes. Not surprisingly, in this situation less was written, and even less managed to be preserved; also, the Latin Church Fathers found it difficult to keep up contact with their counterparts in the eastern half of the Church.

THE LATIN FATHERS OF THE SIXTH THROUGH EIGHTH CENTURIES

During the sixth through eighth centuries, the Latin-speaking Church endured the effects of the Germanic invasions as civilization collapsed, schools were destroyed, and government was in chaos. Not surprisingly, the Latin Church Fathers of the period were limited both in numbers and in training. Their contributions shaped Latin Christianity profoundly as it entered the medieval period. Julianus Pomerius (sixth century) wrote a few works, but the most influential Church Father of this period was Gregory the Great (c. 540–604), who is known as the last great teacher of the Latin Church in antiquity.

THE GREEK FATHERS OF THE SIXTH THROUGH EIGHTH CENTURIES

In this period, marked by additional Christological controversies, the Greek-speaking segment of the Church continued to provide the great leaders in Christian teaching. While not as numerous as in the preceding era, the Greek Church Fathers of this period were profound and insightful. They coordinated what they had received from their predecessors and put the finishing touches on their teaching and practice. Pseudo-Dionysius (early sixth century) produced works that have had a profound influence on mysticism and liturgy. Maximus Confessor (580–662) stalwartly defended the faith and began to pull together in coordinated fashion the teaching of the Greek Church Fathers who had preceded him. This endeavor was carried to completion by John of Damascus (c. 675–749), who is commonly viewed as the last of the Church Fathers.

How to Approach the Readings

In getting ready to turn to the patristic selections that follow, readers should note that, in preparing the selections for this volume, where permitted, I have modernized language and punctuation. In that regard, I have adopted gender-neutral language where possible and appropriate. Biblical references appear in square brackets.

As to format, rather than coordinate the patristic readings under various themes or topics—an approach followed in some other collections—I have kept the readings from each Church Father together and have placed them in the order in which they appear in each writing. Since the Church Fathers lived at different times, in which various questions demanded attention, and since each of the Church Fathers approached the issues of his day from his own vantage point, this approach should allow readers to develop at least a basic acquaintance with the respective Church Fathers and their concerns. Also, this format will help readers get a better sense for what each patristic writing deals with and, to a limited degree, the argument offered in the work. A brief introduction to each Church Father (or document, where the author is unknown) gives background information about his life and works (or about the document).

As readers get set to embark on this journey with the Church Fathers, they should keep three considerations in mind. In the first place, while I have been careful not to distort or misrepresent any of the Church Fathers or their views in the selections I have made, in culling out excerpts some of the thrust of a writing or its overall impact was inevitably left to the side. Reading judiciously chosen selections from the Church Fathers can give good exposure to these classics of Christian literature, but it cannot impart the full impression afforded by reading and pondering a complete patristic work. I hope that many readers will be enticed to read in their entirety some of the works from which excerpts have been taken in the pages that follow.

Secondly, this volume offers a quick tour, not a scholarly study, of patristic literature. While this introduction and the selection process arise from such study, this volume is not intended as a contribution that will advance patristic scholarship. It is intended for readers who want to experience the Church Fathers at first hand. Even so, for someone to develop scholarly facility with the Church Fathers, much more extensive and intensive reading in both primary and secondary sources would be necessary than what this volume offers.

I am convinced, though, that those who have the time and inclination to become experts in patristics are not the only ones who should have some access to the Church Fathers. Reading selections of patristic literature may be all that many busy contemporary Christians—such as students, clergy, and church members—can reasonably hope to achieve. Their concerns in such reading will be different from those of patristic scholars: rather than seeking painstaking examination of the minutiae of patristic scholarship in its multitude of concerns or the wide-ranging interpretive questions with which scholars wrestle, most contemporary Christian readers will be looking for stimulation, comfort, challenge, and inspiration from the Church Fathers. This volume is intended to offer that type of material for such readers; I hope it serves them well.

This leads to a third observation. In approaching the Church Fathers, we need openness to them—that is, we need to meet them where they were and on their terms. We must not expect the Church Fathers to speak with the sort of terminology or nuance that developed subsequently in Church history owing to subsequent controversies, or to be sensitive to the particular issues, tensions, and problems that later agitated the Church. If we are open to the Church Fathers and listen to them on their own terms, we will be enriched by reading selections from their works.

PART I

The Ante-Nicene Fathers

∽ *Clement of Rome*

Clement (c. 30–101) served as the fourth bishop of the church in Rome. According to the early Church, he was the companion of St. Paul mentioned in Philippians 4:3; however, the name was common in the ancient world, and some scholars have rejected the ancient attribution. In defense of the early Church's claim, though, there is nothing particularly incongruous in someone who lived for a while in Philippi later becoming a leader in Rome: Philippi was a Roman colony, so it and its citizens enjoyed special connection to the capital city. Thus, there is no inherent unlikelihood in someone who lived in the colony subsequently moving to and obtaining significant position in Rome.

Clement penned his *Letter of the Romans to the Corinthians* before the end of the first century, probably around AD 95—thus, before the death of the apostle John. In the past, the document was sometimes styled 1 Clement, because it was associated with another document referred to as 2 Clement; however, scholarship has shown the latter document was not written by the same author. Clement's *Letter of the Romans to the Corinthians* manifests profound pastoral concern for the Corinthian church—and gives evidence that the factiousness lamented and sternly addressed by Paul (1 Cor 1:10–13; cf. 3:5–9, 21–23) had not yet disappeared in the church in that bustling seaport community. Clement ended his life in exile, sent to Crimea; his labors there before his death strengthened an already established Christian community.

The Letter of the Romans to the Corinthians[1]

Let us fix our eyes on the blood of Christ and understand how precious it is to His Father: poured out for our salvation, it won for the whole world the grace of repentance. (7:4)

We shall bring upon ourselves no ordinary harm, but rather great danger, if we recklessly surrender ourselves to the purposes of those who launch out into strife and dissension. (14:2)

Let us unite with those who devoutly practice peace, and not with those who hypocritically wish for peace. (15:1)

Boldness and arrogance and audacity are for those who are cursed by God; graciousness and humility and gentleness are with those who are blessed by God. (30:8)

All [the faithful of old] were glorified and magnified, not through themselves or their own works or the righteous actions which they did, but through His will. So we, having been called through His will in Christ Jesus, are not justified through ourselves or through our own wisdom or understanding or piety or works which we have done in holiness of heart, but through faith, by which the almighty God has justified all who have existed from the beginning; to whom be the glory forever and ever. (32:3–4)

Those who follow the instructions of the Master cannot go wrong. (40:4)

Be contentious and zealous, but only about the things that relate to salvation. (45:1)

You have searched the Scriptures, which are true, which were given by the Holy Spirit; you know that nothing unrighteous or counterfeit is written in them. (45:2–3)

Why are there strife and angry outbursts and dissension and schisms and conflict among you? Do we not have one God and one Christ and one Spirit of grace which was poured out upon us? And is there not one calling in Christ? Why do we tear and rip apart the members of Christ, and rebel

---

1 Excerpts taken from *AposFrs* 28–101.

against our own body, and reach such a level of insanity that we forget that we are members of one another? (46:5–7)

Who can describe the bond of God's love? Who is able to explain the majesty of its beauty? The height to which love leads is indescribable. Love unites us with God.... Love knows nothing of schisms, love leads no rebellions, love does everything in harmony.... Without love nothing is pleasing to God. (49:2–5)

For whatever sins we have committed and whatever we have done through any of the tricks of the adversary, let us ask that we may be forgiven. (51:1)

Let us accept correction, which no one ought to resent, dear friends. The reproof which we give to each other is good and exceedingly useful, for it unites us with the will of God. (56:2)

It is better for you to be found small but included in the flock of Christ than to have a preeminent reputation and yet be excluded from His hope. (57:2b)

Grant us, Lord, to hope on Your name, which is the primal source of all creation, and open the eyes of our hearts, that we may know You. (59:3)

Finally, may the all-seeing God and Master of spirits and Lord of all flesh, who chose the Lord Jesus Christ, and us through Him to be His own special people, grant to every soul that has called upon His magnificent and holy name faith, fear, peace, patience, steadfastness, self-control, purity, and sobriety, that they may be pleasing to His name through our High Priest and Guardian, Jesus Christ, through whom be glory and majesty, might and honor to Him, both now and forever and ever. (64)

~ "2 Clement"

Long referred to as *2 Clement*, this document is not a letter, but a sermon. Further, it was not written or preached by Clement of Rome. Thus, it is not rightly styled by its old title; however, since no alternative designation for this work has yet received wide acceptance, we have retained the old name but placed it in quotation marks.

This work is the first post-apostolic sermon to have survived. It was evidently written and proclaimed to the Corinthian church sometime after Clement's letter was received, for it gives evidence that the problems addressed by Clement had been resolved. It has been suggested that the author may have been one of the church leaders who had brought Clement's letter to Corinth; if so, the sermon may be as early as 98–100. Other scholars have discerned slightly later influences, though, and date the work to 120–150. In either case, it offers a striking portrayal of some elements of teaching and church life in the period soon after the death of the apostles.

"2 Clement"[1]

Those who listen as though these [our salvation and hope] are small matters do wrong, and we also do wrong, when we fail to acknowledge from where and by whom and to what place we were called, and how much suffering Jesus Christ endured for our sake. What repayment, then, shall we give to Him, or what fruit worthy of what He has given to us? (1:2–3)

---

1 Excerpted from *AposFrs* 106–127.

He had mercy upon us and in His compassion He saved us when we had no hope of salvation except that which comes from Him, and even though He had seen in us much deception and destruction. For He called us when we did not exist, and out of nothing He willed us into being. (1:7–8)

He Himself says, "Whoever confesses Me before men, him I will also confess before My Father" [Matt 10:32]. This, then, is our reward, if we acknowledge Him through whom we were saved. But how do we acknowledge Him? By doing what He says and not disobeying His commandments, and honoring Him not only with our lips but with all our heart and all our mind [Mark 12:30]. (3:2–4)

This age and the one that is coming are enemies. This one is given to adultery and corruption and greed and deceit, but that one renounces these things. So we cannot be friends of both; we must renounce this one in order to experience that one. (6:3–5)

What assurance do we have of entering the kingdom of God if we fail to keep our baptism pure and undefiled? (6:9)

While we are still on earth, let us repent. (8:1)

While we still have time to be healed, let us place ourselves in the hands of God the physician. (9:7)

Those [who teach evil] do not know what great torment the pleasure of the present brings, and what delight the promise of the future brings. (10:4)

When the pagans hear from our mouths the oracles of God, they marvel at their beauty and greatness. But when they discover that our actions are not worthy of the words we speak, they turn from wonder to blasphemy, saying that it is a myth and a delusion. (13:3)

The apostles declare that the Church not only exists now, but has been in existence from the beginning. (14:2)

Since we have received no small opportunity to repent, let us, while we still have time, turn again to God who has called us, while we still have One who accepts us. (16:1)

Let us help one another to restore those who are weak with respect to goodness, so that we may all be saved, and let us admonish and turn each other back. (17:2)

I make every effort to pursue righteousness, that I may succeed in at least getting close to it. (18:2)

Let us, therefore, practice righteousness, that we may be saved in the end. (19:3)

None of the righteous ever received his reward quickly, but waited for it. For if God paid the wages of the righteous immediately, we would soon be engaged in business, not godliness; though we would appear to be righteous, we would in fact be pursuing not piety but profit. (20:3–4)

~ *Ignatius of Antioch*

Ignatius (c. 30–110) was taught by the Apostle John and served as either the second or third bishop of Antioch, a major center of early Christianity. It was a common opinion in the early Church that Ignatius was the small child set in the midst of the disciples by Christ when He declared, "Unless you are converted and become as little children, you will by no means enter the kingdom of heaven" [Matt 18:2–3]; however, since Ignatius seems to have been a lifelong resident of Syria, this is doubtful. After a long and distinguished career as leader of the church in Antioch, Ignatius was arrested and sent to Rome, where he expected to be martyred for the faith.

All the letters we have from Ignatius were written in the period after his arrest. They show great concern for unity within the churches; clearly, division and factiousness had not subsided, despite earlier apostolic exhortations. As a significant counter to that evil, Ignatius vigorously emphasized the role of the bishop; indeed, he is the earliest explicit proponent of the importance of the episcopal office. Ignatius manifested a deep desire to be martyred for Christ; he saw this (as did many of his Christian contemporaries) as the most desirable way to culminate his Christian experience.

Letter to the Ephesians[1]

In your unanimity and harmonious love Jesus Christ is sung. You must each join this chorus, so that by being harmonious in unanimity and

---

1 Excerpted from *AposFrs* 136–151.

taking your pitch from God you may sing in unison with one voice through Jesus Christ to the Father, in order that He may both hear you and, on the basis of what you do well, acknowledge that you are members of His Son. (4:1–2)

Whoever does not meet with the congregation thereby demonstrates his or her arrogance. (5:3)

There is only one physician, who is both flesh and spirit, born and unborn, God in man, true life in death, both from Mary and from God, first subject to suffering and then beyond it, Jesus Christ our Lord. (7:2)

You are stones of a temple [1 Pet 2:4–5], prepared beforehand for the building of God the Father, hoisted up to the heights by the crane of Jesus Christ, which is the Cross, using as a rope the Holy Spirit; your faith is what lifts you up, and love is the way that leads up to God. (9:1b)

Pray continually for the rest of humanity as well, that they may find God, for there is in them hope for repentance. Therefore allow them to be instructed by you, at least by your deeds. In response to their anger, be gentle; in response to their boasts, be humble; in response to their slander, offer prayers; in response to their errors, be steadfast in the faith; in response to their cruelty, be gentle; do not be eager to retaliate against them. Let us show ourselves their brothers and sisters by our forbearance, and let us be eager to be imitators of the Lord. (10:1–3)

Let us either fear the wrath to come or love the grace which is present, one of the two; either way, let us be found in Christ Jesus, which leads to true life. Let nothing appeal to you apart from Him. (11:1–2)

There is nothing better than peace. (13:2)

For the work [i.e., Christianity] is not a matter of what one promises now, but of persevering to the end in the power of faith. (14:2)

It is better to be silent and be real, than to talk and not be real. (15:1)

God appeared in human form to bring the newness of eternal life. (19:3)

[Regarding the celebration of the Eucharist:] We break one bread, which is the medicine of immortality, the antidote we take in order not to die but to live forever in Jesus Christ. (20:2)

Letter to the Magnesians[2]

It is right, therefore, that we not just be called Christians, but that we actually be Christians. (4:1)

Just as there are two coinages, the one of God and the other of the world, and each of them has its own stamp impressed upon it, so the unbelievers bear the stamp of this world, but the faithful in love bear the stamp of God the Father through Jesus Christ. (5:2)

Be eager to do everything in godly harmony, the bishop presiding in the place of God and the presbyters in the place of the council of the apostles, and the deacons (who are so dear to me) who have been entrusted with the service of Jesus Christ, who before the ages was with the Father and appeared at the end of time. (6:1)

Let no one regard his neighbor in merely human terms but in Jesus Christ love one another always. (6:2)

If God were to imitate the way we act, we would be lost. (10:1)

Be subject to the bishop and to one another, as Jesus Christ in the flesh was to the Father, and as the apostles were to Christ and to the Father, that there may be unity. (13:2)

Letter to the Trallians[3]

Jesus Christ . . . died for us, in order that by believing in His death you might escape death. (2:1)

It is essential . . . that you continue your current practice and do nothing without the bishop, but be subject also to the presbytery as to the apostles

---

2 Excerpted from *AposFrs* 151–159.
3 Excerpted from *AposFrs* 158–167.

of Jesus Christ, our hope, in whom we shall be found, if we so live. (2:2)

Let everyone respect the deacons as Jesus Christ, just as they should respect the bishop, who is a model of the Father, and the presbyters as God's council and as the band of the apostles. Without these no group can be called a church. (3:1)

By gentleness the ruler of this age is destroyed. (4:2b)

Be deaf, therefore, whenever anyone speaks to you apart from Jesus Christ, who was of the family of David, who was the son of Mary; who really was born, who both ate and drank; who really was persecuted under Pontius Pilate, who really was crucified and died while those in heaven and on earth and under the earth looked on; who, moreover, really was raised from the dead when His Father raised Him up, who—His Father, that is—in the same way will likewise also raise us up in Christ Jesus who believe in Him, apart from whom we have no true life. (9:1–2)

Letter to the Romans[4]

Christianity is greatest when it is hated by the world. (3:3)

It is better for me to die for Jesus Christ than to rule over the ends of the earth. Him I seek, who died on our behalf; Him I long for, who rose again for our sake. (6:1)

Do not talk about Jesus Christ while you desire the world. (7:1)

I want the bread of God, which is the flesh of Christ who is of the seed of David; and for drink I want His blood, which is incorruptible love. (7:3)

Letter to the Philadelphians[5]

Do not be misled: if anyone follows a schismatic, that person will not inherit the kingdom of God. (3:3)

God does not dwell where there is division and anger. (8:1)

---

4 Excerpted from *AposFrs* 166–177.
5 Excerpted from *AposFrs* 176–185.

The gospel possesses something distinctive, namely, the coming of the Savior, our Lord Jesus Christ, His suffering, and the Resurrection. For the beloved prophets preached in anticipation of Him, but the gospel is the imperishable finished work. (9:2)

Letter to the Smyrneans[6]

You are established in an unshakable faith, having been nailed, as it were, to the Cross of the Lord Jesus Christ in both body and spirit, and firmly established in love by the blood of Christ, totally convinced with regard to our Lord that He is truly of the family of David with respect to human descent, Son of God with respect to the divine will and power, truly born of a virgin, baptized by John in order that all righteousness might be fulfilled by Him, truly nailed in the flesh for us under Pontius Pilate and Herod the tetrarch (from its fruit we derive our existence, that is from His divinely blessed suffering), in order that He might raise a banner for the ages through His Resurrection for His saints and faithful people, whether among Jews or among Gentiles, in the one body of His Church. (1:1–2)

Flee from divisions, as the beginning of evils. You must all follow the bishop, as Jesus Christ followed the Father, and follow the presbytery as you would the apostles; respect the deacons as the commandment of God. Let no one do anything that has to do with the church without the bishop. (8:1)

Wherever Jesus Christ is, there is the catholic Church. (8:2)

If you want to do well, God is ready to help you. (11:3)

Letter to Polycarp[7]

Wait expectantly for Him who is above time: the Eternal, the Invisible, who for our sake became visible; the Intangible, the Unsuffering, who for our sake suffered, who for our sake endured in every way. (3:2)

Let your baptism serve as a shield, faith as a helmet, love as a spear, endurance as armor. (6:2)

---

6 Excerpted from *AposFrs* 185–195.
7 Excerpted from *AposFrs* 184–201.

~ Polycarp

Taught by St. John the Evangelist, Polycarp (c. 69–155) served as bishop of the church in Smyrna; in that role, he instructed the young Irenaeus. Polycarp's lengthy life and ministry connected the apostles with the Church past the mid-second century.

Polycarp's only extant writing is his Letter to the Philippians. He manifests the early Church's steadfast determination to hold faithfully to the teaching of Christ and the apostles. Interestingly, Polycarp does not emphasize the distinctiveness of the episcopal office, as does Ignatius, his friend and fellow student of St. John. Widely revered throughout the ancient Church for his faithful teaching and piety, Polycarp was infamous for these reasons to non-Christians in the surrounding community. In due course, anti-Christian hostility led to his arrest and martyrdom, in which his faith and boldness for Christ shone brightly. (Obviously, the account of his martyrdom was written by someone other than Polycarp himself.)

Letter to the Philippians[1]

For neither I nor anyone like me can keep pace with the wisdom of the blessed and glorious Paul, who, when he was among you in the presence of the people of that time, accurately and reliably taught the word concerning the truth. And when he was absent he wrote you letters; if you study them carefully, you will be able to build yourselves up in the faith that has been given to you, which "is the mother of us all" [Gal 4:26], while hope follows

---

1 Excerpted from *AposFrs* 206–221.

and love for God and Christ and for our neighbor leads the way. If anyone is occupied with these, that person has fulfilled the commandment of righteousness, for one who has love is far from all sin. (3:2–3)

Let us hold steadfastly and unceasingly to our hope and the guarantee of our righteousness, who is Christ Jesus. (8:1)

Woe to that person through whom the name of the Lord is blasphemed. (10:3)

How can one who is unable to control himself preach self-control to someone else? (11:2)

Now may the God and Father of our Lord Jesus Christ, and the eternal High Priest Himself, the Son of God Jesus Christ, build you up in faith and truth, in all gentleness, in all freedom from anger, in forbearance and steadfastness and patient endurance and purity, and may He give you a share and a place among His saints, and to us with you, and to all those under heaven who will yet believe in our Lord and God Jesus Christ and in His Father who raised Him from the dead. (12:2)

The Martyrdom of Polycarp[2]

Having placed his hands behind him and having been bound, like a splendid ram chosen from a great flock for a sacrifice, a burnt offering prepared and acceptable to God, he [Polycarp] looked up to heaven and said, "O Lord God Almighty, Father of Your beloved and blessed Son Jesus Christ, through whom we have received knowledge of You, the God of angels and powers and of all creation, and of the whole race of the righteous who live in Your presence, I bless You because You have considered me worthy of this day and hour, that I might receive a place among the number of the martyrs in the cup of Your Christ, to the resurrection to eternal life, both of soul and of body, in the incorruptibility of the Holy Spirit. May I be received among them in Your presence today, as a rich and acceptable sacrifice, as You have prepared and revealed beforehand, and have now accomplished, You who are the undeceiving and true God. For this reason, indeed for all things, I praise You, I bless You, I glorify You, through the

---

2 Excerpted from *AposFrs* 226–245.

eternal and heavenly High Priest, Jesus Christ, Your beloved Son, through whom to You with Him and the Holy Spirit be glory both now and for the ages to come. Amen." (14:1–3)

We will never be able either to abandon the Christ who suffered for the salvation of the whole world of those who are saved, the blameless on behalf of sinners, or to worship anyone else. For this one, who is the Son of God, we worship. But the martyrs we love as disciples and imitators of the Lord, as they deserve, on account of their matchless devotion to their king and teacher. (17:2b–3)

~ The Didache

This remarkable document stems from the first century: proposed dates for its writing have varied between 50 and 80. Unquestionably, it reflects the teaching and practice of the earliest Church. The teaching emphasizes the contrasting lifestyles of Christ's faithful disciples and of nonbelievers. It also offers valuable information about early attitudes toward and the practice of baptism and the Eucharist.

The Didache[1]

There are two ways, one of life and one of death, and there is a great difference between these two ways.

This is the way of life: first, "you shall love God, who made you; second, your neighbor as yourself" [see Mark 12:30–31]; and "whatever you do not wish to happen to you, do not do to another" [Tob 4:15; see Matt 7:12]. (1:1–2)

You shall not hate anyone; instead you shall reprove some, and pray for some, and some you shall love more than your own life. (2:7)

Accept as good the things that happen to you, knowing that nothing transpires apart from God. (3:10 [cited verbatim in *The Letter of Barnabas* 20:6])

---

[1] Excerpted from *AposFrs* 250–269.

You shall not turn away from someone in need, but shall share everything with your brother or sister, and not claim that anything is your own. For if you are sharers in what is imperishable, how much more so in perishable things! (4:8)

But the way of death is . . . having no mercy for the poor, not working on behalf of the oppressed, not knowing Him who made them, murderers of children, corrupters of God's creation, turning away from someone in need, oppressing the afflicted, advocates of the wealthy, lawless judges of the poor. (5:1–2)

If you are able to bear the whole yoke of the Lord, you will be perfect. But if you are not able, then do what you can. (6:2)

Baptize as follows: after you have reviewed [with those to be baptized] all these things [regarding faith and life], baptize "in the name of the Father and of the Son and of the Holy Spirit" [Matt 28:19] in running water. But if you have no running water, then baptize in some other water; and if you are not able to baptize in cold water, then do so in warm. But if you have neither, then pour water on the head three times "in the name of the Father and Son and Holy Spirit." And before the baptism, let the one baptizing and the one who is to be baptized fast. (7:1–4)

[Regarding the Eucharist:]
Just as this broken bread was scattered
upon the mountains and then was
gathered together and became one,
so may Your Church be gathered together
from the ends of the earth into Your kingdom;
for Yours is the glory and the power
through Jesus Christ forever. (9:4)

You, almighty Master, created all things for Your name's sake,
and gave food and drink to human beings to enjoy,
that they might give You thanks;
but to us You have graciously given spiritual food and drink,
and eternal life through Your servant. (10:3)

Remember Your Church, Lord,
to deliver it from all evil
and to make it perfect in Your love;
and gather it, the one that has been sanctified,
from the four winds into Your kingdom,
which You have prepared for it;
for Yours is the power and the glory forever.
May grace come, and may this world pass away. (10:5–6a)

Not everyone who speaks in the spirit is a prophet, but only if that person exhibits the Lord's ways. By their conduct, therefore, will the false prophet and the prophet be recognized. (11:8)

If any prophet teaches the truth, yet does not practice what he teaches, he is a false prophet. (11:10)

On the Lord's own day gather together and break bread [i.e., receive the Eucharist] and give thanks, having first confessed your sins so that your sacrifice may be pure. But let no one who has a quarrel with a companion join you until they have been reconciled, so that your sacrifice may not be defiled. For this is the sacrifice concerning which the Lord said, "'In every place incense shall be offered to My name, and a pure offering. . . . For I am a great King,' says the Lord of hosts, 'and My name is to be feared among the nations'" [Mal 1:11, 14]. (14:1–3)

The Letter of Barnabas

This letter was written sometime between 70 and 132 by an otherwise unknown Barnabas. It appears that the author was from the noted intellectual center of Alexandria. The letter tries to show how Christians should appropriate the Jewish Scriptures. His letter manifests the ancient Christian confidence that the Old Testament focused on the coming and work of Christ. Given the prevalence of allegory as an interpretive method in so much of the intellectual culture of the day, it is not surprising that the letter makes wide use of that interpretive device.

The Letter of Barnabas[1]

There are three basic doctrines of the Lord: the hope of life, which is the beginning and end of our faith; and righteousness, which is the beginning and end of judgment; and love shown in gladness and rejoicing, the testimony of righteous works. (1:6)

Let us avoid . . . absolutely all the works of lawlessness, lest they overpower us. And let us hate the deception of the present age, so that we may be loved in the age to come. (4:1)

He Himself submitted, in order that He might destroy death and show the reality of the resurrection of the dead. (5:6)

---

1 Excerpted from *AposFrs* 274–327.

Humanity is earth suffering, for Adam was formed out of the face of the earth. (6:9)

By receiving the forgiveness of sins and setting our hope on the Name, we became new, created again from the beginning. (16:8)

The knowledge which is given to us to walk in is as follows. You shall love Him who made you; you shall fear Him who created you; you shall glorify Him who redeemed you from death. (19:1–2)

Do not be someone who stretches out his hands to receive, but withdraws them when it comes to giving [WSir 4:31; cited also in *The Didache* 4:5]. (19:9)

∽ The Shepherd of Hermas

By far the lengthiest of the documents within the corpus of the Apostolic Fathers is the extraordinary work, *The Shepherd of Hermas*. Comprised of apocalyptic visions followed by mandates for Christian living, the work proved very popular in the early Church and was widely read—some even proposed that it be included within the canon of Christian Scriptures. The work has been dated to around 95–100; its author is unknown.

The Shepherd of Hermas[1]

God . . . dwells in the heavens and created out of nothing the things that are, and increased and multiplied them for the sake of His Holy Church. (1:6)

Bearing a grudge produces death. (7:1)

The Church . . . was created before all things. . . . For her sake the world was formed. (8:1)

First of all, believe that God is one, who created all things and set them in order, and made out of what did not exist everything that is, and who contains all things but is Himself alone uncontained. Believe in Him, therefore, and fear Him, and fearing Him, be self-controlled. Keep these things, and you will cast off all evil from yourself and will put on every virtue of righ-

---

1 Excerpted from *AposFrs* 334–527.

teousness and will live to God, if you keep this commandment. (26:1–2)

Be sincere and innocent, and you will be like little children who do not know the evil that destroys human life. (27:1)

Speak evil of no one, and do not enjoy listening to someone who does. Otherwise you, the listener, will be responsible for the sin of the one speaking evil. (27:2)

Slander is evil; it is a restless demon, never at peace but always at home with dissension. (27:3)

The Lord lives in patience; the devil lives in an angry temper. (33:3)

Turn to the Lord with all your heart and ask of Him unhesitatingly, and you will know His extraordinary compassion, because He will never abandon you but will fulfill your soul's request. For God is not like humans, who bear grudges; no, He is without malice and has compassion on His creation. (39:2–3)

Clothe yourself, therefore, with cheerfulness, which always finds favor with God and is acceptable to Him. (42:1)

Test by life and actions the one who claims to be spirit-inspired. (43:16)

The fear of the Lord lives in the good desire. (45:4)

Luxury and deception have no memories . . . , but . . . punishment and torment have long memories. (65:3)

If . . . you cannot enter the city except through its gate, . . . so too you cannot enter the Kingdom of God except by the name of His Son, who was loved by Him. (89:5)

If you bear the Name but do not bear His power, you will bear His name in vain. (90:2)

For all these things I gave thanks to the Lord: because He had mercy on all those who called upon His name, and sent forth the angel of repentance to us who had sinned against Him and renewed our spirit and, when we were already ruined and had no hope of life, restored our life. (91:3)

The name of the Son of God is great and incomprehensible, and sustains the whole world. (91:5)

If our God and Lord, who rules over all things and has authority over all His creation, holds no grudge against those who confess their sins and is merciful, can a human being, who is mortal and full of sin, hold a grudge against someone, as though he could destroy or save him? (100:4)

The Lord lives among people who love peace, for peace is truly dear to Him, but He keeps His distance from the quarrelsome. (109:2)

All who do not keep His commandments are running away from their own life and oppose Him; . . . they do not follow His commandments, but hand themselves over to death, and every one of them is guilty of his or her own blood. (112:4)

~ *The Letter to Diognetus*

The most eloquently and elegantly written of all the works belonging to the Apostolic Fathers is *The Letter to Diognetus*. It is the earliest extant example of a style of writing that would become increasingly common among Christian intellectuals in the second half of the second and the first half of the third centuries—the apologetic defense of Christianity. Winsomely argued, *The Letter to Diognetus* defends Christian teaching and practice against pagan misunderstandings and false allegations. Neither the author nor the recipient of the work is known. The work dates from somewhere between 150 and 225.

The Letter to Diognetus[1]

He who made the heaven and the earth and all that is in them, and provides us all with what we need, cannot Himself need any of the things that He Himself provides to those who imagine that they are giving to Him. (3:4)

Is it not unlawful to accept some of the things created by God for human use as created good but to refuse others as useless and superfluous? (4:2)

Christians are not distinguished from the rest of humanity by country, language, or custom. For nowhere do they live in cities of their own, nor do they speak some unusual dialect, nor do they practice an eccentric lifestyle. This teaching of theirs has not been discovered by the thought

---

1 Excerpted from *AposFrs* 534–555.

and reflection of ingenious people, nor do they promote any human doctrine, as some do. But while they live in both Greek and barbarian cities, as each one's lot was cast, and follow the local customs in dress and food and other aspects of life, at the same time they demonstrate the remarkable and admittedly unusual character of their own citizenship. They live in their own countries, but only as aliens; they participate in everything as citizens, and endure everything as foreigners. Every foreign country is their fatherland, and every fatherland is foreign. They marry like everyone else, and have children, but they do not expose their offspring. They share their food but not their wives. They are in the flesh, but they do not live according to the flesh. They live on earth, but their citizenship is in heaven. They obey the established laws; indeed in their private lives they transcend the laws. They love everyone, and by everyone they are persecuted. They are unknown, yet they are condemned; they are put to death, yet they are brought to life. They are poor, yet they make many rich; they are in need of everything, yet they abound in everything. They are dishonored, yet they are glorified in their dishonor; they are slandered, yet they are vindicated. They are cursed, yet they bless; they are insulted, yet they offer respect. When they do good, they are punished as evildoers; when they are punished, they rejoice as though brought to life. By the Jews they are assaulted as foreigners, and by the Greeks they are persecuted, yet those who hate them are unable to give a reason for their hostility. (5:1–17)

When God sent Jesus Christ, He did so as one who saves by persuasion, not compulsion, for compulsion is no attribute of God. When He sent Him, He did so as one calling, not pursuing; when He sent Him, He did so as one loving, not judging. But He will send Him again as judge, and who will endure His coming? (7:4–5)

Who had any knowledge at all of what God was, before He [Jesus Christ] came? (8:1)

No one has either seen or recognized God, but He has revealed Himself . . . through faith, which is the only means by which it is permitted to see God. (8:5)

For what else but His righteousness could have covered our sins? In whom was it possible for us, the lawless and ungodly, to be justified, except in the Son of God alone? O the sweet exchange, O the incomprehensible work of God, O the unexpected blessings, that the sinfulness of many should be hidden in one righteous man, while the righteousness of one should justify many sinners. (9:3–5)

God loved humanity, for whose sake He made the world, to whom He subjected everything on earth, to whom He gave reason, to whom He gave mind; them alone He permitted to look up to heaven, them He created in His own image, to them He sent His one and only Son, to them He promised the kingdom in heaven, which He will give to those who have loved Him. (10:2)

Do not be surprised that a person can become an imitator of God; he can, if God is willing. . . . Whoever takes upon himself a neighbor's burden, whoever wishes to benefit another who is worse off in something in which he himself is better off, whoever provides to those in need things that he has received from God, and thus becomes a god to those who receive them, this one is an imitator of God. (10:4, 6)

When you realize what the true life in heaven is, when you despise the apparent death here on earth, when you fear the real death, which is reserved for those who will be condemned to the eternal fire which will punish to the very end those delivered to it, then you will admire those who for righteousness' sake endure the transitory fire, and you will consider them blessed, when you comprehend that other fire. (10:7–8)

Does anyone who has been rightly taught and has come to love the Word not seek to learn exactly the things openly made known by the Word to disciples? (11:2)

This is He who was from the beginning, who appeared as new yet proved to be old, and is always young as He is born in the hearts of saints. (11:4)

The reverence of the law is praised in song, and the grace of the prophets is recognized, and the faith of the gospels is established, and the tradition of the apostles is preserved, and the joy of the Church exults. (11:6)

The tree of knowledge does not kill; on the contrary, disobedience kills. (12:2)

~ Papias

Papias (c. 70–c. 155) served as bishop of Hierapolis in Asia Minor. He carefully collected whatever personal recollections he could recover from anyone who had heard either the Lord Jesus Christ or any of His associates. Papias published these records in a five-volume collection, *Expositions of the Sayings of the Lord,* probably sometime around 130. However, the work has not survived; it is known only in fragments quoted by subsequent authors.

Fragments from Papias's Writings[1]

I did not enjoy those who have a great deal to say, but those who teach the truth. Nor did I enjoy those who recall someone else's commandments, but those who remember the commandments given by the Lord to the faith and proceeding from the truth itself. (§3)

Some of the angels . . . God assigned to rule over the orderly arrangement of the earth, and commissioned them to rule well. . . . But as it turned out, their administration came to nothing. And the great dragon, the ancient serpent, who is called the devil and Satan, was cast out; the deceiver of the whole world was cast down to the earth along with his angels. (§11)

Christ came; and the law, which was impossible for anyone else, He fulfilled in His body, according to the apostle. He defeated sin and condemned Satan, and through His death He spread abroad His righteousness over all. (§24)

---

1 Excerpted from *AposFrs* 562–595.

～ Justin Martyr

By his own testimony, Justin's (c. 100–165) quest for truth eventually led him to embrace Christianity. He had tried various philosophical schools and ended up being most attracted to the variety of Platonism that existed in his day; however, he was still not satisfied. Subsequently challenged by an elderly man to consider the truth claims of Christianity, Justin engaged in a diligent examination, as a result of which he was converted to faith in Christ. Justin set up a school in Rome, where he instructed all who would listen to him in the Christian faith, urging its excellence as the ultimate truth from God Himself. In 165, he was martyred; the excerpts below recounting his martyrdom come from official court reports.

In his writings, Justin Martyr tried to build bridges between Christianity and the intellectual world of his time: he cited and interacted with the poets and philosophers who had influenced the culture in which he lived, while defending Christianity against various accusations and urging its truth claims. His works are rich in insight, offer stimulating presentations of Christian truth, and present some of the earliest information about Christian worship services and, particularly, the administration of baptism and the Eucharist.

The Martyrdom of Justin[1]

Rusticus the prefect asked, "What is the dogma you believe?" Justin answered, "That according to which we worship the God of the Christians, whom we reckon to be One from the beginning, the maker and fashioner of the whole creation, visible and invisible; and the Lord Jesus Christ, the

---
1 Excerpted from ANF 1:305–306.

Son of God, who had been proclaimed beforehand by the prophets as soon coming to dwell with humanity, the herald of salvation and teacher of good disciples. What I can say, as a mere human, is insignificant in comparison with His boundless divinity." (ch. 1)

The God of the Christians is not circumscribed by place; being invisible, He fills heaven and earth, and everywhere He is worshiped and glorified by the faithful. (ch. 2)

No right-thinking person falls away from piety to impiety. (ch. 4)

The First Apology[2]

Impelled by the desire for the eternal and pure life, we seek the abode that is with God, the Father and Creator of all, and are ready to confess our faith, persuaded and convinced as we are that those who have shown God by their works that they followed Him, and loved to abide with Him where there is no sin to cause disturbance, can obtain eternal life. This, then, to speak shortly, is what we expect and have learned from Christ, and what we teach. (ch. 8)

With gratitude to the Maker of the universe, by invocations and hymns, we offer thanks for our creation, for all the means of health, for the various qualities of the different kinds of things, and for the changes of the seasons; and we present petitions before Him that we may exist again in incorruption through faith in Him. (ch. 13)

Not only the one who actually commits adultery is rejected by God, but also the one who desires to commit adultery—since not only our deeds but also our thoughts are open before God. (ch. 15)

Let those who are not found living as Jesus Christ taught be understood to be no Christians, even though they profess with the lip the precepts of Christ; for not those who make profession, but those who do the works, shall be saved, according to His word: "Not everyone who says to Me, 'Lord, Lord,' shall enter the kingdom of heaven, but he who does the will of My Father in heaven" [Matt 7:21]. (ch. 16)

---

2 Excerpted from ANF 1:163–187.

[In the resurrection,] we expect to receive our own bodies again, though they are dead and have been cast into the earth, for we maintain that with God nothing is impossible. (ch. 18)

You are now incredulous because you have never seen a dead person rise again. But as at first you would not have believed it possible that persons could be produced from a small drop [of semen], and yet now you see them thus produced, so also you should judge that it is not impossible that the bodies of people, after they have been dissolved and resolved into earth like seeds, should in God's appointed time rise again and put on incorruption. (ch. 19)

In the books of the prophets we found Jesus Christ foretold as coming, born of a virgin, growing up to maturity, healing every disease and every sickness, raising the dead, and being hated, unrecognized, crucified, dying, and rising again, and ascending into heaven—and being, and being called, the Son of God. (ch. 31)

But when the Spirit of prophecy speaks of things that are about to come to pass as if they had already taken place, . . . this circumstance should afford readers no excuse [for confusion]. . . . The things which He absolutely knows will take place, He predicts as if they had already taken place. (ch. 42)

God did not make humankind like other things (such as trees and four-legged beasts) which cannot act by choice: for they would not be worthy of reward or praise if they did not freely choose the good but did only what they were made to do; nor, if they were evil, would they be worthy of punishment, since they would not have been evil by their choice, but only because they were made to be so. (ch. 43)

We have been taught that Christ is the Firstborn of God, and we have declared that He is the Word of whom every race of humanity were partakers; those who lived by reason are Christians, even though they have been thought atheists—as, among the Greeks, Socrates and Heraclitus, and others like them; and among the barbarians, Abraham, Hananiah, Azariah, Mishael, and Elijah, and many others whose actions and names we now decline to recount, because we know it would be tedious. (ch. 46)

Since, then, we prove that all things which have already happened had been predicted by the prophets before they came to pass, we must necessarily believe also that those things which in like manner have been predicted, but not yet come to pass, shall certainly happen.... For the prophets have proclaimed His two advents: the one, that which is already past, when He came as a dishonored and suffering man; but the second when, according to prophecy, He shall come from heaven with glory, accompanied by His angelic host. Then He shall raise the bodies of all who have lived, and shall clothe the worthy with immortality, and shall send the wicked, endued with eternal sensibility, into everlasting fire with the wicked demons. (ch. 52)

Why should we believe that a crucified man is the Firstborn of the unbegotten God, and that He will pass judgment on the whole human race, unless we had found testimonies concerning Him published before He came and was born as man, and unless we saw that things had happened accordingly? (ch. 53)

[On the practice of baptism:] As many as are persuaded and believe that what we teach and say is true, and promise to live accordingly, are instructed to pray and to entreat God with fasting for the remission of their past sins; we pray and fast with them. Then we bring them where there is water, and they are regenerated in the same manner in which we ourselves were regenerated: in the name of God, the Father and Lord of the universe, and of our Savior Jesus Christ, and of the Holy Spirit, they receive the washing with water. (ch. 61)

No one can utter the name of the ineffable God; and if anyone dare to say that there is a name, he raves with a hopeless madness. (ch. 61)

Having become man by a virgin according to the counsel of the Father for the salvation of those who believe on Him, He endured both to be treated with disdain and to suffer, that by dying and rising again He might conquer death. (ch. 63)

[On the practice of the Lord's Supper:] We call this food the Eucharist, of which none is allowed to partake unless they believe that the things which we teach are true, have been washed with the washing that is for the remission of sins unto regeneration [i.e., baptism], and who are so living as Christ has enjoined. For we do not receive these as common bread and common drink: as Jesus Christ our Savior, having been made flesh by the

Word of God, had both flesh and blood for our salvation, we have been taught that the food which is blessed by the prayer of His word, and from which our blood and flesh by transmutation are nourished, is the flesh and blood of that Jesus who was made flesh. (ch. 66)

For all things with which we are supplied, we bless the Maker of all through His Son Jesus Christ, and through the Holy Spirit. (ch. 67)

[On the order of a worship service:] On the day called Sunday, all who live in cities or in the country gather together to one place, and the memoirs of the apostles or the writings of the prophets are read, as long as time permits. Then, when the reader has ceased, the president verbally instructs and exhorts us to the imitation of these good things. Then we all rise together and pray, and when our prayer is ended, bread and wine and water are brought, and the president in like manner offers prayers and thanksgivings, according to his ability, and the people assent, saying, "Amen." Then these are distributed to each, and each partakes of that over which thanks have been given. (ch. 67)

But Sunday is the day on which we all hold our common assembly, because it is the first day on which God, having wrought a change in the darkness and matter, made the world; and it is the day on which Jesus Christ our Savior rose from the dead. (ch. 67)

The Second Apology[3]

God did not make the world aimlessly, but for the sake of the human race. ... He takes pleasure in those who imitate Him, but He is displeased with those who embrace what is worthless either in word or deed. (ch. 4)

But to the Father of all, who is unbegotten, no name is given. When one is given a name, he has as his elder the person who gives him the name. ... "God" is not a name, but an intuition implanted in the nature of human beings of a thing that can hardly be explained. (ch. 6)

We do not affirm that it is by fate that people do what they do or suffer what they suffer, but that each one by free choice acts rightly or sins. (ch. 7)

---

[3] Excerpted from ANF 1:188–193.

Since God in the beginning made the race of angels and human beings with free will, they will justly suffer in eternal fire punishment for whatever sins they have committed. And this is the nature of all that is made, to be capable of vice and virtue. (ch. 7)

Our doctrines are greater than all human teaching. (ch. 10)

Death is a debt due from everyone who is born. (ch. 11)

Plato . . . , the Stoics, poets, and historians—each of them spoke in proportion to the share he had of the spermatic Word. . . . Whatever things were rightly said among all people are the property of us Christians. (ch. 13)

Adjudged soberly, our doctrines are not shameful; indeed, they are loftier than all human philosophy. (ch. 15)

Dialogue with Trypho[4]

The inability of the female sex to receive fleshly circumcision proves that this circumcision was given for a sign, and not for a work of righteousness. For God has also given women the ability to observe all things which are righteous and virtuous. (ch. 23)

The fact that there are people confessing themselves to be Christians and admitting the crucified Jesus to be both Lord and Christ, yet not teaching His doctrines but those of the spirits of error, causes us who are disciples of the true and pure doctrine of Jesus Christ to be more faithful and steadfast in the hope He announced. (ch. 35)

We pray for you and for all others who hate us, that you, having repented along with us, may not blaspheme Him who by His works, by the mighty deeds even now wrought through His name, by the words He taught, by the prophecies announced concerning Him, is the blameless, and in all things irreproachable, Christ Jesus. We pray further that, believing on Him, you may be saved in His second glorious advent, and may not be condemned to fire by Him. (ch. 35)

---

4 Excerpted from ANF 1:194–270.

The concealed power of God was in Christ the crucified. (ch. 49)

I am entirely convinced that no Scripture contradicts another. I shall admit rather that I do not understand what is recorded, and shall strive to persuade those who imagine that the Scriptures are contradictory to be of the same opinion [about Scripture] as myself. (ch. 65)

When the people waged war with Amalek, and the son of Nave (Nun) by name Jesus (Joshua) led the fight, Moses himself prayed to God, stretching out both hands, and Hur and Aaron supported them during the whole day, so that they might not hang down when he became weary. For if he gave up any part of this sign—which was an imitation of the Cross—the people were beaten, as is recorded in the writings of Moses; but if he remained in this form, Amalek was accordingly defeated. Thus, he who prevailed did so by the Cross. (ch. 90)

For God sets before every race of humankind that which is always and universally just, as well as all righteousness: every race knows that adultery, fornication, homicide, and the like are sinful; and though they all commit such practices, yet they do not escape from the knowledge that they act unrighteously whenever they do so—except for those possessed by an unclean spirit, or who have been debased by education, wicked customs, or sinful institutions, and who have lost (or rather, quenched and put under) their innate ideas. (ch. 93)

The Son of God became human by the virgin, in order that the disobedience which proceeded from the serpent might receive its destruction in the same manner in which it derived its origin. For Eve, who was a virgin and undefiled, having conceived the word of the serpent, brought forth disobedience and death. But the Virgin Mary received faith and joy when the angel Gabriel announced the good tidings to her, "the Holy Spirit will come upon you, and the power of the Highest will overshadow you; therefore, also, that Holy One who is to be born will be called the Son of God"; and she replied, "Let it be to me according to your word" [Luke 1:35, 38]. And by her He has been born, to whom we have proved so many Scriptures refer, and by whom God destroys both the serpent and those angels and people who are like him, but who works deliverance from death to those who repent of their wickedness and believe upon Him. (ch. 100)

The Father wished His Son really to undergo such sufferings for our sakes; we may not say that, being the Son of God, He did not feel what was happening to Him and inflicted on Him. (ch. 103)

Now it is evident that no one can terrify or subdue us who have believed in Jesus throughout all the world. For it is plain that, though beheaded, crucified, thrown to wild beasts, put into chains, thrown into fire, and all other kinds of torture, we do not give up our confession. The more such things happen, the more do others (and in increasing numbers) become faithful, and worshipers of God through the name of Jesus. (ch. 110)

So Christ has come according to the power given Him from the Almighty Father, and has summoned people to friendship, blessing, repentance, and dwelling together. (ch. 139)

I exhort you to give all diligence in this very great struggle for your own salvation, and to be earnest in setting a higher value on the Christ of the Almighty God than on your own teachers. (ch. 142)

The Discourse to the Greeks[5]

These have conquered me—the divinity of the instruction, and the power of the Word. (ch. 5)

Hortatory Address to the Greeks[6]

Accurate investigation of matters, examining the question with a more searching scrutiny, often reveals that things which have passed for excellent are of quite another sort. (ch. 1)

As if with one mouth and one tongue, they [the writers of Scripture] have in succession, and in harmony with one another, taught us concerning God, the Creation of the world, the formation of humankind, the immortality of the human soul, the judgment which is to be after this life, and all things which we need to know. In diverse times and places, they have thus afforded us the divine instruction. (ch. 8)

---

5 Excerpted from ANF 1:271–272.
6 Excerpted from ANF 1:273–289.

God cannot be called by any proper name, for names are given to mark out and distinguish their subject matters, because these are many and diverse; but no one existed before God who could give Him a name, nor did He Himself think it right to name Himself, since He is one and unique. (ch. 21)

Having been duped by the deceiving demon, and having dared to disobey God, our first parents were cast out of Paradise, remembering the name of gods, but no longer being taught by God that there are no other gods. (ch. 21)

The substance of our religion consists in works, not in words. (ch. 35)

Our Savior Jesus Christ, who, being the Word of God, inseparable from Him in power, having assumed that humanity which had been made in the image and likeness of God, restored to us the knowledge of the religion of our ancient forefathers, which those who lived after them abandoned through the bewitching counsel of the envious devil, and turned to the worship of those who were no gods. (ch. 38)

On the Sole Government of God[7]

In the long-suffering of God, forgetfulness—having taken possession of human minds—has acted recklessly in transferring to mortals the name which is applicable to the only true God. From the few the infection of sin has spread to the many, who were blinded by popular usage to the knowledge of that which was lasting and unchangeable. (ch. 1)

On the Resurrection (fragments of the lost work)[8]

Now the Word of Truth is sent from God. The freedom claimed by the truth is not arrogant; even so, since it was sent with authority, it would not be fitting that it should be required to produce proof of what is said. (ch. 1)

Is the soul by itself the human being? No, it is only the soul. Would the body be called the human being? No, it is only called the body. If, then, neither of these is by itself the human being, but that which is made up of the

---

7 Excerpted from ANF 1:290–293.
8 Excerpted from ANF 1:294–299.

two together is called the human being, and God has called human beings to life and resurrection, He has called not a part, but the whole—which is the soul and the body. (ch. 8)

If then the Savior . . . proclaimed salvation to the soul alone, what new thing beyond what we heard from Pythagoras and Plato and all their band did He bring us? But now He has come proclaiming the glad tidings of a new and strange hope to people. For indeed it was a strange and new thing for God to promise that He would not keep incorruption in incorruption, but would make corruption incorruption. (ch. 10)

Other Fragments[9]

We shall not injure God by remaining ignorant of Him, but we shall deprive ourselves of His friendship. (#7)

The unskillfulness of the teacher proves destructive to his disciples, and the carelessness of the disciples entails danger for the teacher. (#8)

Only with difficulty can the soul be recalled to those good things from which it has fallen; with difficulty is it dragged away from those evils to which it has become accustomed. (#9)

What took place in the living water, in which the wood and the hyssop and the scarlet were dipped [Lev 14:49–53], sets forth the bloody Passion of Christ on the Cross for the salvation of those who are sprinkled with the Spirit, and the water, and the blood. (#10)

Sound doctrine does not enter into the hard and disobedient heart. (#16)

To yield and give way to our passions is the lowest slavery; to rule over them is the only liberty. (#18)

That one who by a true faith has come forth from error to the truth, has truly known himself or herself. (#19)

---

9 Excerpted from ANF 1:300–302.

∽ *Athenagoras*

Other than that he lived in the latter half of the second century, little is known about Athenagoras's life; indeed, only one ancient author mentions him. However, Athenagoras has left two striking apologies. They manifest significant rhetorical facility; this, together with his frequent citation of the writings of poets and philosophers of pagan culture, indicates he had received academic training according to the best standards of his time. He used this training capably in defending Christianity.

A Plea for Christians[1]

We know and cherish that being as God by whose Word all things were made and by whose Spirit all things are held in being. (ch. 6)

The Spirit of God moved the mouths of the prophets like musical instruments. (ch. 7)

We acknowledge one God, uncreated, eternal, invisible, impassible, incomprehensible, illimitable; who is apprehended by the understanding only and the reason; who is encompassed by light, beauty, spirit, and power ineffable; by whom the universe has been created through His Word, set in order, and is kept in being. (ch. 10)

Among us you will find uneducated persons, artisans, and old women,

---
1 Excerpted from ANF 2:129–148.

who, if they are unable in words to prove the benefit of our doctrine, yet by their deeds exhibit the benefit arising from their persuasion of its truth: they do not rehearse speeches, but exhibit good works. (ch. 11)

Since we are persuaded that we shall give an account of everything in the present life to God, who made us and the world, we choose a modest, benevolent, and humble life, not deeming it so great an evil in this life if someone robs us of our life, compared with what we shall get back from our great judge for our gentle, benevolent, and moderate way of life.... We know that the life for which we look is far better than can be described in words. (ch. 12)

If, therefore, the world is an instrument in tune, and moving in well-measured time, I adore the Being who gave its harmony, strikes its notes, and sings the accordant strain, but not the instrument. (ch. 16)

It is not the work of God to urge someone to what is against nature. (ch. 26)

For those who are persuaded that nothing will escape the scrutiny of God, but that even the body which has ministered to the irrational impulses of the soul and its desires will be punished along with it, it is not likely that they will commit even the smallest sin. (ch. 36)

On the Resurrection of the Dead[2]

Alongside the truth contained in every dogma and reasoned argument some falsehood will be found growing. This growth comes about, not from any natural cause in the subject matter itself, nor yet from any formal principle in the dogma; rather, it is fostered by those who delight in illegitimate growths to the detriment of the truth. (ch. 1)

It is impossible for God not to know the nature of the bodies destined to rise, in their every part and particle, the destination of every portion of what is dissolved, what part of the element has received that which has been released and returned to its kindred element, even if to human beings it seems quite impossible to separate out that which has once again been united with the common stock of its element. If He was not ignorant of the

---

2 Excerpted from ANF 2:149–162.

nature of the elements that were to be brought into being—out of which the human body was to be formed—even before they each entered into that composition which was proper to them, and if He was not ignorant of the parts of these elements from which He was going to take what was fitting for the composition of the human body, then it is clear that neither, after the complete dissolution of the whole, will He be ignorant of the place to which each part has gone that He took for the completion of each person. (ch. 2)

The completion of each individual body shows that His power is sufficient for the resurrection of these bodies, as well. For if He made human bodies and their constituent elements, even though they did not all come into being right away at the first Creation, then even when they are dissolved in all kinds of ways, He will raise them up with the same ease, for the one is just as possible to Him as the other. (ch. 3)

It is easier to show up a lie than to lay hold of the truth. (ch. 11)

God did not create human beings for no purpose, for He is wise, and no work of wisdom is in vain; nor did He make them because He needed them, for He needs nothing. To a Being who needs absolutely nothing, none of His creatures can offer anything He needs. (ch. 12)

The attention of the Creator reaches to everything—invisible and visible alike, small and great—for all created things require the attention of the Creator. (ch. 18)

The whole human being, therefore, composed of body and soul, is to receive justice for each of his or her acts. But we see that this does not happen in this life, for here in this life final justice is not meted out, for many atheists and consummate villains go to the end of their lives without experiencing hardship; while again many of those who show that their life is lived in the practice of all virtue live in pain, insults, calumnies, outrages, and all kinds of misfortune. Nor does justice happen after death, for there the whole person no longer exists, since the soul is separated from the body and the body itself is scattered again into those elements from which it came, keeping nothing any longer of its former beauty and vivacity or even the memory of its deeds. (ch. 18)

The soul separated from its body does not experience ultimate happiness. ... It is absolutely necessary that the end of every human being be found in another condition of that complete human being, who still remains the same person. (ch. 25)

~ *Theophilus of Antioch*

Theophilus (?–183) served as the sixth bishop of Antioch. He had received a typical education in the Hellenistic mode that prevailed in Asia Minor and Syria. He wrote several works; the only one extant is his *To Autolycus*. This work shows that Theophilus was well trained in rhetoric, knew contemporary literature and philosophy well, and made effective use of metaphor.

To Autolycus[1]

God is seen by those who are enabled to see Him when they have the eyes of their soul opened; for all have eyes, but the eyes of some are clouded by cataracts and do not see the light of the sun. But it does not follow that, because the blind do not see, the light of the sun does not shine; for that, let the blind blame themselves and their own eyes. (1:2)

Iniquities blind you in darkness, so that you cannot see God. (1:2)

The appearance of God is ineffable and indescribable, and cannot be seen by the eyes of flesh. For in glory He is incomprehensible, in greatness unfathomable, in height inconceivable, in power incomparable, in wisdom unrivalled, in goodness inimitable, in kindness unutterable. (1:3)

For as the soul in a human being is not seen, being invisible to us, but

---

1 Excerpted from ANF 2:89–121.

is perceived through the motion of the body, so God cannot be seen by human eyes, but is beheld and perceived through His providence and works. (1:5)

By Him you speak; His breath you breathe, yet Him you know not. And this is your condition, because of the blindness of your soul and the hardness of your heart. (1:7)

Give reverent attention to the prophetic Scriptures, and they will make your way plainer for escaping the eternal punishments, and obtaining the eternal rewards of God. For He who gave the mouth for speech, formed the ear to hear, and made the eye to see, will examine all things and will judge righteous judgment, rendering to each what each deserves. (1:14)

And what great thing is it if God made the world out of existent materials? For even a human artist, when he gets material from someone, makes of it what he pleases. But the power of God is manifested in this, that out of things that are not He makes whatever He pleases; in the same way, the bestowal of life and motion is the prerogative of no other than God alone. (2:4)

With regard to this six days' work [of Creation], no one can give a worthy explanation and description of all its parts—even if that person had ten thousand tongues and ten thousand mouths and lived ten thousand years! Even then, that person could not utter anything worthy of these things, on account of the exceeding greatness and riches of the wisdom of God which there is in the six days' work. (2:12)

On the fifth day [of Creation] the living creatures which proceed from the waters were produced; in this also, the manifold wisdom of God is revealed, for who could count their multitude and various kinds? Moreover, the things proceeding from the waters were blessed by God; this was a sign of humanity's being destined to receive repentance and remission of sin through the water and laver of regeneration—as many as come to the truth, are born again, and receive blessing from God. (2:16)

When God said, "Let Us make man in our image, according to Our likeness" [Gen 1:26], He first intimated the dignity of human beings. For God had made all things by His Word, and had reckoned them all mere by-products of it; but He reckoned the creation of humanity to be the only work worthy of His own hands. Moreover, God says, as if needing help, "Let Us make man in Our image, according to Our likeness." But to no one else than to His own Word and Wisdom [i.e., to the Son and the Spirit] did He thus speak. (2:18)

The tree of knowledge itself was good, and its fruit was good. It was not the tree, as some think, but the disobedience, which had death in it. (2:25)

Far be it from Christians to conceive sinful deeds; for with them temperance dwells, self-restraint is practiced, monogamy is observed, chastity is guarded, iniquity exterminated, sin extirpated, righteousness exercised, law administered, worship performed, God acknowledged: truth governs, grace guards, peace screens them; the Holy Word guides, wisdom teaches, life directs, God reigns. (3:15)

~ Melito of Sardis

Melito (?–c. 190) served as bishop of the church of Sardis in the late second century. Little is known of his life. He wrote some apologies in defense of the Christian faith, but these are no longer extant. His remaining written works—the liturgical homily *On Pascha* (the Passover, seen from its fulfillment in Christ's death and resurrection) and a few fragments cited by other ancient authors—show that he was a gifted rhetorician, prone to allusive and poetic presentation. Well versed in the Old Testament, he understood it as predicting and culminating in Christ. Scholars have ascertained that *On Pascha* must have been written sometime between AD 160 and 170; the dating of the rest of his works is uncertain. Citations from On Pascha are by strophe; those from the fragments are by the number assigned by scholars to the respective fragments.

On Pascha[1]

Old is the law, but new the word;
      temporary the model, but eternal the grace;
      perishable the sheep, imperishable the Lord;
      not broken as a lamb, but resurrected as God.
For although as a sheep he was led to the slaughter,
      yet he was not a sheep;

---

[1] Excerpts taken from Stuart George Hall, trans. and ed., *Melito of Sardis: On Pascha and Fragments* (London: Clarendon Press, 1979), pp. 2–61. (A new edition is planned, but the date is uncertain.)

although as a lamb speechless,
    yet neither was he a lamb.
For the model indeed existed,
    but then the reality appeared.
For instead of the lamb there was a Son,
    and instead of the sheep a Man;
    and in the Man Christ who has comprised all things. (§4–5)

O strange and inexpressible mystery!
The slaughter of the sheep was found to be Israel's salvation,
    and the death of the sheep became the people's life,
    and the blood won the angel's respect.
Tell me, angel, what did you respect?
    The slaughter of the sheep or the life of the Lord?
    The death of the sheep or the model of the Lord?
    The blood of the sheep or the Spirit of the Lord?
It is clear that your respect was won
    when you saw the mystery of the Lord occurring in the sheep,
    the life of the Lord in the slaughter of the lamb,
    the model of the Lord in the death of the sheep. (§31–33)

The law was fulfilled when the gospel was elucidated,
    and the people [of Israel] was made void when the church arose;
    and the model was abolished when the Lord was revealed,
    and today, things once precious have become worthless,
    since the really precious things have been revealed.
Once, the slaying of the sheep was precious,
    but it is worthless now because of the salvation of the Lord. (§43–44)

The Jerusalem below was precious,
    but it is worthless now because of the Jerusalem above.
    the narrow inheritance was precious,
    but it is worthless now because of the widespread bounty.
For it is not on one place nor in a little plot
    that the glory of God is established,
    but on all the ends of the inhabited earth his bounty overflows,
    and there the almighty God has made his dwelling
    through Christ Jesus; to whom be glory for ever. Amen. (§45)

When God in the beginning had made the heaven and the earth
    and all the things in them by his word,
    he fashioned from the earth man,
    and gave him a share of his own breath.
This man he set in the paradise eastward,
    in Eden, there to live in bliss,
    laying down this law for him by his command:
    Of every tree in the paradise by all means eat,
    but of the tree of knowing good and evil you shall not eat;
    and on the day you eat you shall certainly die.
But the man, being naturally receptive of good and evil,
    as a clod of earth is of seed from either side,
    accepted the hostile and greedy adviser,
    and by touching the tree he broke the command and disobeyed God.
So he was cast out into this world,
    as into a convicts' prison.
This man having become very prolific and very long-lived,
    when through the tasting of the tree he was dissolved,
    and sank into the earth,
    an inheritance was left by him to his children;
    for he left his children an inheritance
    not charity but promiscuity,
    not imperishability but decay,
    not honor but dishonor,
    not freedom but slavery,
    not royalty but tyranny,
    not life but death,
    not salvation but destruction. (§47–49)

In every soul sin made a mark,
    and those in whom he made it were bound to die.
So all flesh began to fall under sin,
    and every body under death,
    and every soul was driven out of its fleshly dwelling.
And what was taken from earth was to earth dissolved,
    and what was given from God was confined in Hades;
    and there was separation of what fitted beautifully,
    and the beautiful body was split apart.

For man was being divided by death;
> for a strange disaster and captivity were enclosing him,
> and he was dragged off a prisoner under the shadows of death,
> and desolate lay the Father's image.

This, then, is the reason why the mystery of the Pascha
> has been fulfilled in the body of the Lord. (§54–56)

For the mystery of the Lord is new and old:
> old according to the law, but new with reference to the grace.

But if you look carefully at the model,
> you will perceive him through the final outcome.

Therefore if you wish to see the mystery of the Lord,
> look at Abel who is similarly murdered,
> at Isaac who is similarly bound,
> at Joseph who is similarly sold,
> at Moses who is similarly exposed,
> at David who is similarly persecuted,
> at the prophets who similarly suffer for the sake of Christ.

Look also at the sheep, slaughtered in the land of Egypt,
> which struck Egypt and saved Israel through its blood. (§58–60)

It is he who, coming from heaven to the earth because of the suffering one,
> and clothing himself in that same one through a virgin's womb,
> and coming forth a man,
> accepted the passions of the suffering one
> through the body which was able to suffer,
> and dissolved the passions of the flesh;
> and by the Spirit which could not die
> he killed death the killer of men.

For, himself led as a lamb and slain as a sheep,
> he ransomed us from the world's service as from the land of Egypt,
> and freed us from the devil's slavery as from the hand of Pharaoh;
> and he marked our souls with his own Spirit,
> and the members of our body with his own blood.

It is he that clothed death with shame. (§66–68)

He who hung the earth is hanging;
he who fixed the heavens has been fixed;

he who fastened the universe has been fastened to a tree;
the Sovereign has been insulted.
the God has been murdered. (§96)

"I am the one," says the Christ,
    "I am the one that destroyed death
    and triumphed over the enemy
    and trod down Hades
    and bound the strong one
    and carried off man to the heights of heaven;
    I am the one," says the Christ.
"Come, then, all families of men who are compounded with sins,
    and get forgiveness of sins.
For I am your forgiveness,
    I am the Pascha of salvation,
    I am the lamb slain for you;
    I am your ransom,
    I am your life,
    I am your light,
    I am your salvation,
    I am your resurrection,
    I am your king." (§102–103)

It is he that made heaven and earth
    and fashioned man in the beginning,
    who is proclaimed through the law and prophets,
    who was enfleshed upon a virgin,
    who was hung upon a tree,
    who was buried in the earth,
    who was raised from the dead
    and went up to the heights of heaven,
    who sits at the Father's right hand,
    who has power to save every man,
    through whom the Father did his works from beginning to eternity.
He is the Alpha and the Omega;
    he is beginning and end,
    beginning inexpressible and end incomprehensible.
    he is the Christ. (§104–105)

Fragments[2]

As a ram he was bound, . . .
    and as a lamb he was shorn,
    and as a sheep he was led to slaughter,
    and as a lamb he was crucified;
    and he carried the wood on his shoulders
    as he was led up to be slain like Isaac by his Father.
But Christ suffered, whereas Isaac did not suffer,
    for he was a model of the Christ who was going to suffer.
But by being merely the model of Christ
    he caused astonishment and fear among men.
For it was a strange mystery to behold,
    a son led by his father to a mountain for slaughter. (#9)

On behalf of Isaac the righteous one, a ram appeared for slaughter,
    so that Isaac might be released from bonds.
That ram, slain, ransomed Isaac;
    so also the Lord, slain, saved us,
    and bound, released us,
    and sacrificed, ransomed us. (#10)

For this reason the Father sent his incorporeal Son from heaven,
    so that, enfleshed in the virgin's womb and born as man,
    he might bring man to life and gather his parts,
    which death had scattered when he divided man. . . .
The earth quaked and its foundations shook,
    the sun fled and the elements turned away,
    and the day was changed;
    for they could not bear [to see] their Lord hanging on a tree.
And creation, shuddered, stupefied, and said,
    "What can this strange mystery be?
The judge is judged, and is silent;
    the invisible is seen, and is not ashamed;
    the incomprehensible is seized, and is not vexed;
    the immeasurable is measured, and does not resist;
    the impassible suffers, and does not retaliate;

---

[2] Excerpts taken from Hall, *Melito of Sardis: On Pascha and Fragments,* pp. 62–96.

>> the immortal dies, and takes it patiently;
>> the heavenly one is buried, and submits.
> What is this strange mystery?"
> Creation was stupefied.
> But when our Lord arose from the dead,
>> having trodden down death
>> and bound the strong one
>> and released man,
>> then all creation understood that it was for man's sake
>> that the judge was judged
>> and the invisible was seen
>> and the incomprehensible was seized,
>> and the immeasurable was measured,
>> and the impassible suffered,
>> and the immortal died,
>> and the heavenly one was buried.
> For our Lord, having become man,
>> was judged in order to bestow kindness,
>> was bound in order to release,
>> was seized in order to set free,
>> suffered in order to have compassion,
>> died in order to make alive,
>> was buried in order to raise up. (#13)

> For this cause he came to us;
>> for this cause, though incorporeal, he wove himself a body of our texture.
> He was seen as a lamb, but remained a shepherd;
>> he was reputed a servant, but did not refuse the rank of Son;
>> carried in the womb by Mary, and clothed with his Father;
>> treading the earth, and filling heaven;
>> appearing as a boy, and not falsifying the eternity of his nature;
>> wearing a body, and not restricting the simplicity of his divine nature;
>> seen as poor, and not depriving himself of his wealth;
>> wanting food, inasmuch as he was man,
>> and not ceasing to nourish the world, inasmuch as he was God;
>> putting on the likeness of a servant, and not changing his likeness to the Father;
> He was all things with his nature immutable.

He stood before Pilate, and sat with the Father;
He was fastened to the tree, and held the universe. (#14)

O strange and unspeakable mystery!
They hung on a tree him who founded the earth,
> they fixed with nails on a cross him who fixed the world,
> and they prepared burial for him who measured the heavens,
> and they bound him who frees from sin. . . . (New Fragment #2:9)

When the Savior shut his eyes upon the cross, light shone in hell;
> because the Lord descended to destroy hell, not in body but in soul;
> because the Lord descended and ravished all hell with his soul, but
> > with his body the earth.

When they hung on the tree the Lord with his body,
> then tombs opened, and hell was destroyed,
> and he released many souls, and the dead men arose;
> and creation could not bear it, because they saw their own Lord
> > hung on the cross. (New Fragment #2:12)

He suffered passion for you by the cross to free you from passions,
> he died by the cross to make you alive by the cross,
> he was buried to raise you.

Because the Lord suffered in the likeness of man,
> by that likeness the passions of mankind were destroyed;
> he slew death with death. (New Fragment #2:14)

And every race of men has received life from Christ.
One was judged and many were saved.
One was buried and many arose.
The Lord died for all and rose for all,
> and he put on humanity, ascended to the heights, to heaven,
> and offered the Father a gift, not gold nor silver nor precious pearls,
> but man, whom he made in his image and perfected in his likeness.
> > (New Fragment #2:17)

And because he was God and is God,
> little in body and great in soul,
> despised on earth and glorified in the heavens,
> scorned by men and magnified by the Father,

> this is the Man who was sent by the Father to the world because he is God,
> both Man upon earth and God in heaven,
> and he is God over all creation. (New Fragment #2:22)

Just as from a tree came sin, so also from a tree came salvation.
By the cross death is destroyed,
> and by the cross salvation shines;
> by the cross the gates of hell are burst,
> and by the cross the gates of paradise are opened.

The cross has become the way of saints and martyrs;
> the cross has become the chain of the apostles
> and the shield of faith of prophets.

The cross is the guide of the fallen;
> the cross is the comfort of the possessed,
> and an immovable wall to believers.

The cross is the strength of the weak,
> and the lifting up of the lowly.

The cross is the guide of the faithful robber [Lk 23:40–43];
> the cross is the destroyer of hell. (New Fragment #3:4–5)

∾ *Irenaeus*

Irenaeus (c. 130–202) was the greatest theologian of the second century. Born in Asia Minor, as a young man he listened to the sermons and teaching of Polycarp, the disciple of the Apostle John. At some subsequent point, Irenaeus went to Lyons, where he spent the rest of his life, serving the church there as its bishop. He wrote two important works that have come down to us: his *On the Apostolic Preaching* offers a summary of the message proclaimed by the apostles and handed down from their time within the Church; his massive and influential *Against Heresies* offered both a devastating critique of the various schools of gnosticism and a powerful presentation of the Christian faith. Several other works are no longer extant, apart from some quotations found in the writings of other ancient Christian authors.

On the Apostolic Preaching[1]

Godliness becomes cloudy and loses its luster by bodily impurity, and is broken and stained and loses its integrity when falsehood enters the soul; but it will be preserved in beauty and due measure by the truth constantly abiding in the mind and holiness in the body. For what use is it to know the truth in words, only to defile the body and perform evil deeds? Or what real good at all can bodily holiness do, if truth is not in the soul? (ch. 2)

This is what faith does for us, as the elders, the disciples of the apostles,

---

1 Excerpts taken from ACW 16:47–109.

have handed down to us: first of all, it admonishes us to remember that we have received baptism for the remission of sins in the name of God the Father, and in the name of Jesus Christ, the Son of God, who became incarnate and died and was raised, and in the Holy Spirit of God; and that this baptism is the seal of eternal life and is rebirth unto God, with the result that we are no longer merely children of mortal human beings, but of the eternal and everlasting God. (ch. 3)

And this is the summary of our faith, the foundation of the building, and the support of our way of life: God the Father, uncreated, beyond grasp, invisible, one God the Creator of all; this is the first article of our faith. And the second article is the Word of God, the Son of God, Christ Jesus our Lord, who was revealed by the prophets according to the character of their prophecy and as the Father disposed; all things whatsoever were made through Him. He also, in the end of times, for the recapitulation of all things, became human among humans, visible and tangible, in order to abolish death and bring life to light, and secure the communion of God and humanity. And the third article is the Holy Spirit, through whom the prophets prophesied, the patriarchs learned about God, the righteous were led in the path of justice, and who in the end of times has been poured forth in a new manner upon humanity over all the earth, renewing them to God. (ch. 6)

Therefore the baptism of our regeneration takes place through these three articles, granting us regeneration unto God the Father through His Son by the Holy Spirit: for those who bear the Spirit of God are led to the Word—that is, to the Son; while the Son presents them to the Father; and the Father confers incorruptibility. Thus, without the Spirit there is no seeing the Word of God, and without the Son there is no approaching the Father. (ch. 7)

The sublimity and greatness of this same God is beyond the power of expression. (ch. 8)

Since we were all implicated in the first formation of Adam, and we were bound to death through disobedience, it was fitting that the bonds of death were loosed by the obedience of Him who was made human for us. Because death ruled over the flesh, it was necessary that it should be vanquished by flesh, and so be forced to set humanity free from its oppression. So "the Word became flesh" [John 1:14], in order that sin might be destroyed by means of that same flesh through which it had mastered and seized and dominated humanity. Therefore, our Lord took up the same first formation for an Incarnation, so that He might fight on behalf of His forefathers and vanquish in Adam what had struck us in Adam. (ch. 31)

From this earth, then, while it was still virgin, God took dust and fashioned the man, the beginning of humanity. So the Lord, recapitulating this man, reproduced the scheme of his Incarnation, being born of a virgin by the will and wisdom of God, that He might copy the incarnation of Adam and might become man, as was written in the beginning, "according to the image and likeness of God" [see Gen 1:26]. (ch. 32)

Just as it was through a virgin who disobeyed that humanity was stricken and fell and died, so too it was through a virgin who obeyed the word of God that humanity, resuscitated by life, received life. (ch. 33)

The sin wrought through the tree was undone by the obedience of the tree—that obedience to God by which the Son of Man was nailed to the tree, destroying the knowledge of evil and bringing in and conferring the knowledge of good. . . . So by the obedience He showed unto death, hanging on the tree, He undid the old disobedience wrought in the tree. (ch. 34)

Rich in mercy, God the Father sent the creative Word who, when He came to save us, put Himself in our position, and in the same situation in which we lost life; He loosed the prison bonds, His light appeared and dispelled the darkness of the prison, and He sanctified our birth and abolished death, loosing those same bonds by which we were held. And He showed forth the Resurrection, becoming Himself "the firstborn from the dead" [Col 1:18], and raised in Himself prostrate humanity, being lifted up to the heights of heaven, at the right hand of the glory of the Father. (ch. 38)

It is necessary to believe God in all things, for God is truthful in all things. (ch. 43)

That He who according to the flesh was of the seed of David, the anointed, would be Son of God; that after His death He would rise again; that He would be in figure human, but in power God; and that He would be judge of the whole world and sole worker of righteousness and Redeemer—all this has been declared by [Old Testament] Scripture. (ch. 62)

Sometimes the Spirit of God relates through the prophets as a past event what is to come to pass in the future, for with God what is approved and determined to be is counted as already having happened, and the Spirit uses expressions having in view the time in which the outcome of the prophecy is realized. (ch. 67)

So, if the prophets have prophesied that the Son of God was to appear on earth, and have prophesied also in what place on earth, and how, and as what manner of man He should appear, and the Lord took on Himself all these prophecies, our belief in Him is well founded, and the tradition of the preaching is true—that is, the witness of the apostles who, sent by the Lord, preached to the whole world that the Son of God had come unto sufferings, which He endured for the destruction of death and the giving of life to the flesh; that by casting out hostilities to God (that is, iniquities), we should receive peace with Him, doing what is pleasing to Him. (ch. 86)

A Christian does not need to be commanded to observe a day of rest, for he keeps the Sabbath constantly, celebrating the service of God in the temple of God, which is the human body, and at all times working righteousness. (ch. 96)

This, beloved, is the preaching of the truth, and this is the character of our salvation, and this is the way of life announced by the prophets, ratified by Christ, handed over by the apostles, and handed down by the Church in the whole world to her children. This must be kept in all strictness. (ch. 98)

So error with respect to the three articles of our seal [i.e., baptism] has brought about much wandering away from the truth. For either they despise the Father, or they do not accept the Son, speaking against the dispensation of His Incarnation, or they do not accept the Spirit—that is, they reject prophecy. And we must beware of all such people, and flee their ways, if we really desire to be pleasing to God and receive salvation from Him. (ch. 100)

Against Heresies[2]

Error is never set forth in its naked deformity, lest, being thus exposed, it should immediately be detected for what it is. It is craftily decked out in attractive dress, so that, by its outward form, it might appear to the inexperienced—ridiculous as the expression may seem—truer than truth itself. ... What inexperienced person can readily detect the presence of brass when it has been mixed with silver? ... The language of these deceivers resembles ours, but what they mean with it is very different. (1:Preface,2)

The Church dispersed throughout the whole world to the ends of the earth has received from the apostles and their disciples this faith: We believe in one God, the Father Almighty, Maker of heaven and earth and sea and all that is in them; and in one Christ Jesus, the Son of God, who became incarnate for our salvation; and in the Holy Spirit, who proclaimed through the prophets the works of God, and the advents, and the birth from a virgin, and the Passion, and the Resurrection from the dead, and the ascension into heaven in the flesh of the beloved Christ Jesus, our Lord, and His future manifestation from heaven in the glory of the Father to "gather together in one all things" in Him [Eph 1:10], and to resurrect the entire human race, so that to Christ Jesus, our Lord and God and Savior and King, according to the will of the invisible Father, "every knee should bow, of those in heaven, and of those on earth, and of those under the earth, and ... every tongue should confess" Him [Phil 2:10–11], and that He should execute just judgment on all. At that time He will send the "spiritual hosts of wickedness" [Eph 6:12] (the angels who rebelled and became apostate), along with the ungodly, unrighteous, wicked, and profane among humanity, into everlasting fire; but in the exercise of His grace, He will grant eternal life to the righteous and holy (those who have kept His commandments and persevered in His love, some from the beginning of their lives, but others from their repentance) and will surround them with everlasting glory. (1:10,1)

While scattered throughout the whole world, the Church has received this message and this faith and still, as if living in only one house, carefully preserves it. She believes these points of doctrine as if she had only one soul, and one and the same heart. She proclaims them, teaches them, and

---

[2] Excerpts taken from James R. Payton, Jr., *Irenaeus on the Christian Faith: A Condensation of "Against Heresies"* (Eugene, OR: Pickwick Publications, 2011), pp. 27–194.

hands them down harmoniously, as if she had only one mouth. Although the languages of the world are dissimilar, yet the meaning of the tradition has remained one and the same, for the churches planted in Germany do not believe or hand down anything different than those in Spain or in Gaul or in the East or in Egypt or in Libya or in the central regions of the world. Just as the sun created by God is one and the same throughout the whole world, so also the preaching of the truth shines everywhere and enlightens all those who are willing to come to a knowledge of the truth. No leader in any of the congregations, however highly gifted in eloquence, teaches doctrines different from these (for no one is greater than the master); nor, on the other hand, does even one who is deficient in expression injure the tradition. The faith always remains one and the same: the one who is able to expound it at great length does not add anything to it, and the one who can say only a little does not thereby diminish it. (1:10,2)

The Catholic Church possesses one and the same faith throughout the whole world. . . . (1:10,3)

God needs nothing. . . . He created and made all things by His Word. He did not need the help of angels or any other power inferior to Himself to produce the things which were made. . . . He Himself, by Himself alone, in a way we can neither describe nor understand, having predestined all things, formed them as He chose, bestowing harmony on all things, assigning them their particular place and the beginning of their creation. (2:2,4)

It is not appropriate to say that the one who is God over all, who is free and independent, was a slave to necessity, or that anything takes place with His permission but against His will. In that case, necessity would be greater and more majestic than God, since whatever has the most power is superior. (2:5,4)

By calling on Him, even before the incarnation of our Lord, people were saved from wicked spirits, from all kinds of demons, and from every sort of apostate power. (2:6,2)

God is not as people are, and His thoughts are not like ours [Is 55:8]. The Father of all is at a vast distance from those affections and passions which operate among us. He is a simple, uncompounded being, without separate parts, and entirely like and equal to Himself: He is wholly understanding, wholly spirit, wholly thought, wholly intelligence, wholly reason, wholly hearing, wholly seeing, wholly light, and the whole source of all that is good—as those who are religious and pious are accustomed to say about God. (2:13,3)

He is above all these properties, and therefore indescribable. For He who comprehends all things may well and properly be called "understanding," but He is not therefore like human understanding; and He may most properly be termed "light," but He is nothing like the light with which we are acquainted. And so, in every other regard, the Father of all is not at all like us in our human weakness. (2:13,4)

The Lord suffered so that He might bring those who have wandered from the Father back to knowledge and communion with Him. . . . Having suffered, the Lord granted us salvation, bestowing on us the knowledge of the Father. . . . By His Passion our Lord also destroyed death, dispersed error, put an end to corruption, and destroyed ignorance, while He manifested life, revealed truth, and granted the gift of incorruption. (2:20,3)

He did not despise or evade any human condition. He did not set aside in His own case the order He had appointed for the human race; rather, He sanctified every stage of human development by participating in it Himself. For He came to save all in Himself, all those who are born again to God through Him—infants, toddlers, young children, youths, and the mature. . . . Then, finally, He came on to death itself, so that He would be "the firstborn from the dead, that in all things He may have the preeminence" [Col 1:18], "the Prince of life" [Acts 3:15], existing before all and going before all. (2:22,4)

A healthy mind, one which does not expose its possessor to danger and is devoted to piety and the love of truth, eagerly meditates on those things which God has placed within the power of humankind and has subjected to our knowledge. It will advance in them, learning them easily by daily study. (2:27,1)

The entire Scriptures, the Prophets, and the Gospels can be clearly, unambiguously, and harmoniously understood by all, even if all do not believe them. (2:27,2)

Having the truth itself as our rule and the testimony concerning God set clearly before us, we should not cast away the firm and true knowledge of God by scurrying after a multitude of contradictory responses to questions. It is much more appropriate that we guide our inquiries to investigate the mystery and administration of the living God, and so increase in love for Him who has done and still does such great things for us. (2:28,1)

If, therefore, even with respect to creation, there are some things only God knows, while others come within the range of our knowledge, why should we complain if, in regard to those things which we investigate in the Scriptures (which are thoroughly spiritual), we are able by the grace of God to explain only some of them, while we must leave the rest in the hands of God—and that not only in the present world but also in that which is to come—so that God will forever teach and human beings will forever learn the things God teaches? . . . If, then, . . . we leave some questions in the hands of God, we will keep our faith from injury and will continue without danger. Moreover, we will find all Scripture, which has been given to us by God, to be entirely consistent. Then the parables will harmonize with the passages which are perfectly plain, and the statements which are clear in meaning will help explain the parables, and in all the various utterances of Scripture we will hear one harmonious melody, praising in hymns the God who created all things. So, for instance, if anyone asks, "What was God doing before He made the world?" we reply that the answer to such a question lies hidden with God Himself. (2:28,3)

If anyone asks, "How was the Son produced by the Father?" we reply that no one understands that production, or generation, or calling, or revelation, or whatever term may be used to describe His generation: it is utterly indescribable. (2:28,6)

We have learned from the Scriptures that God holds the supremacy over all things. But Scripture has not revealed to us the way He produced it. . . . In the same way, we must leave unanswered the question why, since all things were made by God, some of His creatures sinned and revolted from a state of submission to God. . . . Since we know only in part [1 Cor 13:12], we must leave all sorts of questions in the hands of Him who gives us grace by measure. (2:28,7)

God alone, who is Lord of all, is without beginning and without end, being truly and forever the same, and always remaining the same unchangeable being. But all things that proceed from Him, everything that has been made and is made, has its own beginning. Consequently, they are inferior to Him who formed them, since they are not unbegotten. (2:34,2)

Life does not arise from us, or from our own nature; it is granted by the grace of God. Therefore the one who takes care of the life received and gives thanks to Him who imparted it will also receive everlasting life. But the one who rejects it and shows himself ungrateful toward his maker, since he has been created and has not recognized Him who bestowed life, deprives himself of ongoing existence. (2:34,3)

All this will enable you to defend the only true and life-giving faith, which the Church has received from the apostles and imparted to her children. The Lord of all gave His apostles the power of the gospel, and we have come to know the truth through them. That truth is the teaching of the Son of God, who declared, "He who hears you hears Me, he who rejects you rejects Me, and he who rejects Me rejects Him who sent Me" [Luke 10:16]. (3:Preface)

We have learned the plan of our salvation from no one else than the ones through whom the gospel has come down to us. At first, they proclaimed it in public, but later on, in accordance with God's will, they handed it down to us in the Scriptures, to be the ground and pillar of our faith [1 Tim 3:15]. ... After our Lord rose from the dead, the apostles received power from on high [Luke 24:49] when the Holy Spirit came down upon them [Acts 1:8], were filled with all His gifts, and thus received complete knowledge. They departed to the ends of the earth, preaching the glad tidings of the good things sent from God to us, and proclaiming the peace of heaven toward humankind [Luke 2:14]. They all equally and individually possessed the gospel of God. Matthew produced a written Gospel for the Hebrews in their own language, while Peter and Paul were preaching at Rome, laying the foundations of the church there. After their departure, Mark, the disciple and interpreter of Peter, handed down to us in writing what Peter had preached. Luke also, the companion of Paul, recorded in a book the gospel Paul preached. Afterwards, John, the disciple of the Lord, who had leaned upon his breast [John 13:23], also published a Gospel while he was living at Ephesus in Asia. (3:1,1)

When we refer them to the tradition which originated from the apostles, which has been preserved through the succession of presbyters in the Churches, they object to tradition.... It comes down to this, that these people will not yield, either to Scripture or to tradition. (3:2,2)

While it is not an easy thing for a soul under the influence of error to repent, yet, on the other hand, it is not altogether impossible to escape from error when the truth is brought alongside it. (3:2,3)

Everyone who wants to see the truth can behold the tradition of the apostles in any church anywhere in the world. We can list all those whom the apostles instituted as bishops in the churches, and the succession from them down to our own times. (3:3,1)

The faith they [the apostles] preached to humanity has come down to our time through the successions of bishops. (3:3,2)

Having founded and built up the church in Rome, the blessed apostles [Peter and Paul] committed the office of bishop there into the hands of Linus. Paul mentions this Linus in his letters to Timothy [2 Tim 4:21]. Anacletus succeeded him; and next, in the third place from the apostles, Clement received the bishopric. He had seen the blessed apostles and conversed with them, so he might be said to have the preaching of the apostles still echoing in his ears and their traditions before his eyes. He was not alone in this: many were still alive who had been taught by the apostles. In Clement's time, a serious conflict arose in the church at Corinth; the church in Rome sent a vigorous letter to the Corinthians, exhorting them to peace and renewing their faith by declaring again the tradition which it had recently received from the apostles. That apostolic Tradition proclaims that there is one God Almighty, the Maker of heaven and earth, the Creator of humankind, who sent the flood, who called Abraham, who led the people from the land of Egypt, who spoke with Moses and gave the law, who sent the prophets, and who has prepared fire for the devil and his angels. Whoever wants to may learn from this letter that the Father of our Lord Jesus Christ was preached by the churches; that person can then understand the apostolic Tradition of the Church.... After Clement came Evaristus; Alexander followed Evaristus. Then, sixth from the apostles, Sixtus was appointed; after him, Telephorus, who was gloriously martyred; then Hyginus; after him, Pius; then after him, Anicetus. Soter having succeeded Anicetus, Eleutherus—in the twelfth place from the apostles—now has the inheritance of the episcopate. In this order and via this succession, the ecclesiastical tradition from the apostles, the preaching of the genuine truth, has come down to us. This is most abundant proof that there is one and the same life-giving faith, which has been handed down and faithfully preserved in the Church from the apostles until now. (3:3,3)

Further, Polycarp was instructed by apostles and conversed with many who had seen Christ; the apostles in Asia appointed him bishop of the church in Smyrna. I saw him in my early youth, for he lived a long time. As a very old man, he endured a glorious and noble martyrdom and departed this life. He had always taught what he had learned from the apostles—which is what the Church has handed down, and which alone is true. All the Asiatic churches testify to these things, as do those who have succeeded Polycarp down to the present time. . . . There is also a very powerful letter of Polycarp written to the Philippians, from which those who are eager to learn about salvation can get to know the character of his faith and the preaching of the truth. Furthermore, the church in Ephesus, founded by Paul, among whom John remained until the times of Trajan, is a faithful witness of the tradition of the apostles. (3:3,4)

Since we have such proofs, we do not need to seek from others the truth which is easy to get from the Church: the apostles, like a rich man depositing his wealth in a bank, placed everything related to the truth in her hands, so that whoever wants to can draw the water of life out of her [Rev 22:17]. She is the door to life; all others are thieves and robbers [John 10:7–8]. Consequently, we should turn away from the heretics and be sure to turn to the Church, so that we may lay hold of the tradition of the truth. . . . What would we do if the apostles had not left us writings? Would it not be necessary, in that case, to follow the course of the tradition which they handed down to those to whom they committed the churches? (3:4,1)

This is what the numerous barbarian nations who believe in Christ do. Salvation has been written in their hearts by the Spirit, without paper or ink, but they carefully preserve the ancient tradition—believing in one God, the Creator of heaven and earth, and everything in them, through Christ Jesus, the Son of God; who, because of His surpassing love towards His creation, condescended to be born of the virgin, thus uniting humanity in Himself to God; having suffered under Pontius Pilate, and rising again, and having been received up in splendor, He will come again in glory as the Savior of those who are saved and the Judge of those who are judged, and will send into eternal fire those who pervert the truth and despise His Father and His advent. As regards our language, those who have believed this faith without recourse to written documents are barbarians, but as regards doctrine, manner, and tenor of life, they are very wise indeed because of faith: they please God, living their lives in all righteousness, chastity, and wisdom. (3:4,2)

Since then the tradition from the apostles exists and is preserved in the Church, let us turn to the scriptural proof furnished by the apostles who wrote the gospel, in which they recorded the doctrine about God, pointing out that our Lord Jesus Christ is the Truth [John 14:6], and that no lie is found in Him. . . . Since they were disciples of the Truth, the apostles would not stoop to falsehood, for a lie has no fellowship with the truth, just as darkness has none with light [2 Cor 6:14]; one drives the other out. (3:5,1)

With His Incarnation everything entered a new phase. The Word arranged His coming in the flesh in a unique way, so that He might win back to God that human nature which had departed from God. (3:10,2)

Throughout the world, the entire Church, firmly rooted in the apostles' teaching, perseveres in the very same conviction about God and His Son. (3:12,7)

His only begotten Word—who is always present with the human race, who was united to and mingled with His own creation, according to the Father's pleasure, and became flesh—is Himself Jesus Christ our Lord, who suffered for us and rose again on our behalf, and who will come again in His Father's glory to resurrect all who have lived, to show His salvation, and to judge with consummate justice everything He has made. (3:16,6)

The Son of God did not then begin to exist, since He was with the Father from the beginning. When He became incarnate and was made human, He began anew the long line of human beings and, to state it briefly, furnished us with salvation. Consequently, what we had lost in Adam—namely, the image and likeness of God—we recovered in Christ Jesus. (3:18,1)

It was impossible that those who had once for all been conquered, and who had been destroyed through disobedience, could reform themselves and grasp the prize of victory. It was impossible that those who had fallen under the power of sin could attain salvation. So the Son accomplished both these things. As the Word of God He descended from the Father, became incarnate, humbled Himself, even to death [Phil 2:8], and fulfilled the plan of our salvation. (3:18,2)

As man contending for humanity, the Lord fought and conquered. Through obedience He completely did away with disobedience: He bound the strong man [Matt 12:29], set the weak free, and granted salvation to His own handiwork by destroying sin. He is a most holy and merciful Lord, and He loves humanity. (3:18,6)

He caused human nature to cleave to and become one with God. On the one hand, unless a human being had overcome the enemy of humanity, the enemy would not have been justly defeated. On the other hand, unless it had been God who had freely given salvation, we could never have possessed it securely. Unless humanity had been joined to God, humanity could never have become a partaker of incorruptibility. So, it was incumbent upon the Mediator between God and humanity [1 Tim 2:5], via His relationship to both, to bring them to friendship and peace, and so to present humankind to God, while revealing God to humankind. This is also why He passed through every stage of life, restoring all of them to communion with God. (3:18,7)

It behooved Him who was to destroy sin and redeem humankind under the power of death to be made human, for humanity had been drawn by sin into bondage and was held by death, so that sin should be destroyed by man, and humankind should be delivered from death. For as by the disobedience of the one man who was originally molded from virgin soil, many were made sinners and forfeited life, so it was necessary that, by the obedience of one man, who was originally born from a virgin, many should be justified [Rom 5:19] and receive salvation.... What He appeared to be He also was: God recapitulated in Himself the ancient formation of humanity, so that He might kill sin, deprive death of its power, and give life again to humankind. (3:18,7)

This was why the Word of God was made human, and He who was the Son of God became the Son of Man—that human beings, taken into the Word and receiving adoption, might become the children of God. By no other means could we have attained incorruptibility and immortality, unless we had been united to incorruptibility and immortality. How could we be joined to incorruptibility and immortality unless incorruptibility and immortality had first become what we are, so that the corruptible might be swallowed up by incorruptibility, and the mortal by immortality [1 Cor 15:53], so that we might receive adoption as children [Gal 4:5]? (3:19,1)

The Word of God lived among us and became the Son of Man, so that He might accustom humankind to receive God, and God to dwell in humanity, as the Father intended. (3:20,2)

The first-formed himself, Adam, received his substance from untilled and as yet virgin soil ("for the Lord God had not caused it to rain on the earth, and there was no man to till the ground" [Gen 2:5]), and was formed by the hand of God (that is, by the Word of God, for "all things were made through Him" [John 1:3]), for the Lord took dust from the earth and formed man. The same was true of the Word, who recapitulated Adam in Himself and received a genuine birth, so that He could gather up Adam into Himself from Mary, who was still a virgin. If, then, the first Adam had a man for his father and was born of human seed, it would have been appropriate to say that the second Adam was begotten of Joseph. But if the former was taken from the dust and God was his maker, it was incumbent that the latter also, making a recapitulation in Himself, should be formed as man by God Himself, to have an analogy with the former as to His origin. (3:21,10)

In due course, Mary the virgin was found obedient, saying, "Behold the maidservant of the Lord! Let it be to me according to your word" [Luke 1:38]. Eve had been disobedient, for she did not obey when she was still a virgin. (To be sure, she had a husband, Adam, but she was still a virgin. In Paradise "they were both naked, the man and his wife, and were not ashamed" [Gen 2:25], since they had only been created a short time previously and at that point had no understanding of the procreation of children. It was necessary that they should first come to adult age, and then they would begin to multiply [Gen 1:28].) Becoming disobedient, Eve became the cause of death, both for herself and for the entire human race; but Mary, engaged to a man but still a virgin, yielded obedience and so became the cause of salvation, both for herself and for the whole human race. . . . This is also how the knot of Eve's disobedience was untied by the obedience of Mary: what the virgin Eve had bound fast through unbelief, the Virgin Mary set free through faith. (3:22,4)

After Adam transgressed, as Scripture relates, God pronounced no curse upon Adam, but upon the ground, which he was to work. . . . Similarly, the woman received her share of toil—specifically, labor, groans, the pain of childbirth, and a state of subjection in which she would serve her husband [Gen 3:16]. . . . But the curse in all its fullness fell upon the serpent, which had beguiled them. (3:23,3)

God drove them out of Paradise, separating them from the tree of life—not because He wanted to protect the tree of life from them, as some teach, but because God pitied them. He did not want them to continue to live forever as sinners, or for the sin which had engulfed them to last forever, or for evil to have no end or remedy. So, God set a bound to sin by interposing death, thus causing sin to cease [Rom 6:7]. (3:23,6)

Anyone who wants to convert these heretics to the truth needs to have a good understanding of their systems or schemes of teaching. It is impossible for anyone to heal the sick if he has no knowledge of the disease afflicting the patient. (4:Preface,2)

The serpent beguiled Eve, by promising her what he did not have himself. (4:Preface,4)

On frequent subsequent occasions He performed cures on the Sabbath, and for this reason many used to seek Him out on the Sabbath days. The law commanded them to abstain from every servile work—that is, from all grasping after wealth which is procured by trading and by other worldly business—but it exhorted them to attend to the exercises of the soul (which consist in reflection) and the instruction that would enable them to serve their neighbors' benefit. This is why the Lord reproved those who unjustly blamed Him for healing on the Sabbath days [Matt 12:1–13], since He did not violate but fulfilled the law by performing the work of a high priest, propitiating God for human beings, cleansing lepers, healing the sick, and Himself suffering death, so that exiled humanity might escape condemnation and return without fear to its inheritance. (4:8,2)

As God is always the same, so also humans, when found in God, will always go on towards God. God never stops conferring benefits upon and enriching humankind, and humanity never ceases to receive those benefits and to be enriched by God. (4:11,2)

In the beginning, God formed Adam, not as if He needed humanity, but so that He might have someone upon whom to confer His benefits.... The service we render to God profits Him nothing, and God does not need our obedience. He grants life and incorruption and eternal glory to those who follow and serve Him, bestowing benefits on those who serve Him because they serve Him and on His followers because they follow Him. He does not receive any benefit from them, though, for He is rich, perfect, and in need of nothing. The reason God demands service from human beings is so that, since He is good and merciful, He may benefit those who continue in His service. While God needs nothing, humans need fellowship with God, and this is the glory of a human being, to continue and remain permanently in God's service. (4:14,1)

Sacrifices do not sanctify anyone, for God does not need sacrifice. What moves God to accept an offering is the conscience of the offerer, which sanctifies the sacrifice when it is pure. But He says, "He who sacrifices a lamb [is] as if he breaks a dog's neck" [Is 66:3]. (4:18,3)

Since the Church offers with single-mindedness, her gift is appropriately reckoned a pure sacrifice by God.... It is indeed right for us to make an oblation to God, and in all things to be grateful to God our Maker—in a pure mind, in faith without hypocrisy, in well-grounded hope, and in fervent love, offering the first-fruits of His own created things. Only the Church offers this pure oblation to the Creator, offering to Him, with thanksgiving, the things taken from His creation. (4:18,4)

The Eucharist ... establishes our view. For we offer Him His own, faithfully proclaiming the fellowship and union of flesh and Spirit. For as the bread, which is produced from the earth, when it receives the invocation of God, is no longer common bread, but the Eucharist, consisting of two realities, earthly and heavenly, so also our bodies, when they receive the Eucharist, are no longer corruptible, since they now have the hope of the resurrection to eternity. (4:18,5)

God cannot be measured in the heart, and He is incomprehensible by the mind. (4:19,2)

So there is one God, who by the Word and Wisdom created and arranged all things. This is the Creator who has granted this world to the human race and who, as to His greatness, is unknown to all whom He has made—for no one has searched out His height, whether among the ancients who have gone to their rest or any of those who are now alive. But in His love, He is always known through Him by whose means He ordained all things. (4:20,4)

As His greatness is past finding out, so also His goodness is beyond expression; having been seen through His goodness, He grants life to those who see Him. Without life it is impossible to live, and the means of life is found in fellowship with God. But fellowship with God is to know God and to enjoy His goodness. (4:20,5)

The glory of God is a human being fully alive, and the life of a human being consists in beholding God. (4:20,7)

It was not only for those who believed on Him in the time of Tiberius Caesar that Christ came; nor did the Father direct His providence only for those who are alive now; but for all those who from the beginning, according to their capacity, in their generation have feared and loved God, have practiced justice and piety towards their neighbors, and have earnestly desired to see Christ and hear His voice. (4:22,2)

Every prophecy, before its fulfillment, is enigmatic and ambiguous, but when its time of fulfillment has arrived and the prediction has come to pass, then the prophecies have a clear and certain exposition. (4:26,1)

It is necessary to obey the presbyters who are in the Church. They have the succession from the apostles; together with the succession of the episcopate, they have received the certain gift of truth, according to the good pleasure of the Father. We need to view with suspicion those who turn from the primitive succession and assemble themselves together elsewhere, for they are either heretics of perverse minds, schismatics puffed up and self-pleasing, or hypocrites who act this way for money or vainglory. (4:26,2)

Where the gifts of the Lord have been placed, there it behooves us to learn the truth—namely, from those who possess that succession of the Church which is from the apostles, and among whom exists what is sound and blameless in conduct, as well as what is unadulterated and incorrupt in speech. These people preserve this faith of ours in one God who created all things; and they increase our love for the Son of God, who accomplished such marvelous dispensations for our sake; and they expound the Scriptures to us without danger, neither blaspheming God, nor dishonoring the patriarchs, nor despising the prophets. (4:26,5)

He will also judge those who cause schisms, people destitute of the love of God, who desire their way more than the unity of the Church, and who for trifling reasons or any kind of reason which occurs to them cut in pieces and divide the great and glorious body of Christ and, as far as lies in them, destroy it. People like that speak about peace but bring on war; they strain out a gnat but swallow a camel [Matt 23:24]. They will not be able to achieve any reformation adequate to make up for the mischief they cause by their schism. (4:33,7)

True knowledge is the doctrine of the apostles, which is the ancient constitution of the Church throughout the entire world. The body of Christ is clearly manifest by the successions of bishops, by whom the Church existing in every place has been faithfully taught, so that the truth has come down also to us. It has been guarded and preserved by a thorough presentation of doctrine, without any spurious scriptures and without receiving either addition or subtraction. It consists in reading the Word of God without falsification, a legitimate and diligent exposition in harmony with the Scriptures, without either danger or blasphemy, and the preeminent gift of love [1 Cor 13:13], which is more precious than knowledge, more glorious than prophecy, and which excels all the other gifts of God. (4:33,8)

If some had been made bad by nature and others good, the latter would not deserve praise for being good, for that is the way they were created; nor would the former be reprehensible, for that would be the way they were made. But since all humanity has the same nature, able both to retain and do what is good, as well as the power to cast it from them and not do it, some justly receive praise, even among those who are guided by good laws (and much more from God), and obtain deserved testimony for their good choices in general and for persevering in them. But the others are blamed and receive a just condemnation because they rejected what is fair and good. (4:37,2)

Submission to God is eternal rest, but those who shun the light receive a place worthy of their flight, and those who fly from eternal rest find a place suited to their fleeing. Since all good things are with God, those who by their own determination fly from God rob themselves of all good things. Having been thus robbed of all good things with respect to God, they consequently fall under the just judgment of God. (4:39,4)

Our Lord Jesus Christ . . . through His transcendent love became what we are, that He might make us to be what He is. (5:Preface)

There is no other way we could have learned the things of God, unless our master, who is the Word, had become human. No other being had the power to reveal to us the things of the Father except His own proper Word. (5:1,1)

The Lord has redeemed us through His own blood, giving His soul for our souls and His flesh for our flesh, and has poured out the Spirit of the Father for the union and communion of God and humankind, imparting God to humanity by means of the Spirit. On the other hand, He has united humanity to God by His own Incarnation and, through communion with God, genuinely and lastingly bestowed immortality on us by His coming. (5:1,1)

The Holy Spirit came upon Mary, and the power of the Most High overshadowed her, so that what was generated was a holy child, the Son of the Most High God the Father of all [Luke 1:35], who accomplished this Incarnation. He thus showed forth a new kind of generation—that, as through the former generation we inherited death, so by this new generation we might inherit life. (5:1,3)

As by means of a tree we were made debtors to God, so also by means of a tree we may obtain the remission of our debt. (5:17,3)

As the former was led astray by the word of an angel, so that she fled from God when she had transgressed His Word, so the latter, by an angelic communication, received the glad tidings that she should bear God, being obedient to His Word. While the former disobeyed God, the latter was persuaded to be obedient to God; thus, the Virgin Mary became the patroness of the virgin Eve. And so, as the human race fell into bondage to death by means of a virgin, so it is rescued by a virgin, virginal disobedience being balanced in the opposite scale by virginal obedience. (5:19,1)

Heretics, since they are blind to the truth and turn aside from the right way, walk in various paths. Because of that the footsteps of their doctrine are scattered here and there, without agreement or connection. But the path of those belonging to the Church circumscribes the whole world, since the Church possesses the sure Tradition from the apostles. She thus enables us to see that the faith of all is one and the same, since all receive one and the same God the Father, believe in the same dispensation regarding the Incarnation of the Son of God, know the same gift of the Spirit, recognize the same commandments, preserve the same form of ecclesiastical constitution, expect the same advent of the Lord, and await the same salvation of the total person—that is, of soul and body. And without question the preaching of the Church is true and steadfast, in which one and the same way of salvation is shown throughout the whole world. God has entrusted the light to her. (5:20,1)

The enemy would not have been vanquished fairly unless he had been conquered by a man born of a woman, since it was by means of a woman that he got the advantage over humanity at first, thus setting himself up as humanity's opponent. And so the Lord presents Himself as the Son of Man, comprising in Himself that original man out of whom the woman was fashioned, so that, as our species went down to death through a vanquished man, so we might also ascend to life again through a victorious one. As it was through a man that death received the palm of victory over us, so it was also by a man that we received the palm against death. (5:21,1)

Justly is he led captive who had led humanity unjustly into bondage, while humankind, which had been led captive in times past, was rescued from the grasp of its possessor. This comes through the tender mercy of God the Father, who had compassion on His own handiwork and granted it salvation, restoring it by means of the Word—that is, by Christ—so that human beings might learn by actual proof that they receive incorruptibility not by their own efforts, but by the free gift of God. (5:21,3)

Fragments from the Lost Writings of Irenaeus[3]

I can describe the place where the blessed Polycarp used to sit and discourse—his going out, too, and his coming in—his general mode of life and personal appearance, together with the discourses which he delivered to the people; also how he would speak of his familiar conversation with the Apostle John and with the rest of those who had seen the Lord; and how he would call their words to remembrance. Whatever he had heard from them with regard to the Lord, about both His miracles and His teaching, Polycarp—having thus received it from the eyewitnesses of the Word of life—would recount it all in harmony with the Scriptures. These things, through God's mercy which was upon me, I then listened to attentively and treasured up, not on paper but in my heart. (#2)

As long as anyone has the means of doing good to his neighbors and does not do so, that person shall be reckoned a stranger to the love of the Lord. (#4)

The will and the energy of God is the effective and foreseeing cause of every time and place and age, and of every nature. (#5)

God not only bursts the limits of human understanding and surpasses our powers of mind, reason and speech, time and place, and that in every age; He is also beyond substance, beyond fullness, and beyond perfection. (#6)

Ever, indeed, speaking well of the deserving, but never ill of the undeserving, we also shall attain to the glory and kingdom of God. (#9)

The business of the Christian is nothing else than to be ever preparing for death. (#11)

If you say that the serpent attacked the woman because she was the weaker of the two, I reply that, on the contrary, she was the stronger, since she appears to have been the helper of the man in the transgression of the commandment. For by herself alone she resisted the serpent, and it was only after holding out for a while and offering resistance that she ate of the tree, and that because she was deceived; but Adam, offering no resistance whatsoever, nor refusal, partook of the fruit handed to him by the woman—

---
3 Excerpts taken from ANF 1:568–578.

an indication of the utmost stupidity and weakness of mind on his part. As for the woman, since she was vanquished in the contest by a demon, she deserves pardon; but Adam deserves none, since he was worsted by another human being—and he was the one who, in his own person, had received the command from God! (#16)

The Word of God became one with flesh by a physical and hypostatic union; after the Resurrection, the heavy and terrestrial part, having been rendered immortal, was borne up into heaven by the divine nature. (#28)

It was not pointless that Naaman of old, when suffering from leprosy, was purified upon his being baptized: it served as an indication to us. For we are lepers in sin, and we are cleansed of our old transgressions by means of the sacred water and the invocation of the Lord; we are spiritually regenerated as newborn babes, as the Lord has declared: "Unless one is born of water and the Spirit, he cannot enter the kingdom of God" [John 3:5]. (#34)

The oblation of the Eucharist is not carnal, but spiritual; and in this respect it is pure. For we make an oblation to God of the bread and the cup of blessing, giving Him thanks for commanding the earth to bring forth these fruits for our nourishment. And then, when we have completed the oblation, we invoke the Holy Spirit, that He may exhibit this sacrifice, both the bread, the body of Christ, and the cup, the blood of Christ, in order that the receivers of these antitypes may obtain remission of sins and life eternal. (#37)

He [Jesus Christ] was sold with Joseph and guided Abraham; He was bound along with Isaac and wandered with Jacob; with Moses He was leader and, as regards the people, legislator. He preached in the prophets, was incarnate of a virgin, born in Bethlehem, received by John and baptized in the Jordan, was tempted in the desert, and proved to be the Lord. He gathered the apostles together and preached the Kingdom of heaven. (#54)

He is the salvation of the lost, the light to those dwelling in darkness, and redemption to those who have been born. (#54)

~Hippolytus

Hippolytus (c. 170–235), bishop of Pontus (near Rome), was an eminent and learned scholar who wrote voluminously in the early third century. Since he was unusually well versed in Greek philosophy, the Hellenistic mystery religions, and the teachings of the Apologists, it seems clear that, like Irenaeus, Hippolytus came from the eastern half of the Roman Empire. He professed himself to be a disciple of Irenaeus and, like his teacher, Hippolytus wrote his works in Greek; indeed, he was the last Christian author in Rome to do so. He died a martyr.

Hippolytus's writings include several widely different fields of Christian concern. His *Refutation of All Heresies* engaged pagan culture and philosophy extensively. In his *Apostolic Traditions,* Hippolytus handed on what had become customary practice within the Church by his day. Topics covered include particulars regarding Christian life, details about the administration and celebration of the sacraments of baptism and the Eucharist, and some information about the responsibilities of clergy.

The Refutation of All Heresies[1]

In these last days, the Father sent this Logos forth, no longer to speak by a prophet, and not wishing that the Word, being obscurely proclaimed, should be made the subject of mere conjecture, but that He should be manifested, so that we could see Him with our own eyes. (10:29)

---

1 Excerpts taken from ANF 5:9–153.

We know that this Logos received a body from a virgin, and that He remodeled the old man by a new creation. And we believe that the Logos passed through every period in this life, in order that He Himself might serve as a law for every age, and that, by being present among us, He might exhibit his own humanity as an aim for all. (10:29)

Through the knowledge of Christ, you will escape the approaching threat of the fire of judgment, and the rayless scenery of gloomy Tartarus, where no beam from the irradiating voice of the Word ever shines! You will escape the boiling flood of hell's eternal lake of fire, and the eye of fallen angels, ever fixed in menacing glare, who are chained in Tartarus as punishment for their sins; and you shall escape the worm that ceaselessly coils for food around the body whose scum has bred it. Now you will escape these torments if you are instructed in the knowledge of the true God. And you will possess an immortal body, one placed beyond the possibility of corruption, just like the soul. And you will receive the kingdom of heaven if, while living this life, you know the celestial king. (10:30)

This is the ultimate significance of the proverb, "Know yourself"—i.e., discover God within yourself, for He formed you in His own image. For with knowledge of self is conjoined being an object of God's knowledge, for you are called by God Himself. (10:30)

The Apostolic Tradition[2]

We give thanks to you God, through your beloved child Jesus Christ, whom, in the last times, you sent to us as savior and redeemer and angel of your will, who is your inseparable Word through whom you made all things and who was well pleasing to you. You sent him from heaven into the womb of a virgin, and he was conceived and made flesh in the womb and shown to be your Son, born of the Holy Spirit and the virgin. He fulfilled your will and won for you a holy people, opening wide his hands when he suffered that he might set free from suffering those who believed in you. When he was handed over to voluntary suffering, in order to dissolve death and break the chains of the devil and harrow hell and illuminate the just and fix a boundary and manifest the resurrection, he took bread and giving

---

2   Excerpts taken from Alister Stewart, trans., *Hippolytus: On the Apostolic Tradition* (Crestwood, NY: St. Vladimir's Seminary Press, 2001), pp. 53–182.

thanks to you he said: "Take, eat, this is my body which will be broken for you" [Matt 26:26]. Likewise with the cup saying: "This is my blood which is poured out for you. Whenever you do this, you perform my commemoration" [Matt 26:27–28]. (ch. 4:4–10)

[Prayer of consecration for the Eucharist:] And we ask that you should send your Holy Spirit . . . . Gathering us into one, may you grant to all the saints who receive for the fullness of the Holy Spirit, for the confirmation of their faith in truth, that we may praise and glorify you through your child Jesus Christ, through whom be glory and honor to you, with the Holy Spirit in your holy church both now and to the ages of the ages. Amen. (ch. 4:12–13)

[Regarding administration of baptism:] You are to baptize the little ones first. All those who are able to speak for themselves should speak. With regard to those who cannot speak for themselves their parents, or somebody who belongs to their family, should speak. Then baptize the grown men and finally the women. (ch. 21:4–5)

When the one being baptized goes down into the waters the one who baptizes, placing a hand on him, should say thus: "Do you believe in God the Father Almighty?" And he who is being baptized should reply: "I believe." Let him baptize him once immediately, having his hand placed upon his head. And after this he should say: "Do you believe in Jesus Christ, the son of God, who was born of the Holy Spirit and Mary the virgin and was crucified under Pontius Pilate and was dead [and buried] and rose on he third day alive from the dead and ascended in the heavens and sits at the right hand of the Father and will come to judge the living and the dead?" And when he says, "I believe," he is baptized again. And again he should say: "Do you believe in the Holy Spirit and the holy church and the resurrection of the flesh?" And he who is being baptized should say: "I believe." And so he should be baptized a third time. (ch. 21:12–18)

[Prayer over those who have been baptized:] Lord God, you have made them worthy to deserve the remission of sins through the laver of regeneration: make them worthy to be filled with the Holy Spirit, send your grace upon them that they may serve you in accordance with your will; for to you is glory, to the Father and the Son with the Holy Spirit in the holy church both now and to the ages of the ages. Amen. (ch. 22:21)

The faithful, as soon as they have woken and got up, before they go to their work, shall pray to God and then hasten to their work. (ch. 35:1)

Everybody should be concerned that one who is not of the faithful, nor a mouse nor any other animal, should eat of the Eucharist, and that none of it should fall and be altogether lost. For it is the body of Christ to be eaten by the faithful, and not to be despised. (ch. 37)

Every faithful man and woman, when they have risen from sleep in the morning, before they touch any work at all, should wash their hands and pray to God, and so go to their work. But if instruction in the word of God takes place, each one should choose to go to that place, reckoning in his heart that it is God whom he hears in the one who instructs. For he who prays in the church will be able to pass by the wickedness of the day. He who is God-fearing should think it a great loss if he does not go to the place where instruction is given. (ch. 41:1–2)

Pray also before your body rests on the bed. (ch. 41:10)

If you are tempted, reverently sign yourself on the forehead [with the sign of the cross]. For this sign of the passion is shown and is proven against the Devil if you make it in faith, and not so that you may show it to people, but present it through knowledge like a shield. For when the adversary sees the power which comes from the heart, and when he sees that the inner man, who is rational, outwardly displays the likeness of the Word which is impressed on him internally, he is put to flight . . . . This Moses showed in the paschal sheep which was slaughtered. He sprinkled the blood on the threshold and anointed the doorposts, and showed forth that faith in the perfect Sheep which now is in us. By signing forehead and eyes with the hand we shall escape the one who is seeking our destruction. (ch. 42:1–4)

Extant Fragments of Hippolytus's Works[3]

There is one God, the knowledge of whom we gain from the Holy Scriptures, and from no other source. For just as a person who wishes to be skilled in the wisdom of this world will find it impossible to get at it in any other way than by mastering the teachings of philosophers, so all of us who

---

3   Excerpts taken from ANF 5:223–241.

wish to practice piety will be unable to learn it from any other quarter than the oracles of God. (*Against the Heresy of Noetus*, #9)

For the Father is indeed One, but there are two Persons, because there is also the Son; and then there is the third, the Holy Spirit. The Father decrees, the Word executes, and the Son is manifested, through whom the Father is believed on.... And we cannot otherwise think of one God, but by believing in truth in Father and Son and Holy Spirit. (*Against the Heresy of Noetus*, #14)

Let us believe, then, according to the tradition of the apostles, that God the Word came down from heaven, and entered into the holy Virgin Mary, in order that, taking the flesh from her, and assuming also a human—by which I mean a rational—soul, and becoming thus all that humans are with the exception of sin, He might save fallen humanity and confer immortality on those who believe on His name. (*Against the Heresy of Noetus*, #17)

But between God the Maker of all things and what is made, between the infinite and the finite, between infinitude and finitude, there can be no kind of comparison, since these differ from each other not in mere comparison or relatively, but absolutely in essence. (*Against Beron and Helix*, #1)

The God of all things became human for this purpose, that by suffering in the flesh, which can suffer, He might redeem our whole race, which was sold to death; and that by working wondrous things by His Divinity, which cannot suffer, through the medium of the flesh He might restore it to that incorruptible and blessed life from which it fell away by yielding to the devil. (*Against Beron and Helix*, #2)

The one who comes down in faith to the laver of regeneration, and renounces the devil, and joins himself or herself to Christ; who denies the enemy, and makes the confession that Christ is God; who puts off the bondage, and puts on the adoption—that one comes up from the baptism brilliant as the sun, flashing forth the beams of righteousness and, the most important thing, becomes a child of God and joint-heir with Christ. (*Discourse on the Holy Theophany*, #10)

He who rescued from the lowest hell the first-formed man of earth when he was lost and bound with the chains of death; He who came down from above, and raised the earthy on high; He who became the evangelist of the dead, and the Redeemer of souls, and the Resurrection of the buried—He was constituted the helper of vanquished humanity, being made human Himself, so that the firstborn Word acquainted Himself with the first-formed Adam in the virgin; He who is spiritual sought out the earthy in the womb; He who is the ever living One sought out him who through disobedience became subject to death. (from a homily on a Psalm)

∽Novatian

Novatian (c. 200–c. 258) served as a priest in Rome and was the first Roman theologian to write in Latin. His best-known work is his treatise on the Trinity. Novatian fell into disgrace for causing a schism when he set himself up as an antibishop of Rome. Even so, his treatise on the Trinity continued to be respected as a major contribution on the doctrine.

Treatise Concerning the Trinity[1]

And after these things [the rest of the Creation], He placed humanity as the head of the world. He made humankind in the image of God, and He granted them mind and reason and foresight, so that they might imitate God. And although the first elements of the human body were earthly, the substance was inspired by a heavenly and divine breathing. And when He had given humanity all things for its service, He willed that humans alone should be free. (ch. 1)

By envy, mortality came back upon humankind, since, although they could have escaped it by obedience, they rushed into it by hurrying to be God under the influence of perverse counsel. Still, God indulgently tempered their punishment by cursing, not humanity, but its labors upon earth. (ch. 1)

He [God] is always unbounded, because nothing is greater than He; always eternal, because nothing is more ancient than He. For that which is

---
1 Excerpts taken from ANF 5:611–644.

without beginning can be preceded by none since He has no time. (ch. 2)

Concerning Him and those things which are of Himself and are in Him, the human mind cannot worthily conceive what they are, how great they are, and what they are like. Nor does the eloquence of human discourse set forth a power that approaches the level of His majesty, for to conceive and speak of His majesty, all eloquence is as mute as all mind is poor. He is greater than mind itself: it cannot even be conceived how great He is, since if He could be conceived, He would be smaller than the human mind in which He could be conceived. He is greater, moreover, than all discourse, so He cannot be declared; for if He could be declared, He would be less than human discourse, by which He had been encompassed and contained. (ch. 2)

We can in some degree be conscious of Him in silence, but we cannot unfold Him as He is in our speech. For if you would call Him "Light," you would be speaking of His creature rather than of Himself, so you would not declare Him. If you should call Him "Strength," you would be speaking about and bringing out His power rather than speaking about Him. If you would call Him "Majesty," you would be describing His honor rather than Him. (ch. 2)

What can you fittingly either say or think about Him who is greater than all discourses and thoughts? (ch. 2)

Since by the gaze of our eyes we cannot see Him, we rightly learn about Him from the greatness, power, and majesty of His works. (ch. 3)

He has gone beyond the contemplation of the eyes who has surpassed the greatness of thought. (ch. 3)

If He [the Son of God] came to human beings that He might be "mediator between God and men" [1 Tim 2:5], it behooved Him to be with humanity, and the Word to be made flesh, so that in Himself He might link together earthly things with heavenly things, by associating in Himself pledges of both natures, and uniting God to humanity and humanity to God; so that reasonably the Son of God might be made by the assumption of flesh the Son of Man, and the Son of Man by the reception of the Word of God the Son of God. This most profound and recondite mystery, destined before the worlds for the salvation of the human race, is found to be fulfilled in the Lord Jesus Christ, both God and man, that the human race might be placed within reach of the enjoyment of eternal salvation. (ch. 23)

This is He [the Holy Spirit] who places prophets in the Church, instructs teachers, directs tongues, gives powers and healings, does wonderful works, offers discrimination of spirits, affords powers of government, suggests counsels, and orders and arranges whatever other gifts there are of charismata. (ch. 29)

He [the Holy Spirit] it is who by water effects the second birth, as a certain seed of divine generation, and a consecration of a heavenly nativity, the pledge of a promised inheritance, and as it were a kind of handwriting of eternal salvation. (ch. 29)

[The Holy Spirit is] given to inhabit our bodies and to effect their holiness. Working in us for eternity, He is also able to produce our bodies at the resurrection unto life, accustoming them already now to be associated in Himself with heavenly power, and to be allied with divine eternity. (ch. 29)

~ *Minucius Felix*

Little is known about the third-century Christian author Minucius Felix. He may have been born in North Africa, but he lived most of his life in Rome. A lawyer by profession, he was one of the earliest Christian authors to write in Latin. His only extant work is *Octavius,* a dialogue in which friends (one pagan and one Christian) debate the truth claims of Christianity.

Octavius[1]

Human beings are possessed of neither reason nor any sense, nor even eyesight, when they refuse to regard the whole of this beautiful universe as the finished work of a divine intelligence, but rather consider it as a random collection and conglomeration of bits and pieces. Lift your eyes heavenwards and survey what is beneath and about you: there can be nothing more evident, more undeniable, more obvious than that some divine being exists, endowed with transcendent intelligence, who sustains the whole of nature with breath and with movement, with guidance and with nourishment. (17:3–4)

Now if you went into a house and saw that everything in it was splendidly cared for, arranged, and appointed, you would think that there must be a master in charge of it and that he must be far superior to all those fine possessions. Likewise in this house of the world: when you discern in heaven and on earth order, law, providence, you must believe that there is a master, a father of the universe, and that He actually surpasses in beauty the con-

---

1 Excerpts taken from ACW 39:51–126.

stellations and the separate parts of the whole world. (18:4)

He is too great for our senses—a boundless infinity, sharing with Himself alone the knowledge of His vastness. But the understanding we have is too limited to comprehend Him, and that is why we measure Him worthily when we say that He is immeasurable. (18:8)

Now you [the pagan opponents of Christianity] think that if we have neither temples nor altars we are concealing the object of our worship? But what image would I fashion for God, since humanity can be rightly considered as the image of God? What temple would I erect to Him, since the entire universe, the work of His hands, cannot contain Him? Would I enclose the might of such majesty within the confines of a single chapel, while I, a mere human being, may lodge more spaciously? (32:1)

[Defending the Christian doctrine of the resurrection:] Is there anyone so senseless and stupid as to dare to object to the claim that man can be reshaped by God anew, just as he was fashioned by Him in the first place? That he is nothing after death, just as before birth he was nothing? That it is, therefore, equally possible for him to be restored from nothing as it was for him to be born from nothing? (34:9)

Do you think that simply because our weak sight does not see something it is also lost to God? A corpse may dry into dust or dissolve into liquid or reduce into ashes or fade into smoke; whatever the case, all its elements are preserved in God's sight. (34:10)

Consider how all nature consoles us by the suggestion of our future resurrection. The sun sets and rises again, the stars rise and set, flowers die and live again, shrubs grow old and then blossom again, seeds can only sprout after they have died. (34:11)

Christians' burials are distinguished by the same sense of peace as our lives. (38:4)

Tranquil, moderate, confident in the generosity of our God, we enliven our hopes for happiness in the future by our faith in the majesty He manifests at present. And so, blessed is the state to which we rise again, and blessed is the state in which we now live, meditating on that future. (38:4)

~ Clement of Alexandria

Clement (c. 150–c. 215) became the head of a Christian catechetical school in the intellectual center of the ancient Roman Empire, Alexandria. He sought to present Christianity in a winsome way to the learned elite of his culture: less confrontational than many previous Christian authors, he tried to show how Christianity meshed with the best of what ancient pagan philosophy and literature had produced. He was well educated for the task: his works include citations from more than three hundred pagan authors, plus copious references to both the Old Testament Scriptures and the writings of the apostles.

In his major works, Clement urged his contemporaries to see that the truth and beauty of which poets and philosophers had written were found in Christ, that special knowledge has been granted to Christians, and that Christ is a wise educator who molds the character of His students.

Poem[1]

Shepherd of tender youth, guiding in love and truth
    through devious ways:
Christ our triumphant King, we come Your name to sing;
    hither our children bring,
    to shout Your praise.

---

1 This hymn is in the public domain.

You are the holy Lord, the all-subduing Word,
> healer of strife:
You did Yourself abase, that from sin's deep disgrace
> You might then save our race,
> and give us life.

You are the great High Priest, You have prepared the feast
> of heavenly love:
while in our mortal pain, none calls on You in vain:
> help You do not disdain,
> help from above.

O ever be our guide, our shepherd and our pride,
> our staff and song:
O Jesus, Christ of God, by Your everlasting Word,
> lead us where You have trod;
> make our faith strong.

So now and till we die, we'll sound Your praises high,
> and joyful sing:
infants, and the glad throng who to Your Church belong,
> unite to swell the song
> to Christ our King.

Christ the Educator[2]

The Word forcibly draws people from their natural, worldly way of life and educates them to the only true salvation, which is faith in God. . . . Let us call Him, then, by the one title: educator of little ones, an educator who does not simply follow behind, but who leads the way, for His aim is to improve the soul, not just to instruct it; He guides to a life of virtue, not merely to one of knowledge. (1:1)

There is nothing more important for us than first to be rid of sin and weakness, and then to uproot any habitual sinful inclination. The highest perfection, of course, is never to sin in any least way; but this can be said of God alone. The next highest is never deliberately to commit wrong; this

---

[2] Excerpted from FC 23:3–275.

is the state proper to the one who possesses wisdom. In the third place comes not sinning except on rare occasions; this marks one who is well educated. Finally, in the lowest degree, we must place delaying in sin for a brief moment; but even this, for those who are called to recover their loss and repent, is a step on the path to salvation. (1:4)

The Word is our educator who heals the unnatural passions of our soul with his counsel. (1:6)

Since humans are the creation of God, they are naturally dear to Him. Other things God made by a simple word of command, but humanity He fashioned by His own direct action and breathed into them something proper to Himself. (1:7)

Let us recognize that both men and women practice the same sort of virtue. Surely, if there is but one God for both, then there is but one educator for both.
    One Church, one virtue, one modesty, a common food, wedlock in common, breath, sight, hearing, knowledge, hope, obedience, love—all are alike in man and woman. They who possess life in common, grace in common, and salvation in common have also virtue in common and, therefore, education too. (1:10)

A mother draws her children near her; we seek our mother, the Church.... The Father of all draws near to those who seek His aid, giving them a new birth and making them His own adopted children. He recognizes them as His little ones, He loves only them, and He comes to the aid of such as these and defends them. (1:21)

When we are baptized, we are enlightened; being enlightened, we become adopted children; becoming adopted children, we are made perfect; and becoming perfect, we are made divine. It is written, "I say, 'You are gods, children of the Most High, all of you'" [Ps 82:6].

This ceremony is often called "free gift," "enlightenment," "perfection," and "cleansing"—"cleansing," because through it we are completely purified of our sins; "free gift," because by it the punishments due to our sins are remitted; "enlightenment," since by it we behold the wonderful holy light of salvation (that is, it enables us to see God clearly); finally, we call it "perfection" as needing nothing further, for what more does the one need who possesses the knowledge of God? (1:26)

As His will is creation, and is called the universe, so His desire is the salvation of humanity, and is called the Church. (1:27)

Perfection lies ahead, in the resurrection of the faithful, but it consists in obtaining the promise which has already been given to us. (1:28)

The perfection of knowledge is faith. . . . Assuredly, if we who believe already have life everlasting, what more remains but the enjoyment of that life everlasting? (1:29)

Sins are forgiven through one divine remedy, baptism in the word. All our sins, in fact, are washed away; instantaneously we are no longer bad. (1:29–30)

Those whom the Word does not heal through persuasion He will heal with threats; and those whom threats do not heal the rod will; and those whom the rod does not heal fire will consume. (1:61)

Reproof is like surgery performed on the passions of the soul. . . . Then there is admonition which is like the diet given one who is sick, counseling what should be taken and forbidding what should not. (1:64–65)

Because He is the good educator, He wisely assumes the task of correcting by means of reproach, as though to arouse by the whip of sharp words minds which have become sluggish, and then He attempts to encourage the same people. Those whom praise does not stimulate blame arouses; and those whom blame does not stir up to seek salvation, as if they were already dead, denunciation raises to the light of truth. . . . The Word adapts Himself completely to the disposition of each, being strict with one, forgiving another. (1:66)

It is not inconsistent that the Word who saves should make use of reproof in his care for us. As a matter of fact, reproof is simply the antidote supplied by the divine love for humankind, because it awakens the blush of confusion and shame for sins committed. And if there is need for reproach and for harsh words, then there is also occasion to wound—not to death, but to its salvation—a soul grown callous; in such a way He inflicts a little pain, but spares it eternal death. (1:74)

We need the Savior, for we are sick; the guide, for we are wandering; Him who gives light, for we are blind; the life-giving spring, for we are parched with thirst, and, once we have tasted of it, we will never thirst again. We are in need of life, for we are dead; of the shepherd, for we are sheep; of the educator, for we are children. In a word, throughout the whole of our human lives, we need Jesus, that we may not go astray and at length merit condemnation as sinners, but may be separated from the chaff and gathered into the storehouse of the Father. (1:83)

As the mirror is not unjust to an ugly man for showing him exactly the way he looks, and as the doctor is not unjust to the sick man for diagnosing his fever (for he is not responsible for the fever, but simply states it is present), so he who corrects is not ill-disposed toward one sick of soul. He does not put the sins there, but only shows that they are present, so that similar sins may be avoided in the future. (1:88)

A human being's duty is to cultivate a will that is in conformity and united throughout life to God and Christ, properly directed to eternal life. (1:102)

It is fitting to bless the Maker of all things before we partake of food. . . . Again, it is a holy duty to give thanks to God for the favors and the love we have received from Him, before we fall asleep. (2:44)

Like everything that is beautiful, the flower gives pleasure by being seen, and we should glorify the Creator by looking at and enjoying its beauty. (2:70)

God has given us the power to use our possessions, I admit, but only to the extent it is necessary: He wishes them to be in common. It is unbecoming that one person live in luxury when there are so many who labor in poverty. How much more honorable it is to serve many than to live in wealth! (2:120)

To know oneself has always been, so it seems, the greatest of all lessons. For, if anyone knows himself, he will know God; and, in knowing God, he will become like Him. (3:1)

Wealth is like a snake; unless a person knows how to grasp it properly, ... the snake will twist about to the hand and strike. Wealth, too, twisting in the grasp, whether experienced or not, can cling to the hand and bite unless one rises superior to it and uses it with discretion; that is to say, one may train the beast by the invocation of the Word and remain unharmed. (3:35)

A gem is not worth much, nor is silver, nor clothes, nor beauty of body; but virtue is, because it is reason translated into deeds under the guidance of the educator. (3:35)

[Regarding possessions:] We should travel light on our road toward truth. (3:38)

The benign educator bestows aid on us in different ways, now offering advice, now rebuke; He holds up to us the dishonor reaped by those who have sinned, and reveals the punishment they have merited, both to attract our notice and to warn us. In this way He devises a gentle means of restraining us from evil.... For who is there who, following someone down a path and seeing him fall into a ditch, would not be careful not to stumble over the same obstacle, and would not avoid the consequences of sin? (3:43)

We have the Cross of the Lord as our boundary line, and by it we are fenced around and shut off from our former sins. (3:85)

Who Is the Rich Man Who Is Saved?[3]

Because of His love He voluntarily subjected Himself to human experience, so that by bringing Himself to the measure of our weakness whom He loved, He might correspondingly bring us to the measure of His own strength. (§33)

God Himself is love; and out of love to us God became feminine. In His ineffable essence He is Father; in His compassion to us He became Mother. (§37)

He left us a new covenant: I give you my love. What kind of love is this, and

---

3   Excerpted from ANF 2:591–604.

what is its dimension? For each of us He laid down a life that was worth the entire universe. And He demands in return that we lay down our lives for one another. (§37)

It is probably impossible to eradicate inbred passions all at once; but by God's power and human intercession, the help of brothers and sisters, sincere repentance, and constant care, they are corrected. (§40)

Fragments[4]

Feigned praise is worth less than true censure. (cited by Antonius Melissa)

To the weak and infirm, what is moderate appears excessive. (cited by Antonius Melissa)

It is not those who abstain from wickedness because of compulsion, but those who abstain by choice, that God crowns. (cited by Maximus the Confessor)

---

4 Excerpts taken from ANF 2:571–587.

~ Origen

Origen (c. 185–c. 254) became head of the catechetical school in Alexandria. A humble but wide-ranging scholar, Origen wrote commentaries on many books of Scripture as well as numerous works on doctrine and practical piety, and he excelled in textual critical scholarship. A bent for speculation led him to espouse a number of ideas that were later repudiated by the Church as untenable, but his genius as a Christian scholar could not be denied and his contributions to Christian thought could not be doubted.

On First Principles[1]

So, when a ship has overcome the dangers of the sea, although the result was accomplished by great labors on the sailors' part, by everyone's efforts in navigation, by the expertise and care of the pilot, by the favorable influences of the winds, and the careful observation of the stars, no one in his right mind ascribes the vessel's safety—after it has been tossed by the waves and wearied by the billows, but has finally reached safe harbor—to anything else than to the mercy of God. . . . Not that they feel that they contributed no skill or labor to save the ship, but because they know that while they contributed their labor, the safety of the vessel was in the hands of God. So it is in the race of our life, with our salvation: we ourselves have to

---

[1] Except for the first (from ANF 4:322), excerpts are from Rowan A. Greer, trans., *Origen: An Exhortation to Martyrdom; Prayer; First Principles: Book IV, Prologue to the Commentary on the Song of Songs; Homily XXVII on Numbers* (Mahwah, NJ: Paulist Press, 1979), pp. 171–216.

expend labor and be diligent and zealous; but it is from God that salvation is to be hoped for. (2:1,18)

Although a great many lawgivers were eminent among Greeks and barbarians, as well as numerous teachers and philosophers who promised they were declaring the truth, we remember no lawgiver so influential that he was able to inspire the minds of other nations with zeal either to adopt his laws willingly or to defend them with the entire effort of their minds. Therefore, no one was able to introduce and to implant what seemed to him the truth even in one nation, to say nothing of many other foreign nations, in such a way that his knowledge or his belief should reach everyone. . . . Nevertheless, in every part of the world, in all of Greece and in every foreign nation, there are numberless throngs of people who have left their ancestral laws and those they supposed gods, and who have dedicated themselves to the observance of Moses' law and to the discipleship and worship of Christ. . . . And it is all the more amazing that while their [Christians'] teachers are neither very capable nor very many, nevertheless this word is preached throughout the whole world [Matt 24:14], so that Greeks and barbarians, wise and foolish [Rom 1:14], uphold the religion of Christ's teaching. Because of this it cannot be doubted that it is not because of human powers or abilities that the word of Christ Jesus grows strong with all authority and persuasion in the minds and souls of all. (4:1,1–2)

Although it is certain that everything that exists or happens in this world is ordered by God's providence, nevertheless certain things show quite openly that they are arranged by the governance of providence, while others are unfolded in so obscure and incomprehensible a fashion that the reason of divine providence lies hidden deep within them. (4:1,7)

[Regarding the Scriptures:] The treasure of divine wisdom is hidden in the baser and rude vessel of words. (4:1,7)

The right way of understanding Scripture is to observe the rule and discipline which was delivered by Jesus Christ to the apostles and which they delivered in succession to their followers who teach the Church. (4:2,2)

Hear him [St. Paul] say, "How unsearchable are His judgments and His ways past finding out" [Rom 11:33]. He did not say that it was difficult to search out the judgments of God, but that it was altogether impossible. Nor did he say that it was difficult to investigate His ways, but that they could not be investigated. (4:3,14)

We do not say, as the heretics imagine, that there was a time when He [the Son of God] was not. (4:4,1)

But what we have said, that there never was a time when He was not, must be taken with a qualification. For the very words "when" and "never" bear a meaning implying the notion of time. But what is said about the Father, the Son, and the Holy Spirit must be understood above all time, above all ages, and above all eternity. The Trinity alone surpasses every sense of our understanding, not only temporal but also eternal. (4:4,1)

David points out the mystery of the entire Trinity in the creation of everything when he says, "By the word of the Lord the heavens were made, and all the host of them by the breath [Spirit] of His mouth" [Ps 33:6]. (4:4,3)

The aim for which we hope is that so far as it can happen we may be made participants in the divine nature [2 Pet 1:4] by imitating Him, as it is written, "He who says he abides in Him [Christ] ought himself also to walk just as He walked" [1 John 2:6]. (4:4,4)

There is nothing uncreated except the nature of the Father, Son, and Holy Spirit. God, who is good by nature, wishing to have those whom He might benefit and who might enjoy the benefits received from Him, made creatures . . . who could receive Him. (4:4,8)

An Exhortation to Martyrdom[2]

Those deceive themselves who suppose that it is sufficient for gaining the goal in Christ to believe with the heart for justification, even if confession with the mouth for salvation is not added. (§5)

If, therefore, the one who breaks agreements with other human beings is outside any truce and alien to safety, what must be said of those who by denying made null and void the agreements they made with God, and who run back to Satan, whom they renounced when they were baptized? (§17)

---

2 Excerpts taken from Greer, *Origen,* pp. 41–79.

Let us also remember the sins we have committed, and that it is impossible to receive forgiveness of sins apart from baptism, that it is impossible according to the laws of the gospel to be baptized again with water and the Spirit for the forgiveness of sins, and that the baptism of martyrdom has been given to us. (§30)

[Reflecting on Matt 10:32:] We must recognize that the person who confesses the Son before others commends, as far as it is his to do so, Christianity and the Father of Christianity to those before whom he confesses. But the one who is confessed by the Firstborn of all creation and by the Son of Man is commended through the confession of the Son of God and the Son of Man to the Father in heaven and to the angels of God. (§35)

On Prayer[3]

It is impossible to persuade someone that in human actions his or her will is not free. (6:2)

God necessarily knew what our free choice would be before it existed, together with all the other creatures that were to be from the creation and foundation of the world. In all the things that God has foreordained in accordance with His foreknowledge of our free actions, He arranged all in accord with each of our free choices, both what was to be the result of His providence and what was to take place in the natural order of things. At the same time, God's foreknowledge is not the cause of everything that will be, and indeed not of the results of our free actions following our own impulses. Even if God did not know what would happen, we would still be able to choose one thing or another; but because He does have foreknowledge, the free actions of everyone are harmonious with the structure of the whole, and this is necessary for the existence of the world. (6:3)

Not only does the High Priest pray with those who pray genuinely, but so do the angels who rejoice in heaven over one sinner who repents more than over ninety-nine righteous persons who need no repentance [Luke 15:7; Matt 18:13]. So do the souls of the saints who have already fallen asleep. (11:1)

---

3 Excerpts taken from Greer, *Origen*, pp. 81–170.

One of the most supreme virtues according to the divine Word is the love of neighbor. And we must suppose that it is far more present in the saints who have already fallen asleep toward those struggling in life than in those who are still in human weakness and struggle alongside their inferiors. For it is not only here below that there applies to those who love their brothers and sisters in Christ the saying, "And if one member suffers, all the members suffer with it; or if one member is honored, all the members rejoice with it" [1 Cor 12:26]. Indeed, it is fitting also for the love of those outside this present life to speak about the "deep concern for all the churches. Who is weak, and I am not weak? Who is made to stumble, and I do not burn with indignation?" [2 Cor 11:28–29]. (11:2)

God is not Lord of base slaves, but of those who to begin with were in fear because of their childishness, but who have been made noble and afterwards serve more blessedly by love than they did in fear. (16:1)

Who would any longer call what is constantly spoken of by people "noble birth" in its true sense, once that person has known the noble birth of the children of God? (17:2)

Hypocrites work hard at boasting before others of their piety or generosity. (19:2)

The very thing which is supposed to be good and praiseworthy is defiled when we act so that we may receive glory from others or so that we may be seen by others [Matt 6:2, 5]. And consequently we receive no reward from God for it. (19:2)

[Playing on the Greek word *hypokritai*, which means both "actors" and "hypocrites":] Those who pretend to the false appearance of good are not righteous but only actors of righteousness, "hypocrites" who act in their own theater. (20:2)

The good is one, but shameful things are many; and truth is one, but lies are many; and true righteousness is one, but there are many ways of counterfeiting it; and the wisdom of God is one, but many are the wisdoms—doomed to pass away—of this age and of the rulers of this age [1 Cor 2:6]; and the Word of God is one, but many are the words foreign to God. (21:2)

[Regarding the opening address of the Lord's Prayer, "Our Father in heaven":] It is right to examine what is said in the Old Testament quite carefully to see whether any prayer may be found in it calling God "Father." Up till now, though I have looked as carefully as I can, I have not found one. I do not mean that God was not called Father or that those who are supposed to have believed in God were not called children of God; but nowhere have I found in a prayer the boldness proclaimed by the Savior in calling God "Father." (22:1)

Even if God is called Father and those who are begotten by the word of faith in Him are called His children, the certainty and immutability of sonship cannot be seen in the Old Testament. (22:2)

[Regarding the petition, "Hallowed be Your name":] The one who fits his idea of God to things he ought not takes the name of the Lord in vain. (24:1)

[Regarding the petition, "Your Kingdom come":] The one who prays that the Kingdom of God may come prays that the Kingdom of God may spring up in him, bear fruit, and be rightly perfected. (25:1)

[Regarding the petition, "Your will be done on earth as in heaven":] We may infer that through prayers He [Jesus Christ] wishes to take His disciples as His fellow workers with the Father, so that like the things in heaven that had been subjected to truth and to the Word, He might correct the things on earth by the authority He received on earth as in heaven and might lead them to the blessed perfection of things subject to His power. (26:4)

Since a quick and too brief healing causes some to think lightly of the diseases into which they have fallen, as though they were easy to heal, and since this results in their falling into the same diseases a second time after they have been healed, God in such cases will reasonably overlook the evil as it increases to a certain point, even disregarding it when it progresses so far in them as to be incurable. His purpose is that they may become satiated by long exposure to evil, and by being filled with the sin they desire may so perceive the harm they have suffered. Then they hate what they previously welcomed; and since they have been healed more firmly, they are able to profit from the health of their souls, which is theirs by the healing. (29:1)

When we have accomplished all we can by ourselves, God will fulfill what is lacking because of human weakness. (29:19)

The person who is about to come to prayer should withdraw for a little and prepare himself, and so become more attentive and active for the whole of his prayer. He should cast away all temptation and troubling thoughts and remind himself so far as he is able of the majesty whom he approaches, and that it is impious to approach Him carelessly, sluggishly, and disdainfully; and he should put away all extraneous things. (31:2)

[On preparing for prayer:] All malice toward anyone who seems to have wronged him he should put away as far as he would wish God to put away His malice toward him. (31:2)

Although there are a great many different positions for the body [in prayer], we should not doubt that the position with the hands outstretched and the eyes lifted up is to be preferred above all others, because it symbolizes in the body the characteristics befitting the soul in prayer. I mean that this position must be preferred, barring any chance circumstance. For in certain instances, it is allowed to pray properly sometimes sitting down because of some disease of the feet that cannot be disregarded, or even lying down because of fever or some such sickness. . . . Kneeling is necessary when someone is going to speak against his own sins before God, since he is making supplication for their healing and their forgiveness. (31:2–3)

Now concerning the place [for prayer], let it be known that every place is suitable for prayer if a person prays well. For "in every place incense shall be offered to My name" [Mal 1:11], and "I desire therefore that the men pray everywhere" [1 Tim 2:8]. But everyone may have, if I may put it this way, a holy place set aside and chosen in his own house, if possible, for accomplishing his prayers in quiet and without distraction. (31:4)

And a place of prayer, the spot where believers assemble together, is likely to have something gracious to help us, since angelic powers are placed near the throngs of believers, as well as the powers of our Lord and Savior Himself, and the spirits of the saints—I think both of those who have already fallen asleep and clearly of those who are still alive, even though it is not easy to say how. (31:5)

Now concerning the direction in which one ought to look when praying, a few things must be said. Since there are four directions—north, south, west, and east—who would not immediately acknowledge that it is perfectly clear we should make our prayers facing east, since this is a symbolic expression of the soul's looking for the rising of the true Light? (32:1)

It seems to me there are four topics that need to be sketched out and that I have found scattered in the Scriptures. Each person should organize his prayer according to these topics. This is what they are: in the beginning and preface of the prayer something having the force of praise should be said of God through Christ, who is praised with Him, and by the Holy Spirit, who is hymned with Him. After this each person should place general thanksgivings, bringing forward for thanksgiving the benefits given many people and those he himself has received from God. After thanksgiving it seems to me that he ought to blame himself bitterly before God for his own sins and then ask, first, for healing that he may be delivered from the habit that brings him to sin and, second, for forgiveness of the sins that have been committed. And after confession, the fourth topic that seems to me must be added is the request for great and heavenly things, both private and general, and concerning his household and his dearest. And, finally, the prayer should be concluded with a doxology of God through Christ in the Holy Spirit. (33:1)

Discussion with Heraclides[4]

We ... believe that Christ took flesh, that He was born, that He reascended into heaven in the flesh in which He rose again, that He sits at the right hand of the Father, whence He will come "to judge the living and the dead" [2 Tim 4:1], and that He is both God and man. (1:16-22)

We must keep in mind that we are judged at the divine tribunal not on our faith alone as if we did not have to answer for our conduct [cf. James 2:24], nor on our conduct alone as if our faith were not subject to examination. It is from the correctness of both that we are justified; it is from the noncorrectness of both that we are punished for both. (8:24-31)

---

4 Excerpts taken from ACW 54:57–64.

~ *Tertullian*

Tertullian (c. 155–c. 220) lived in North Africa. Thoroughly trained in rhetoric and law—the two chief emphases of Roman higher education—Tertullian used his great learning and sharp mind to defend the Christian faith against heresies and impurities of all kinds. A vigorous and uncompromising controversialist, Tertullian was rigorous with himself as well: he lived and urged on others a life of unsparing asceticism. In the last years of his life, he embraced Montanism, a movement that arose to challenge perceived laxity in Christian practice and eventually became schismatic.

To Scapula[1]

It is a fundamental human right, a privilege of nature, that everyone should worship according to his own convictions: one person's religion neither harms nor helps someone else. It is assuredly no part of religion to compel religion. (ch. 2)

A Christian is enemy to none, least of all to the emperor of Rome, whom he knows to be appointed by his God, and so cannot but love and honor; and whose well-being, moreover, he must desire, with that of the empire over which he reigns so long as the world shall stand—for that is how long Rome shall continue. (ch. 2)

---

1 Excerpts taken from ANF 3:105–108.

We therefore sacrifice for the emperor's safety, but to our God and his, and after the manner God has enjoined—in simple prayer. (ch. 2)

Apology[2]

Our very incapacity of fully grasping God opens up to us the idea of what He really is. He is presented to our minds in His transcendent greatness, as at once known and unknown. And this is the crowning guilt of human beings, that they will not recognize one of whom they cannot possibly be ignorant. (ch. 17)

So that we might attain a fuller and more authoritative knowledge of Himself, and of His counsels and will, God has bestowed a written revelation to help all whose heart is set on seeking Him—that seeking they may find, and finding believe, and believing obey. (ch. 18)

People are made, not born, Christians. (ch. 18)

All these things Pilate did to Christ; and now in fact a Christian in his own convictions,[3] he sent word of Him to the reigning Caesar, who was at the time Tiberius. (ch. 21)

There is nothing as old as the truth. (ch. 47)

The rule of truth comes down from Christ by transmission through His companions. (ch. 47)

The oftener we are mown down by you, the more we grow in number. The blood of Christians is seed. (ch. 50)

Prescriptions Against the Heretics[4]

No one is a Christian unless he perseveres to the end. (§3)

---

2   Excerpted from ANF 3:17–55.
3   Tertullian is referring to the content of "The Letter of Pontius Pilate" allegedly written to Emperor Tiberius. The letter has been reproduced in ANF 8:459; see also related materials at ANF 8:460–467.
4   Excerpts taken from S. L. Greenslade, trans., *Early Latin Theology: Selections from Tertullian, Cyprian, Ambrose, and Jerome* (Louisville, KY: Westminster

Heresy is a Greek word meaning choice, the choice which anyone exercises when he teaches heresy or adopts it. That is why Paul calls a heretic self-condemned [Titus 3:10–11]; he chooses for himself the cause of his condemnation. We Christians are forbidden to introduce anything on our own authority or to choose what someone else introduces on his own authority. Our authorities are the Lord's apostles, and they in turn chose to introduce nothing on their own authority. They faithfully passed on to the nations the teaching which they had received from Christ. (§6)

It is philosophy that supplies the heresies with their equipment. (§7)

A plague on Aristotle, who taught them [heretics] dialectic, the art which destroys as much as it builds. (§7)

What has Jerusalem to do with Athens, the Church with the Academy, the Christian with the heretic? (§7)

After Jesus Christ we have no need of speculation, after the gospel no need of research. (§7)

All the Lord's sayings, I admit, were set down for all people. They have come through the ears of the Jews to us Christians. Still, many were aimed at particular people and constitute for us an example rather than a command immediately applicable to ourselves. (§8)

No word of God is so unqualified or so unrestricted in application that the mere words can be pleaded without respect to their underlying meaning. (§9)

Christ laid down one definite system of truth which the world must believe without qualification, and which we must seek precisely in order to believe it when we find it. Now you cannot search indefinitely for a single definite truth. You must seek until you find, and when you find, you must believe. Then you have simply to keep what you have come to believe. (§9)

The Rule of Faith—to state here and now what we maintain—is . . . that by which we believe that there is but one God, who is none other than the

---

John Knox Press, 1956), pp. 31–64.

Creator of the world who produced everything from nothing through His Word, sent forth before all things; that this Word is called His Son, and in the Name of God was seen in diverse ways by the patriarchs, was ever heard in the prophets, and finally was brought down by the Spirit and power of God the Father into the Virgin Mary, was made flesh in her womb, was born of her, and lived as Jesus Christ; who thereafter proclaimed a new law and a new promise of the Kingdom of heaven, worked miracles, was crucified, on the third day rose again, was caught up into heaven, and sat down at the right hand of the Father; that He sent in His place the power of the Holy Spirit to guide believers; that He will come with glory to take the saints up into the fruition of the life eternal and the heavenly promises and to judge the wicked to everlasting fire, after the resurrection of both good and evil with the restoration of their flesh. (§13)

Provided the essence of the Rule [of Faith] is not disturbed, you may seek and discuss as much as you like. (§14)

Faith is established in the Rule [of Faith]. There it has its law, and it wins salvation by keeping the law. (§14)

To know nothing against the Rule [of Faith] is to know everything. (§14)

Any given heresy rejects one or another book of the Bible. What it accepts, it perverts with both additions and subtractions to suit its own teaching, and if, in some cases, it keeps books unmaimed, it nonetheless alters them by inventing interpretations different from ours. (§17)

They are themselves reckoned apostolic, since they are the offspring of apostolic churches. Things of every kind must be classed according to their origin. These churches, then, though numerous, are identical with that one primitive apostolic Church from which they all come. All are primitive and all apostolic. . . . [They] are governed by no other principle than the single tradition of a common creed. (§20)

Is it likely that so many churches would have erred into one faith? (§28)

Where uniformity is found among many, it is not error but tradition. Will anyone venture to affirm that the error lay in the authors of the tradition? (§28)

The real thing always exists before the representation of it; the copy comes later. (§29)

Truth comes first and falsification afterwards. (§31)

Are we to believe that those who learned from the apostles preached something different [than the apostles]? (§32)

This Rule [of faith, of truth] the Church has handed down from the apostles, the apostles from Christ, and Christ from God. (§37)

Corruption of the Scriptures and of their interpretation is to be expected wherever difference in doctrine is discovered. (§38)

Every falsehood about God is a kind of idolatry. (§40)

To abandon the truth ill befits anyone who is mindful of the judgment to come, when we must all stand before the judgment seat of Christ, rendering an account above all of our faith. (§44)

The Five Books Against Marcion[5]

Marcion has quenched the light of his faith, and so has lost the God whom he had found. His disciples will not deny that he held his first faith along with us; a letter of his own proves this. So, for the future a heretic may from his case be designated as one who, forsaking what was prior, afterwards chose out for himself something which did not previously exist. Since what was delivered in times past and from the beginning will be held as truth, what is brought in later must be accounted heresy. . . . Heretics . . . can be refuted even without considering their doctrines; they are shown to be heretical by the novelty of their opinions. (1:1)

Living and perfect Deity has its origin neither in novelty nor in antiquity, but in its own true nature. Eternity has no time; it is itself all time. It acts; it cannot then suffer. It cannot be born, so it has no age. If old, God forfeits the eternity that is to come; if new, the eternity which is past. (1:8)

---

5   Excerpted from ANF 3:271–474.

We maintain that God must first be known from nature, and afterwards authenticated by instruction: from nature, by His works; from instruction, through what He has revealed. (1:18)

No other teaching has the right to be received as apostolic than what is at present proclaimed in the churches of apostolic foundation. (1:21)

[Addressing Marcion directly:] If the churches prove to have been corrupt from the beginning, where will the pure ones be found? Will it be among the adversaries of the Creator? Show us, then, one of your churches which can trace its descent from an apostle, and you will have gained the day. (1:21)

By conceding permission for the operation of his [the devil's] designs, He [God] acted consistently with the purpose of His own goodness, deferring the devil's destruction for the same reason as He postponed humanity's restitution. He made space for a conflict, in which man might crush his enemy with the same freedom of will which had made him succumb to him (proving that the fault was his own, not God's), and so worthily recover his salvation by a victory. In this also the devil would receive a more bitter punishment, by being vanquished by him whom he had previously injured. And in this God is shown to be so much the more good, for He waits for humankind to return from this present life to a more glorious Paradise, with a right to pluck from the tree of life. (2:10)

Justice is the very fullness of the Deity Himself, manifesting God as both a perfect father and a perfect master: a father in His mercy, a master in His discipline; a father in the mildness of His power, a master in its severity; a father who must be loved with dutiful affection; a master who must needs be feared; be loved, because He prefers mercy to sacrifice; be feared, because He dislikes sin; be loved, because He prefers the sinner's repentance to his death; be feared, because He dislikes the sinners who do not repent. Accordingly, the divine law enjoins duties in respect of both these attributes: "You shall love God," and "You shall fear God." It proposed one for the obedient person, the other for the transgressor. (2:13)

Although you allow, with others, that man was in-breathed by God into a living being, not God by man, it is yet palpably absurd for you to place human characteristics in God rather than divine ones in humankind. (2:16)

He [God] did not actually curse Adam and Eve, for they were candidates for restoration, and they had been relieved by confession. (2:25)

God conversed with humanity, that humanity might learn to act like God. (2:27)

In a battle fought in the name of that Lord who was one day to fight against the devil, the shape was necessary of that very Cross through which Jesus was to win the victory. Why . . . did Moses, after prohibiting the likeness of everything, set up the golden serpent on the pole, and as it hung there, propose it as an object to be looked at for a cure? Did he not here also intend to show the power of our Lord's Cross, by which that old serpent the devil would be vanquished—by which also to everyone who was bitten by spiritual serpents but who yet turned to it with an eye of faith, was proclaimed a cure from the bite of sin, and health forevermore? (3:18)

Of the apostles, John and Matthew first instill faith into us, while of apostolic men, Luke and Mark renew it afterwards. These all start with the same principles of the faith, as far as relates to the one only God the Creator and His Christ, that He was born of the virgin and came to fulfill the Law and the Prophets. Never mind if you find some variation in the order of their narratives, provided there is agreement in the essential matter of the faith—in which there is disagreement with Marcion. (4:2)

What . . . comes down from the apostles . . . has been kept as a sacred deposit in the churches of the apostles. (4:5)

These are the summary arguments which we use when we take up arms against heretics for the faith of the gospel, maintaining both that order of periods which rules that a late date is the mark of forgers, and that authority of churches which lends support to the tradition of the apostles, for truth must needs precede the forgery and proceed straight from those by whom it has been handed on. (4:5)

In treating of the gospel, we have proved from the sacrament of the bread and the cup the verity of the Lord's body and blood, in opposition to Marcion's phantom. (5:8)

If the Father "[sent] His own Son in the likeness of sinful flesh" [Rom 8:3], it must not be said that the flesh which He seemed to have was only a phantom. For in a previous verse he [St. Paul] ascribed sin to the flesh and made it out to be "law of sin which is in my members" and "warring against the law of my mind" [Rom 7:23]. This is why he means to say that the Son was sent in the likeness of sinful flesh: that He might redeem this sinful flesh by a like substance, a fleshly one, which resembles sinful flesh, although it was itself free from sin. This is the very perfection of divine power: to accomplish salvation in a nature like that of humanity.... So, the likeness has reference to the quality of the sinfulness, not to any falsity of the substance. (5:14)

No man will love the picture of his wife without taking care of it and honoring and crowning it. The likeness partakes with the reality in the privileged honor. (5:18)

My practice in my prescription against all heresies is to fix a summary criterion of truth in the testimony of time, claiming priority in it as our rule and alleging lateness to be the characteristic of every heresy. (5:19)

Against Hermogenes[6]

When dealing with heretics, to shorten the discussion, we follow the practice of laying down against them a peremptory rule based on the lateness [of their appearance]. Since the rule of truth was earlier, warning ahead of time as it did that heresies would arise in the future [1 Cor 11:18–19], consequently all later doctrines can be regarded a priori as heresies, for their future existence was announced by the older rule of truth. (1:1)

That person is turbulent who takes talkativeness for eloquence, regards impudence as staunchness of character, and considers the slandering of individuals the normal task of a good conscience. (1:2)

The patriarchs of the heretics are the philosophers. (8:2)

Heretics generally have a habit of twisting everything simple.... We, on the other hand, assert for every word its proper meaning. (19:1, 2)

---

6 Excerpts taken from ACW 24:26–85.

The Soul's Testimony[7]

We will have nothing to do with the literature and the teaching, perverted in its best results, which is believed in its errors rather than its truth. (ch. 1)

A person becomes a Christian; he is not born one. (ch. 1)

Satan we hold to be the angel of evil, the source of error, the corrupter of the whole world, by whom in the beginning humankind was deceived into breaking the commandment of God. And humanity being given over to death on account of sin, the entire human race, tainted in their descent from our first parents, were made a channel for transmitting his condemnation. (ch. 3)

On Baptism[8]

Water was the first to produce that which had life [see Gen 1:20], that it might be no wonder if waters know how to give life in baptism. (ch. 3)

The Spirit of God, who hovered over the waters from the beginning [Gen 1:2], continues to linger over the waters of baptism. (ch. 4)

The nature of the waters, sanctified by the Holy One, itself conceived the power of sanctifying. (ch. 4)

If in the mouth of three witnesses every word shall stand [Deut 19:15], and through the benediction we have the same three [the Father, the Son, and the Holy Spirit] as witnesses of our faith whom we have as sureties of our salvation, then how much more does the number of the divine names assure us in our hope! (ch. 6)

The act of baptism itself is physical: we are plunged in water; but the effect is spiritual: we are freed from sins. (ch. 7)

---

7 Excerpted from ANF 3:175–179.
8 Excerpted from ANF 3:669–679.

On Patience[9]

So is patience set over the things of God, that one can obey no precept, fulfill no work well-pleasing to the Lord, if estranged from it. (ch. 1)

God suffers Himself to be conceived in a mother's womb and awaits the time for birth; and, when born, bears the delay of growing up; and, when grown up, is not eager to be recognized. (ch. 3)

I detect the nativity of impatience in the devil himself, at that very time when he impatiently bore that the Lord God subjected the universal works which He had made to His own image—that is, to humanity. For if he had accepted that, he would not have grieved, and he would not have envied humankind if he had not grieved. (ch. 5)

Let us not interpret covetousness as consisting merely in the desire for what is another's, for even what seems ours is another's—for nothing is ours, since all things are God's, whose are we also ourselves. (ch. 7)

On Idolatry[10]

The principal charge against the human race, the world's deepest guilt, the all-inclusive cause of judgment, is idolatry. (§1)

All sins are discovered in idolatry, and idolatry in all of them. (§1)

What a variety of precautions have to be taken against it [idolatry], so wide is its scope. It overthrows the servants of God in countless ways, both when they do not recognize it and when they shut their eyes to it. (§2)

If unrighteousness is summed up in idolatry, it is important to guard ourselves in advance against its abundance by recognizing idolatry even where it is not at once evident. (§2)

Idolatry . . . can go on without temple or idol. (§3)

---

9 Excerpted from ANF 3:707–717.
10 Excerpts taken from Greenslade, *Early Latin Theology,* pp. 83–110.

It must not be supposed that only effigies consecrated in human form count as idols. (§3)

Human error worships everything but the very Creator of everything. (§4)

Need I quote more from Scripture? When the Holy Spirit has spoken, that is surely enough. (§4)

That an offense was committed by another does not lessen my guilt, if it was committed by my agency. At no point ought I to be an indispensable instrument to someone else doing what I may not do myself. (§11)

Walking according to God's moral law is endangered by words as well as deeds. (§20)

It is cowardly to keep quiet in order to escape recognition as a Christian. (§21)

Many say, no one is obliged to proclaim himself a Christian. Nor, I think, to deny that he is one. For you are denying it, if you dissemble your Christianity when for any reason you are taken for a pagan. (§22)

On Repentance[11]

Where there is no fear, there is likewise no conversion, and where there is no conversion, repentance is in vain. (ch. 2)

A good deed has God as its debtor. (ch. 2)

Even if human shortsightedness considers no sins wrong but those of deed, since it is incapable of penetrating the hidden places of the will, we should not on this account ignore its sins as God sees them. (ch. 3)

For all sins, therefore—whether committed by the flesh or by the spirit, whether in deed or in desire—He who has appointed that chastisement follow upon judgment, has also promised that pardon will follow upon repentance. (ch. 4)

---

11 Excerpted from ACW 28:14–37.

Lay hold on repentance and grip it fast, as one who is shipwrecked holds to a plank of salvation. It will buoy you up when you are plunged into a sea of sin and bear you safely to the haven of divine mercy. (ch. 4)

The essence of obedience consists in a union of wills. (ch. 4)

It is presumptuous to debate about the goodness of a divine decree, for we ought to obey it, not because it is good, but rather because God has decreed it. . . . The authority of the One who commands is of greater significance than the advantage of the one who obeys. (ch. 4)

Willful disobedience destroys the fear of God. (ch. 5)

What folly it is, what perversity, to practice an imperfect repentance and then to expect a pardon for sin! This is to stretch forth one's hand for merchandise and not to pay the price. (ch. 6)

Let no one be worse because God is better, sinning just as often as he is forgiven. (ch. 7)

Most of those who are saved from shipwreck divorce both ship and sea from that time on, and they show their appreciation for the gift of God—that is, their salvation—by remembering their peril. (ch. 7)

When a disease recurs the medicine must be repeated. (ch. 7)

On Prayer[12]

In the [Lord's] Prayer is comprised an epitome of the whole gospel. (ch. 1)

Do the ears of God wait for sound? What advantage will they who pray too loudly gain, except that they annoy their neighbors? (ch. 17)

---

12 Excerpts taken from ANF 3:681–691.

On Purity[13]

The virtue of which we are beginning to speak has become so obsolete now that purity is thought of as the moderation of lust, not its complete renunciation, and one is considered to be sufficiently chaste who is not too unchaste. (ch. 1)

The foundations of Christian purity are shaken, that purity which draws from heaven all that it has—its nature from the laver of regeneration, its schooling from the ministry of preaching, its rigor from verdicts pronounced in both testaments, firmly sanctioned by the fear of an eternal fire and the desire of an eternal kingdom. (ch. 1)

I am not ashamed that I have abandoned an error. . . . Nobody blushes when he makes progress. (ch. 1)

Freedom in Christ does no injury to virtue. (ch. 6)

We do not take the parables as sources of doctrine; rather, we take doctrine as a norm for interpreting the parables. (ch. 9)

If need be, we prefer an incomplete to an incorrect understanding of the Scripture. (ch. 9)

How ruthlessly the apostle Paul puts the axe of censure to every thicket of lust. (ch. 16)

On the Shows[14]

When entering the water [of baptism], we make profession of the Christian faith in the words of its rule [of faith]; we bear public testimony that we have renounced the devil, his pomp, and his angels. (ch. 4)

We despise the teachings of secular literature as foolishness in God's eyes. (ch. 17)

---

13 Excerpted from ACW 28:53–125.
14 Excerpted from ANF 3:79–91.

What could be more delightful than to have God the Father and our Lord at peace with us, than revelation of the truth, than confession of our errors, than pardon of the innumerable sins of our past life? (ch. 29)

To His Wife[15]

Marriage is conceded to us on the principle that marry we may because marry we must.... To be sure, marriage is better because burning is worse! Even so, how much better it is neither to marry nor to burn! (1:3)

Nothing should be sought simply because it is not forbidden. (1:3)

You ought to choose things that are good for you rather than things which are merely not bad for you. (1:3)

You may take it for granted that you will need nothing, if you serve the Lord; all things are yours if you possess the Lord of all. (1:4)

It is more difficult to sacrifice something we actually have than to be indifferent about something we no longer possess. (1:6)

Satan has discovered how to turn the cultivation of virtue itself to one's destruction, and it makes no difference to him whether he ruins souls by lust or by chastity. (1:6)

We ought to make the most of a situation which removes what necessity imposed. (1:7)

It is easy not to desire that of which you are ignorant and easy to turn your back on what you have never desired. (1:8)

Failure is easy to excuse wherever success is difficult to achieve. (2:1)

In proportion as the sin was easier to avoid, the burden of our guilt will be greater for obstinately committing it. (2:3)

---

15 Excerpted from ACW 13:10–36.

An Exhortation to Chastity[16]

So you too [like Adam], if you disobey the Lord who gave you the power of free choice along with His command, will of your own volition turn aside to what He forbids. And you imagine that in acting thus you have been overcome by the devil who, though he wishes you to make a choice against the will of God, does not actually cause you so to choose! Satan did not force our first parents to choose sin. The opposite is true, since they were not acting against their own wills, nor were they ignorant of what it was that God did not want them to do. He certainly did not want something to be done which, if done, He had decreed should be punished by death. So, there is just one thing the devil does: he makes trial of you, to see whether you will choose what it is in your power to choose—if you will! But when you have once made your choice, then he makes you his slave, not by actually having willed your choice for you, but by seizing upon the opportunity given him in the choice you made yourself. (ch. 2)

Since we alone have the power of making our own decisions, and since in so doing we show how we are disposed towards God (i.e., by choosing or not choosing to do His will), we need to reflect deeply and seriously on the will of God, even in matters which are not perfectly plain. (ch. 3)

The apostles had the Holy Spirit in a unique, special, personal way—not partially, as all others have, but fully, in prophecy, miracles, and the gift of tongues. (ch. 4)

To resist temptation is to prove one's mettle. (ch. 8)

Monogamy[17]

Faith is always the precursor of right conduct. (ch. 2)

Our one Father, God, lives, and so does our mother, the Church. (ch. 7)

For us, it is clear, life itself does not begin until we begin to believe. (ch. 11)

---

16 Excerpted from ACW 13:42–64.
17 Excerpted from ACW 13:70–108.

~ Cyprian

Cyprian (195–258) served as bishop of Carthage. He had received an excellent education. Converted, in large part, through the reading of Tertullian's works, Cyprian devoted himself to serving the needy. In due course, he was chosen bishop. During his episcopate, persecution was renewed. This resulted, on the one hand, in some members of the Church renouncing their faith, and, on the other, in the arising of a rigorist party that refused to readmit repentant people who had thus fallen. This rigorist group eventually became schismatic. Cyprian's writings dealt with these issues.

The Unity of the Catholic Church[1]

It is not persecution alone that we ought to fear, nor those forces that in open warfare range abroad to overthrow and defeat the servants of God. It is easy enough to be on one's guard when the danger is obvious; one can stir up one's courage for the fight when the enemy shows his true colors. There is more need to fear and beware of the enemy when he creeps up secretly, when he beguiles us by a show of peace and steals forward by those hidden

---

1 Some excerpts taken from ACW 25:43–68; others taken from S. L. Greenslade, trans., *Early Latin Theology: Selections from Tertullian, Cyprian, Ambrose, and Jerome* (Louisville, KY: Westminster John Knox Press, 1956), pp. 124–142. The sources will each be indicated at the end of the citation by "ACW" or "LCC" (the unnumbered Library of Christian Classics series, to which the Greenslade volume belongs) in curled parentheses.

approaches which have earned him the name "Serpent." This is his way: lurking in the dark, he ensnares us by trickery. (§1) {ACW}

The devil was defeated precisely through being detected and unmasked. (§1) {ACW}

It is our duty to stand upon His [Christ's] words, to learn and do all that He taught and did. How can anyone profess faith in Christ without doing what Christ commanded? How can he come to the reward of faith without keeping faith with the commandments? (§2) {LCC}

What could be more clever and cunning than the enemy's moves after being unmasked and defeated by Christ's coming? Light had come to the nations and the lamp of salvation was shining for the deliverance of humankind, so that the deaf began to hearken to the Spirit's call of grace, the blind to open their eyes to the Lord, the sick to recover their health unto eternity, the lame to hasten to the Church, and the dumb to raise their voice aloud in prayer. Thereupon the enemy, seeing his idols abandoned and his temples and haunts deserted by the ever growing number of the faithful, devised a fresh deceit, using the Christian name itself to mislead the unwary. He invented heresies and schisms so as to undermine the faith, to corrupt the truth, to sunder our unity. (§3) {ACW}

Satan snatches away people from within the Church herself, and while they think that coming close to the light they have now escaped the night of the world, he plunges them unexpectedly into darkness of another kind. They still call themselves Christians after abandoning the gospel of Christ and the observance of His law; though walking in darkness, they think they still enjoy the light. (§3) {ACW}

If one does not hold fast to this oneness of the Church, does he imagine that he still holds the faith? If he resists and withstands the Church, can he still have confidence that he is in the Church, when the blessed Apostle Paul gives us this very teaching and points to the mystery of oneness when he writes that "there is one body and one Spirit, . . . one hope of your calling; one Lord, one faith, one baptism; one God" [Eph 4:4–6]? (§4) {ACW}

The episcopate is a single whole, in which each bishop's share gives him a right to and a responsibility for the whole. (§5) {LCC}

Whoever breaks with the Church and enters into an adulterous union cuts himself off from the promises made to the Church; and the one who has turned his back on the Church of Christ shall not come to the rewards Christ has promised: that one is an alien, a worldling, and an enemy. You cannot have God for your Father if you do not have the Church for your mother. (§6) {ACW}

He who rends and divides the Church cannot possess the garment of Christ. (§7) {LCC}

Can anyone be so criminal and faithless, so mad in his passion for quarrelling, as to believe it possible that the oneness of God, the garment of the Lord, the Church of Christ, should be divided, or dare to divide it himself? (§8) {ACW}

How can a Christian breast harbor the fierceness of wolves and the madness of dogs and the deadly venom of snakes and the bloodlust of wild beasts? It is a blessing when such people break away from the Church: it prevents their preying upon the doves and sheep of Christ with their savage and poisonous influence. (§9) {ACW}

Let no one think that good people can leave the Church. It is not the grain that the wind carries away, nor the solidly rooted tree that the storm blows down. It is the empty chaff that is swept away by the storm, the weakling trees that are overturned by the blast of the whirlwind. (§9) {ACW}

This all was foretold by the Holy Spirit through the apostle when he said, "For there must also be factions among you, that those who are approved may be recognized among you" [1 Cor 11:19]. In this way, the faithful are proved and the faithless discovered; thus too even before the day of judgment, already here below, the souls of the just and unjust are distinguished, and the wheat is separated from the chaff. (§10) {ACW}

Born of a lie, they cannot inherit what the truth has promised; begotten by the faithless, they are deprived of the grace of faith. (§11) {ACW}

No one whose furious discord breaks the Lord's peace can come to the reward of peace. (§11) {LCC}

One who has violated the love of Christ by faithless dissension cannot attain to the reward of a Christ who said, "This is My commandment, that you love one another as I have loved you" [John 15:12]. (§14) {LCC}

Those who have refused to be of one mind in the Church of God cannot abide with God. (§14) {ACW}

The one who does not stand fast in Christ's gospel and the true faith cannot be reckoned a Christian. (§14) {LCC}

Just as the devil is not Christ, although he tricks people by the name, so the one who does not stand fast in Christ's gospel and true faith cannot be counted a Christian. (§14) {LCC}

One who separates himself from the Church is to be avoided and fled from. He is perverted, sinful, self-condemned. (§17) {LCC}

Confession [of faith in Christ] is the beginning of glory, but it does not earn the crown at once. It does not perfect praise, but initiates honor. Scripture says, "He who endures to the end will be saved" [Matt 10:22]. (§21) {LCC}

God is one, and Christ is one, and His Church is one; one is the faith, and one the people cemented together by harmony into the strong unity of a body. (§23) {ACW}

The Lapsed[2]

When persecution rages, the mind of none escapes free and unscathed. (ch. 4)

If we know what made us fall we can learn how to heal our wounds. (ch. 5)

Many were defeated before the battle was joined. (ch. 8)

No one could be overcome by the world if he had nothing in the world to overcome him. (ch. 11)

---

2 Excerpts taken from ACW 25:13–42.

But how can those who are tethered to their inheritance be following Christ? And can those who are weighed down by earthly desires be seeking heaven and aspiring to the heights above? They think of themselves as owners, whereas it is they rather who are owned: enslaved as they are to their own property, they are not the masters of their money but its slaves. (ch. 12)

The one who soothes the sinner with comforting flatteries only encourages the sinful appetite; he is not checking crime, but fostering it. . . . He is a poor doctor whose timid hand spares the swelling, festering wound, and who, by letting the poison remain buried deep in the body, only aggravates the illness. The wound must be cut open, the infected parts cut out, and the wound treated with stringent remedies. No matter how much the patient shouts and cries, no matter how much he protests in exasperation at the pain—later he will be grateful, when he feels his health restored. (ch. 14)

It is an innocent-seeming pestilence which masquerades as compassion. (ch. 15)

No one is in union with the Church who cuts himself off from the gospel. (ch. 16)

We cannot take it for granted that because someone has made a promise [that we are forgiven] the same has been granted by the majesty of God. (ch. 18)

The gospel cannot in part stand and in part fail. (ch. 20)

If certain doubters have too little faith in what the future holds in store, let them learn to tremble from what is happening even now. (ch. 23)

The penalty of a few is a warning to all. (ch. 23)

Let each one consider not what has befallen someone else but what affliction he deserves himself; and let him not think that he has escaped because no penalty has yet overtaken him. (ch. 26)

God cannot be mocked or outwitted; no clever cunning can deceive Him. (ch. 28)

Can anyone count himself a Christian if being a Christian makes him blush and afraid to admit it? (ch. 28)

Through the presumption of certain folk who beguile with false promises of salvation, all true hope of salvation is destroyed. (ch. 34)

Let the earnestness of our repentance correspond to the gravity of our sin. (ch. 35)

Letter 73[3]

There is no salvation outside the Church. (§21)

---

3 This is in the public domain.

~ Lactantius

Lactantius (c. 250-c. 320) lived through the last great persecution of the Church, under Diocletian, and during the reign of the first Christian emperor, Constantine the Great; indeed, Lactantius served as tutor to one of Constantine's sons. He was widely learned in the mythology, philosophy, and literature of the Hellenic, Hellenistic, and Roman cultures; he had served as a teacher of rhetoric. Converted in his adulthood, he turned his considerable persuasive skills to the service of the Christian faith, which he defended to the cultured world of his day, not by reference to Scripture, but by appeal to and argument with the works of that culture. Lactantius was an able rhetorician and has been praised for his eloquence.

The Divine Institutes[1]

The thought of God especially slips out of human memory, when, enjoying His benefits, they ought to give honor to divine indulgence. But whenever serious necessity falls upon them, then they remember God. (2:1)

When God finally revealed the truth to humans, He wished us to know only those things which we need to know in order to attain life. (2:8)

The whole Scripture is divided into two testaments. That which preceded the coming of Christ and His Passion—that is, the Law and the Prophets—is called the Old Testament; those things which were written after his

---

1 Excerpted from FC 49:15–541.

Resurrection are called the New Testament. The Jews use the Old, we the New. They are not opposed, however, because the New is the fulfillment of the Old, and in both the testator is Christ, who by the death He underwent for us makes us heirs of the eternal kingdom. (4:20)

[Having repudiated several heretics and schismatics, Lactantius urges:] Therefore, the catholic Church alone is the one which retains true worship. This is the fount of truth; this is the domicile of faith; this is the temple of God. And if one does not enter this and go out from it, that person is cut away from the hope of life and salvation. (4:30)

If by chance any of the erudite were converted to that truth [i.e., Christianity], they did not measure up for its defense [to unbelievers]. Among those who are known to me, Minucius Felix was not of mean repute among the case-pleaders of the place. His book, which has the title *Octavius*, shows how suitable a defender of the truth he could have been if he had devoted himself entirely to that pursuit. Septimius Tertullian also was an expert in every sort of learning, but he had little ease in eloquence, was not polished, and was quite obscure. So, not even here did he earn high praise. There was, however, one exceptional and brilliant one, Cyprian, who acquired great glory for himself in the profession of the art of oratory, and who wrote many wonderful works in his own manner. For he had an ability in speaking, easy, fluent, pleasant, and—what is of prime importance in speech—so clear that you cannot distinguish whether he was more ornate in eloquence or more successful in explanation or more powerful in persuasion. Still, he is not able to please those who do not know the mystery [i.e., are not believers], since the things which he spoke are mystical matters and were prepared for the purpose of being heard by the faithful. (5:1)

Religion cannot be forced. It is a matter that must be managed by words rather than by blows, so that it may be voluntary. (5:19)

Religion ought to be defended, not by killing but by dying, not by fury but by patience, not by crime but by faith. The former action each time belongs to evil, the latter to good, and it is necessary that the practice of religion be good, not evil. If you wish, indeed, to defend religion by blood, if by torments, if by evil, then it will not be defended; it will be polluted and violated. (5:19)

This is the first step of wisdom, to know who our true Father is, that we may honor Him alone with due piety, that we may obey Him and most devoutly serve Him, that all our acts and care and attention be focused on doing so. (6:9)

If we have all sprung from one man whom God made, then surely we are relatives, and for this reason it must be considered the greatest crime to hate a man or to do him harm. (6:10)

The first step of righteousness is to refrain from evil deeds; the second, from evil words; and the third, from consideration or thinking of evil things. He who has ascended the first step is righteous in a sufficient or moderate degree; he who makes the second is already of perfect virtue, since he fails in neither deeds nor words; but he who reaches the third seems, in truth, to have attained likeness to God. (6:13)

Passion is . . . a sort of natural richness of souls. . . . When God made the first humans, He implanted emotions in them. (6:15)

We ought to direct the passions, which it is a vice to use evilly, into the right channels. (6:17)

Just as water which is always still and quiet is unhealthful and more disordered, so a mind unmoved and torpid is useless even to itself. . . . Those who urge immobility of soul wish to deprive the soul of life, since life is full of activity, and death is quiet. (6:17)

God warns that the worker of righteousness should not be boastful, lest he seem to have performed the work of mercy, not so much from a desire of obeying the heavenly commands as from one of pleasing other people [Matt 6:1], and lest he already thus have the price of glory which he has gained and so not receive the prize of that heavenly and divine reward. (6:18)

There are three emotions which drive people headlong into all crimes: anger, desire, and passion (or lust). For this reason the [ancient pagan] poets said that there were three Furies which attack human minds: anger seeks for revenge; desire riches; passion pleasure. But for all of these God has set fixed limits. . . . What these limits are, however, it is not a great task to show. Desire has been given to us for procuring those things which are necessary for life. Passion has been given for the propagation of the race. The emotion of anger is for checking the sins of those who are under our authority—that is, so that with stricter discipline the younger might be formed to justice and probity. (6:19)

When God invented the plan of the two sexes, He placed in them the desire of each other and joy in union. So He put in bodies the most ardent desire of all living things, so that they might rush most avidly into these emotions and be able by this means to propagate and increase their kind. (6:23)

Let each one, then, as far as he is able, train himself to modesty, cultivate shame, and protect chastity of both conscience and mind. (6:23)

If we take up our children again, and cherish and embrace them when we see them repent of their faults, and when we think that they have corrected them and cast them from them, why should we not hope that the clemency of our true Father can be won by repentance? The same Lord and most indulgent Father, therefore, promises that He will remit the sins of those repenting of them, and that He will wipe away all the iniquities of the one who will begin at length to do righteousness. (6:24)

He in whose sight we live knows all things, and even if we are able to hide from all other people, we cannot shut out God, to whom nothing can be hidden, nothing secret. (6:24)

Human eyes are stopped by walls, but the divine glance of God cannot be kept away even from the innermost regions of the heart—on the contrary, He beholds and knows the whole person. (6:24)

Whoever obeys all these heavenly commands is the true worshiper of God. His sacrifices are meekness of soul, an innocent life, and good deeds. The one who displays all of these makes a sacrifice as often as he does something good and pious. (6:24)

So the highest rite of worshiping God is praise from the mouth of the righteous person directed to God. In order, however, that it may be acceptable to God, this must be done with humility and fear and the greatest devotion, lest anyone flaunting confidence in integrity and innocence might incur the crime of pride and arrogance, and thereby lose the grace of virtue. But in order that he may be dear to God and lack all stain, let him always implore the mercy of God and pray for nothing else than the forgiveness of his sins, even though there be none of which he is conscious. If he desires something else, there is no need of words for One who knows what we wish. If anything good happens to him, let him give thanks; if anything evil, let him make satisfaction and acknowledge that it has happened to him on account of his sins. And, nevertheless, let him give thanks even in evils, and in prosperity make reparation, that he may remain the same, stable, immutable, and unshaken. And let him not think that he must do this only in a temple, but also at home and even in his very bedroom. (6:25)

We can take nothing with us except a life well spent, lived without any harm. That one will come rich to God, that person will be wealthy, in whose favor there will stand continence, mercy, patience, charity, faith. This is our inheritance which cannot be snatched from anyone or transferred to another. (7:27)

The Workmanship of God[2]

It is neither possible to grasp with our senses nor to expound in words God's divine providence and all-perfect power. (ch. 1)

And does one wonder if the divine mind of God, intent upon all the parts of the world, discourses over and rules all things, governs all things, is everywhere present and everywhere diffused, when the force and power of the human mind enclosed within a mortal body is so great that not even by the barriers of this heavy and sluggish body with which it is encumbered can it be in any way restrained from granting to itself, impatient of rest, the free power of wandering? (ch. 16)

The Wrath of God[3]

Without religion . . . we are leveled to either the inhumanness of beasts or the stupidity of cattle; for in religion alone—that is, in the acknowledging of the supreme God—is wisdom. (ch. 22)

---

2 Excerpted from FC 54:5–56.
3 Excerpts taken from FC 54:61–116.

If we have wealth, if we have resources at hand, let them be used, not for the pleasure of one, but for the welfare of many. (ch. 24)

Let God be hallowed by us, not in temples, but in our hearts, for all things are destructible which are made by hand. Let us clean this temple which is defiled, not by smoke, not by dust, but by evil thoughts, this temple which is lighted, not by burning wax, but by the brightness of God and the light of wisdom. (ch. 24)

PART II

The Nicene and Post-Nicene Fathers

~ *Eusebius of Caesarea*

Eusebius (c. 260–c. 340) served as bishop of Caesarea from about 315 to his death. His life spanned the last (and worst) of the imperial persecutions of the Church and the remarkable turn of events as Emperor Constantine first legalized the practice of, and then himself favored, Christianity. Indeed, Eusebius enjoyed Constantine's favor and was often at the imperial court as an adviser. He wrote a biography and a panegyric of the emperor, and recorded the address the emperor gave to the Council of Nicea in 325 (in which Eusebius himself participated).

Prior to that, he wrote the major work for which he is known, *Ecclesiastical History*. This work is the first history of the Church ever written, covering the period from the coming of Christ to the opening years of Constantine's reign (but not including the Nicene Council). Eusebius's work is a valuable source for much information that has otherwise been lost (including descriptions of and excerpts from the writings of some early church leaders). He often relates his history to that of Josephus, the Jewish historian, and to the change of emperors in Rome; he gives information about several leading figures within the Church and among the heretics; at several points he relates viewpoints, and himself shows considerable critical insight, regarding the canon of the Old and the New Testaments; and he gives extensive treatment to the martyrs. *Ecclesiastical History* is comprised of ten books; between the eighth and the ninth Eusebius placed a small work, *The Book of Martyrs*.

Given the nature of *Ecclesiastical History*, we do not include many excerpts below, since the regular narrative—interesting as it otherwise is—does not often correlate to the selection criteria for the present volume.

The Life of Constantine[1]

The sign [the cross] which appeared [to Constantine] was the symbol of immortality, the trophy of the victory over death which He [Christ] had gained. (1:32)

[In a letter from Emperor Constantine to Eusebius]: It is a proof of genuine piety to stand firm in what appears at the same time pleasing to God and accordant with apostolic Tradition. (3:51)

Oration in Praise of Constantine[2]

No one can worthily comprehend God's being, and the ineffable splendor of the glory which surrounds Him repels the gaze of every eye from His divine majesty. (1:2)

The sacred doctrine teaches that He who is the supreme source of good and cause of all things is beyond all comprehension, and therefore inexpressible by word, speech, or name; surpassing the power not only of language but even of thought. Uncircumscribed by place or body; neither in heaven, nor in ethereal space, nor in any other part of the universe; but completely independent of everything else, He pervades the depths of unexplored and secret wisdom. The sacred oracles teach us to acknowledge Him as the only true God. (12:1)

Why did the incorporeal Word of God assume this mortal body as a way to interact with humanity? How else than in human form could that divine and impalpable, that immaterial and invisible essence manifest itself to those who sought God in created and earthly objects, unable or unwilling otherwise to discern the author and maker of all things? So, as a fitting means to communicate with humankind, He assumed a mortal body, something with which they were familiar—for like, it is proverbially said, loves like. So, to those whose affections were engaged by visible objects,

---

1 Excerpts taken from NPNF (2nd) 1:481–559.
2 Excerpts taken from NPNF (2nd) 1:581–610.

who looked for gods in statues and lifeless images, who imagined the deity to have material and corporeal substance, who even conferred on human beings the title of divinity, the Word of God presented Himself in this form. (14:1–2)

In arming His disciples against the power of this last enemy, He did not deliver His teaching merely by verbal precepts; nor did He try to prove the soul's immortality by persuasive and probable arguments; but He displayed to them in His own person a real victory over death. (15:8)

He was the victim offered to the supreme sovereign of the universe for the whole human race—consecrated for the need of the human race, and for the overthrow of the errors of demon worship. For as soon as the one holy and mighty sacrifice, the sacred body of our Savior, had been slain for humankind, to be a ransom for all nations, which had until then been involved in the guilt of impious superstition, from that point on the power of impure and unholy spirits was utterly abolished, and every earthborn and deluding error was weakened and destroyed. Thus, then, this salutary victim taken from among themselves (I mean the mortal body of the Word) was offered on behalf of the common race of humanity. (15:11–12)

How wondrous must that power be deemed which summoned obscure and unlettered men from their fisher's trade and made them the legislators and instructors of the human race! And how clear a demonstration of His deity do we find in the promise so abundantly fulfilled, that He would make them fishers of men; in the power and energy which He bestowed, so that they composed and published writings of such authority that they were translated into every civilized and barbarous language, were read and pondered by all nations, and the doctrines contained in them accredited as the oracles of God! (17:9–10)

Constantine's Oration to the Assembly of the Saints[3]

To trace the secret reasons of all these things is a task which exceeds the power of human faculties. For how can the intellect of a frail and perishable being arrive at the knowledge of perfect truth, or apprehend in its purity the counsel of God from the beginning? (§8)

---

3 Excerpts taken from NPNF (2nd) 1:561–580.

O Christ, Savior of humankind, be present to aid me in my holy task! Direct the words which celebrate Your virtues and instruct me worthily to sound Your praises. (§11)

[In considering the death to which Christ yielded:] It is beyond the bounds of folly itself that people should be able to persuade themselves that the incorruptible God yielded to the violence of human beings, and not rather to that love alone which He bore to the human race. (§11)

What higher blessing can we speak of than this, that God should set forth the way of righteousness and make those who are counted worthy of His instruction like Himself; that goodness might be communicated to all classes of humankind and eternal blessedness be the result? (§11)

From infancy possessing the wisdom of God; received with reverential awe by the Jordan, in whose waters He was baptized; gifted with that royal anointing, the Spirit of universal intelligence; with knowledge and power to perform miracles and heal diseases beyond the reach of human art; He granted swift and unhindered assent to the prayers of human beings—to whose welfare, indeed, His whole life was devoted without reserve. His doctrines instilled not only prudence but real wisdom: His hearers were instructed, not just in social virtues, but in the ways which lead to the spiritual world, with the result that they devoted themselves to the contemplation of immutable and eternal things, the knowledge of the supreme Father. The benefits He bestowed were no common blessings: for blindness, the gift of sight; for helpless weakness, the vigor of health; in place of death, restoration to life. I will not dwell on the abundant provision in the wilderness, when a scanty measure of food became a complete and enduring supply for the needs of a mighty multitude. We offer thanks to You, our God and Savior, according to our feeble power—to You, O Christ, supreme providence of the mighty Father, You who save us from evil and impart to us Your most blessed doctrine; for I say these things not to praise but to give thanks. For what mortal can worthily declare Your praise, who called Creation into being out of nothing and illumined it with Your light, who regulated the confusion of the elements by the laws of harmony and order? (§11)

Ecclesiastical History[4]

No language is sufficient to express the origin, the dignity, even the substance and nature of Christ. . . . For who but the Father has thoroughly understood that light which existed before the world was—that intellectual and substantial wisdom, and that living Word which in the beginning was with the Father, before all Creation and any production visible or invisible, the first and only offspring of God? (1:2)

[Regarding the extremes to which some inhabitants of Jerusalem fell during the terrible famine suffered by the Jews when besieged by Emperor Titus:] Famine surpasses all other evils, but it destroys nothing so effectually as shame. (3:6)

[Regarding persecutions suffered by Christians:] There is nothing terrifying where the love of the Father, nothing painful where the glory of Christ prevails. (5:1)

The confusion of the [Roman] empire, which prevailed to a great extent, did not cease before the Christians received full liberty of conscience to profess their religion. (8:14)

The power of God is always present to help aid those who have to bear any hardship for the sake of religion, to lighten their labors, and to strengthen their ardor. (*The Book of Martyrs*, ch. 2)

Thanks be to God, the omnipotent and universal sovereign, thanks also to the Savior and Redeemer of our souls, Jesus Christ, through whom we pray that peace will be preserved to us at all times, firm and unshaken by any temporal molestation from without, and troubles from the mind within. (10:1)

Him also we would extol, and bear His name constantly upon our lips, the second cause of our mercies, the instructor in divine knowledge, teacher of true religion, destroyer of the impious, slayer of tyrants, the reformer of the world, and the Savior of us when our condition was desperate, our Lord

---

[4] Excerpts taken from Isaac Boyle, trans., *The Ecclesiastical History of Eusebius Pamphilius* (1850; repr., Grand Rapids, MI: Baker Book House, 1969), pp. 13–439.

Jesus. For He alone as the only all-gracious Son of the all-gracious Father, according to the purpose of His Father's benevolence, readily and freely assumed our nature who lay prostrate in the depths of destruction. Like an excellent physician, who, for the sake of saving those who are suffering from a dreadful disease, examines their sufferings, touches their foul sores, and from other miseries brings upon himself their griefs and pains, He has saved us, not only struggling with our dreadful sores and our wounds already putrid, but even lying among the dead, and rescued us to Himself from the very jaws of death. For none of those in heaven had such power at command, as to promote the salvation of so many without detriment. But He alone, after having reached the deplorable corruption of our race, He alone taking upon Himself our burdens, and bearing the punishment of our iniquities, recovering us, not merely half-dead, but altogether fetid and offensive, in tombs and sepulchers, both of old and new, by His gracious love saves us still beyond the hope and expectation of others, and even of ourselves, and liberally imparts to us the abundance of His Father's blessings. (10:4)

～The Desert Fathers and Mothers

Beginning in the later third century, monasticism developed in Egypt and spread into Syria and Palestine. Both men and women left the civilized world behind and headed into the desert in the desire to draw nearer to God. Through strenuous asceticism, unceasing prayer, and diligent labor, they sought to devote themselves entirely to an awareness of and openness toward God. This monastic impulse attracted large numbers of men and women for several centuries, until invasions devastated the regions.

Many of the monks and nuns became known for spiritual and theological insight; they came to be known as the Desert Fathers and Desert Mothers. Often sought out for guidance by Christians living in cities, monastic leaders also gave counsel to those whom they led in the movement. The Desert Fathers and Mothers flourished until well into the sixth century (although monasticism has continued through all centuries up to the present). Many of the Desert Fathers' and Mothers' teachings and the stories of their lives were written down and copied for spiritual guidance. They have come down to us in various collections.

The Letter of Palladius[1]

There is One alone who has no need of doctrine or learning—God. {p. 77}

---

1 Excerpts taken from Ernest A. Wallis, trans. and ed., *The Paradise or Garden of the Holy Fathers, Being Histories of the Anchorites, Recluses, Monks, Coenobites, and Ascetic Fathers of the Deserts of Egypt Between A.D. 250 and A.D.*

This is doctrine: the correction of the natural habits and disposition, and the leading of a life of spiritual excellence. {p. 78}

It is better to be under subjection to the barbarians than to evil passions. {p. 81}

Constant prayer is the strength, the armor, and the wall of the soul. {p. 81}

In truth, neither eating food nor abstaining from it is anything, but the faith and love which are made perfect in works. {p. 86}

The Histories of Holy Men, by Palladius[2]

Abba Dorotheos of Thebes taught, "Where the sign of the cross is, the wickedness of Satan has no power to do harm." (1:2)

Abba Didymus of Alexandria declared, "If you would walk in the life of excellence and in the love of God, remove yourself from contention." (1:4)

Now I write down these things in order that, if anyone be observing a correct rule of life of any kind whatsoever which is pleasing unto God, he may take heed lest he fall, and that even if he be tripped up in a snare and fall he may not come to despair, and remain in his fallen condition, but that by leaning upon the staff of the hope of the divine mercy, and by arraying himself through repentance in the apparel of simplicity and humility, he may again become strong enough to stand up, for we should not despise those who truly repent. (1:28)

Abba Paphnutius said, "Every lapse or calamity which takes place, whether through the tongue, some feeling, or some action, or through the whole body, takes place in proportion to the measure of one's pride, and by the permission of God." (1:52)

Palladius asked, "How is it possible for the human mind to be with God continually and uninterruptedly?" The monk Diocles answered, "The

---

400: *Compiled by Athanasius, Archbishop of Alexandria; Palladius, Bishop of Helenopolis; Saint Jerome, and Others* (New York: Burt Franklin, 1907 [1972 reprint ed.]), 1:77–87.

2 Excerpted from Wallis, *The Paradise*, 1:89–281.

mind of that soul which lives in the thought or deed of the fear of God, no matter what it may be, is with God." (1:55)

Lord, You always show Your compassion upon the miserable soul, and You spare it. (2:13)

Abba Malchus said, "Hold in contempt the fire of time, that you may flee from the fire of eternity." (2:15)

Abba Malchus also taught, "I was afraid lest, having been victorious in the time of war, I might receive a severe wound through the arrows of the enemy in the time of peace." (2:15)

Abba Malchus declared further, "By the help of God, patient endurance and implicit obedience will deliver one from all temptations. Obedience to the commandments of God is everlasting life, and the patient endurance which is perfect produces everlasting life in us; for "the one who endures to the end will be saved" [Matt 10:22]. (2:15)

We bless You, our Lord Jesus Christ, for ten thousand times ten thousand sins are too few for Your mercy to forgive in one hour. (2:27)

Abba Poeman taught, "If you repent with all your heart, I believe that God will grant you forgiveness; do not despair of your redemption." (2:33)

Abba Macarius the Egyptian declared, "Glory to You, O Christ, for You are the refuge of those who are overtaken by storms, the straight way of those who err, the Redeemer of those who flee unto You for refuge, now, always, and forever and ever." (2:42)

Now therefore, O Christians, since we know from the Holy Scriptures and from divine revelation how great the grace is which God dispenses to those who truly run to Him for refuge, and who blot out their former sins by repentance, and also how, according to His promise, He rewards with good things and neither takes vengeance according to what is just nor brings upon us a punishment for our former sins, let us not be in despair of our lives. For as He promised through the prophet Isaiah, He will make clean those who have toiled in sin, and will make them bright and white like clean wool and snow [Is 1:18], and will make them happy with the blessings of heaven. Moreover, through the Prophet Ezekiel, God asserts with oaths that He does not desire their destruction, for He says, "As I live, says the Lord, I have no pleasure in the death of the wicked, but that the wicked turn from their ways and live" [Ezek 33:11]. (2:44)

The Rule of Pachomius at Tabenna[3]

Do you not know that the mother of the beginning of wickednesses is pride? (§1)

O, what a great and wonderful thing it is that God humbled Himself, and took upon Himself the form of a servant, and put on his body and dwelt in him, and became obedient even unto death for our sakes! And yet we who are by nature low puff ourselves up with pride! (§1)

Since God is a fountain of grace, He seeks excuses to pour out upon us the abundant streams of His grace. (§3)

O Lord who sustains the universe, send Your mercies to me, and never take them away from me, for I know that without Your mercy nothing can possibly exist. (§9)

Before the hour comes when we will weep for our souls, let us cultivate spiritual excellence with a ready mind. And I tell you that, if you knew the good things in heaven, and the glory laid up for the saints, and how those who have fallen are punished by God, and the tortures laid up for those who have been neglectful, and especially for those who having known the truth have not, as was right, guided themselves by it, instead of inheriting the blessedness which is reserved for the saints, you would do so. (§10)

Let us weep for ourselves while we still have the time, so that when our departure comes near we may not be found asking God for more time to repent. (§10)

Let us not allow this world, which is a small and a contemptible thing, and which resembles a fleeting shadow, to steal away from us blessed and immortal life. (§10)

---

3 Excerpted from Wallis, *The Paradise*, 1:283–316.

History of the Monks of Egypt[4]

When certain priests came to visit him [Abba Paphnutius], he made known to them all that the Lord had revealed to him, saying to them that no one in this world ought to be despised, let him be a thief, or an actor on the stage, or one that tilled the ground, and was bound to a wife, or was a merchant and served a trade. For in every condition of human life, there are souls that please God and have their hidden deeds wherein He takes delight. Whence it is plain that it is not so much profession or habit that is pleasing to God as the sincerity and affection of the soul and honesty of deed. {pp. 51–52}

The Life of St. Pelagia the Harlot[5]

[Spoken before Pelagia's conversion, just after she had passed by the place where bishops were assembled:] He [Bishop Nonnus] spoke to the [his fellow] bishops: "What think you? How many hours has this woman spent in her chamber, bathing and adorning herself with all solicitude . . . , that there may be no stain or flaw in all that body's beauty and its wearing, that she may be a joy to all men's eyes, nor disappoint those paltry lovers of hers who are but for a day and tomorrow are not? And we who have in heaven a Father Almighty, an immortal Lover, with the promise of riches eternal and rewards beyond all reckoning, since eye has not seen nor ear has heard nor has it ascended into the heart of man to conceive the things that God has prepared for them that love Him—but what need is there of further speech? With such a promise, the vision of the Bridegroom, that great and splendid and ineffable face, whereon the Cherubim dare not look, we adorn not, we care not so much as to wash the filth from our miserable souls, but leave them lying in their squalor." {p. 179}

The Life of St. Mary the Harlot[6]

Be not mistrustful, daughter, of the mercy of God; let your sin be as mountains, His mercy towers above His every creature. We read that an unclean woman came to Him that was clean, and she did not soil Him, but was

---

4 Excerpts taken from Helen Waddell, *The Desert Fathers* (London: Constable & Co., 1936), pp. 45–57.
5 *Op. cit.*, pp. 177–178.
6 *Op cit.*, pp. 190–201.

herself made clean by Him: she washed the Lord's feet with her tears, and dried them with her hair [Luke 7:36–48]. If a spark can set on fire the sea, then can your sins stain His whiteness. It is no new thing to fall in the mire, but it is an evil thing to lie there fallen. {p. 198}

Fear not: mortal man is apt to slip. But if he be swift to fall, swift is he to rise again with the succor of God who desires not the death of a sinner, but rather that he be healed and live. {p. 198}

[St. Mary the Harlot's concluding prayer:] Have mercy upon me, You that alone are without sin, and save me, who alone is pitiful and kind. For beside you, the Father most blessed, and Your only begotten Son who was made flesh for us, and the Holy Ghost who gives life to all things, I know no other, and believe in no other. And now be mindful of me, Lover of men, and lead me out of the prison-house of my sins, for both are in your hand, O Lord, the time that You did will me to come into this world, and the time that You shall bid me go out from it elsewhere. Remember me that am without defense, and save me a sinner. And may Your grace, that was in this world my aid, my refuge, and my glory, gather me under its wings in that great and terrible day. . . . Holy Lord, I beseech you, bring me into Your kingdom, and deign to bless me with all that have found grace before You, for with You is magnificence, adoration, and honor, Father, Son, and Holy Spirit. Amen. {p. 201}

The Histories of the Monks, by St. Jerome[7]

Blessed be God, who desires the welfare of all humankind, who wishes that they may live and come to the knowledge of the truth. (§1)

The hearing of the ears is less trustworthy than the sight of the eyes, and frequently error makes its way into what is heard by the ears, while the remembrance of what one has seen can never be blotted out from the heart, and it will be permanently fixed in the mind. (§2).

[From John the Recluse:] Even were you to possess all the virtues (which is difficult to accomplish), still you must not be confident in yourselves, for those who have become puffed up with pride, and who thought they had

---

7 Excerpted from Wallis, *The Paradise*, 1:317–382.

arrived to the point where they were worthy of praise, have subsequently fallen from their high estate. (§2)

[From John the Recluse:] Do not let your thoughts wander around when you are praying to God; do not let any other thought enter into your mind and turn it away from that glorious sight of God which rises upon the pure heart during prayer, and which enlightens the understanding and makes it shine; and do not let the remembrance of evil thoughts disturb your minds while you pray. (§2)

[From John the Recluse:] It is not fitting for anyone to think that he has found knowledge with absolute certainty.... We should always draw near to God with humble ideas and in faith, so far as it is possible to approach Him in the mind, and so far as mere humans are able to attain unto Him. (§2)

[From John the Recluse:] The person who is worthy of a little of the knowledge of God (for no one is able to receive the whole of it) is able to acquire the knowledge of many things, and to see those mysteries which the knowledge of God will show him. (§2)

[From John the Recluse:] It is the cunning of the evil one that, having vanquished someone in the strife, brings that person to a senseless state of despair . . . , for behold, many have been in despair about themselves, but the compassion of God has not forsaken them. (§2)

[From John the Recluse:] I beseech each of you before all things to lead a life of humility, for that is the foundation of all the glorious virtues. (§2)

[From Petarpemotis:] Now that your life has come to an end you ask for time for repentance! What have you been doing all your life long? (§16)

The Sayings of the Fathers[8]

One person appears to be silent, but his heart judges and condemns others, and so that person actually speaks continually; someone else speaks from morning to evening, but that one keeps silence, because he speaks only what is helpful. (1:27)

---

8 Excerpted from Wallis, *The Paradise*, 2:3–336.

A brother asked an aged monk, "What is humility?" And the old man answered, "That you not pay back evil for evil." (1:32)

I have many times repented that I spoke, but I have never repented that I held my peace. (1:53)

Poemen said, "As smoke drives bees away and people take the sweetness of the bees' work, in the same way ease of the body drives the fear of God from the heart and carries away all the benefit of its labor." (1:95)

Whenever one reads the divine books, the demons are afraid. (1:107)

Epiphanius said, "The holy person who sees someone sin weeps bitterly, saying, 'It is this one who sins now, but sometime subsequently it may be me.' So, however much someone may sin before you, do not condemn him, but count yourself a sinner far greater than he is, even though he may be a child of this world, and he may have sinned greatly against God." (1:119)

Epiphanius said, "Know yourself, and you will never fall. Give your soul work—that is to say, constant prayer, and love of God—before another can give it evil and filthy thoughts; and pray that the spirit of error may be far from you." (1:120)

Epiphanius said, "The one who shuts up the memory of evil things within himself is like one who hides fire in straw." (1:122)

Epiphanius said, "Pray to the Lord God as if He were standing before you, for He is near you and looks upon you." (1:125)

Three old men once came to Abba Sisoes because they had heard that he was a great man. And the first one asked him, "Father, how can I escape from the river of fire?" And Abba Sisoes answered him not a word. Then the second old man asked him, "Father, how can I escape from the gnashing of teeth, and from the worm which never dies?" And Abba Sisoes answered him not a word. Then the third old man asked him, "Father, what shall I do? The remembrance of the outer darkness troubles me." And Abba Sisoes answered and said to them, "I never think about any of these things, but I believe that God is merciful, and that He will show mercy to me." (1:138)

Poemen said, "The one who does not weep for himself in this world must weep forever in the next. He may weep here voluntarily, or there because of the punishments which he will receive, but it is impossible for anyone to escape weeping." (1:152)

When the mind is weighed down with the care of the world it cannot receive the holy Word of God. (1:164)

We do not advance because we do not know our capacity, we do not have sufficient patience in the work we begin, and we wish to possess spiritual excellences without working for them. (1:195)

Poemen said, "Satan has three kinds of power which precede all sin. The first is error, the second is laxity, and the third is lust. When error has come it produces neglect, and from neglect springs lust, and by lust humanity fell. If we watch against error, neglect will not come; if we are not negligent, lust will not appear; and if we do not engage in lust, we will, through the help of Christ, never fall." (1:247–248)

Because I set the judgement of God before my eyes I cannot be negligent, for I keep in mind the realization that my sins are many. (1:252)

One of the old men came to another old man who was his companion, and as they were talking one of them said, "I have died to the world." His companion said, "Have no confidence in yourself that this is so until you go forth from the world, for although you say, 'I have died,' Satan is not dead." (1:259)

Poemen said, "Teach your heart to practice what your tongue teaches." (1:297)

Poemen said, "We need nothing except a watchful and strenuous heart." (1:306)

Let no one do anything whatsoever without first of all trying his heart to see that what he is about to do will be done for God's sake. (1:339)

How can you teach another what you do not observe yourself? (1:352)

From the greatest to the least of the things I do, I carefully consider the fruit it will produce, in thoughts, words, or deeds. (1:358)

Through holding small wickednesses in contempt we fall into great ones. (1:360)

For one to commit sin is not so destructive as for one to cut off hope from his soul. The one who repents in a fitting manner and according to what is right blots out his offences, but the one who cuts off hope from his soul perishes because he will not offer it the medicine of repentance. (1:360)

Poemen said, "Think lightly of no one; think no evil in your heart; condemn no one and curse no one. Then God will give you rest, and your habitation shall be without trouble." (1:366)

Poemen said, "The chief of all wickednesses is the wandering of the thoughts." (1:370)

Sisoes advised, "With every trial that comes upon you, say, 'It has come because of my sins'; but if something good happens to you, say, 'This has come by the providence of God.'" (1:382)

Palladius said, "The blessed Anthony never deemed it right to do something that was convenient for himself to the same extent as something profitable for his neighbor." (1:404)

Mother Sarah said, "It is a good thing to give alms, even if you do so for the approval of others, because from this you will eventually come to do it for God's sake." (1:428)

It is right for one to take up the burden for those who are near him, whatever it may be, and, so to speak, to put one's own soul in the place of the neighbor's, and to become, if possible, a double person. One must suffer, weep, and mourn with him, and finally view the matter as if one had himself put on the actual body of his neighbour, and as if one had acquired his countenance and soul, and one must suffer for him as one would for oneself. (1:434)

Defeat comes to you if, when you are reviled and treated with contempt by someone, you do not show him evenness of heart, even before he repents and asks you to forgive him. (1:437)

A certain brother came to Abba Macarius the Egyptian, and said to him, "Father, speak to me a word whereby I may live." Abba Macarius said to him, "Go to the cemetery and revile the dead"; and he went and reviled them, and stoned them with stones, and he came and informed the old man that he had done so. And the old man asked him, "What did they say to you?" and the brother said, "Nothing." Again the old man said unto him, "Go tomorrow and praise them, and call them apostles, saints, and righteous." He did so, and he came to the old man and said, "I have praised them." And the old man said unto him, "And what did they say to you?" and he said, "Nothing." And the old man said to him, "You see how you have praised them, and they said nothing to you, and that, although you reviled them, they made no response. Let it be so with yourself. If you wish to live, become dead, so that you care neither for the reviling of others nor for their praise, for the dead care for nothing; in this way you will be able to live." (1:446)

John said, "We relinquish a light burden when we condemn ourselves, but we take upon ourselves a heavy burden when we attempt to justify ourselves." (1:460)

A brother asked an old man, "What should I do? The love of praise is killing me." The old man said, "You do well, for behold, you made the heavens and the earth." Then the brother was sorry because of what the old man had said unto him, and he expressed contrition and said, "Father, forgive me, but I have done nothing of the kind"; the old man said to him, "If He who did make them came into this world in humility, why do you who are mud boast yourself?" (1:467)

Theodore said, "There is no spiritual excellence greater than that of one who does not despise his neighbor." (1:486)

An elderly monk said, "I would rather have defeat with humility than conquest with boasting." (1:514)

When the thought of pride arises within you, and you become arrogant, examine your conscience and see if you have kept all the commandments, and if you love your enemies, and if you love the approval of your enemy, and if you are grieved when he is afflicted, and if you consider yourself an unprofitable servant, and a sinner greater than anyone else. . . . Then you will not be proud: as you know, proud thoughts abrogate all the virtues and make them unprofitable. (1:515)

Poemen said, "As the sword-bearer stands before the king, always ready to smite, so the soul needs to be prepared to resist the demon of fornication." (1:565)

An old monk was asked by one who toiled, "Is the repentance of sinners accepted by God?" And after he had taught him with many words, the old monk said to him, "Tell me, O my beloved one: if your cloak were torn in rags, would you throw it away?" And he said, "No, I would sew up the tears, and then I could use it again." And the old monk said to him, "If you would show pity on your garment which has no feeling, shall not God show pity on what He has fashioned, on what is His work?" (1:599)

Abba Ammon of Ritheaon asked Abba Poemen about the impure thoughts which are produced in a man, and about lust; and Abba Poemen said to him, "It belongs to Satan to sow them, but it is our affair not to welcome them." (1:603)

Poemen said, "I prefer one who has sinned, done wickedly, and repented, to one who has not sinned and has not manifested repentance; for the former possesses a humble mind, but the latter esteems himself in his thoughts a righteous man." (1:609)

Poemen taught, "Water is by nature soft, and stone is hard. Nevertheless if you suspend a vessel full of water above a stone, and pour water out upon it drop by drop, the water will wear away the stone. In the same way the Word of God is soft, and our heart is hard, but if it hears continually the Word of God, the heart will be opened, and will turn to the fear of God." (1:628)

Macarius said, "Truly, virginity by itself is nothing, nor is marriage; life as a monk is nothing, nor is life in the world. God seeks one's desire, and gives the Spirit unto everyone." (2:4)

We abstain from certain things not because the things themselves are bad, but because the passions are mighty, and when they have become strong they kill us. (2:6)

One of the Fathers asked Abba Nastir, the friend of the blessed Anthony, saying, "What is the best work for me to do?"... And he answered, "Whatsoever work your soul wishes to do, provided that it be of God, do that, and keep your heart from evil things." (2:21)

Gregory taught, "God demands three things from the one who has been baptized: true faith from the soul, truth from the tongue, and chastity from the body." (2:29)

Anthony said, "A person's life or death comes from his neighbor; if we benefit our brother we benefit ourselves, and if we offend him we sin against God." (2:33)

The brothers asked an old monk, "How is it that God promises in the Scriptures good things to the soul, but that the soul does not desire them, but turns aside to impurity?" And he answered, "It is my opinion that it is because it has not yet tasted the good things which are above, and therefore the good things which are here are dear to it." (2:46)

If when you are sitting down, or standing up, or when you are doing anything else, you set God before your eyes continually, no act of the enemy can terrify you; if this thought abides with you, the power of God will abide with you also. (2:84)

The person who has his death continually before his eyes will overcome littleness of soul. (2:85)

Poemen taught, "Keep aloof from everyone who is contentious in speech." (2:89)

A brother asked a certain old monk, "How can one tell if the fear of God dwells in the soul?" The old monk answered, "If one possesses humility, and practices abstinence, and judges no one, the fear of God dwells in that soul." (2:111)

The perfection of all spiritual excellences is for one not to judge one's neighbor.... If we allow ourselves to view our own sins closely, we shall not see those of our neighbor. (2:126)

Jacob said, "As a lamp illumines a dark chamber, so the fear of God—if it abides in one's heart—illumines him, and teaches him all the excellences of the commandments of God." (2:146)

Elijah asked, "What is sin able to do where repentance is found? And what will love profit where there is pride?" (2:164)

Do nothing without prayer, and afterwards you will never be sorry. (2:192)

Put no confidence in your own righteousness, and do not regret or reflect on something which is past, and be persistent in restraining your tongue and your belly. (2:197)

Arsenius said, "If we seek God He will be revealed to us, and if we lay hold on Him, He will remain with us." (2:203)

Poemen taught, "It is impossible for one who believes rightly, and who works in the fear of God, to fall into the impurity of the passions, and into the error of demons." (2:205)

John Kolob said, "I see evil thoughts coming against me, and because I cannot stand against them I flee and take refuge in God by prayer, and I am delivered from the enemies, and I live forever." (2:211)

Strife delivers one over to anger, and anger delivers one over to blindness of the mind, and blindness of the mind makes one do everything which is bad. (2:214)

Muthues taught, "Satan does not know by means of what passion the soul may be conquered, so he sows, not knowing whether he will reap; but with the thoughts of fornication, and of calumny, and of all the passions towards which he sees the soul incline, he fights against the soul and fetters it." (2:248)

A brother said to Abba Poemen, "If I stumble and commit a few minor sins, my mind afflicts me, and blames me, and makes accusations against me, saying, 'Why did you fall?'" The old man said to him, "Every time one falls into any shortcoming or folly, if one says, 'I have sinned,' God will immediately receive him." (2:252)

Poemen said, "Unless Moses had been gathering together sheep into the fold he would never have seen Him that was in the bush." (2:255)

Poemen taught, "Everything which is immoderate is from the demons." (2:289)

God demands nothing from Christians except that they shall hearken unto the divine Scriptures, and shall carry into effect the things which are said in them, and shall be obedient unto their governors and the orthodox Fathers. (2:290)

Theodore taught, "There is no spiritual excellence so sublime as that which consists in not despising someone else and treating him with contempt." (2:294)

An old monk was asked, "How can the soul acquire humility?" And he answered, "By examining and enquiring into its own wickednesses only." (2:295)

Agathon taught, "Do the demons make war upon you? But they do not make war against us so fiercely as we ourselves do with our own wishes, though they do make war against us in proportion as our wishes do. Our desires become demons, and they force us to fulfil them." (2:308)

Guard yourself against the thoughts which praise you, and which hold your neighbor in contempt. (2:347)

Judas, who wrought mighty deeds with the apostles, in one night lost all his labor, and fell from heaven to Sheol. Therefore let not him who conducts himself uprightly boast. (2:348)

A brother asked an old monk, "What shall I do? For there is no feeling in my soul, and I have no fear of God." The old monk said to him, "Seek out a person who fears God, and then cling closely to him, and from him you will learn to fear God." (2:361)

A brother asked an old monk, "What shall I do about those things I love, but which are not beneficial to me?" The old monk answered, "Do not approach them, do not touch them, and they will of their own accord become alien to you." (2:367)

Copres taught, "Whosoever loves to gratify his own will more than to gratify the will of God has no fear of God." (2:371)

Amonis taught, "Bear with everyone in such a way that God may also bear with you." (2:373)

True obedience is like a chaste woman who is betrothed, and who is not drawn aside after strange voices. The ear which turns away, ever so little, from the truth, is like an adulterous woman who turns away from her husband, and the mind which is led by every teaching of error is like a harlot, who obeys everyone who calls her. Let us then rebuke the wandering mind which is corrupted by strange voices, and which loves the voice of its seducer instead of that of the true Bridegroom. (2:380)

If you have prayed for your companion, you have also prayed for yourself; but if you have prayed only for yourself, you have impoverished your prayer. (2:381)

Poemen said, "One is constrained to humility and to the fear of God at all times, even as he is constrained to draw the breath which goes forth from his mouth." (2:399)

If you desire to learn to know your neighbor, praise him more than you rebuke him. (2:400)

Anthony declared, "I do not fear God; on the contrary, I love him." (2:403)

Abba Isaac said, "I was on one occasion sitting with Abba Poemen, and I saw that he was in a state of great stupefaction, and because I possessed some influence over him, I asked him, 'Father, where is your mind?' And after I had pressed him greatly, he answered, 'My mind was in the place of the crucifixion, where the holy woman Mary, the God-bearer, was standing and weeping by the Cross of our Redeemer, and I was wishing that I might at all times feel like that.'" (2:408)

For your sake Christ was born, and the Son of God came that He might make you live; He became a babe, He became a child, and He became a man, being at the same time God in His nature, and the Son of God. (2:426)

He was beaten for your sake, He was crucified for your sake, and He died for your sake, yet for His sake you will not even bear disgrace! He rose as God, and He ascended as God. He wrought all things for us, fittingly and in order, that He might redeem us. Let us, then, be watchful, and zealous, and constant in prayer; let us do all things which are pleasing to Him, and which gratify those who love Him, so that we may be redeemed and live. (2:431)

Take care each day to stand before God without sin, and draw near to Him with tears as the sinful woman did; and pray to the Lord God as if He were standing before you, for He is near and looks at you carefully. (2:450)

Love does not know how to keep a storehouse full of possessions. (2:467)

Anthony advised, "When we rise up in the morning each day let us think that we shall not abide until the evening, and when we come to lie down also let us think that we shall not abide until the morning; for we do not know the days of our life, but they are known to God. If we do this each day we shall not sin, and we shall do nothing wicked before God, and we shall not lust eagerly for anything belonging to this world, and we shall not be angry with anyone, but in everything we shall be regarding our souls, even as those who await death." (2:471)

Theona said, "Because we put ourselves out of the sight of God, we are led captive by the passions of the body." (2:498)

It is impossible that one who is of God should not love, and it is impossible for one who does not love to work aright, and it is impossible to believe that the one who teaches but does not work is a true believer. (2:546)

How can one overcome lust? By spiritual remembrance. If the desire for the delights which are to come does not obliterate that for the things that are here, one cannot conquer lust. (2:554)

The impurity of the world is a dark covering over the face of the soul, one that keeps the soul from discerning spiritual wisdom. (2:558)

[Regarding the Eucharist:] The body of our Lord is given to us for our happiness, and His blood is the drink of our redemption. (2:559)

Pure prayer is little in speech and great in deeds. (2:563)

We ought to pray to God for the return of those who are afar off, and friendliness towards those who wrong us, and love towards those who persecute us, and a sorrowful care for those who provoke us to wrath; if one does these things, truly there is repentance in one's mind. (2:568)

The one in whose dwelling the kingdom of God and its righteousness are found lacks nothing, even when one does not ask. (2:568)

Unless the world dies in one's heart, humility cannot dwell in it, and unless the body be deprived of its lusts, the soul cannot be cleansed from evil thoughts. (2:570)

We need to make the sign of the cross for the protection of our life. (2:575)

Whenever an evil thought comes against the soul, we must flee immediately from doing what it suggests and take refuge in supplication to God. That will dissolve the thoughts, just as wax is dissolved before fire, for our God is a consuming fire. (2:580)

When a thought has come against the soul, and the soul has, with great difficulty, been able to drive it out, another thought gets ready to come. In this way the soul is occupied the whole day long in a war against the thoughts, and it is unable to occupy itself with the sight of God, and to enjoy it continually. (2:582)

If one prays continually, that will bring correction to the mind immediately. (2:593)

Be an enemy to all folly and sin. (2:600)

Dejection drives away the fear of God, and captivity to sin drives away the virtues from the soul. (2:600)

The fear of God drives away all evil things, but dejection drives away the fear of God. (2:601)

Evagrius Ponticus taught, "After the vanquishing of all the other passions, there still remain two which will wage war against the perfect person until death—namely, vainglory and pride." (2:603)

Nastir said, "All rules of conduct are not alike. Abraham was a lover of strangers, David was a humble man, Elijah loved silence, and God accepted the work of all of them. Whatever work is acceptable to God, if your soul desires it, do it, and God will be with you." (2:605)

Paphnutius and James the Lame taught, "Every lapse which takes place through the tongue, or through lust, or through an action, or through the whole body, is in proportion to the measure of one's pride." (2:614)

It is right for those who have arrived at a correct conduct of the mind, and who think continually about God, and who pray to Him without wandering, when they are exhausted by this severe labor, to bring down their minds from time to time and to relieve it by means of thought concerning some profitable subject which is less exalted than thinking about God. (2:615)

Diocles said, "When the soul meditates with understanding upon some profitable subject, or upon some profitable action, its mind is with God." (2:615)

Without the power of the Spirit which our Lord gave us in baptism for the fulfilling of His commandments, which is confirmed in us each day by partaking of His body and blood, we cannot be purified from the passions, and we cannot vanquish demons, and we cannot perform the works of spiritual excellence. (2:617)

The demons fear and tremble, not only because of the crucifixion of Christ, but even at the sign of the cross, wherever it is made. (2:627)

The Fathers gave the admonition, "Whenever a demon appears in any form whatsoever, make the sign of the cross, and pray." . . . Since our Redeemer was crucified for us, and since he exposed to disgrace the rulers and dominions (which are evil demons), and put them to shame openly by his Person, even as it is written, from that time onwards, whenever they have made themselves visible to the adorers of Christ in various ways to do them harm, as soon as one made mention of the name of Christ, and signed himself with the sign of the cross, the demons fled straightway, and they have disappeared. And this happens not only in the case of holy and perfect people, but also in respect of ordinary people who possess shortcomings. (2:628)

God dwells in the saints through the constant remembrance with which they remember Him, as they marvel at Him and His works. (2:634)

The brothers asked, "What should be the beginning of the fight against sin?" The old monk answered, "In all the contests against sin and its lusts the labor of fasting is the first thing to undertake, and it is so especially in the case of the one who fights against the sin which is within him." (2:640)

Whoever loves the occupation of fasting all the days of his life is a friend of chastity. . . . Fasting is the strengthener of all spiritual excellences. . . . Fasting is the abode of all spiritual excellences, and the one who holds it in contempt disturbs them all. . . . For who should treat with contempt or hold lightly the armor which has been forged by God? If He who laid down the law fasted, who is there among those who would keep the law that has no need to fast? (2:640)

As merchants cannot save up riches without labor and trouble, so the righteous person cannot expect the crown and the reward without anguish and labor for the sake of righteousness. (2:640)

Evagrius Ponticus taught, "Against the monks who lead a life of silent contemplation the demons wage war in person, but against those who lead a life of spiritual excellence within a church, the demons only stir up and incite the lazy." (2:667)

The brothers asked, "Is everyone who is destitute of works also destitute of love?" The old monk answered, "It is impossible for one who is in God not to love, and it is impossible that one who loves should not work." (2:678)

The brothers asked, "How can we vanquish lust?" The old monk said, "By remembering the good things of the Spirit; for, if the desire for the good things which are to come does not abrogate the lust for the delights of this world, one cannot overcome it at all." (2:686)

The one who loves money has a doubt in his mind concerning God, and he prepares the means of life before God gives them to him; and, although in his words he rejoices in the promises, he makes them a lie by his deeds. (2:691)

The world troubles you because the cares of it are in your mind, and love for it is in your body, and its delights are in your heart. (2:694)

The brothers asked, "What is pure prayer?" The old monk answered, "That which is of few words and is abundant in deeds." (2:695)

The brothers asked, "How ought we to pray before God?" The old man answered, "For the repentance of sinners, and the finding of the lost, and the drawing near of those who are afar off, and friendliness towards those who do us harm, and love towards those who persecute us, and sorrowful care for those who provoke God to wrath." (2:700)

The Sayings of the Fathers (a second collection)[9]

[Abba Hyperichius said,] "The monk that cannot master his tongue in time of anger will not be master of the passions of his body at some other time." (4:49)

Once a brother [i.e., monk] in Scete was found guilty, and the older brethren [i.e., monks] came in assembly and sent to the abbot Moses, asking him to come: but he would not. Then the priest sent to him, saying, "Come: for the assembly of brethren awaits you." And he rose up and came. But taking with him a very old basket, he filled it with sand and carried it behind him. And they went out to meet him, asking, "Father, what is this?" And the old man said to them, "My sins are running behind me and I do not see them, and I am come today to judge the sins of another man." And they heard him, and said naught to the brother, but forgave him. (9:4)

---

9 Excerpts taken from Waddell, *The Desert Fathers,* pp. 62–129.

A brother asked the abbot Pastor, saying, "If I should see my brother's fault, is it good to hide it?" The old man said to him, "In what hour we do cover up our brother's sins, God shall cover ours: and in what hour we betray our brother's shames, in like manner God shall betray our own." (9:6)

[Abba Agatho said,] "If an angry man were to raise the dead, because of his anger he would not please God." (10:13)

The brethren asked the abbot Agatho, saying, "Father, which virtue in this [monastic] way of life is most laborious?" And he said to them, "Forgive me, but to my mind there is no labor so great as praying to God: for when a man wishes to pray to his God, the hostile demons make haste to interrupt his prayer, knowing that their sole hindrance is in this, a prayer poured out to God. With any other labor that a man undertakes in the life of religion, however instant and close he keeps to it, he has some rest: but prayer has the travail of a mighty conflict to one's last breath." (12:2)

They [some monks] asked the abbot Macarius, saying, "How ought we to pray?" and the old man said, "There is no need of speaking much in prayer, but often stretch out your hands and say, 'Lord, as You will and as You know, have mercy upon me.' But if there is war in your soul, add, 'Help me.' And because He knows what we need, He shows us His mercy." (12:10)

[Abba Mathois said,] "The nearer a man approaches to God, the greater sinner he sees himself to be. For the prophet Isaiah saw God, and he said that he was unclean and undone [Is 6:5]." (15:28)

He [Abba Anthony] said, that with our neighbor there is life and death: for if we do good to our brother, we shall do good to God: but if we scandalize our brother, we sin against Christ. (17:2)

A brother asked a certain old man, saying, "There be two brothers, and one of them is quiet in his cell, and prolongs his fast for six days, and lays much travail upon himself: but the other tends the sick. Whose work is the more acceptable to God?" And the old man answered, "If that brother who carries his fast for six days were to hang himself up by the nostrils, he could not equal the other, who does service to the sick." (17:18)

The Sayings of the Fathers (a third collection)[10]

"What is it to hate evil?" And the old man said, "He hates evil, who hates his own sins, and who blesses and loves every one of his brethren." (3:132)

The abbot Isaac once came into the monastery and saw there a careless monk and in anger commanded that he be expelled from the monastery. And when he had gone out and was nearing his own house, there came God's angel and stood before the door of his cell, saying, "I shall not suffer you to enter." Then he asked that he might be shown his fault. And the angel made answer and said, "God sent me, saying, 'Go, and say to Isaac, Where do you command Us to send this brother who has sinned?'" Then did he straightway repent, saying, "Lord, I have sinned, have mercy upon me." And the angel said, "Arise, the Lord will have mercy. But do not the like again, to condemn any, before God has judged him." (3:137)

It chanced that a certain brother in a monastery fell into disgrace; and whilst the others were upbraiding him, he made his way to the abbot Anthony. And the brethren followed him, wishful to bring him back, and began to cover him with reproaches, he meantime denying that he had committed that fault. Now the abbot Paphnutius was there, whose surname was Cephalus, and he told the brethren in assembly a parable that they had never heard. "I saw," said he, "on the bank of the river a man sunk to his knees in the mud; and some came up with outstretched hands to pull him out, and sank him up to the neck." Then said the blessed Anthony of the blessed Paphnutius, "Behold a man who truly can heal the soul." And the brethren, cut to the heart by his discourse, did penance and restored to the community the brother who had gone from it. (3:138)

[An old monk said,] "That which is done for God's sake is manifestly a work of God: and that which was ordained for pride's sake is manifestly the authority of men. Whatsoever things are from God, have their spring in humbleness: but such things as spring from authority and anger and strife, these are of the Enemy." (3:142)

---

10 Excerpted from Waddell, *The Desert Fathers*, pp. 131–146.

The Sayings of the Fathers (a fourth collection)[11]

The blessed Anthony was wont to say, "The Fathers of old went out into the desert, and when they themselves were made whole, they became physicians, and returning again they made others whole: but if it should come to pass that any of us go into the desert, we offer a cure to men before we be cured ourselves: and our infirmity returns upon us and our last sins are worse than our first: for which cause it is commanded to us, 'Physician, look first to yourself.'" (7:35)

A certain brother asked Abba Pimenion, "What is faith?" And the old man said, "To live ever in loving-kindness and humility, and to do good to one's neighbor." (7:17)

[Abba Poemen said,] "With the imagination of lust and the disparaging of your neighbor, with these two speak not in your heart, nor consent to any of their befouling in your soul. For if you have suffered your heart to dwell on these, you shall soon feel their poisoning: it is the stirring of perdition: but by prayer and good actions bring the malignant spirit to naught, and do you fight them off more hardily, and you shall have quiet." (7:3)

A brother asked an old man saying, "What shall I do, Father, against thoughts of passion?" He answered, "Pray to the Lord that the eyes of your soul may behold the help that is from God, that does go round about a man and keep him safe." (7:4)

An old man said, "There is no stronger virtue than to scorn no man." (7:91)

An old man said, "The man that has every hour death before his eyes, will conquer meanness of soul." (7:94)

---

11 Excerpted from Waddell, *The Desert Fathers*, pp. 149–155.

~ Pseudo-Macarius

For many centuries, *The Fifty Spiritual Homilies* and *The Great Letter* were thought to be from the Desert Father Macarius of Egypt (c. 300–c. 390). However, scholarly examination has shown that the background presupposed and the approach to godliness espoused were both Syrian, rather than Egyptian; thus, these works could not have been from that Desert Father. While the works stem from the late fourth century, it is not known who the author was. Since the works circulated so long under Macarius's name, and there is nothing approaching a scholarly consensus as to who their author may have been, the pseudonymous designation has been retained.

The works of Pseudo-Macarius reflect the wisdom of a seasoned Desert Father. In these works, he addresses other monks—and, with them, other conscientious Christians—on how to live before God. The spirituality espoused is ascetic, but its orientation reflects the rich piety of Syriac Christianity. Since only a few works of that remarkable tradition have been published in English, the works of Pseudo-Macarius are especially valuable for their witness to a vibrant stream of Christian lifestyle and thought.

The Fifty Spiritual Homilies[1]

Adam violated the command of God and obeyed the deceitful serpent. He sold himself to the devil and that evil one put on Adam's soul as his

---

1 Excerpted from George A. Maloney, trans., *Pseudo-Macarius: The Fifty Spiritual Homilies and the Great Letter* (Mahwah, NJ: Paulist Press, 1992), pp. 37–246.

garment—that most beautiful creature that God had fashioned according to His own image. (1:7)

The soul is united in will with whatever it is joined and bound to as its master. Either it has, therefore, the light of God in it and lives in that light with all of its powers, abounding with a restful light, or it is permeated by the darkness of sin, becoming a sharer in condemnation. (1:8)

Satan clothed the soul and all its substance with sin. That evil prince corrupted it completely, not sparing any of its members from slavery—not its thoughts, neither the mind nor the body—but he clothed it with the purple of darkness. . . . And so the entire body fell a victim to passion and corruption. (2:1)

And just as in that other state of error the old man put on the whole, complete man and wears the garment of the kingdom of darkness, the cloak of blasphemy, unbelief, audacity, vainglory, pride, avarice, concupiscence, and all the other similar adornments of the kingdom of darkness, ragged, impure, and contaminated—so on the contrary, all who have put off the old and earthly man and from whom Jesus has removed the clothing of the kingdom of darkness have put on the new and heavenly man, Jesus Christ, so that once again the eyes are joined to new eyes, ears to ears, head to head, to be completely pure and bearing the heavenly image. (2:4)

And the Lord has clothed them with the garments of the Kingdom of unspeakable light, the garment of faith, hope, love, joy, peace, goodness, human warmth, and all the other divine and living garments of light, life, and ineffable tranquillity. The result is that, as God is love and joy and peace and kindness and goodness, these the new man may become by grace. (2:5)

To uproot sin and the evil that is so imbedded in our sinning can be done only by divine power, for it is impossible and outside human competence to uproot sin. To struggle, yes, to continue to fight, to inflict blows, and to receive setbacks is in your power. To uproot, however, belongs to God alone. If you could have done it on your own, what would have been the need for the coming of the Lord? (3:4)

If the soul perseveres without letting down its guard in any area, it begins to emerge victorious as it sees through the deceits, and so it wins the crown of victory over sin. (3:5)

Those who strive to live the Christian life with great zeal must above all else develop with greatest care their soul's faculty of understanding and discerning so that, having acquired an exact discernment between good and evil, always distinguishing those things with which nature has been unnaturally tainted, we may conduct ourselves properly and without offense. (4:1)

God indeed gives help to one who turns away from sordid pleasures and from his former habits, who centers with might and main all his thoughts always on the Lord, and who denies himself and ardently seeks only the Lord. (4:5)

We have received into ourselves something foreign to our nature—namely, the corruption of our passions through the disobedience of the first man—which has strongly taken over in us, as though it were a certain part of our nature by custom and long habit. This must be expelled again by what is also foreign to our nature, namely, the heavenly gift of the Spirit, and so the original purity must be restored. (4:8)

Even though we, in our supreme ignorance, childishness, and tendency toward evil, turn away from true life and place many impediments along our path because we really do not like to repent, nevertheless the Lord has great mercy on us. He patiently waits for us until we will be converted and return to Him and be enlightened in our inner selves so that our faces may not be ashamed in the day of judgment.

    If that seems difficult and troublesome to us because practicing virtue is hard, but, more so, because of the insidious suggesting of the adversary, still God is very full of compassion, long-suffering, and patient as He waits for our conversion, and when we do sin He is ready to lift us up, for He desires our repentance. And when we fall, He is not ashamed to take us back, as the prophet said, "Will they fall and not rise? Will one turn away and not return?" [Jer 8:4]. We only need to have a sincere heart and live in vigilance and be converted immediately after seeking His help, and He Himself is most ready to save us. For He looks for our ardent will, as best we can, to turn toward Him. When we show good faith and promptness glowing from our desiring, then He works in us a true conversion.

    Let us then, O beloved, as children of God, be diligent and prompt to follow Him. (4:16–17)

Look at all the loving dispositions of God manifested in the times of the fathers and the prophets! What promises! And what exhortations! What great mercy of the Lord has been shown us from the very beginning! Finally, in His own coming on this earth He has shown us an ineffable kindness though His crucifixion in order to convert us and bring us into life. And yet we are not willing to give up our love for the world nor our evil tendencies and habits. In this way we show that we are persons of little or absolutely no good faith. And in spite of all this, He still shows Himself kind to us. He protects and cherishes us invisibly, not turning us over, as our sin deserves, to the deceits of evil and the world. In His great compassion and long-suffering, He watches from above, waiting for the time we shall return to Him. (4:18)

But if we abuse His long-suffering and kindness and forbearance and we add still more sins, and by our carelessness and contempt we store up for ourselves still more serious judgments, that saying will be fulfilled: "But in accordance with your hardness and your impenitent heart you are treasuring up for yourself wrath in the day of wrath and revelation of the righteous judgment of God" [Rom 2:5]. (4:19)

If anyone, receiving such immense goodness and gentleness of God shown him, would not accept the remission of his every offense, hidden or manifest, while God regards him without a word as He holds out to him repentance, such a person, I say, would be abusing God's kindness by remaining hardened in his sins. In fact, he would add sin to sin. (4:21)

Let us, therefore, strive to approach Him with a truly converted heart, not despairing that we will ever attain salvation, for such a thought itself is evil and depraved. The remembrance of our past sins can easily lead us to despair, to sloth, negligence, and resignation that we may not be converted to the Lord and ever attain salvation, even though the great goodness of the Lord covers the whole human race.

But if it truly seems difficult and impossible to us that we can ever be converted from such a great multitude of sins because we are caught in their grasp, a temptation . . . of evil and a sure obstacle to our salvation, let us recall and seriously consider how our Lord, while on this earth, restored sight to the blind, cured the paralytics, healed every sickness. He raised the dead, already decaying and disintegrating. He made the deaf to hear and drove out a legion of devils from one man and restored him to full mental health after such madness. How much more, therefore, will He not convert a soul that turns back to Him, seeking mercy from Him and needing His help? (4:24–25)

The world of Christians is of a special kind, their style of living, their thinking, their speech, and all their actions. That of the people of this world is completely different. (5:1)

As the wheat in the sieve is shaken by the sifter and is continually tossed up and down, so the prince of evil holds all people engrossed in earthly concerns. By these concerns he disturbs people, keeps them anxious and in a state of nervous action. The result is that they are disturbed by vain thoughts and base passions and are in bondage to earthly attachments to this world. (5:2)

The prince of this world keeps each soul that is not reborn of God tossed on the waves of various passions and lusts. (5:2)

For just as from one Adam humankind was multiplied over the earth, so one depravity of passion infiltrated the entire human race. (5:3)

Christians possess a glory and beauty and an indescribable heavenly richness that come to them with hard work and sweat, acquired in times of temptations and in many trials. All of this must be ascribed to divine grace. (5:4)

Just as God has made great, ineffable, and indescribable promises, so too they demand on our part great faith, hope, and effort and great struggles. (5:6)

Regardless of how anyone is bound, whether by a small or a great chain to the world, he is possessed by that attachment and is unable to extricate himself from it. (5:6)

The soul that truly tends toward the Lord completely forces itself to a total love of Him. It is held fast in a willed dedication, as far as is possible, to God alone. From Him it obtains the help of grace. (5:6)

Those who do not obey the commandments of the Lord and do not deny themselves, refusing to love God above all else, freely decide to be held by earthly bonds. (5:6)

Those are able to endure conflict to the end who have completely and with their whole heart loved God alone and who have freed themselves from all other loves for the world. However, few are found who enjoy such a love, turning away from all pleasures and desires of the world and who bravely endure the assaults and temptations of the evil one. (5:6)

Most want to possess the kingdom without labors and struggles and sweat, but this is impossible. (5:6)

When we read in Scripture how such and such a righteous person pleased God, how he was made a friend and companion of God and how all the fathers were considered friends and participators of God, we forget one thing—namely, the great afflictions they had to suffer, how much they had to endure on behalf of God, the great courage with which they struggled and fought battles! We congratulate them and we wish to enjoy rewards and honors equal to theirs. We desire ardently to receive their outstanding gifts, but we fail to notice their labors, struggles, afflictions, and crucifixions. We eagerly want honors and dignities such as they received from God, but we are not ready to accept their labors and struggles. (5:6)

One needs effort and patience, restraint and every kind of watchfulness, alacrity and perseverance in prayer to the Lord, so that one can rise above earthly desires and the snares and traps of sense pleasures, above the enticements of the world, and avoid the attacks of evil spirits. (5:6)

What the soul now stores up within will be revealed on the final day as its treasure. (5:7)

Christians live in another world, eat from another table, are clothed differently, prefer different enjoyment, different dialogue, and a different mentality. (5:11)

A person ought to labor to concentrate on his thoughts. He must cut away everything that leads to evil thoughts, urging himself toward God. He should not allow his thoughts to control his will, but he needs to collect them whenever they wander off in all directions, discerning natural thoughts from those that are evil. (6:3)

God...has permitted evil in order to develop humankind. (7:2)

Question: When sin is transformed into "an angel of light" [2 Cor 11:14] and seemingly appears as grace, in what way can one recognize the deceits of the devil? And how can one receive and discern the ways of grace?
 Answer: The signs accompanying grace are much joy, peace, love, and truth. Such truth impels one to seek truth. But the signs of sin are accompanied by turmoil, not joy and love toward God. Take the example of the plant endive. It looks like lettuce. But the latter is sweet, the former bitter. Also in the matter of grace, some things resemble truth, but they are different from the genuine substance of truth. (7:3)

There are times when grace burns more brightly, consoles and refurbishes more completely. (8:5)

But who has ever attained perfection and tasted and directly experienced that world? I have not yet seen any perfect Christian or one perfectly free. ... There may be some who, because of the immense grace and light that they receive, consider themselves perfect and free, but they are deceived because of lack of experience. (8:5)

One cannot possess his soul and the love of the heavenly Spirit unless he cuts himself off from all the things of this world and surrenders himself to seek the love of Christ. (9:10)

The mind that never ceases to be attentive to itself and to seek the Lord can possess its soul, which loses itself otherwise in the passions. (9:11)

Persons who love truth and God, who thoroughly wish to put on Christ with great hope and faith, do not need so much encouragement or correction from others. They never give up their longing for heaven and their love of the Lord, granted that from time to time they bear patiently a bit of diminishment in that love. (10:1)

The person...who truly loves God and Christ, even though he may perform a thousand good works, considers himself as having done nothing because of his insatiable longing for the Lord. . . . But daily he perseveres in prayer with a hungering and a thirst in faith and love. He has an insatiable desire for the mysteries of grace and for every virtue. (10:4)

Truly the soul is incapable by itself of studying its own thoughts and discerning them. (11:4)

He who fashioned the body and soul comes and undoes all the cunning of the wicked devil and all that he had wrought in the thoughts of humankind. He renews and forms a heavenly image and recreates the soul anew so that Adam again may be king over death and lord over all creatures. (11:6)

In the shadow of the Law Moses was called the savior of Israel, for he led the Israelites out of Egypt. So also now the true Redeemer, Christ, enters into the depths of the soul and leads it out of dark Egypt with its burdensome yoke and bitter slavery. (11:6)

But what is the meaning of that dead serpent that was fixed on top of the pole and healed those that had been bitten [Num 21:9]? The dead serpent conquered over the living serpents, as a type of the body of the Lord. The body which He took from Mary He raised up on the Cross. He hung it and fastened it to the tree. And so the dead body conquered and slew the serpent, living and creeping in the hearts of men. . . . Thus a dead body overcame the live serpent. (11:9)

The Lord comes to death and argues with death. He orders that death release, from hell and death, the souls and give them back to Him.
    Behold, death is shaken by these words and approaches his servants and gathers together into a group all his powers and princes of evil. And the prince of evil bears forth the signed documents of indentured slaves and declares, "Look, these people have obeyed my word! See how they have bowed down in adoration to us!" But God, who is a just judge, shows then His justice and says to him, "Adam obeyed you, and then through him you captured all human hearts. Humanity obeyed you. But My body, what is it doing here? It is sinless. That body of the first Adam was in bondage to you, and you legally held the writ of indenture. But all bear witness to Me that I have not sinned. I owe you nothing. And that I am the Son of God all universally bear witness. For from above out of the heavens there came

upon earth a voice bearing testimony: 'This is My beloved Son' [Matt 3:17]. John gives witness: 'Behold! The Lamb of God who takes away the sin of the world' [John 1:29]. And again Scripture says, '[He] committed no sin, nor was deceit found in His mouth' [1 Pet 2:22]. And again, 'The ruler of this world is coming, and he has nothing in Me' [John 14:30]. And, moreover, you yourself, Satan, witness to Me in saying, 'I know who You are—the Holy One of God' [Mark 1:24]. And again: 'What have we to do with You, Jesus, You Son of God? Have You come here to torment us before the time?' [Matt 8:29]. There are, therefore, three who bear witness to Me: He that sends down from the heavens a voice; and those who are on earth; and you yourself [Deut 19:15]. I, therefore, bought back the body that was sold to you by the first Adam. I tore up the contract that enslaved humanity to you. Indeed, I satisfied Adam's debts when I was crucified and I descended into hell. And I command you, O Hell, O Darkness, O Death, release the imprisoned souls of the children of Adam." And so, at last, the wicked powers, struck with fear, restore the imprisoned children of Adam. (11:9, 10)

Death has its grip on the children of Adam and their thoughts are imprisoned in darkness. And when you hear mention made of tombs, do not at once think only of visible ones. For your heart is a tomb and a sepulcher. When the prince of evil and his angels have built their nest there and have built roads and highways on which the powers of Satan walk about inside your mind and in your thoughts, then are you not really a hell and a sepulcher and a tomb dead to God? (11:11)

But the Lord descends into the souls of those who seek Him. He goes into the depths of the hellish heart and there He commands death: "Release those captive souls that seek after Me, those that you hold by force in bondage." He breaks through the heavy stones that cover the soul. He opens the tombs. He truly raises the dead person to life and leads that captive soul forth out of the dark prison. (11:11)

It sometimes happens that Satan carries on a dialogue within your heart, such as: "See what great evils you have committed; see how your soul is full of so many follies. See how you are weighed down by sins so that you can hardly expect to be saved." These things he does to lead you to despair, thinking that your repentance has not been acceptable. For since evil through transgression entered into the human heart, afterward evil argues day and night with the soul, as one person to another. Answer him in this way: "I have the Lord's testimonies in Scripture: 'I have no pleasure in the death of the wicked, but that the wicked turn from his way and live'" [Ezek 33:11].

The Lord descended so that He might save sinners, raise up the dead, bring new life to those wounded by death, and enlighten those who lay in darkness. The Lord truly came and called us to be God's adopted children, to enter into a holy city, ever at peace, to possess a life that will endure forever, to share an incorruptible glory. Let us singly strive to come to a good end after a good beginning. (11:15)

Grace works in individual Christians in diverse ways. (12: 4)

The more you wish by knowledge to search and penetrate God, the more deeply you descend away from Him and you comprehend nothing. (12:11)

God created all visible things and gave them to us for recreation and enjoyment. (13)

Evil is cut out little by little and diminished, not all at once. (15:7)

Purity of heart is, when you see the sinners and the weak, you have compassion and show mercy toward them. (15:8)

That is, indeed, the way of the Christian religion. Where the Holy Spirit is, there follows, as a shadow, persecution and struggle. . . . It was the same with the apostles. From that time when Jesus was crucified, the Spirit, the Paraclete, passed the cross down through the ages to the Christians. (15:12)

The enemy never stops waging war against humanity. Satan is without mercy and hates humans. For this reason he never is hesitant to war against everyone. But he does not attack all in the same ways. (15:18)

As water runs through a pipe, so sin runs through the heart and the thoughts. (15:21)

Christians look on this world with the eyes of children, despising its worldliness and seeing the presence of grace. They are strangers to this world. (15:26)

All of us look like Adam. (15:32)

The enjoyment of God is insatiable, and the more anyone tastes and eats, the more he hungers. (15:38)

As the body of the Lord was glorified when He climbed the mount and was transfigured into the divine glory and into infinite light [Matt 17:1-2], so also the bodies of the saints are glorified and shine like lightning. Just as the interior glory of Christ covered His body and shone completely, in the same way also in the saints the interior power of Christ in them in that day will be poured out exteriorly upon their bodies. For even now at this time they are in their minds participators of His substance and nature [2 Pet 1:4]. (15:38)

There are some who, even though they have begun to develop a taste for divine things, nevertheless are disturbed and hassled by the adversary, so that they are surprised (still lacking experience) that after God has so touched them, they should still harbor doubts about the mysteries of the Christian religion. Those who have grown old in them are not surprised at all. (16:3)

When ... one is deep and rich in grace, there still remains inside of him a remnant of evil. But he has close at hand One who can help him. (16:4)

God is without limits and is incomprehensible. (16:5)

Like a bee that secretly fashions its comb in the hive, so also grace secretly forms in hearts its own love. It changes to sweetness what is bitter, what is rough into what is smooth. (16:7)

A godly person regards himself as the greatest of all sinners. He carries this thought ever with him as a part of his very makeup. And the more he progresses in knowledge of God, the more simple and unlearned he considers himself. And the more he studies and learns, the less he feels he knows. (16:12)

The genuine struggle and battle of man, his testing and his good will toward God, then appear when grace is withheld, and he shows himself brave as he cries out to God. (16:13)

Everything that belongs to the Lord, no matter how much it is, He entrusts to you. He came to your aid in person to call you back to what once was yours. (16:13)

There are some people in whom grace is operative and working in peace. Within, however, evil is also present hiddenly, and the two ways of existing—namely, according to the principles of light and darkness—vie for dominance within the same heart. (17:4)

Simple-minded and foolish persons, when grace begins to some degree to work in them, believe that they are simply freed from sin. But those who have discretion and prudence would never dare to deny that, even when we are gifted by divine grace, we are still tested by wicked and obscene thoughts. (17:5)

No one in his sane mind should dare to say, "Because I am in grace, I am thoroughly freed of sin." (17:6)

Certain persons endowed with grace have only one concern, about their own affairs. Others seek also to help others. The latter are more outstanding than the former. (17:8)

Some in pursuing virtue seek glory and honors from others, saying that they are Christians and participate in the Holy Spirit. In contrast, others strive to hide themselves, even from encountering other human beings. These far excel the first. (17:8)

Those who speak about spiritual topics without tasting or experiencing are like one who, walking in the desert, has an overwhelming raging thirst, so to satisfy that thirst draws a picture of a fountain flowing with water, while all the while his lips and tongue burn for thirst. (17:12)

The Christian religion is a food and drink. The more one eats of it, the more strongly one's mind is enticed by its sweetness, so much so that one can never be restrained or satisfied, but insatiably asks for more and continually eats more. If one has a great thirst and is given a pleasing drink, then, and one begins to taste of it, the more one wants to have it, the more eagerly one drinks of it. So is the taste of the Spirit; it can hardly be stopped or satisfied. (17:13)

Where truth begins ever so gradually to show itself, there error attacks and seeks to conceal and cover over the truth. (17:13)

We must inquire how and by what means we can obtain purity of heart. There is no other way than through Him who was crucified for us. (17:15)

We must first beg of God with struggle in the heart through faith that He grant us to discover His riches, the true treasure of Christ in our hearts, in the power and energy of the Spirit. (18:6)

Those who have been deemed worthy to become children of God and to be reborn by the Holy Spirit from above, who have Christ within themselves, illuminating and bringing them rest, are guided in many and various ways by the Spirit. They are invisibly acted upon in the heart, in spiritual tranquillity, by grace. (18:7)

Grace affects us in various ways and leads the soul in so many different paths, refreshing it in accord with the will of God. Grace exercises the soul differently in order to restore it to the heavenly Father perfect and faultless and pure. (18:9)

The person who wishes to come to the Lord and to be deemed worthy of eternal life and to become the dwelling place of Christ and to be filled with the Holy Spirit so that he may be able to bring forth the fruits of the Spirit and perform the commandments of Christ purely and blamelessly ought to begin first by believing firmly in the Lord and giving himself completely to the words of His commands and renouncing the world in all things, so that his whole mind may not be taken up with anything ephemeral. And he ought to persevere constantly in prayer, always waiting in faith that expects His coming and His help, keeping the goal of his mind ever fixed upon this. Then he ought to push himself to every good work and to doing all the commandments of the Lord, because there is sin dwelling within him. (19:1)

He fills him with the Holy Spirit. And gradually without force or struggle he keeps all the Lord's commandments in truth—or, rather, the Lord keeps in him His very own commandments—and then that person brings forth purely the fruits of the Spirit. (19:2)

One coming to the Lord must at first force himself to do good and, even if he should not be so inclined in his heart, he must constantly await His mercy with unshaken faith and push himself to love, even if he does not have love. He ought to push himself to meekness, even if he has none, to mercy and to have a merciful heart. (19:3)

The Lord Himself does all these things in truth in him without labor and force, which before he could not perform, even by his own determination, because of sin that dwelled in him. And now all the practice of virtues comes to him as though the virtues were a part of his nature. The reason is really that the Lord comes and dwells in him and he is in the Lord. The Lord Himself operates in him to accomplish His own commandments, effortlessly now, filling him with the fruit of the Spirit. (19:6)

It is necessary that whoever wishes truly to please God and receive from Him the heavenly grace of the Spirit and to grow and be perfected in the Holy Spirit should force himself to observe the commandments of God and to make his heart submissive, even if he is unwilling. (19:7)

A proud mind is a great humiliation, while humility is a great uplifting of the mind and an honor and dignity. (19:8)

Christ . . . gives and adorns with glory in ineffable light. (20:2)

If anyone stands solely on his own righteousness and redemption, he labors in vain and to no purpose. For every imagination of one's own righteousness will appear on the last day as a filthy rag, as the Prophet Isaiah says, "All our righteousnesses are like filthy rags" [Is 64:6]. Let us, then, beg and implore God to clothe us with "the garments of salvation" [Is 61:10]—namely, our Lord Jesus Christ, the ineffable Light, which those who have borne it will never put off for all eternity. (20:3)

No self-justification had power to heal human beings until the Savior came, the true Physician, who cures without costs. He gave Himself as a ransom on behalf of the human race. He liberated them from slavery and led them out of darkness by shedding His light upon them. (20:6)

Just as that blind man, unless he had cried out, and that woman who had suffered from the issue of blood, unless she had approached the Lord, would not have received a cure, in the same way, unless a person comes to the Lord of his own movement and with firm desire and begs Him with fullness of faith, in no way can that person receive a cure. (20:8)

Everywhere in the visible as well as in the invisible there is opposition which has come down to us from the fall of the first man. (21:2)

No one can deliver himself by his own power from the opposition and error of temptations, interior passions, and the wiles of the evil one. (21:4)

We have not yet accepted the happiness in Christ's salvation. (25:4)

Consider your dignity and nobility, since not on behalf of angels but for you the Lord came to your protection in order to call you back when you were lost, when you were wounded, and He restored to you the first created condition of the pure Adam. (26:1)

By the power of the Spirit and spiritual regeneration, humans not only come to the measure of the first Adam, but they also reach a greater state than he possessed. (26:2)

This is the sign of Christianity: however much one may do, and however many righteous works one should perform, to feel that one has accomplished nothing. (26:11)

In many cases Satan, under the pretext of good thoughts, such as "In this way you can please God," suggests to a person and cunningly leads him astray to subtle and half truths. Such a person does not know how to detect that he is secretly being seduced, and so he "fall[s] into reproach and the snare of the devil" [1 Tim 3:7]. (26:12)

The coming of the Lord and His providence have had this purpose—to free those who were held captive by evil and bound and in submission to it and to make them conquerors over death and sin. (26:22)

All the righteous ones have pleased God on the narrow way full of afflictions by their persevering right to the end. (26:25)

It is not right that the Bridegroom came to suffer and to be crucified while the Bride, for whom the Bridegroom came, should live in luxury and worldly distraction. (27:2)

It is one thing to lecture with a certain intellectual knowledge and ideas, but another thing to do so in substance and reality—in full faith, in the inner person, and in the consciousness to have the treasure and the grace and the taste and the working of the Holy Spirit. (27:12)

The devil is very cunning and has many tricks and loopholes and all sorts of deceits. He captures the grazing lands of the soul and the thoughts and does not allow it to pray properly and to draw near to God. For human nature itself tends to form a fellowship with the demons and the evil spirits equally as well as with the angels and the Holy Spirit. (27:19)

This is the foundation of the road to God: in much patience, in hope, in humility, in poverty of spirit, in gentleness to travel along the road of life. By such means one can possess justification for oneself. We mean by justification the Lord Himself. These commandments, which so enjoin us, are like milestones and signposts along the royal highway that leads a journeyer to the heavenly city. (27:23)

God, being angry with the human soul because of violating His command, turned it over to its enemies, to the demons as well as to the passions. And so, when these had seduced it, they completely ruined it and there was no longer any feast or incense or offering sent up by it to God. (28:1)

Adam transgressed the commandment and fell from his former glory and became subject to the spirit of the world. The veil of darkness came upon his soul. And from his time until the last Adam (the Lord), humankind did not see the true heavenly Father and the good and kind mother, the grace of the Spirit, and the sweet and desired brother, the Lord, and the friends and relatives, the holy angels with whom he was rejoicing, dancing, and celebrating. (28:4)

Everyone should realize that there are eyes deeper within than these physical eyes and there is a hearing deeper within than this hearing. (28:5)

The wisdom of God, since it is infinite and incomprehensible, brings about in an incomprehensible and unsearchable way the dispensations of grace toward the human race in various ways. (29:1)

Each person will be responsible for the fruits of virtue in proportion to the benefits bestowed on him by God, whether natural or given by divine grace. Therefore, everyone is without excuse before God in the day of judgment. For each person will be required to correspond with his choice and will, according to what he knew, to produce the fruits of faith and love and every virtue in relationship to God, whether he heard or had never heard the word of God. (29:6)

Our Lord Jesus Christ was concerned with humanity's salvation. He exercised from the beginning every providential planning and diligence through the fathers, the patriarchs, through the Law and the Prophets. Finally He Himself came and suffered the ignominy of the Cross and endured death. (30:1)

The good portrait painter, Christ, for those who believe in Him and gaze continually toward Him, at once paints a heavenly man according to His own image. . . . It is necessary that we gaze on Him, believing and loving Him, casting aside all else and attending to Him so that He may paint His own heavenly image and send it into our souls. (30:4)

In that day when Adam fell, God came walking in the garden. He wept, so to speak, seeing Adam and He said, "After such good things, what evils you have chosen! After such glory, what shame you now bear! What darkness you are now! What ugly form you are! What corruption! From such light, what darkness has covered you!" When Adam fell and was dead in the eyes of God, the Creator wept over him. The angels, all the powers, the heavens, the earth and all creatures bewailed his death and Fall. For they saw him who had been given to them as their king now become a servant of an opposing and evil power. (30:7)

We are all his children of that dark race and we all inherit the same stench. Therefore, the passion that he suffered, all of us, who are of Adam's seed, suffer also. For such a suffering has hit us, as Isaiah says, "From the sole of the foot even to the head, there is no soundness in it, but wounds and bruises and putrefying sores" [Is 1:6]. Thus we were wounded with an incurable wound. Only the Lord could heal it. For this He came in His own person, because none of the ancients nor the law itself nor the prophets was able to heal it. He alone, when He came, healed that sore, the incurable sore of the soul. (30:8)

If we do not dissolve ourselves in sloth and turn over the pastures of our minds to the disorderly thoughts of evil, but if we force our mind to obey our will, compelling our thoughts toward the Lord, without doubt the Lord will come to us with His will and take us unto Himself in truth. . . . Therefore, strive to please the Lord, always waiting expectantly for Him from within, seeking Him in your thoughts and forcing and compelling your own will and deliberation to stretch out always toward Him. And see how He comes to you and makes His abode in you [John 14:23]. For as much as you concentrate your mind to seek Him, so much more He, by His own tender compassion and goodness, comes to you and gives you rest. (31:3)

As without the vine, the branch is dried up, so is he who desires justification without Christ. (31:4)

The soul is nourished where it feeds, either from this world or from the Spirit of God. (31:5)

When you are in prayer, be attentive to yourself, observing your thoughts and your activities, and where they come from—God or the adversary. (31:6)

As Christians walk in this creation, they discover newer, heavenly insights and glories and mysteries, receiving them from the things that hit their senses. (32:1)

But just as the shadow of the body is from the body itself, but is unable to perform any physical service, for a shadow cannot bind up wounds or give food or speak, and yet it has its existence from the body, and proceeding before it manifests the presence of the body, so also the ancient Law is a shadow of the New Covenant. The shadow manifests the truth in advance, but it does not possess the service of the Spirit. (32:4)

Just as neither the ages above nor the ages below can grasp the greatness of God and His incomprehensibility, so also neither the worlds above nor the worlds on earth can understand the humility of God and how He renders

Himself little to the humble and small. Just as His greatness is incomprehensible, so also is His littleness. (32:7)

For a certain hidden and subtle power of darkness is revealed that has been entrenched in the heart. And the Lord is near to your soul and body, seeing your battle. And He puts in you secret, heavenly thoughts and He begins to give you rest within. He allows you to be disciplined, and grace directs you in these very afflictions. (32:10)

The person who has his Lord abiding with him . . . is full of every beauty and uprightness. (33:3)

There is no other way to be saved except through the neighbor. (37:3)

The head of every good endeavor and the guiding force of right action is perseverance in prayer. (40:2)

If, therefore, the working of divine grace overshadows the soul according to the degree of each person's faith and he receives help from above, grace still overshadows him only in a certain degree. Let no one think that his whole soul has been enlightened. (41:2)

The one who is rich in the grace of God ought to be grounded in great humility and possess a contrite heart. And he ought to regard himself as poor and possessing nothing. What is his belongs to another. Another gave it to him and takes it away whenever he wishes. (41:3)

Those who journey cannot go through without temptations. (42:2)

For this reason He was called Christ in order that we also, being anointed with the same oil as He was anointed, may become Christs. (43:1)

Like thick smoke in a one-room house, so is sin with its filthy thoughts. (43:7)

And now on account of its Fall the mind is clothed with shame and the eyes of the heart are blinded so as not to see that glory which our father Adam beheld before his disobedience. (45:1)

There is no other family tie and helpfulness like that between the soul and God and between God and the soul. (45:4)

Anyone who obeys the Word of Truth must prove himself and examine himself or be examined and tested by spiritual persons as to how he has believed and dedicated himself to God, whether really and truly according to God's Word, or whether by his own idea of the justification and faith that he entertains within himself. (48:2)

There is nothing common to God's nature and that of the soul. But by means of His infinite and ineffable and incomprehensible love and compassion, it pleased Him to make His indwelling in this created thing. (49:4)

The Great Letter[2]

God calls to Christ all who willingly undergo the contest of accepting the cross. {p. 259}

We must fear lest we who have received gifts of the Spirit and rightly would begin acting virtuously were to use that as an occasion of growing in pride and vanity before we have reached the goal of the things we hoped for. {p. 259}

We must show ourselves to be humble and most diffident, since we are far away from attaining the promises and still a great way from the perfect love of Christ. {pp. 259–260}

The substance of faith is poverty of spirit and an infinite love toward God. {p. 260}

The upright and solicitous servant ought to submit himself to the judgment of the Lord and not set himself up before the Lord as judge and flatterer of his virtuous life. {p. 263}

If the love of God dwells within you, it is necessary that such love bring forth other fruit, such as fraternal love, meekness, sincerity, perseverance in prayer, and zeal and all virtues. But since the treasure is precious, so

---

2   Excerpts from Maloney, *Pseudo-Macarius*, pp. 253–271.

also great are the labors necessary to obtain it. {p. 264}

We must strengthen ourselves with thoughts of piety, lest the adversary find an entrance or a place for deceits. Much struggle is needed, therefore, and much inward and unseen travail, much scrutiny of our thoughts and training of our soul's enfeebled organs of perception, before we can discriminate between good and evil. {p. 264}

The devil strives by every means to drive the fear of the Lord out of our hearts. By means of earthly forms and seductions, he seeks to distract our love for God by turning away our soul from what is truly good toward what only appears to be good. {p. 265}

In prayer we should not be satisfied with merely standing or kneeling, seemingly to be agreeing with Scripture and well pleasing to God, while the mind wanders far from him. We must guard against every neglect of thoughts and unseemly attitude, and turn the whole soul with the body back to prayer. {p. 268}

Through their continued conversion and the gift of the Holy Spirit to maturity, by the grace that is given to them, Christians prefer above the glory, pleasures, and all that is delightful, the greater desire to be held in contempt for the sake of Christ, to bear all insults and ignominy through faith in God. {p. 270}

The grace of the Spirit permeates the entire soul and floods the dwelling place with joy and virtue. The Spirit makes sweet the sufferings of the Lord by extinguishing the feeling of present sorrow through the hope of future blessings. {p. 270}

Athanasius

Athanasius (296–372) played a leading role at the Council of Nicea. He was the great defender of the Christian faith against the heresy of Arius, which allowed the Son of God only a secondary divine status; in contrast, Athanasius affirmed without reservation the full deity of the Son of God. For his steadfastness in this, he was repeatedly banished from Alexandria by imperial order; however, he refused compromise and was restored after each exile. The phrase *Athanasius contra mundum* ("Athanasius against the world") was coined to describe his sturdy insistence on the deity of Christ in the face of all opposition. Athanasius was a remarkable theologian of penetrating insight and winsome expression.

The Life of Anthony[1]

None of us is judged for what he does not know, any more than one is counted blessed because he is learned and possesses knowledge. Rather, each of us faces judgment on these questions: whether we have kept the faith and sincerely observed the commandments. (§33)

Live as though dying daily. (§91)

---

1 Excerpts taken from Robert C. Gregg, trans., *Athanasius: The Life of Antony and the Letter to Marcellinus* (Mahwah, NJ: Paulist Press, 1980), pp. 29–99.

Letter to Marcellinus[2]

From the Psalms the one who wants to do so can learn the emotions and dispositions of the soul, finding in them also the therapy and correction suited for each emotion. (§13)

On Luke 10:22[3]

Humanity sinned and fell, and by its fall all things are in confusion: death prevailed from Adam to Moses, the earth was cursed, Hades was opened, Paradise was shut, heaven was offended, and humanity was corrupted. (§2)

"The Father loves the Son, and has given all things into His hand" [John 3:35]—so that, just as all things were made by Him [John 1:3], so in Him all things might be renewed. (§2)

By His suffering, He gave us rest; by His hungering, He nourished us; and by His descent into Hades, He brought us back from it. (§2)

Against the Nations[4]

Every manifestation of demons is driven away by this sign [the cross]. (1:5)

The soul is made not merely to move, but to move in the right direction. (4:5)

Speaking generally, all the nations that have given themselves over to idols have different opinions and religions; consistency is never found. This is not surprising, for since they have fallen away from contemplating the one God, they have descended to many differing objects; and since they have turned away from the Word of the Father, Christ the Savior of all, they inevitably end up with their understanding wandering in many directions. (23:4–5)

It is possible to attain to the knowledge of God from the things which are seen, since creation, as though in written characters, declares its Lord and

---

2 Excerpted from Gregg, *Athanasius*, pp. 101–129.
3 Excerpted from NPNF (2nd) 4:87–90.
4 Excerpted from NPNF (2nd) 4:4–30.

Creator in a loud voice by its order and harmony. (34:4)

God did not remain in His invisible nature ... and leave Himself utterly unknown to humankind. He structured creation so that, although He is invisible by nature, He may nonetheless be known by His works. (35:2)

Since everywhere one finds not disorder but order, proportion and not disproportion, arrangement rather than chaos—and all of that in an entirely harmonious order—we must infer and come to perceive the master who put together and coordinated everything, producing harmony in it all. Although He cannot be seen with the eyes, nevertheless from the order and harmony of all things it is possible to perceive their Ruler, Arranger, and King. (38:1)

The nature of created things, since it is brought into being out of nothing, is fleeting, weak, and mortal. (41:2)

On the Incarnation of the Word[5]

The renewal of creation has been the work of the very same Word that made it at the beginning. (1:4)

Out of nothing, and without its having any previous existence, God made the universe to exist through His Word. (3:1)

God showed special concern for humanity. Since it had a beginning, it would be unable to live forever, so He gave humanity a further gift: He did not merely create human beings as He did all the other creatures on earth, but He made them according to His own image ..., so that ... they might be able to live everlastingly. (3:3)

He brought them into His own garden and gave them a commandment, so that if they kept the grace and remained good, they might still keep the life in Paradise without sorrow or pain or care, and have the promise of incorruption in heaven. If, though, they transgressed and turned away and became evil, they would know that they were incurring that corruption in death which was theirs by nature. They would no longer live in Paradise,

---

5 Excerpted from NPNF (2nd) 4:36–67.

but would be cast out of it to die and would remain in death and corruption. (3:4)

It was our sin that was the cause of His descent; our transgression called forth the loving-kindness of the Logos, that He might come to us and manifest Himself as Lord among humankind. We then were the occasion for His incarnation; it was for our salvation that He so showed His love for humanity as to be born a man and to be revealed in a body. (4:3–4)

Humans are by nature mortal, since they are made out of what is not. (4:6)

Since they rejected things eternal and by the counsel of the devil turned to the things of corruption, humans became the cause of their own corruption in death. (5:1)

[At the sin of Adam and Eve,] death gained from that time onwards a legal hold over us. (6:2)

What was God in His goodness to do? Allow corruption to prevail against them and death to hold them fast? If so, what would be the profit of their having been made in the first place? For it would have been better for them not to have been made than, once made, to be left to neglect and ruin. . . . It was, then, out of the question to leave humankind to the current of corruption, because this would be unfitting, and unworthy of God's goodness. (6:7, 10)

Since He was the Word of the Father and exalted above all, He alone had the ability to recreate all things, and He alone was worthy to suffer for all and be ambassador for all with the Father. (7:5)

He took pity on our race and had mercy on our infirmity and condescended to our corruption. Unwilling to allow that death should have the final mastery, lest the creature perish and His Father's handiwork in humankind come to nothing, He took unto Himself a body like ours. (8:2)

Being Himself mighty, and the maker of everything, He prepares the body in the virgin as a temple for Himself. (8:3)

Thus taking from our bodies one of like nature, because all were under penalty of the corruption of death, He gave it over to death in the place of all, and offered it to the Father. He did this out of His loving-kindness, to the end that, firstly, all being held to have died in Him, the law involving the ruin of humankind might be undone (since its power was fully spent in the Lord's body and had no longer right to hold onto humanity, His peers); and that, secondly, whereas human beings had turned toward corruption, He might turn them again toward incorruption, and quicken them from death by the appropriation of His body and by the grace of the Resurrection. (8:4)

He takes to Himself a body capable of death, so that it, by partaking of the Word who is above all, might be worthy to die in the place of all, and might, because of the Word which had come to dwell in it, remain incorruptible, and that from then on corruption might be kept away from all by the grace of the Resurrection. By offering to death the body He had taken, an offering and sacrifice free from any stain, He put away death from all His peers by offering an equivalent. . . . He satisfied the debt by His death. (9:1–2)

Whereas the grace of the divine image was in itself sufficient to make known God the Word, and through Him the Father, still God, knowing human weakness, made provision for their carelessness; so that if they did not care to know God through themselves, they might be enabled to avoid ignorance of the maker through the works of Creation. (12:1)

The Word of God came in His own person, that, as He was the image of the Father, He might be able to create humankind afresh after the image. (13:7)

He was not, as might be imagined, circumscribed in the body, nor, while present in the body, was He absent elsewhere; nor, while He moved the body, was the universe left void of His working and providence; but—marvelous as it is to consider—Word as He was, so far from being contained by anything, He rather contained all things Himself. (17:1)

While known from the body by His works, He was nonetheless manifest from the working of the universe as well. (17:2)

When the virgin bore Him He did not endure any change, and by being in the body His glory was not dulled; on the contrary, He sanctified the body also. (17:5)

His trophy over death was the Cross. (19:3)

For the sun hid its face, and the earth quaked and the mountains were rent; all people were awed. Now these things showed that Christ on the Cross was God, while all creation was His slave, and was witnessing by its fear to its master's presence. (19:3)

Since it was necessary that the debt owed by all should be paid . . . , He offered up His sacrifice on behalf of all, yielding His temple [His body] to death in the place of all. (20:2)

By virtue of its union with the Word, Christ's humanity was no longer subject to corruption according to its own nature, but by reason of the Word that had come to dwell in it, it was placed beyond the reach of corruption. And so two marvels came to pass at once: the death of all was accomplished in the Lord's body, and death and corruption were wholly done away with because of the Word that was united with it. (20:5)

Death had to be suffered on behalf of all, if the debt owed by all was to be paid. So, since it was impossible for Him to die [as God] . . . , He took to Himself a body which could die, so that He might offer it as His own in the place of all and, suffering through His union with it on behalf of all, might "destroy him who had the power of death, that is, the devil" [Heb 2:14]. (20:6).

He awaited death to destroy it and hastened to accomplish the death offered Him for the salvation of all. (22:2)

The Lord was especially concerned for the Resurrection of the body, which He was set to accomplish. He would manifest it as a monument of victory over death. (22:4)

The death which they thought to inflict as a disgrace was actually a monument of victory against death itself. (24:4)

That death has been destroyed, that the Cross conquered it, and that it no longer has power but is truly dead itself, we have no small proof, but a clear declaration, in that death is despised by all Christ's disciples. They defy it and no longer fear it, but by the sign of the cross and by faith in Christ they tread upon it. (27:1)

The Cross of the Lord is a sign of victory over death. (30:1)

How could death have been shown as destroyed unless the Lord's body had risen? (30:2)

It was impossible for it [the Lord's body] to remain dead, because it had been made the temple of life. (31:4)

The Savior clothed Himself with a body, so that the body, becoming closely bound to the life, might no longer have to remain in death, but having been clothed with everlasting life, should rise again and live forever. (44:6)

The reason He put on a body was so that He might find death in the body and blot it out. For how could the Lord have proved Himself to be the life, if He had not given life to what was mortal? (44:6)

If one uses the sign of the cross, he will drive out the demons' deceits. (47:2)

But as to the nations' wisdom, and the sounding pretensions of the philosophers, we hardly need any argument: the wonder is before the eyes of all that, while the wise among the Greeks had written so much, they were unable to persuade even a few from their own neighborhood concerning immortality and a virtuous life. However, Christ alone, by ordinary language and by men not clever with the tongue, has throughout all the world persuaded whole churches full of people to despise death and to be concerned for the things of immortality. (47:5)

What human doctrine ever has prevailed everywhere, one and the same, from one end of the earth to the other? (49:5)

He became man so that man might become God. (54:3)

In a word, the achievements of the Savior, resulting from His becoming man, are of such a kind and number that, if one desired to count them all, he would be like someone looking out over the expanse of the sea and wanting to count its waves. (54:4)

The Scriptures were spoken and written by God through men who spoke of God. (56:2)

And you will also learn about His second glorious and truly divine appearing to us, when no longer in lowliness but in His own glory, no longer in humble guise but in His own magnificence, He comes, not to suffer, but to render to all the fruit of His own Cross (that is, the Paradise and incorruption) and no longer to be judged, but to judge all, by what each has done in the body, whether good or evil. (56:3)

In order rightly to search the Scriptures and come to a genuine understanding of them, an honorable life, a pure soul, and that virtue which follows Christ are necessary: the mind of the one who guides his path thus will be able to attain what it desires and understand, as far as it is accessible to human nature, the Word of God. Without a pure mind and a life modeled after the saints, though, no one can comprehend the words of the saints. (57:1–2)

The one who wants to understand the mind of those who speak of God must begin by washing and cleansing his soul by the way he lives. He must approach the saints by imitating their lives, so that, sharing in a common life with them, he may understand what God has revealed to them. (57:3)

Festal Letters[6]

All those who invent heresies refer to the Scriptures, to be sure, but they do not accept the teachings handed down by the saints, dismissing them as merely human traditions. In this they err, understanding neither those teachings nor their power. This is why Paul justly praises the Corinthians, because their opinions were in accordance with the traditions [1 Cor 15:11]. (#2)

Let us not forget what Paul delivered, declaring it to the Corinthians—Christ's Resurrection, by which He destroyed the one that had the power of death, that is, the devil [Heb 2:14]. He raised us up together with Him, having loosed the bands of death, and granted a blessing instead of a curse, joy instead of grief, a feast instead of mourning, in this holy joy of Easter,

---

6 Excerpts taken from NPNF (2nd) 4:506–553.

which continually fills our hearts, so that we always rejoice. (#2)

Beloved, our will ought to keep pace with the grace of God. (#3:3)

He freed the world by the blood of the Savior, trod down the grave by the Savior's death, and opened the way to the heavenly gates. (#5:3)

The Lord was sacrificed, that by His blood He might abolish death. (#6:4)

If there is joy in heaven over one sinner who repents [Luke 15:7], what must there be over the abolition of sin and the resurrection of the dead? Oh, what a feast and how great the gladness in heaven! How must all its hosts joy and exult, as they rejoice and watch in our assemblies, those that are held continually, and especially those at Easter? (#6:10)

Although place separates us, yet the Lord the Giver of the feast, who is Himself our feast, who is also the bestower of the Spirit, brings us together in mind, harmony, and the bond of peace [Eph 4:3]. For when we mind and think the same things, and offer up the same prayers for each other, no place can separate us, but the Lord gathers and unites us together. (#10:2)

God works in various manners for our salvation by means of His Word, who is not restricted or hindered as He deals with us. Since His grace is rich and manifold [1 Pet 4:10], He varies Himself according to the individual capacity of each soul. (#10:4)

He suffered to prepare freedom from suffering for those who suffer in Him; He descended that He might raise us up; He took on Himself the trial of being born, that we might love Him who is unbegotten; He went down to corruption, that corruption might put on immortality; He became weak for us, so that we might rise with power; He descended to death, that He might bestow on us immortality and give life to the dead. (#10:8)

It is truly a reason for joy, that we can see the signs of victory over death, even our own incorruptibility, in the body of the Lord. For since He rose gloriously, it is clear that the resurrection of all of us will take place; and since His body remained without corruption, there can be no doubt regarding our incorruption. (#11:14)

Letters[7]

Although it is impossible to comprehend what God is, yet it is possible to say what He is not. . . . It is the same with the Son of God: although we are by nature far from being able to comprehend Him, yet it is possible and easy to condemn what the heretics assert about Him, and to say that the Son of God is not as they teach. (#52:2)

Know this, most religious Augustus [Emperor Jovian], that these things have been preached from the beginning, and this is the faith confessed by the Fathers who met at Nicea; and to it all the churches everywhere have assented, those in Spain, Britain, the Gauls, all Italy, Dalmatia, Dacia and Moesia, Macedonia and all Greece, all Africa, Sardinia, Cyprus, Crete, as well as Pamphylia, Lycia, and Isauria, and those in Egypt and the Libyas, Pontus and Cappadocia, and those who are near us, and the churches in the East. (#56:2)

The faith there [at the Council of Nicea, 325] confessed by the Fathers according to the divine Scriptures is enough by itself at once to overthrow all impiety and establish religious faith in Christ. (#59:1)

How can they wish to be called Christians who say that the Word has descended upon a holy man as upon one of the prophets, and has not Himself become man, taking the body from Mary, but that Christ is one Person, while the Word of God, who before Mary and before the ages was Son of the Father, is another? (#59:2)

This is not the teaching of the catholic Church, nor did the Fathers hold this. . . . If you wish to be children of the Fathers, do not hold the contrary of what they wrote. (#59:3–4)

A great advantage has accrued to the human body itself from the fellowship and union of the Word with it: instead of mortal, it has become immortal; and although it is a physical body, it has become spiritual; and although made from earth it has entered the heavenly gates. (#59:9)

We do not worship a creature—perish the thought! Such an error belongs to heathens and Arians! We worship the Lord of creation, Incarnate, the

---
7 Excerpts taken from NPNF (2nd) 4:554–580.

Word of God. The flesh is itself a part of the created world, but it has become God's body. We do not divide the body from the Word and worship it by itself; nor, as we worship the Word, do we separate Him from His flesh. But knowing that "the Word became flesh" [John 1:14], we recognize Him as God also, after having come in the flesh. (#60:3)

He has become man, that He might deify us in Himself. He has been born of a woman and begotten of a virgin, in order to transfer to Himself our erring generation, and that we might become henceforth "a holy nation," and "partakers of the divine nature," as blessed Peter wrote [1 Pet 2:9; 2 Pet 1:4]. (#60:4)

Our faith is right, and starts from the teaching of the apostles and the tradition of the Fathers, being confirmed both by the New Testament and the Old. (#60:6)

We always give thanks in the name of Jesus Christ, and we do not set aside the grace which came to us through Him. For the coming of the Savior in the flesh has been the ransom and salvation of all creation. (#60:6)

In worshiping the Lord in the flesh we do not worship a creature, but the Creator who has put on the created body. (#60:6)

We know that, while "in the beginning was the Word, and the Word was with God" [John 1:1], now that He has become also man for our salvation we worship Him, not as though He had come in the body and equalized Himself with it, but as master, assuming the form of the servant, the maker and creator coming in a creature, so that in the body delivering all things, He might bring the world near to the Father and make all things to be at peace, things in heaven and things on earth. (#60:8)

We are deified not by partaking of the body of some man, but by receiving the body of the Word Himself. (#61:2)

If the Word became man by His deity alone, the commemoration of Mary would be superfluous. (#61:3)

While as a babe He lay in a manger, He subjected the Magi and was worshiped by them; and while as a child He came down to Egypt, He brought to nothing the handmade objects of its idolatry; and crucified in the flesh, He raised the dead long since turned to corruption. (#61:4)

∽ Cyril of Jerusalem

Cyril (c. 315–387) served as bishop of the church in Jerusalem. He played a leading role at the Council of Constantinople in 381. Only one of his sermons survives, on the healing of the paralytic at the pool of Bethesda, as recorded in John 5:2–18. The work for which Cyril is best known is his *Catechetical Lectures*. Saturated with citations from both Old and New Testaments, these lectures were delivered in the Lenten season to those preparing to profess their faith and receive baptism. Scholars have questioned whether the *Mystagogical Lectures,* which lay out for the recently baptized how to appropriate baptism and the Eucharist, are Cyril's work or that of his successor, John. In either case, they show what the fourth-century church in Jerusalem taught about baptism and the Eucharist; consequently, selections from these lectures have been included at this point.

The Sermon on the Paralytic at the Pool[1]

Wherever Jesus appears, there is salvation. If He sees a revenue officer sitting in his office, He makes him an apostle and evangelist. Laid in the grave, He raises the dead to life. He bestows sight on the blind, hearing on the deaf. (§1)

"Do you want to be healed?" [John 5:6]. What mighty power that implied in the physician, making relief depend only on the patient's willing! (§4)

---

1 Excerpted from FC 64:209–222.

The blind men kept on crying out, "Have mercy on us, Son of David" [Matt 20:30]. Those whose eyes did not serve them to read recognized Him whom the students of the Law failed to see. (§5)

There by the waters of the pool stood the Ruler and Maker of the waters. To Him the cripple said, "I have no one to put me into the pool when the water is stirred up" [John 5:7]. (§9)

Jesus said to him, "Stand up, take your mat and walk" [John 5:8]. The disease was long-standing, the remedy swift. The paralysis had lasted for years; the strengthening of the sinews was instantaneous. . . .
Where he simply said, "Stand up, take your mat and walk," what astonishment, do you think, seized the beholders! Yet, marvelous as the sight was, it was the faithlessness of the onlookers [John 5:9–18] that was really strange. A years-old disease is healed, but an obstinate incredulity was not healed. (§13)

Great is God's forbearance, lavish His grace. But do not let His great patience breed contempt. Do not make God's long-suffering a pretext for continuing in sin. (§17)

Let us not be slaves, but masters, in our own house [i.e., in our bodies]. Let us be moderate in our eating, not allowing ourselves to be carried away by gluttony. So, bridling our appetite, we shall govern also its henchman, lust. Let the soul rule the body and not be at the beck and call of animal instinct. (§18)

The Catechetical Lectures[2]

Do not suppose that it is a small thing that you are being given. You, a pitiable creature, are receiving the family name of God. (Introductory Lecture:6)

Great is the prize set before you in baptism: ransom for captives; remission of sins; death of sin; a new, spiritual birth; a shining garment; a holy seal inviolable; a heaven-bound chariot; delights of Paradise; a passport

---

2 Excerpts from Cyril's "Introduction" and Lectures 1–12 taken from FC 61:91–249; excerpts from Lectures 13–18 taken from FC 64:4–180.

to the Kingdom; the grace of adoption. (Introductory Lecture:16)

Never be idle, day or night, but as soon as sleep falls from your eyes let your mind occupy itself with prayer. (Introductory Lecture:16)

It is mine to speak, yours to translate my words into action, and God's to perfect the work. (Introductory Lecture:17)

Sin is a terrible thing, and the most grievous disease of the soul is iniquity. ... But it is not incurable, being grievous only to the one who cherishes it, but easy to cure for the one who puts it away by repentance. (2:1)

It is when you forget God that you begin to entertain evil thoughts and commit wicked deeds. (2:2)

The sum of your sins does not surpass the magnitude of God's mercies. Your wounds are not beyond the healing skill of the great physician. Only surrender to Him with faith, and tell the physician of your malady. (2:6)

Would you see the loving-kindness of God and the extent of His forbearance? Listen to the story of Adam. Adam, the first creature of God, was disobedient. Could God not have condemned him to death at once? But see what the Lord in His great loving-kindness does. Although He casts him out of Paradise—for he was not worthy, because of his sin, to live there—He settles him over against Paradise, so that he might see whence and from what bliss he had fallen, in order that he might be saved thereafter through repentance. (2:7)

God is merciful and quick to forgiveness, but slow to vengeance. Therefore let no one despair of salvation. (2:19)

[Regarding baptism:] Do not regard the laver merely as fresh water, but look to the spiritual grace given with the water. For just as the offerings on the pagan altars, though morally neutral in themselves, become defiled by the invocation of the idols, so contrariwise the plain water, after the invocation of Holy Spirit, Christ, and Father, acquires a power of sanctification.
    For since human nature is twofold, compounded of soul and body, the purification is also twofold—incorporeal for the incorporeal part, bodily for the body. For as the water purifies the body, so the Spirit seals the soul,

that "with our hearts sprinkled clean from an evil conscience and our bodies washed with pure water" [Heb 10:22] we may draw near to God. (3:3–4)

With water the world began [Gen 1:2]; the Jordan saw the beginning of the Gospels. The sea was the means of Israel's liberation from Pharaoh; and freedom for the world from sin comes through the laver of water in the Word of God. (3:5)

True religion consists of these two elements: pious doctrines and virtuous actions. God does not accept doctrines apart from good works or works divorced from godly doctrine. (4:2)

He was crucified not for His own sins, but that we might be freed from ours. He was despised and buffeted by men at that time as man, but was acknowledged as God by creation—for the sun, seeing its Master dishonored, was darkened and trembled, not enduring the sight. (4:10)

Let us not be ashamed of the Cross of Christ. But even if someone else hides it, may you seal it openly on your brow, so that the demons, seeing the royal sign, may tremble and flee far away. Make this sign when eating and drinking, when sitting, lying down, rising, speaking, or walking—in a word, on every occasion. For He who was crucified is in heaven above. (4:14)

This saving faith of ours does not depend on ingenious reasoning, but on proof from the inspired Scriptures. (4:17)

Don't tell me that the body is the cause of sin! If the body is the cause of sin, how is it that a corpse does not sin? (4:23)

Treat this body with care and understand that with this body you will rise from the dead to be judged. But, if any doubt should steal into your mind, as though the thing [i.e., resurrection] were impossible, judge the things unseen from your own experience. Just think where you yourself were a hundred or more years ago. From what an extremely small and insignificant substance you have come to such magnitude of stature and to such dignity of form! Cannot He, who brought what was not into being, raise up again what has already existed but has decayed? Will He, who raises up the corn for us when it dies year by year, have difficulty in raising us up, for whose sake the corn was raised? (4:30)

There is one God of the two testaments, who foretold in the Old Testament the Christ who appeared in the New, and who, through the preparatory school of the Law and the Prophets, led us to Christ. For "before faith came, we were . . . guarded under the law" and the Law trained us for Christ's school [Gal 2:23, 24]. (4:33)

It is not only among us who are marked with the name of Christ that the dignity of faith is great; all the business of the world, even of those outside the Church, is accomplished by faith. By faith, marriage laws join in union persons who are strangers to each other; the spouses, though previously strangers, give each other their bodies and material possessions, because of faith in the marriage contract. By faith agriculture is sustained; for one does not endure the toil involved unless he believes that he will reap a harvest. By faith, seafarers, entrusting themselves to a tiny wooden craft, exchange solid land for the unstable motion of the waves, surrendering themselves to uncertain hopes and carrying about with them a faith more sure than any anchor. Indeed, most human affairs depend on faith. (5:3)

We do not declare what God is, but we frankly confess that we have no exact knowledge concerning Him. (6:2)

Someone may ask, "If the divine nature is incomprehensible, then why do you discourse about it?" In answer: Because I cannot drink up the whole stream, may I not drink as much as I need? Or because I cannot take in all the sunlight, owing to the constitution of my eyes, may I not gaze upon what is sufficient for my needs? On entering a vast orchard, because I cannot eat all the fruit in it, should I go away completely hungry? I praise and glorify God who made us; for it is a divine command which says, "Let everything that breathes praise the Lord!" [Ps 150:6]. I am endeavoring now to glorify the Lord, not to describe Him, although I realize that I will fall short of glorifying Him worthily. Nevertheless, it is a godly work to try! (6:5)

But I will be asked, "Is it not written, 'in heaven their [the little children's] angels continually see the face of my Father in heaven'" [Matt 18:10]? To be sure, the angels see God—not as He is in Himself, though, but in the measure of their capacity. For Jesus himself said, "Not that anyone has seen the Father except the one who is from God; he has seen the Father" [John 6:46]. (6:6)

Let no one be ashamed to confess ignorance in this regard. I am speaking now, and all do on occasion. Yet how we speak we cannot tell; how then can I describe Him who gave the power of speech? How shall I, who have a soul and yet cannot declare its characteristics, set forth its giver? (6:6)

If the very least of His works cannot be comprehended, can the One who made all things be comprehended? (6:9)

The history of godless heresies is a maze; to stray from the one straight way is to find oneself faced with precipices at every step. (6:13)

He [Marcion] was the first to dare to cut out the Old Testament testimonies cited in the New and thus to leave the preaching of the Word without witness. He fancied that he had disposed of God with a pair of scissors, and hoped thus to corrupt the faith of the Church—as if there were no tradition of the gospel to be reckoned with. (6:16)

This is the Church's traditional instruction against heresies; she touches the mire to save you from defilement. She speaks of the wound to save you from actual wounds. For you the knowledge is enough; avoid the experience. (6:34)

It is impossible to perceive the divine nature with bodily eyes, but from his divine works we may gain some impression of His power, according to the words of Solomon: "From the greatness and beauty of created things comes a corresponding perception of their Creator" [WSol 13:5]. (9:2)

Learn, then, that it is impossible to comprehend God's nature. . . . It is impossible to examine closely into the nature of God; but, for His works which we see, we can offer Him praise and glory. (9:3)

Great, indeed, is the testimony of Peter and John, yet open to suspicion, because they were His friends. But when he who was formerly His enemy [i.e., Saul/Paul] afterwards dies for His sake, who can entertain doubts about the truth?
    I confess my amazement at the wise dispensation of the Holy Spirit, in limiting the letters of the others to a small number, but granting the grace to Paul, the former persecutor, to write fourteen. For it was not as though Peter or John were less than Paul that the Holy Spirit withheld the gift in

their case. Rather, so that his doctrine might be beyond question, He gave the grace to the former enemy and persecutor to write more, that thus we might all be confirmed in our faith. (10:17–18)

Our Savior said, "Blessed are you, Simon son of Jonah! For flesh and blood has not revealed this to you, but my Father in heaven" [Matt 16:17]. And anyone who acknowledges our Lord Jesus Christ as the Son of God shares this blessing. (11:3)

[Regarding the generation of the Son of God by the Father:] "God is spirit" [John 4:24]; He who is spirit begot spiritually, being incorporeal, by an unsearchable and incomprehensible generation. For the Son Himself says of the Father, "He said to me, 'You are my son; today I have begotten you'" [Ps 2:7]. Now this "today" is not recent, but eternal; this "today" is timeless, before all ages. (11:5)

"God is spirit" [John 4:24], and His generation is spiritual; for bodies beget bodies, and for the generation of bodies an interval of time is necessary; but there is no intervening time in the generation of Son from Father. In natural generation what is begotten is begotten imperfect; but the Son of God was begotten perfect; for what He now is, this He was begotten from the beginning. (11:7)

He was not first God without a Son, but afterwards, in time, became Father: He has the Son eternally, having begotten Him not as humans beget children, but as He Himself alone knows who begot Him before all ages, true God. (11:8)

Therefore, the Father begot in a manner no one could understand, but as He Himself only knows. We do not claim to declare how He begot Him; we merely affirm that it was not in this way or that. (11:11)

Why do you busy yourself about things which the Holy Spirit has not written of in the Scriptures? When you cannot understand what is written, why are you curious about what is not written? There are many questions in the divine Scriptures; if we do not understand what is written, why do we weary ourselves about what is not written? (11:12)

The Father, having begotten the Son, remained Father, and He is not changed. He begot Wisdom, but did not Himself become devoid of wisdom; He begot Power, but He did not become weak; He begot God, but He was not deprived of His own Godhead; neither did He lose anything by way of decrease or change, nor did He who was begotten have any defect. Perfect is He who begot, perfect that which was begotten. (11:18)

Believe that God has a Son, but do not eagerly search out how, for seeking you will not find. (11:19)

[Regarding worshiping Christ:] It is neither holy to worship the mere man, nor pious to speak of Him as God only, apart from His manhood. For if Christ is God, as He truly is, but did not assume humanity, then there is no salvation. (12:1)

[Representing Christ as speaking:] From my conflict on the Cross I will give to each of My soldiers a royal sign to bear upon his or her forehead. (12:8)

For our part, let us believe in Jesus Christ, who came in the flesh and was made human; for we could not receive Him otherwise. Since we could not behold or enjoy Him as He is, He became what we are, that we might be allowed to enjoy Him. For if we cannot look full upon the sun, which was made on the fourth day, could we behold God, its Maker? (12:13)

Through Eve, still a virgin, came death; there was need that through a virgin—or rather from a virgin—life should appear; that as the serpent deceived the one, so Gabriel should bring the good news to the other. Humanity, having abandoned God, fashioned images like themselves. Since, therefore, the image of man was falsely worshiped as God, God became truly man, that the falsehood might be destroyed. (12:15)

There is nothing corrupt in the human frame unless one defiles it with adulteries and wantonness. He who formed Adam formed Eve also; and both male and female were fashioned by the divine hands. None of the members of the body as fashioned from the beginning is corrupt. (12:26)

Now then, if Eve was born without a mother, from the side of a man, may not a child be born without a man, from the womb of a virgin? (12:29)

If Adam and Eve were cast out of Paradise because of the tree from which they ate, should not believers more easily enter into Paradise because of the tree of Jesus [i.e., the Cross]? If the first man, fashioned out of the earth, brought universal death, shall not He who fashioned him, being the Life, bring everlasting life? (13:2)

Adam received the sentence, "Cursed is the ground because of you; . . . thorns and thistles it shall bring forth for you" [Gen 3:17, 18]. So Jesus assumes the thorns to remove the condemnation; so also He was buried in the earth, to have the earth which had been cursed receive a blessing instead of the curse. (13:18)

We have touched on the story of Paradise, and I am truly amazed at the correspondence of the types. In Paradise (the garden of Eden) was the fall, and in a garden our salvation. From the tree came sin, and until the tree sin lasted. When the Lord was walking in Paradise in the afternoon, Adam and Eve hid themselves [Gen 3:8]; and in the afternoon the robber is brought into Paradise by the Lord [Luke 23:43]. (13:19)

The originator of sin was a woman, formed from the side of Adam; but when Jesus came to grant pardon freely to men and women alike, He was pierced in the side for woman's sake, to undo the sin. (13:21)

The iniquity of sinners was not as great as the righteousness of Him who died for them. (13:33)

Let us not be ashamed to confess the Crucified. Let us boldly make the cross as our seal upon our brow on all occasions: over the bread we eat, over the cups we drink; in our comings and in our goings; before sleep; on lying down and rising up; when we are on the way and when we are still. It is a powerful safeguard; it is without price, for the sake of the poor; without toil, because of the sick; for it is a grace from God, a badge of the faithful, and a terror to demons; for "He made a public display of them, triumphing over them in the cross" [Col 2:15]. For when they see the cross, they are reminded of the Crucified. (13:36)

Death was panic-stricken on seeing a new visitant descending into the nether world, One not subject to the bonds of the place. Why, O you porters of hell, were you terrified on seeing Him? (14:19)

May the God of all Himself, the Father of Christ, and our Lord Jesus Christ, who descended and ascended, and sits with the Father, guard your souls; may He preserve unshaken and unchangeable your hope in Him who rose again; and may He raise you up together with Him from your dead sins to His heavenly gift, and deem you worthy to be "caught up in the clouds ... to meet the Lord in the air" [1 Thess 4:17] in His good time; and until that time of His glorious second coming arrives, may He write all your names in the book of the living and, after writing them, never blot them out. (14:30)

We preach not one coming of Christ, but a second as well, far more glorious than the first. The first gave us a spectacle of His patience; the second will bring with it the crown of the Kingdom of God. In general all things are twofold in our Lord Jesus Christ. His birth is twofold, one of God before the ages, and one of a virgin in the consummation of the ages. His descent is twofold, one lowly, "like rain that falls on the mown grass" [Ps 72:6], and a second, His manifest coming, which is yet to be. In His first coming He was wrapped in swaddling clothes in the manger; in His second He will be "wrapped in light as with a garment" [Ps 104:2]. In His first coming He "endured the cross, disregarding its shame" [Heb 12:2]; in His second He will come in glory, attended by a host of angels. We do not rest, therefore, in His first coming, but we look also for His second. (15:1)

Let us assert of the Holy Spirit, therefore, only what is written; let us not busy ourselves about what is not written. The Holy Spirit has authored the Scriptures; He has spoken of Himself all that He wished, or all that we could grasp. Let us confine ourselves to what He has said, for it is reckless to do otherwise. (16:2)

[Of the day of Pentecost:] A flaming sword of old barred the gates of Paradise; a fiery tongue, bringing salvation, restored the grace. (17:15)

The multitude of those listening was confounded; it was a second confusion, in contrast to the first evil confusion at Babel. In that former confusion of tongues there was a division of purpose, for the intention was impious; here there was a restoration and union of minds, since the object of their zeal was pious. Through what occasioned the fall came the recovery. (17:17)

[In defense of the resurrection:] Do not because of your own weakness charge God with impotence. (18:3)

Do not wonder at the delay of the [final] judgment. Everyone who contends for a prize is crowned or put to shame only after the contest is over; never does the presiding judge crown the competitors while they are still contending; he waits until all the contestants have finished, intending afterwards, having sifted them, to award the prizes and the crowns. So God also, while the strife in this world goes on, assists the righteous only in part; but afterwards He bestows on them their rewards in all fullness. (18:4)

Since in this life only is the appointed time for repentance and pardon—for which those who enjoy it praise God—it is no longer possible for those who have died in sin to offer praise, but only to grieve for themselves. For praise comes from those who give thanks, but lamentation from those who are punished. Therefore, while the righteous will then offer praise, those who have died in sin will have no further season for confessing God's goodness. (18:14)

We shall all rise again, all with eternal bodies, though not all with the same kind of bodies. A righteous person will receive a heavenly body, to dwell worthily with the angels; whereas the sinner will receive an eternal body, and so never be consumed, even though it burn eternally in fire. Justly does God make this dispensation of both classes, for nothing is done without the body. We blaspheme with the mouth, with the mouth we pray. We commit fornication through the body, and through the body we preserve our purity. We rob by the hand, and by the hand we give alms, and so forth. Since the body has ministered to us in everything, it will share our lot hereafter. (18:19)

The Church is called "catholic" because it is spread throughout the world, from end to end of the earth; also because it teaches universally and completely all the doctrines which should be known concerning things visible and invisible, heavenly and earthly; and because it subjects to right worship all humankind, rulers and ruled, literate and illiterate; further because it treats and heals universally every sort of sin committed by soul and body, and it possesses in itself every conceivable virtue, whether in deeds, words, or in spiritual gifts of every kind. (18:23)

Mystagogical Lectures[3]

Pass from the old to the new, from the figure to the reality. There Moses was sent by God to Egypt; here Christ is sent from the Father into the world. Moses' mission was to lead a persecuted people out of Egypt; Christ's, to rescue all the people of the world who were under the tyranny of sin. There the blood of a lamb was the charm against the destroyer; here, the blood of the unspotted Lamb, Jesus Christ, is appointed your inviolable sanctuary against demons. Pharaoh pursued that people of old right into the sea; this outrageous spirit [i.e., Satan], the impudent author of all evil, followed each of you up to the very verge of the saving streams [i.e., your baptisms]. That other tyrant is engulfed and drowned in the Red Sea; this one is destroyed in the saving water. (1:3)

[Regarding baptism:] You were asked, one by one, whether you believed in the name of the Father and of the Son and of the Holy Spirit; you made that saving confession, and then you dipped three times under the water and three times rose up again, therein mystically signifying Christ's three days' burial. (2:4)

The strange, the extraordinary, thing, is that we did not really die, nor were we really buried or really crucified; nor did we really rise again; this was figurative and symbolic; yet our salvation was real. Christ's crucifixion was real, His burial was real, and His Resurrection was real; and all these He has freely made ours, so that by sharing His sufferings in a symbolic enactment we may really and truly gain salvation. (2:5)

[Regarding the Eucharist:] Once at Cana in Galilee He changed water into wine by His sovereign will; is it not credible, then, that He changed wine into blood? If as a guest at a physical marriage He performed this stupendous miracle, shall He not far more readily be confessed to have bestowed on the friends of the Bridegroom [Matt 9:15] the fruition of His own body and blood?

With perfect confidence, then, we partake as of the body and blood of Christ. For in the figure of bread His body is given to you, and in the figure of wine His blood, that by partaking of the body and blood of Christ you may become of one body and blood with Him. For when His body and blood become the tissue of our members, we become Christ-bearers and,

---

3 Excerpted from FC 64:153–203.

as the blessed Peter said, "partakers of the divine nature" [2 Pet 1:4]. (4:2–3)

Do not then think of the elements as bare bread and wine; they are, according to the Lord's declaration, the body and blood of Christ. Though sense suggests the contrary, let faith be your stay. Instead of judging the matter by taste, let faith give you an unwavering confidence that you have been privileged to receive the body and blood of Christ. (4:6)

"Our Father in heaven": O, the greatness of the mercy of God! To those who had revolted from Him and been reduced to the direst straits He has granted so liberal a pardon for their crimes, He has been so prodigal of His favor, that they may even call him "Father." (5:11)

"Hallowed be Your name": God's name is by nature holy, whether we call it so or not. But because it is sometimes profaned among sinners (according to the words, "The name of God is blasphemed among the nations because of you" [Rom 2:24]), we pray that the name of God may be hallowed in us: not that from not being holy it becomes holy, but because it becomes holy "in us" when we are sanctified [i.e., "hallowed"] and our actions correspond to our holy profession. (5:12)

"Your will be done on earth as it is in heaven": God's heavenly, blessed angels do the will of God. So, what you mean by this petition is, "As Your will is done in the angels, so on earth may it be done in me, O Lord." (5:14)

"And forgive us our debts, as we forgive our debtors": Bearing in mind the disproportion of this *quid pro quo,* let us not delay or put off forgiving one another. The offenses committed against us are small, paltry and easily settled; but the offenses we have committed against God are great—too great for any mercy except His. Beware, then, lest, on account of slight and trifling transgressions against you, you debar yourself from God's forgiveness of your grievous sins. (5:16)

[Regarding receiving the Eucharist:] "O taste and see that the Lord is good" [Ps 34:8]. Entrust not the judgment to your bodily palate, but to unwavering faith. For in tasting you taste, not bread and wine, but the body and blood of Christ. (5:20)

~ Basil of Caesarea

Among the Cappadocian Fathers, Basil (329–379) excelled as a high-ranking clergyman and a church administrator. He served as bishop of Caesarea (in Cappadocia). Prior to taking on these responsibilities, he had received an excellent education and had traveled throughout Syria, Palestine, and Egypt in order to study monasticism. Upon his return, he set up a monastic community. His pattern for that community commended itself to subsequent monastic groups within Eastern Christianity and is followed to this day.

Basil was a faithful theologian, especially known for his defense of the full deity of both the Son and the Holy Spirit. An able preacher, Basil retained a lifelong fascination with the natural world. Among his best-known works is his *In Hexaemeron*, a series of sermons on the six days of Creation.

In Hexaemeron[1]

The Maker of the universe—whose creative power, far from being bounded by one world, could extend to the infinite—needed only the impulse of His will to bring the immensities of the visible world into being. (1:2)

Is not this the nature of time, where the past is no more, the future does not exist, and the present escapes before being recognized? (1:5)

"In the beginning God created" [Gen 1:1]: this teaches us that at the will

---
1 Excerpts taken from NPNF (2nd) 8:52–107.

of God the world arose in less than an instant. (1:6)

Let us glorify the supreme Artificer for all that was wisely and skillfully made; by the beauty of visible things let us raise ourselves to Him who is above all beauty; by the grandeur of bodies, sensible and limited in their nature, let us conceive of the infinite Being whose immensity and omnipotence surpass all the efforts of the imagination. (1:11)

The corrupters of the truth are incapable of submitting their reason to Holy Scripture. (2:2)

[God's power in creating is] a power as incomprehensible to human reason as it is unutterable by human voice. (2:2)

In saying, "In the beginning God created the heavens and the earth," the sacred writer passed over many things in silence—e.g., water, air, fire, and their effects—which, all forming in reality the true complement of the world, were without doubt made at the same time as the universe. By this silence, the text plainly wishes to train the activity of our intelligence, giving it a weak point for starting, to impel it to the discovery of the truth. (2:3)

That evil exists, no one living in the world will deny. What shall we say then? Evil is not a living animated essence; it is the condition of the soul opposed to virtue. . . . So, do not go beyond yourself to seek for evil, nor imagine that there is an original nature of wickedness. Let us all acknowledge that each of us is the first author of our own vice. . . . Do not look for the guiding cause beyond yourself, but recognize that evil, rightly so called, has no other origin than our voluntary falls. (2:4–5)

[With regard to God's creative words:] It must be well understood that when we speak of the voice, of the word, of the command of God, this divine language does not mean to us a sound which escapes from the organs of speech, a collision of air struck by the tongue; it is a simple sign of the will of God, and, if we give it the form of an order, it is only the better to impress the souls whom we instruct. (2:7)

The time which you lend to God is not lost: He will return it to you with abundant interest. (3:1)

Do not let anyone compare the simple and inartificial character of the utterances of the Spirit with the inquisitive discussions of philosophers about the heavens; as the beauty of chaste women surpasses that of a harlot, so our arguments are superior to those of our opponents. (3:8)

But why torment ourselves to refute the errors of philosophers, when it is sufficient to produce their mutually contradictory books and, as quiet spectators, to watch the war? (3:8)

You must raise yourselves from visible things to the invisible Being: let the grandeur and beauty of creatures give you a just idea of the Creator. (3:10)

We shall not give occasion to sin, we shall not give place to the enemy within us, if we remember God and keep Him ever dwelling in our hearts. (3:10)

And shall we, whom the Lord, the great worker of marvels, calls to the contemplation of His own works, tire of looking at them, or be slow to hear the words of the Holy Spirit? Shall we not rather stand around the vast and varied workshop of divine Creation and, carried back in mind to the times of old, view all the order of Creation? (4:1)

A word of God makes the nature, and this order is a direction for the future course of the creature. (4:2)

"And God saw that it was good" [Gen 1:10]. Scripture does not merely wish to say that a pleasing aspect of the sea presented itself to God. It is not with eyes that the Creator views the beauty of His works. He contemplates them in His ineffable wisdom. . . . It is the purpose of the work which makes the goodness. (4:6)

"Then God said, 'Let the earth bring forth grass, the herb that yields seed, and the fruit tree that yields fruit according to its kind, whose seed is in itself, on the earth'" [Gen 1:11]. . . . The voice that was then heard and this command were as a natural and permanent law for the earth, giving fertility and the power to produce fruit for all ages to come. (5:1)

I want Creation to penetrate you with so much admiration that everywhere, wherever you may be, the least plant may bring to you the clear remembrance of the Creator. (5:2)

A single plant, a blade of grass, is sufficient to occupy all your intelligence in the contemplation of the skill which produced it. (5:3)

Everywhere, in mystic language, history is sown with the dogmas of theology. (6:2)

[Regarding astrology:] What madness! But, above all, what impiety! For the evil stars throw the blame of their wickedness upon Him who made them. If evil is inherent in their nature, the Creator is the author of evil. (6:7)

If the origin of our virtues and of our vices is not in ourselves, but in the fatal consequence of our birth, it is useless for legislators to prescribe for us what we ought to do, and what we ought to avoid; it is useless for judges to honor virtue and to punish vice. The guilt is not in the robber, not in the assassin: it was willed for him; it was impossible for him to hold back his hand, urged to evil by inevitable necessity. Those who laboriously cultivate the arts are the maddest of people. The laborer will make an abundant harvest without sowing seed and without sharpening his sickle. Whether he wishes it or not, the merchant will make his fortune, and will be flooded with riches by fate. As for us Christians, we shall see our great hopes vanish, since from the moment that one does not act with freedom, there is neither reward for justice nor punishment for sin. Under the reign of necessity and of fate there is no place for merit, the first condition of all righteous judgment. (6:7)

Recognize here the wisdom of the Artificer. See how He made the heat of the sun proportionate to its distance from the earth. Its heat is so regulated that it neither consumes the earth by excess, nor lets it grow cold and sterile by defect. (6:10)

May He who has given us intelligence to recognize in the smallest objects of creation the great wisdom of the Contriver make us find in great bodies a still higher idea of their Creator.... Even so, the whole universe cannot give us a right idea of the greatness of God. (6:11)

See how the divine order embraces all and extends to the smallest object. A fish does not resist God's law—but we human beings cannot endure His precepts of salvation! (7:4)

I myself have seen these marvels, and I have admired the wisdom of God in all things. If beings deprived of reason are capable of thinking and of providing for their own preservation; if a fish knows what it ought to seek and what to shun, what shall we say, who are honored with reason, instructed by law, encouraged by the promises, and made wise by the Spirit, but who show less sense about our own affairs than do fish? They know how to provide for the future, but we renounce our hope of the future and spend our life in indulgence worthy only of brute animals. (7:5)

If ever you hear anyone laugh at our mystery [i.e., the Christian faith], as if it were impossible and contrary to nature that a virgin should become a mother without losing the purity of her virginity, remember that He who would save the faithful by the foolishness of preaching [1 Cor 1:23] has given us beforehand in nature a thousand reasons for believing in the marvelous. (8:6)

Our God has created nothing unnecessarily and has omitted nothing that is necessary. (8:7)

Leisure without the fear of the Lord is a school of vice. (8:8)

He has passed over in silence, as useless, all that is unimportant for us. Shall I then prefer foolish wisdom to the oracles of the Holy Spirit? Shall I not rather exalt Him who, not wishing to fill our minds with these vanities, has regulated all the economy of Scripture in view of our edification? (9:1)

"Let the earth bring forth the living creature" [Gen 1:24]: this command has continued and earth does not cease to obey the Creator. (9:2)

What language can attain to the marvels of the Creator? What ear could understand them? (9:3)

Virtues exist in us also by nature, and the soul has affinity with them not by education, but by nature herself. We do not need lessons to hate illness, but by ourselves we repel what afflicts us; the soul has no need of a master to teach us to avoid vice. Now all vice is a sickness of the soul, as virtue is its health.... Thus, without having need of lessons, the soul can attain by herself to what is fit and conformable to nature. (9:4)

In all beings there is nothing disorderly, nothing unforeseen. All bear the marks of the wisdom of the Creator, and show that they have come to life with the means of assuring their preservation. (9:4)

In truth the most difficult of sciences is to know oneself. (9:6)

"Then God said, 'Let Us make man'" [Gen 1:26]. Does not the light of theology shine in these words, as through windows? And does not the Second Person show Himself in a mystical way, without yet manifesting Himself until the great day?... Tell me, is there then only one Person? It is not written, "Let man be made," but "Let Us make man." The preaching of theology remains enveloped in shadow before the appearance of the humanity who was to be instructed, but now that the Creation of humankind is expected, that faith unveils herself and the dogma of truth appears in all its light.... To whom does He say, "in Our image": to whom if it is not to Him who is "the brightness of His glory and the express image of His person" [Heb 1:3], to Him who is "the image of the invisible God" [Col 1:15]? It is then to His living image, to Him who has said, "I and My Father are one" [John 10:30] and "He who has seen Me has seen the Father" [John 14:9], that God says, "Let Us make man in Our image." (9:6)

On the Holy Spirit[2]

Truth is always a hard quarry to hunt, so we must look everywhere for its tracks. (§2)

"In the beginning was the Word" [John 1:1]: thought cannot travel outside "was" nor imagination beyond "beginning." (§14)

How do we become Christians? "By faith," would be the universal answer. And in what way are we saved? Put plainly, we are regenerated through the grace given in our baptism. How else could we be? This salvation is established through the Father and the Son and the Holy Spirit. (§26)

---

2 Excerpts taken from NPNF (2nd) 8:2–50.

Count, if you must—but you must not by counting do damage to the faith. Either let the ineffable be honored by silence, or let holy things be counted consistently with true religion. There is one God and Father, one Only Begotten, and one Holy Spirit. We proclaim each of the hypostases singly; and, when count we must, we do not let an ignorant arithmetic carry us away to the idea of a plurality of Gods. (§44)

Honor paid to the image [the incarnate Son of God] passes on to the prototype [God the Father]. (§45)

Should I lament more the ignorance or the blasphemy of those who try to insult the doctrines that concern the divine nature by comparing them with the human? (§51)

Ancient dogmas inspire a certain sense of awe, venerable as they are with a hoary antiquity. (§71)

[Speaking about tensions within the Church:] We have become more brutish than the brutes; at least they herd with their fellows, but our most savage warfare is with our own people. (§78)

By the tradition of the Fathers doctrine has been preserved by an unbroken sequence of memory down to our own day. (§79)

~ Gregory Nazianzen

Gregory Nazianzen (330–390) was one of the Cappadocian Fathers. A gifted orator and a poet of some distinction, he composed nearly four hundred poems, many of which became hymns used through the ages by the Church. He valiantly defended the completeness of both the deity and the humanity of Christ in, respectively, the Arian and the Apollinarian controversies, and he played a leading role in the Council of Constantinople in 381. Indeed, his stalwart defense of the faith has led to his being called, among the Eastern Orthodox, Gregory the Theologian—an epithet accorded to only two others in the history of the Church.

Poetry[1]

POEM 1.1.2, "ON THE SON"

He lost nothing of the Godhead
    and yet became my salvation.
The Healer stooped down to my unbearable pains.
He was mortal, yet God;
    of the race of David, yet the maker of Adam;
    He wore flesh, yet was beyond bodily form;
    He had a mother, yet she was a virgin;

---

[1] Excerpted from John A. McGuckin, trans., *Saint Gregory Nazianzen: Selected Poems* (Oxford: Sisters of the Love of God Press, 1986), pp. 1–20; and from Peter Gilbert, trans., *On God and Man: The Theological Poetry of St. Gregory of Nazianzus* (Crestwood, NY: St. Vladimir's Seminary Press, 2001), pp. 37–171.

He was circumscribed, yet had no limit. . . .
He came to the contest as a mortal,
> but as the unconquerable One
> He vanquished the Tempter. . . .
He was sacrifice and celebrant,
> sacrificial priest and God himself.
He offered blood to God to cleanse the entire world.
The Cross lifted Him up
> but it was the trap that nailed sin fast.
And yet how can I speak of all His works?

POEM 1.1.4, "CONCERNING THE WORLD"

He thought, and things came to be, in-formed: the divine thought
> is the complicated womb of all that is. . . .
All things are immediate to God, as much things future as things past,
> as well as things now present. Time for me is fractured in this way,
> with some things earlier, others later: but for God it all comes in one,
> and the great Godhead engulfs it in his arms.

POEM 1.1.9, "ON THE TWO COVENANTS, AND THE APPEARING OF CHRIST"

This is how God does things. For his custom is to persuade, not to manhandle mortal men. What's forced has no reward, it seems to me. . . .
But, seeing as Christ had set in the human body a piece of heaven,
> when he saw it blasted with heart-gnawing evil,
> and the twisted dragon lording it over men,
he did not, to raise again his portion, send yet
> other aids to treat the disease (for a little cure
> is inadequate against great illnesses); but, emptying himself
> of his glory as the immortal God the Father's motherless Son,
> he appeared for me himself, without a father, a strange son;
> yet no stranger, since from my own kind came this immortal, being made
> man by a virgin mother, so that the whole of him might save the whole of me.

POEM 1.1.11, "ON THE INCARNATION OF CHRIST"

The Word of the Father,
    made man for us, is God—
compounded of the union
    of God and mortal things—
one God in both,
    mortal so that he might offer us divinity
    in exchange for our mortality.
Be merciful, O wounded One on high,
    for how great you are!
How could human mind ever grasp
    this union beyond all words?

POEM 1.1.29, "TO GOD"

You are above all things
    and what way can we rightly sing of You?
How can words sing Your praise,
    when no word can speak of You?
How can the mind consider You,
    when no mind can ever grasp You?
You alone are unutterable
    from the time You created all things that can be spoken of.
You alone are unknowable
    from the time You created all things that can be known.
All things cry out about You—
    those which speak, and those which cannot speak;
all things honor You—
    those which think, and those which cannot think.
For there is one longing, one groaning, that all things have for You.

POEM 1.1.33, "THANKSGIVING"

O Son of God, according to the Spirit,
and Son of Man, according to the flesh—
    in which as mortal man
        You suffered the fate of man
        upon a Cross;

but as immortal God, on the third day,
> came out of the gates of hell,
>> snapping all the chains of death in your Paradise.

And so You graced our mortal race
> with a nature that might live forever
> and forever sing Your praise.

POEM 1.2.14, "ON HUMAN NATURE"

A mind cloaked round with sorrows doesn't want to sing back happily.
But privately, my mind is a whirlpool spinning,
I had this sort of battling round of words:
Who was I? Who am I? What shall I be? I don't know clearly.
Nor can I find one better stocked with wisdom.
But, as through thick fog, I wander
> every which way, with nothing, not a dream, of the things I long for....

No one among mortals has ever made this boast, that,
> unvanquished, he has left life's hateful pains.

Feebleness, poverty, birth, death, enmity, rogues,
> sea-beasts and land-beasts, sufferings: all this is life.

I have known many woes and utter unhappiness,
> but of good things, nothing wholly free from pain,
> from the time that that bitter price got wiped on me
> by the destroying taste, and the adversary's spite.

Well, so much, flesh, for you, incurable, an agreeable
> enemy, who never lets up warring,
> a beast sharply biting, a fire that chills, what a wonder!

It'll be a great wonder, if ever you end up agreeable to me....
I am an image of God, and have turned out a son of shame;
> I blush at honor's mother, craving lust....

Christ, blending his own form with ours, so that
> God, by his passion, might give me a defense against my passions,
> and perfect me as god by his human image.

POEM 1.2.15, "ON THE CHEAPNESS OF THE OUTWARD MAN"

If what we are were this alone, which had been shown to all,
> and life's destroyed, I should have nothing more....

What things shall the unrighteous receive on that last day:
> fire that roars, a gruesome darkness, to be far away from light,
> the worm, the ceaseless remembrance of our own evil.

Better had it been for you, vile man, if you'd never crossed life's gates—
> or if, having crossed them, like the beasts you'd perished utterly,
> rather than to find again, after all your sufferings here,
> yet worse punishments than those you've already met.

POEM 1.2.16, "ON THE DIFFERENT WALKS OF LIFE"

In human matters, no good exists without its mix of evil. . . .
Everything here is trouble for us mortals. All's laughter,
> powder, shadows, illusions, dew, a breath, a wing, a puff, a dream,
> a wave's heave, a river's flow, a schooner's trail, a breeze, fine dust,
> a still-rolling circle, turning all alike,
> the slow, the swift, the failures, the successful,
> for hours, days, nights, with pains, deaths, sufferings
> and pleasures, in illnesses, mishaps, triumphs.

And this, Creator Word, is of your wisdom, that instability
> should be in everything, so we might have a love for what is stable.

POEM 1.2.17, "BLESSINGS OF VARIOUS LIVES"

Blessed is he, whoever leads a solitary life, not at all mixing
> with worldly folk, but has divinized the mind.

Blessed is he who, dwelling amidst many people, does not turn towards
> the many, but directs his whole heart to God.

Blessed is he who purchases Christ with all his belongings
> and has, as his only possession, the cross, which he raises on high.

Blessed is he who, administering his cleanly-gained possessions,
> extends God's hand to those who are in need. . . .

Blessed is he who honors the Lord by much-toiling hands: and,
> for many people, this is the law of life. . . .

There is not one common food that pleases all alike,
> neither is there but one way of life appropriate to Christians.

POEM 1.2.18, "CONCERNING HUMAN LIFE"

From dirt to mud, then back to dust again.
For earth is reunited again with earth,
    and in earthly swaddling-clothes is swaddled,
    and dirt once more flies forward with the dust
    which the violent twisting of the winds
    lifts up on high, then throws back down.
And so it is with our much-swirling life
    which the heady winds of wickedness
    raise up on high, to spurious acclaim.
But again the dirt drops down, and stays below,
    until the Creator's Word accords
    the things conjoined their necessary parting.
But now there peers out, as if from some depth,
    the dirt, made spiritual by the divine image,
    and cries aloud in earthly tragedies,
    and weeps this life, which seems to be a joke.

POEM 2.1.39, "ON HIS OWN VERSES"

I've found this to be
    the single sweetest counsel, that,
    pitching out all other words, one hold
    on only to those inspired by God,
    as a calm harbor for those who flee the storm. . . .
A world fragmented into sects,
    where all find grounds for their own straying
    in those writings they've set above themselves.

POEM 2.1.45, "LAMENTATION CONCERNING THE SORROWS OF HIS OWN SOUL"

Therefore I wage an unending battle of war, with
    flesh and soul opposed to one another.
I am the image of God, and am drawn to wickedness.

The worse attacks its better with irreverence.
Or else I escape wickedness, and stand, not without struggling,
    exercised many ways, with the help of heaven's hand.
For there is, in me, there is a double law: on the one hand there is good,
    which follows what is good; but what is worse
    follows evil things; for, while the mind is ready
    to follow Christ, and will approach the light,
    the other, of flesh and blood, is eager
    to entertain Belial, and be dragged headlong to darkness.
And it delights in material things, things unstable
    and fleeting, as if they were good. . . .
By Christ's sufferings,
    he drew me away from bitter passion,
    taking flesh, being nailed to the cross, nailing also
    the creature's black transgression, and Belial's strength,
    so that, reborn and racing out of the tomb,
    we should have glory anew with the great Christ.

POEM 2.1.78, "TO HIS OWN SOUL"

You have a job to do, soul, and a great one, if you like:
    examine yourself, what it is you are and how you act,
    where you come from, and where you're going to end,
    and whether to live is this very life you're living, or something else
        besides.
You have a job to do, soul; by these things cleanse your life.
Make me to know God and God's mysteries.
What was there before this universe, and why is this universe here for you?
Where has it come from, and where is it going?
You have a job to do, soul, by these things cleanse your life.
How does God guide and turn the universe:
    or why are some things permanent, while other things flow away,
    and us especially, in this changing life?
You have a job to do, soul: look to God alone.
What was my former glory, what is this present arrogance?
What will be my crown, and what the end of my life?
Of these things inform me, and check the mind from wandering.
A job you have to do, soul: lest you suffer in deep trouble.

HYMN TO THE TRINITY[2]

O Light that knew no dawn, that shines to endless day,
all things in earth and heaven are lustered by Your ray;
no eye can to Your throne ascend,
    nor mind Your brightness comprehend.

O Father, give me grace to live in holy fear;
most urgently I pray: grant me Your voice to hear.
From sin restore my life anew,
    and let me dwell in light with You.

That, cleansed from stain of sin, I may pure homage give
to You, and then behold Your beauty while I live.
My hands in holy worship raise
    and You, O Christ my Savior, praise.

In supplication meek to You I bend the knee;
O Christ, when You shall come, in love remember me.
Within Your kingdom, by Your grace,
    grant me a humble servant's place.

O Spirit, give me grace, I humbly ask of You;
shed light upon my way and keep me ever true;
for gifted by Your holy fire,
    my heart and life Your praise desire.

Epigrams[3]

I would hate to be held in good esteem by wicked people. (Epigram #7)

The Theological Orations (Orations 27–31)[4]

Not to everyone, my friends, does it belong to philosophize about God...,
and, I will add, not before every audience, nor at all times, nor on all points;

---

2 This hymn is in the public domain.
3 Excerpted from McGuckin, *Saint Gregory Nazianzen*, p. 19.
4 Excerpts taken from Edward E. Hardy, trans., *Christology of the Later Fathers* (Louisville, KY: Westminster John Knox Press, 1954), pp. 128–214.

but on certain occasions, and before certain persons, and within certain limits. (1:3)

We ought to think of God more often than we draw our breath. (1:5)

It is not the continual remembrance of God that I would hinder, but only the talking about God. (1:5)

It is difficult to conceive God, but to define Him in words is an impossibility, as one of the Greek teachers of divinity taught, not unskillfully, as it appears to me. . . . But in my opinion it is impossible to express Him, and yet more impossible to conceive Him. For what may be conceived may perhaps be made clear by language, if not well, at lest to some degree, to anyone who is not unable to hear or slothful in understanding. But to comprehend the whole of so great a subject is utterly impossible and unattainable, not just for the utterly careless and ignorant, but even for those who are highly exalted, and who love God. (2:4)

It is not only "the peace of God which surpasses all understanding" [Phil 4:7], nor only the things which God has stored up in promise for the righteous, which "no eye has seen, nor ear heard, nor the human heart conceived" [1 Cor 2:9] except in a very small degree, nor the accurate knowledge of the Creation. . . . Far beyond them all is that nature which is above them, and out of which they spring, the incomprehensible and illimitable—not, I mean, as to the fact of His being, but as to its nature. . . . For it is one thing to be persuaded of the existence of a thing, and quite another to know what it is. (2:5)

God would be altogether circumscript if He were comprehensible in thought. (2:10)

To make clear the point at which my argument has aimed from the first: the divine nature cannot be apprehended by human reason, and we cannot even represent to ourselves all its greatness. (2:11)

It is quite impracticable for those who are in the body to be conversant with objects of pure thought apart altogether from bodily objects. (2:12)

Our mind faints to transcend corporeal things, and to consort with the incorporeal, stripped of all clothing of corporeal ideas, as long as it has to look with its inherent weakness at things above its strength. (2:13)

Usage when confirmed by time was held to be law [WSol 14:16]. (2:14)

Reason . . . leads us up to God through visible things. (2:16)

The truth, then—and the whole word—is full of difficulty and obscurity; and, as it were, with a small instrument we are undertaking a great work, when with merely human wisdom we pursue the knowledge of the self-existent. (2:21)

Granted, you understand orbits and periods, and waxings and wanings, and settings and risings, and some degrees and minutes, and all the other things which make you so proud of your wonderful knowledge. But with all this you have not arrived at comprehension of the realities themselves, but only at an observation of some movement. When this has been confirmed over a period of time, and the observations of many other individuals have been collated into a generalization, a law is deduced. This has acquired the name of science (as the lunar phenomena have become generally known to us), being the basis of this knowledge. But if you will be scientific on this subject, to have a just claim to admiration, tell me: what is the cause of this order and this movement? (2:29)

We cannot set forth that which is above time, if we avoid as we desire any expression which conveys the idea of time. (3:3)

How then, was the Son of God begotten? This generation would have been no great thing, if you could have comprehended it who have no real knowledge even of your own generation, or at least who comprehend very little of it. (3:8)

The begetting of God must be honored by silence. It is a great thing for you to learn that He was begotten. But the manner of His generation we will not admit that even angels can conceive, much less you. Shall I tell you how it was? It was in a manner known to the Father who begot, and to the Son who was begotten. Anything more than this is hidden by a cloud, and escapes your dim sight. (3:8)

How do you describe the essence of God? Not by declaring what it is, but by rejecting what it is not. (3:11)

In the beginning He was, uncaused; for what is the cause of God? But afterward for a cause He was born—and that so that you might be saved. (3:19)

His inferior [nature], the humanity, became God, because it was united to God, and became one [Person] because the higher nature prevailed . . . in order that I too might be made God so far as He is made man. (3:19)

In His human nature He had no father, and in His divine nature no mother. (3:19)

He was baptized as man, but He remitted sins as God. . . . He was tempted as man, but He conquered as God. . . . He hungered, but He fed thousands. . . . He thirsted, but he cried, "Let anyone who is thirsty come to me, and let the one who believes in me drink" [John 7:37, 38]. . . . He was wearied, but He is the rest of those who are weary and heavy-laden. (3:20)

He asks where Lazarus was laid, for He was man; but He raises Lazarus, for He was God. He is sold, and very cheap, for only thirty pieces of silver; but He redeems the world, and that at a great price, for the price was His own blood. . . . He is bruised and wounded, but He heals every disease and every infirmity. . . . He dies, but he gives life, and by His death destroys death. (3:20)

What greater destiny can befall humanity's humility than that it should be intermingled with God, and by this intermingling should be deified? (4:3)

Look at it this way: for my sake He was called a curse, who destroyed my curse; and sin, who takes away the sin of the world; and became a new Adam to take the place of the old. In the same way He makes my disobedience His own, as head of the whole body. (4:5)

He honors obedience by His action, and proves it experimentally by His Passion. (4:6)

We . . . shall be entirely like God, ready to receive [into our hearts] the whole God and Him alone. This is the perfection to which we press on. (4:6)

His human will cannot be opposed to God, since it is altogether taken into God. (4:12)

He still pleads even now as man for my salvation; for He continues to wear the body which He assumed, until He make me God by the power of His Incarnation. (4:14)

The Deity cannot be expressed in words. (4:17)

No one has yet breathed the whole air, nor has any mind entirely comprehended, or speech exhaustively contained, the being of God. But we sketch Him by His attributes, and so obtain a certain faint and feeble and partial idea concerning Him, and our best theologian is the one who has, not indeed discovered the whole, for our present chain does not allow of our seeing the whole, but conceived of Him to a greater extent than another, and gathered in himself more of the likeness or adumbration of the truth, or whatever we may call it. (4:17)

Being is in its proper sense peculiar to God, and belongs to Him entirely, and is not limited or cut short by any before or after, for in Him there is no past or future. (4:18)

So He is called man, not only that through His body He may be apprehended by embodied creatures, which otherwise would have been impossible because of His incomprehensible nature; but also that by Himself He may sanctify humanity, and be as it were a leaven to the whole lump; and by uniting to Himself that which was condemned may release it from all condemnation, becoming for all human beings all things that we are, except sin. . . . [He is] God in visible form. . . . He is Son of Man, both on account of Adam, and of the virgin from whom He came: from the one as a forefather, from the other as a mother, both in accordance with the law of generation, and apart from it. (4:21)

I would have them clearly understand that their love for the letter is but a cloak for their impiety. (5:3)

What then, is procession [i.e., of the Holy Spirit]? If you will tell me what the unbegottenness of the Father is, then I will explain to you the physiology of the generation of the Son and the procession of the Spirit—and we shall both be frenzy-stricken for prying into the mystery of God. And who are we to do these things, we who cannot even see what lies at our feet, or number the sand of the sea, or the drops of rain, or the days of eternity, much less enter into the depths of God, and supply an account of that nature which is so unspeakable and transcends all words? (5:8)

But since God is one and the supreme nature is one, how can I present to you a likeness? Will you seek one in lower regions or in your surroundings? It is shameful, and not only shameful but foolish, to take from things below a guess at things above, and from a fluctuating nature at the things that are unchanging. (5:10)

To us there is one God, for the Godhead is one, and all that proceeds from Him is referred to One, though we believe in three Persons. For One [Person] is not more and another less God; nor is One before and another after; nor are they divided in will or parted in power; nor can you find here any of the qualities of divisible things; but the Godhead is, to speak concisely, undivided in separate Persons. . . . When, then, we look at the Godhead, or the first cause, or the monarchia, that which we conceive is One; but when we look at the Persons in whom the Godhead dwells, and at those who timelessly and with equal glory have their being from the first cause, there are three whom we worship. (5:14)

We have given names according to our own comprehension from our own attributes to those of God. (5:22)

It is no easy matter to change from those habits which custom and use have made honorable. (5:25)

The Old Testament proclaimed the Father openly, and the Son more obscurely. The New Testament manifested the Son, and suggested the deity of the Spirit. Now the Spirit Himself dwells among us, and supplies us with a clearer demonstration of Himself. (5:26)

By baptism and resurrection the Creator-spirit creates anew. (5:29)

I have very carefully considered this matter, and have looked at it in every point of view, in order to find some illustration of this most important subject, but I have been unable to discover anything on earth with which to compare the nature of the Godhead. (5:31)

Orations[5]

Let us become like Christ, since Christ became like us. Let us become God's for His sake, since He for ours became human. He assumed the worse that He might give us the better; He became poor that we through His poverty might be rich; He took upon Himself the form of a servant that we might receive back our liberty; He came down that we might be exalted; He was tempted that we might conquer; He was dishonored that He might glorify us; He died that He might save us; He ascended that He might draw to Himself us, who were lying low in the fall of sin. Let us give all, offer all, to Him who gave Himself a ransom and a reconciliation for us. (1:5)

It is in this that wickedness especially has the advantage over goodness, and it is most distressing to me to perceive it—that vice is something attractive and ready at hand, and that nothing is so easy as to become evil, even without anyone to lead us on to it, while the attainment of virtue is rare and difficult, even where there is much to attract and encourage us. (2:11)

It is only by the aid of the Spirit that we are able to perceive, expound, or embrace the truth in regard to God. (2:39)

We account piety to consist, not in often speaking about God, but in silence for the most part, for the tongue is a dangerous thing to humans, if it is not governed by reason. Believe that listening is always less dangerous than talking, just as learning about God is more pleasant than teaching. (3:7)

I must be buried with Christ, become the son of God, yea, God himself.... This is the purpose of the great mystery for us. This is the purpose for us of God, who for us was made man and became poor—to raise our flesh and recover His image and remodel humanity, that we might all be made one in Christ. (7:23)

The departed have not in the grave confession and restoration, for God has confined life and action to this world, and to the future the scrutiny of what has been done. (16:7)

---

5 Excerpts taken from NPNF (2nd) 7:203–434.

Its [the divine being's] every quality is incomprehensible and beyond the power of our intellect. How can we either perceive or express by definition on such a subject, which is beyond our ken? How can the immeasurable be measured, and the Godhead be reduced to the condition of finite things, and measured by degrees of greater or less? (18:16)

Deification . . . is conferred by true philosophy. (21:2)

This is the way illegitimate priests, unworthy of their vocation, intrude upon it: their preparation for the priesthood has cost them nothing; they have endured no inconvenience for the sake of virtue; they only begin to study religion when appointed to teach it; and they undertake the cleansing of others before being cleansed themselves; yesterday sacrilegious, today sacerdotal; yesterday excluded from the sanctuary, today its officiants; proficient in vice, novices in piety; the product of the favor of human beings, not of the grace of the Spirit. (21:9)

On doubtful points, I am disposed to think we ought to incline to the charitable side, and acquit rather than condemn the accused. . . . One who is not ready to do ill is not inclined even to suspect it. (21:15)

The one who suffers has a better memory. (33:5)

We are brought back by the tree of shame to the tree of life. (33:9)

It is ours to be living temples of the living God—living sacrifices, reasonable burnt-offerings, perfect sacrifices, yea, gods through the adoration of the Trinity. (33:15)

Laws are unequal and irregular. For what was the reason why they restrained the woman, but indulged the man, and that a woman who practices evil against her husband's bed is an adulteress, and the penalties of the law for this are very severe; but if the husband commits fornication against his wife, he has no account to give? I do not accept this legislation; I do not approve this custom. They who made the law were men, and therefore their legislation is hard on women. (37:6)

Even to wish well needs help from God; . . . even to choose what is right is divine and a gift of the mercy of God. For it is necessary both that we should be our own masters and also that our salvation should be from God. (37:13)

[On the celebration of Christ's birth:] God was manifested to humanity by birth. On the one hand, being (and eternally being) of the eternal being, above cause and word, for there was no word before the Word; and on the other hand for our sakes also becoming, that He who gives us our being might also give us our well-being—or rather, might restore us by His Incarnation, when we by wickedness had fallen from well-being. (38:3)

The divine nature is boundless and hard to understand, and all that we can comprehend of Him is His boundlessness. (38:7)

[Regarding death and sin:] Death is a gain, for it cuts off sin, so that evil may not be immortal. Thus God's punishment is changed into a mercy; for it is in mercy, I am persuaded, that God inflicts punishment. (38:12)

The first and last of all evils is idolatry, the transfer of worship from the Creator to creatures. (38:13)

[Regarding Christ's birth:] Adore the birth by which you were loosed from the chains of your birth. (38:17)

Let us not remain what we are, but let us become what we once were. (39:2)

Since that deceiver [Satan] thought that he was unconquerable in his malice, after he had cheated us with the hope of becoming gods, he was himself cheated by God's assumption of our nature: in attacking Adam (as he thought), he encountered God, and thus the new Adam saved the old, and the condemnation of the flesh was abolished, death being slain by flesh. (39:13)

John baptized, and Jesus came to him ... to bury the whole of the old Adam in water. (39:15)

But further, Jesus went up out of the water. With Himself He carried up the world, and He saw the heaven opened which Adam had shut against himself and all his posterity. (39:16)

Too great length in a sermon is as much an enemy to people's ears as too much food is to their bodies. (40:1)

If after your baptism the persecutor and tempter of the light assails you..., defend yourself with the water. (40:10)

This is the way he fights: the robber is skilled in Scripture. (40:10)

If good could be bought, you would spare no money; but if mercy is freely at your feet, you despise it for its cheapness. (40:13)

If you always pass over today and wait for tomorrow, by your little procrastinations you will be cheated without knowing it by the evil one, as his manner is. "Give to me," he says, "the present, and to God the future; to me your youth, and to God old age." (40:14)

Do not take your enemy [Satan] as your counselor. (40:16)

Do you have an infant child? Do not let sin get any opportunity, but let him be sanctified [i.e., baptized] from his childhood; from his very tenderest age let him be consecrated by the Spirit. Do you fear the seal because of the weakness of your infant's nature? . . . Give your child the Trinity, that great and noble guard. (40:17)

Some will ask regarding baptism, "What about those who are only children, and conscious neither of the loss nor of grace? Are we to baptize them, too?" Certainly, if any danger presses. . . . A proof of this is found in the circumcision on the eighth day, which was a type of this seal and was conferred on children before they had the use of reason. . . . But I give my advice in regard to others, to wait until the end of the third year or so, when they may be able to listen and to answer something about the sacrament, so that, even though they do not yet entirely understand it, still at any rate they may know the outlines; and then to sanctify them in soul and body with the great sacrament of our consecration . . . , for at that time they begin to be responsible for their lives, as reason is maturing and they learn the mystery of life. (40:28)

[Regarding Jesus' baptism:] He had no need of cleansing; it was for you that He was purified, just as it was for you that, although He had not flesh, yet He was clothed with flesh. (40:29)

Nothing is so magnificent in God's sight as pure doctrine, and a soul perfect in all the dogmas of the truth. (42:8)

Virtue, that it may remain virtue, is without reward, its eyes fixed alone on that which is good. (42:12)

It is no disgrace to change, while it is fatal to cling to evil. (42:27)

I take it as admitted by all sensible people that the first of our advantages is education—and not only this our more noble form of it [the Christian faith], which disregards rhetorical ornaments and glory, and holds to salvation, and beauty in the objects of our contemplation, but even that external culture which many Christians ill-judgingly abhor, as treacherous and dangerous and keeping us far from God. For we should not neglect the heavens, earth, and air, and all such things, because some have wrongly seized upon them and honored God's works instead of God; instead, we should reap whatever advantage we can from them for our life and enjoyment, while we avoid their dangers, not raising creation as foolish people do in revolt against the Creator, but from the works of nature apprehending the Worker and, as the divine apostle says, "taking every thought captive to obey Christ" [2 Cor 10:5]. (43:11)

He [Basil of Caesarea] is in heaven where, if I am not mistaken, he is offering sacrifices for us and praying for the people—for though he has left us, he has not entirely left us. (43:80)

God is pleased when we do what we can. (43:82)

The gates of hell are opened, and death is destroyed, and the old Adam is put aside, and the new is fulfilled. Anyone in Christ is a new creature [2 Cor 5:17]—so be renewed! (45:1)

We had fallen in consequence of the original sin. (45:12)

If He was numbered among the transgressors for you and your sin, you should become law-abiding for His sake. (45:24)

We needed an incarnate God, a God put to death, that we might live. (45:28)

Many indeed were the miracles of that time: God crucified; the sun darkened and again rekindled, for it was fitting that the creatures should suffer with their Creator; the veil torn; ... the rocks rent for the Rock's sake; ... and yet none of these equal the miracle of my salvation. A few drops of blood recreate the whole world! (45:29)

Letters on the Apollinarian Controversy[6]

We do not sever the man from the Godhead, but we lay down as a dogma the unity and identity [of Person], who of old was not man but God, and the only Son before all ages, unmingled with body or anything corporeal; but who in these last days has assumed humanity also for our salvation; passible in His flesh, impassible in His Godhead; circumscript in the body, uncircumscript in the Spirit; at once earthly and heavenly, tangible and intangible, comprehensible and incomprehensible; that by one and the same [Person], who was perfect man and also God, the entire humanity fallen through sin might be created anew.

If anyone does not believe that holy Mary is the mother of God, he is severed from the Godhead. If anyone should assert that He passed through the virgin as through a channel, and was not at once divinely and humanly formed in her (divinely, because without the intervention of a man; humanly, because in accordance with the laws of gestation), he is in like manner godless. If any assert that the manhood was formed and afterward was clothed with the Godhead, he too is to be condemned. For this were not a generation of God, but a shirking of generation. If any introduce the notion of two sons, one of God the Father, the other of the mother, and discredits the unity and identity, may he lose his part in the adoption promised to those who believe aright. (#101)

If any should say that It [the Godhead] wrought in Him [Jesus Christ] by grace as in a prophet, but was not and is not united with Him in essence—let him be empty of the higher energy, or rather full of the opposite. If any worship not the Crucified, let him be anathema and be numbered among the deicides. (#101)

That which He has not assumed [in the Incarnation] He has not healed; but that which is united to His Godhead is saved. If only half Adam fell, then

---

6   Excerpts taken from Hardy, *Christology*, pp. 215–232.

that which Christ assumes and saves may be half also; but if the whole of his nature fell, it must be united to the whole nature of Him that was begotten, and so be saved as a whole. (#101)

I never have honored and never can honor anything above the Nicene faith, that of the Holy Fathers who met there to destroy the Arian heresy; but am, and by God's help ever will be, of that faith, completing in detail that which was incompletely said by them concerning the Holy Spirit; for that question had not then been mooted—namely, that we are to believe that the Father, Son, and Holy Spirit are of one Godhead, thus confessing the Spirit also to be God. (#102)

I join in one the Son, who was begotten of the Father, and afterward of the Virgin Mary, and . . . I do not call Him two sons, but worship Him as one and the same in undivided Godhead and honor. (#102)

We must worship, not a God-bearing man, but a flesh-bearing God. (#102)

Nothing is or ever has been more valuable in our eyes than peace. (#102)

~ Gregory of Nyssa

Gregory of Nyssa (c. 330–395), the younger brother of Basil of Caesarea, was the most brilliant and subtle thinker of the three Cappadocian Fathers. He developed a distinctive approach to Christian mysticism and was a stalwart defender of orthodox Christianity; he played a prominent role at the Council of Constantinople in 381. Widely learned himself, he taught that pagan learning could be well used for the benefit of Christianity, provided it was purified of its defilements and integrated faithfully into genuinely Christian approaches to thought and life.

Gregory produced many works—commentaries, treatises, and controversial literature. His *On Religious Instruction* stands as a solid summary of the Christian faith, and his *The Life of Moses* opened up new paths for mystical practice and teaching. He wrote *On the Making of Humanity* to serve as the completion of his brother Basil's *In Hexaemeron:* Basil had lamented not giving fuller attention to humanity's creation in his treatment, and Gregory set about to fill that gap.

An Answer to Ablabius: That We Should Not Think of Saying There Are Three Gods[1]

No damage arises from a misguided use of words about humanity. However, in teaching about God the indiscriminate use of words entails no similar freedom from danger: trifles here are far from trifling. {p. 258}

---

[1] Excerpts taken from Edward E. Hardy, trans., *Christology of the Later Fathers* (Louisville, KY: Westminster John Knox Press, 1954), pp. 256–267.

Following the suggestions of Holy Scripture, we have learned that God's nature cannot be named and is ineffable. We say that every name, whether invented by human custom or handed down by the Scriptures, is indicative of our conceptions of the divine nature, but does not signify what that nature is in itself. {p. 259}

Whatever terms there are to lead us to the knowledge of God, each of them contains a particular idea of its own; and you will not find any word among the terms especially applied to God which is without some meaning. From this it is clear that the divine nature in itself is not signified by any of these terms; rather, some attribute is declared by what is said. For we say, perhaps, that the Divine is incorruptible or powerful or whatever else we are in the habit of saying. But in each of these terms we find a particular idea which by thought and expression we rightly attribute to the divine nature, but which does not express what that nature essentially is. {p. 259}

We do not learn that the Father does something on His own, in which the Son does not cooperate. Or again, that the Son acts on His own without the Spirit. Rather, every operation which extends from God to creation and is designated according to our differing conceptions of it has its origin in the Father, proceeds through the Son, and reaches its completion by the Holy Spirit. {pp. 261–262}

We believe that the divine nature is unlimited and incomprehensible, and hence we do not conceive of its being comprehended. But we declare that the nature is in every way to be thought of as infinite. . . . Therefore that which is without limit is certainly not limited by the word we use for it. In order, then, that our conception of the divine nature should remain unlimited, we say that the Divine transcends every name for it. {p. 264}

We must realize that Scripture uses the prevailing mode of speech. It does not lay down rules about how words ought to be used in one way or another. It does not record these phrases by way of giving technical instruction in the use of language. But it uses the word according to prevailing custom, having only this in view, that the word may be helpful to those who receive it. It does not use language with precision in matters where no harm arises in the understanding of the phrases. Indeed, it would be a lengthy task to list the inaccurate expressions from Scripture to prove my point. But where there is danger of a point of truth being perverted, we no longer find this careless and indifferent use of words in Scripture. {p. 265}

Although we acknowledge the divine nature is undifferentiated, we do not deny a distinction with respect to causality. That is the only way by which we distinguish one Person from the other. {p. 266}

The principle of causality distinguishes the Persons of the Holy Trinity. It affirms that the one is uncaused, while the other depends on the cause. But the divine nature is in every way understood to be without distinction or difference. {p. 267}

An Address on Religious Instruction (also known as Catechetical Oration)[2]

The same method of teaching... is not suitable for everyone who approaches this word.... We must adapt our method of therapy to the form of the disease. (Introduction)

If someone willfully closes his eyes in broad daylight, the sun is not responsible for his failure to see. (§7)

He who is able to grasp all things within His knowledge, and sees the future equally with the past, was not ignorant that humanity would deviate from the good. But just as He saw humankind's perversion, so He perceived its restoration once more to the good. Which, then, was better? Not to have brought our nature into being at all, since He knew in advance that the one to be created would stray from the good? Or, having brought it into being, to restore it by repentance, sick as it was, to its original grace? (§8)

By Adam's turning from life, death came in instead. Privation of light engendered darkness. Absence of virtue brought in wickedness; and in the place of every form of goodness there was now to be reckoned the list of opposing evils. By thoughtlessness, humankind fell into this condition. (§8)

If you inquire how the Deity is united with human nature, it is appropriate for you first to ask in what way the soul is united to the body. If the manner

---

2 Excerpted from Hardy, *Christology,* pp. 268–325.

in which your soul is joined to your body is a mystery, you must certainly not imagine the former question is within your grasp. (§11)

While we believe that the corporeal and intelligent creation owes its being to the incorporeal and uncreated nature, our faith in this regard does not involve an examination of the source and manner of this. The fact of creation we accept; but we renounce a curious investigation of the way the universe was framed as a matter altogether ineffable and inexplicable. (§11)

Of God's very existence one can get no other proof than the testimony of His actions themselves. (§12)

Every objection of unbelievers would be removed, if we could actually see what we only hope for. But our hopes await the ages to come, so that there may then be revealed what at present our faith alone apprehends. (§17)

Throughout the world, churches and altars have been erected in the name of Christ; and the holy and bloodless priesthood and the sublime philosophy which consists in deeds rather than words now flourishes. (§18)

[Regarding how God accomplished salvation:] In what, then, did God's justice consist in this matter? In his not exercising an arbitrary authority over the one who held us in bondage. Also, in His not wresting us from the one who held us, by His superior power, and so leaving the one who had enslaved humankind through pleasure with a just cause of complaint. (§22)

When once we had voluntarily sold ourselves, He who undertook out of goodness to restore our freedom had to contrive a just and not a dictatorial method to do so. And some such method is this: to give the master the chance to take whatever he wants as the price of the slave. (§22)

What, then, would he exchange for those in his power, if not something clearly superior and better? Thus, by getting the better of the bargain he might the more satisfy his pride. (§23)

When the enemy saw such power, he recognized in Christ a bargain which offered him more than he held. For this reason he chose Him as the ransom for those he had shut up in death's prison. Since, however, he could not look upon the direct vision of God, he had to see Him clothed in some part of that flesh which he already held captive through sin. Consequently the Deity was veiled in flesh, so that the enemy, by seeing something familiar and natural to him, might not be terrified at the approach of transcendent power. So when he saw this power softly reflected more and more through the miracles, he reckoned that what he saw was to be desired rather than feared. (§23)

God's transcendent power is not so much displayed in the vastness of the heavens, or the luster of the stars, or the orderly arrangement of the universe or His perpetual oversight of it, as it is in His condescension to our weak nature. We marvel at the way the sublime entered a state of lowliness and, while actually seen in it, did not leave the heights. We marvel at the way the Godhead was entwined in human nature and, while becoming man, did not cease to be God. (§24)

In that way, as it is with greedy fish, he might swallow the Godhead like a fishhook along with the flesh, which was the bait. Thus, when life came to dwell with death and light shone upon darkness, their contraries might vanish away. For it is not in the nature of darkness to endure the presence of light, nor can death exist where life is active. (§24)

What is there improbable in what we learn from the gospel revelation? Purity lays hold of those stained with sin, life lays hold of the dead, and guidance is given to those astray, so that the stain may be cleansed, the error corrected, and the dead may return to life. (§24)

He united Himself with our nature, in order that by its union with the divine it might become divine. . . . With His return from death, our mortal race begins its return to immortal life. (§25)

Justice is evident in the rendering of due recompense, by which the deceiver was in turn deceived. The purpose of the action, on the other hand, testifies to the goodness of Him who brought it about. For it is the mark of justice to render to everyone the results of what he originally planted, just as the earth yields fruits according to the types of seed sown. It is the mark of wisdom, however, by the way in which it returns like for like, not to exclude a higher aim. (§26)

So it is with the Incarnation. By the principle of justice the deceiver reaps the harvest of the seeds he sowed with his own free will. For he who first deceived man by the bait of pleasure is himself deceived by the camouflage of human nature. But the purpose of the action changes it into something good. For the one practiced deceit to ruin our nature; the other, being at once just and good and wise, used a deceitful device to save the one who had been ruined. (§26)

Certainly it was in keeping with His intimate union with our nature that He should be united with us in all our characteristics. Those who wash dirt off garments do not leave some of the stains and remove others. But, from top to bottom, they cleanse the whole garment of the stains, to give it a consistent character and a uniform brightness from the washing. It is the same with our human life, which from beginning to end and throughout was stained with sin. The cleansing power had to penetrate it entirely. One part could not be healed by cleansing while another was overlooked and left uncured. (§27)

The Most High . . . , by reason of His transcendent nature, is unapproachable. The whole universe is uniformly beneath His dignity. . . . Earth is not more below His dignity, and heaven less. Nor do the creatures inhabiting each of these elements differ in this respect, that some have a direct contact with His inaccessible nature, while others are distant from it. (§27)

The only thing alien to the divine is evil. Nature is not evil. (§28)

Now had we, in the course of our argument, contended that the divine will allots faith to people in such a way that some are called, while others fail to share in the calling, there would be occasion to prefer such a charge against our religion. But all are equally called without respect to rank, age, or nationality. . . . Out of His high regard for humanity, the Sovereign of the universe left something under our own control and of which each of us is the sole master. I mean the will, a faculty which is free from bondage and independent, and is grounded in the freedom of the mind. (§30)

If the will is inactive, virtue of necessity vanishes, being precluded by the inertness of the will. (§31)

The fact that faith has not taken root in all people is not to be charged against God's goodness, but against the disposition of those to whom the gospel is preached. (§31)

What has come down to us from tradition is as follows: everything spoken and done in the gospel has a higher, divine meaning. There is no exception to this principle whereby a complete mingling of the divine and the human is indicated. The word and the act proceed in a human way, but their secret meaning reveals the Divine. (§32)

We do not doubt the presence of what He has promised, because His promise is true. (§34)

It is the same with those who are altogether persuaded by the truthfulness of His promise that His grace is present in those who are born again through this sacramental act [of baptism]. . . . For we are convinced that grace accompanies the rite in any case, since He who made the promise is God. (§34)

The manner of our salvation owes its efficacy less to instruction by teaching than to what He who entered into fellowship with humankind actually did. (§35)

Thus the reason we have to enact in advance and by water the grace of the resurrection is to assure us that it is just as easy to be baptized in water as it is to rise again from the dead. (§35)

Both common sense and the teaching of Scripture indicate that one cannot enter the divine fellowship unless that person has entirely washed away all stains of sin. (§36)

You observe how small a thing it is to begin with and how easily accomplished—just faith and water: faith which is a matter of our own choice, and water which is natural to human life. But what a blessing springs from these things—no less than kinship with God Himself. (§36)

The reason that God, when He revealed Himself, united Himself with our mortal nature was to deify humanity by this close relation with Deity. In consequence, by means of His flesh, which is constituted by bread and wine, He implants Himself [in the Eucharist] in all believers, following out the plan of grace. (§37)

Existence is divided into what is created and what is uncreated. (§39)

The change our life undergoes through rebirth would not be a change were we to continue in our present state. I do not, indeed, see how one who continues the same can be reckoned to have become different, when there is no noticeable alteration in him. For it is patent to everyone that we receive the saving birth for the purpose of renewing and changing our nature. Yet baptism produces no essential change in human nature. (§40)

If, then, as the prophet says, when we undergo this sacramental "washing" we become "clean" in our wills and wash away "the iniquities" of our souls, we become better and are changed for the better. But if the washing has only affected the body, and the soul has failed to wash off the stains of passion, and the life after initiation is identical with that before, despite the boldness of my assertion I will say without shrinking that in such a case the water is only water, and the gift of the Holy Spirit is nowhere evident in the action. (§40)

If this sort of thing characterizes someone's life as much after baptism as before it, I cannot see that he has undergone any change, since he appears just the same person as before. (§40)

The gospel says of the regenerate that "He gave all those who received him the power to become children of God" [John 1:12]. Now the child born of someone certainly shares his parent's nature. If, then, you have received God and become His child, let your way of life testify to the God within you; make it clear who your Father is! (§40)

Those, therefore, who are wise should set their eyes, not on this present life, but on that to come. In this short and fleeting existence they should lay the foundations of untold blessedness. (§40)

On the Making of Humanity[3]

When the Maker of all had prepared beforehand, as it were, a royal lodging for the future king (the land and islands and sea, and the heaven arching like a roof over them), and when all kinds of wealth had been stored in this palace (and by wealth I mean the whole creation—all that is in plants and trees, and all that has sense, and breath, and life; and [if we are to account materials also as wealth] all that for their beauty are reckoned precious in the eyes of humankind, as gold and silver, and the substances of your jewels which people delight in [having concealed, I say, abundance of all these also in the bosom of the earth as in a royal treasure-house]), He thus manifests humanity in the world, to be the beholder of some of its wonders and the lord of others; that by his enjoyment he might have knowledge of the Giver, and by the beauty and majesty of the things he saw might trace out that power of the Maker which is beyond speech and language.

For this reason humankind was brought into the world last after the creation, not being rejected to the last as worthless, but as one whom it behooved to be king over his subjects at his very birth. (2:1–2)

God gave humanity the instincts of a two-fold organization, blending the divine with the earthy, that by means of both he may be naturally and properly disposed to each enjoyment, enjoying God by means of his more divine nature, and the good things of earth by the sense that is akin to them. (2:2)

The creation was, as it were, made off-hand by God and came into existence at once on His command, but divine counsel preceded the making of humankind. (3:1)

As painters transfer human forms to their pictures by means of certain colors, laying on their copy the proper and corresponding tints, so that the beauty of the original may be accurately transferred to the likeness, so I would have you understand that our Maker also, painting the portrait to resemble His own beauty, by the addition of virtues, as it were with colors, shows in us His own sovereignty. (5:1)

He who said, "Let us make humankind after our image" [Gen 1:26] revealed the Holy Trinity by the plural signification. (6:3)

---

[3] Excerpts taken from NPNF (2nd) 5:387–427.

Humankind was made last after the animals, as nature advanced in an orderly course to perfection. (8:5)

"Who has known the mind of the Lord?" [Rom 11:34], the apostle asks; and I ask further, who has understood his own mind? Let those tell us who consider the nature of God to be within their comprehension, whether they understand themselves—if they know the nature of their own mind. (11:2)

One of the attributes we contemplate in the divine nature is incomprehensibility. (11:3)

The life of our bodies, material and subject to flux, always advancing by way of motion, finds the power of its being in this, that it never rests from its motion. (13:1)

"Let us make humankind in our image, according to our likeness" [Gen 1:26]. How mean and unworthy of the majesty of humankind are the fancies of some heathen writers, who magnify humanity, as they supposed, by comparing it to this world! They say that humanity is a little world [i.e., "microcosm"], composed of the same elements with the universe. Those who bestow on human nature such praise as this by a high-sounding name forget that they are dignifying humans with the attributes of the gnat and the mouse.... In what then does the greatness of humanity consist, according to the doctrine of the Church? Not in its likeness to the created world, but in being in the image of the Creator. (16:1–2)

The image is properly so called if it keeps its resemblance to the prototype. (16:3)

There is in us the principle of all excellence, all virtue and wisdom, and every higher thing that we conceive: but preeminent among all is the fact that we are free from necessity, and not in bondage to any natural power, but have decision in our own power as we please. (16:11)

What difference do we discern between the Divine and that which has been made like to the Divine? We find it in the fact that the former is uncreated, while the latter has its being from Creation. And this distinction of property brings with it a train of other properties; for it is certainly acknowledged that the uncreated nature is also immutable, and always remains the same, while the created nature cannot exist without change. (16:12)

The image of God is not in part of our nature. (16:17)

Humanity seems to me to bear a double likeness to opposite things—being molded in the divine element of his mind to the divine beauty, but bearing, in the passionate impulses that arise in him, a likeness to the animals. (18:3)

Wickedness is not so strong as to prevail over the power of good; nor is the folly of our nature more powerful and more abiding than the wisdom of God. (21:1)

It is one's duty, as the proclamation is clearly made to all that the time of change will come [i.e., the final day], not to trouble oneself about times (for he said that "it is not for us to know the times and the periods that the Father has set by his own authority" [Acts 1:7]), nor to pursue calculations, for by these one will surely sap the hope of the resurrection in the soul. (22:8)

Our reason suggests difficulties on many points, offering no small occasions for doubt as to the things which we believe. (23:2)

We believe that all things are of God, as the Scripture says. However, the question how they were in God is a question beyond our reason, and we do not seek to pry into it. (23:4)

[Regarding prophecies:] The Lord foretold these things and others like them, not for the sake of the matters themselves—for what great advantage would it have been to the hearers, at any rate, to have a prediction of what was about to happen? They would have known by experience, even if they had not previously learned what would come. But He foretold them, so that by these means faith on their part might follow concerning more important matters [which He would declare to them]. (25:4)

[Regarding the future resurrection:] There are some who, owing to the feebleness of human reasoning, and judging the divine power by the compass of our own, maintain that what is beyond our capacity is not possible even to God. (26:1)

[With regard to the resurrection of human bodies:] If you are not ignorant of any of the things in your hand, do you deem the knowledge of God to be feebler than your own, that it should fail to discover the most minute of the things that are within the compass of the divine span? (26:2)

Now may we all return to that divine grace in which God at the first created humanity, when He said, "Let us make humankind in our image, according to our likeness" [Gen 1:26]; to Him be glory and might forever and ever. (34)

Against Eunomius[4]

In the faith which was delivered by God to the apostles we admit neither subtraction, nor alteration, nor addition. . . . Whatever is said otherwise than in exact accord with the truth is assuredly false, not true. (2:1)

As to essence, He [God] is one; that is why the Lord ordained that we should look to one name. But through what is said about the Persons, our belief in Him is distinguished into belief in the Father, the Son, and the Holy Spirit. He is divided without separation and united without confusion. (2:2)

The benevolent dispensation of the Holy Spirit, in delivering to us the divine mysteries, imparts that instruction which transcends reason by such methods as we can receive. . . . Its expression must stoop to our low capacity. (2:9)

In the tradition of the faith delivered by the truth, we are taught to believe in Father, Son, and Holy Spirit. (2:9)

Now sin is nothing else than alienation from God, who is the true and only life. Accordingly, the first man lived many hundred years after his disobedience, and yet God did not lie when he said, "In the day that you eat of it you shall die" [Gen 2:17]. For in being alienated from the true life, the sentence of death was ratified against him that very day; after this, at a much later time, there followed also the bodily death of Adam. (2:13)

The same person is Son of God and was made, in the Incarnation, Son

---

4 Excerpts taken from NPNF (2nd) 5:33–248.

of Man, so that by His communion with each He might link together by Himself what were divided by nature. (3:4)

Since the Deity is too excellent and lofty to be expressed in words, we have learned to honor in silence what transcends speech and thought. (3:5)

We believe, as those "who from the beginning were eyewitnesses and servants of the word" [Luke 1:2] delivered to us by the Holy Scriptures, that the God who was in the beginning "afterwards," as Baruch says, "appeared on earth and lived with humankind" [Bar 3:37]. Becoming a ransom for our death, He loosed the bonds of death by His own Resurrection, and by Himself made the resurrection a way for all flesh. And being on the same throne and in the same glory with His own Father, on the day of judgment He will give sentence upon those who are judged, according to what they have deserved by the lives they have led. (5:3)

For this reason we do not cease to extol Him exceedingly, as much as we can, that He who because of His unspeakable and unapproachable greatness is not comprehensible by any, except by Himself and the Father and the Holy Spirit, was able even to descend to community with our weakness. (5:3)

To the Ephesians, he [St. Paul] describes by the figure of the Cross the power that controls and holds the universe together, when he expresses a desire that they may be exalted to know the exceeding glory of this power, calling it height and depth and breadth and length [Eph 3:18], speaking of the several projections we behold in the figure of the Cross by their proper names—he calls the upper part "height," and that which is below, on the opposite side, "depth," while by the terms "length" and "breadth" he indicates the cross-beam projecting to either side—that thereby might be manifested this great mystery, that both things in heaven, and things under the earth, and all the furthest bounds of the things that are, are ruled and sustained by Him who gave an example of this unspeakable and mighty power in the figure of the Cross. (5:3)

The Scripture "inspired by God," as the apostle says, is the Scripture of the Holy Spirit, and its intention is the profit of humankind. For "all scripture is inspired by God and is useful," to varied and manifold purposes—"for teaching, for reproof, for correction, and for training in righteousness" [2 Tim 3:16]. . . . The divine intention lies hidden under the body of the

Scripture, as it were under a veil, some legislative enactment or some historical narrative being cast over the truths that are contemplated by the mind.... That is why he says, "the letter kills, but the Spirit gives life" [2 Cor 3:6], showing that often the obvious interpretation, if not taken according to the proper sense, has an effect contrary to that life which is indicated by the Spirit. (7:1)

As the hollow of one's hand is to the whole deep, so is all the power of language in comparison with that nature which is unspeakable and incomprehensible. (7:4)

The loving dispensation of the Holy Spirit, in delivering to us the divine mysteries, conveys Its instruction on those matters which transcend language by means of what is within our capacity as It does also constantly elsewhere, when It portrays the Divinity in bodily terms, making mention, in speaking concerning God, of His eye, His eyelids, His ear, His fingers, His hand, His right hand, His arm, His feet, His shoes, and the like—none of which can be said to belong in its primary sense to the divine nature. But turning Its teaching to what we can easily perceive, It describes by terms well worn in human use facts that are beyond every name, while by each of the terms employed concerning God we are led analogically to some more exalted conception. (8:4)

The ultimate division of all that exists is made by the line between created and uncreated. (8:5)

He has taken all that was ours, on the terms of giving to us in return what is His. (10:4)

Having learned from the holy voice of Christ that unless one is born again of water and of the Spirit he shall not enter into the kingdom of God [John 3:3, 6], and that whoever eats His flesh and drinks His blood shall live forever [John 6: 51, 54], we are persuaded that the mystery of godliness is ratified by the confession of the divine names—the names of the Father, the Son, and the Holy Spirit—and that our salvation is confirmed by participation in the sacramental customs and tokens. (11:5)

The sacramental tokens... secure spiritual blessings and avert from believers the assaults directed against them by the wiles of the evil one. (11:5)

Since, as the apostle tells us, "the woman was deceived and became a transgressor" [1 Tim 2:14] and was by her disobedience foremost in the revolt from God, woman became the first witness of the Resurrection, that she might retrieve by her faith in the Resurrection the overthrow caused by her disobedience. By making herself at the beginning a minister and advocate to her husband of the counsels of the serpent, she brought into human life the beginning of evil and its train of consequences; so, by ministering to his disciples the words of Him who slew the rebel dragon, she became to men the guide to faith, whereby with good reason the first proclamation of death is annulled. (12:1)

Answer to Eunomius's Second Book[5]

There is no faculty in human nature adequate to the full comprehension of the divine essence. {p. 257}

With regard to the Creator of the world, we know that He exists, but of His essential nature we cannot deny that we are ignorant. {p. 257}

The desire of investigating what is obscure and tracing out hidden things by the operation of human reasoning gives an entrance to false no less than true notions, since the one who aspires to know the unknown will not always arrive at truth, but may also conceive of falsehood itself as truth. {p. 260}

For in speculative inquiry fallacies readily find place. But where speculation is entirely at rest, the necessity of error is precluded. And that this is true may be seen if we consider how it is that heresies in the churches have wandered off into many and various opinions in regard to God, people deceiving themselves as they were swayed by one mental impulse or another. {p. 260}

In the canon [of Scripture], in revealing God—so long unknown to humanity because of the prevalence of idolatry—and making Him known to humanity, both from the wonders which manifest themselves in His works and from the names which express the manifold variety of His power, the sacred writers lead human beings, as by the hand, to the understanding of the divine nature, making known to them the bare grandeur of the thought

---

5 Excerpts taken from NPNF (2nd) 5:250–314.

of God, while they dismiss the question of His essence, as impossible to grasp, and bearing no fruit for the curious inquirer, without any attempt at its solution. . . . Concerning God Himself, they exhort people to "believe that he exists and that he rewards those who seek him" [Heb 11:6], but in regard to His nature, as being above every name, they neither name it nor concern themselves about it. For if we have learned any names expressive of the knowledge of God, all these are related and have analogy to such names as denote human characteristics. {p. 260}

How can one who is ignorant of himself take knowledge of anything that is above himself? If one recognizes his own self-ignorance, is that not enough to teach him plainly not to be astonished at any of the mysteries that are without? {p. 262}

Reason supplies us with only a dim and imperfect comprehension of the divine nature. Even so, the knowledge that we gather from the terms which piety allows us to apply to it is sufficient for our limited capacity. {p. 263}

Whatever be the nature of God, He is not to be apprehended by sense and transcends reason, even though human thought, busying itself with curious inquiry, with such help of reason as it can command, stretches out its hand and just touches His unapproachable and sublime nature, being neither keen-sighted enough to see clearly what is invisible, nor yet so far withheld from approach as to be unable to catch some faint glimpse of what it seeks to know. . . . It is a sort of knowledge to know that what is sought transcends knowledge. {p. 264}

Whatever discovery has been made in human life, conducive to any useful purposes of peace or war, came to us from nowhere else but an intelligence conceiving and discovering according to our several requirements—and that intelligence is a gift of God. {p. 268}

[Regarding God's speaking Creation into existence:] Who does not know, even if he is the merest simpleton, that there is a natural correlation between hearing and speech, and that, as it is impossible for hearing to discharge its function when no one is speaking, so also speech is ineffectual unless directed to hearing? If, then, he means literally that "God said," let him tell us also to what hearing His words were addressed. Does he mean that God said them to Himself? If so, the commands which He issues, He issues to

Himself. Yet who will accept this interpretation, that God sits upon His throne prescribing what He Himself must do, and employing Himself as His minister to do his bidding? {pp. 270–271}

We assert that the words, "He said," do not imply voice and words on the part of God, but that the writer, in showing the power of God to be concurrent with His will, renders the idea easier for us to understand. For since by the will of God all things were created, and it is the ordinary way of human beings to signify their will first of all by speech, and so to bring their work into harmony with their will, and since the scriptural account of the creation is the learner's introduction, as it were, to the knowledge of God, representing to our minds the power of the divine being by objects easier for us to comprehend (for sensible apprehension is an aid to intellectual knowledge), for this reason Moses, by saying that God commanded all things to be, signifies to us the inciting power of His will—and by adding, "and it was so," he shows that in the case of God there is no difference between will and performance. {p. 273}

We maintain that the grace of God "spoke . . . in many and various ways by the prophets" [Heb 1:1], ordering their voices conformably to our capacity and the modes of expression with which we are familiar, and that by such means it leads us, as with a guiding hand, to the knowledge of higher truths, not teaching us in terms proportioned to their inherent sublimity (for how can the great be contained by the little?), but descending to the lower level of our limited comprehension. {p. 275}

But before the Creation of the world, since there was no one to hear the word, and no bodily element capable of accentuating the articulating voice, how can one who says that God used words give any air of probability to his assertion? {p. 275}

If God spoke in human language before the Creation, whom was He to benefit by using it? {p. 276}

Though exalted far above our nature and inaccessible to all approach, like a tender mother who joins in the inarticulate utterances of her baby, [God] gives to our human nature what it is capable of receiving. Thus, in the various manifestations of God to humanity He adapts Himself to humankind and speaks in human language and assumes wrath and pity and other emotions, so that through feelings corresponding to our own, our infantile life might be led as by the hand and lay hold of the divine nature by means of the words which His foresight has given. {p. 292}

The divine being suffers no loss because we are at a loss for a naturally appropriate name. Our inability to find a way to express such unutterable things, while it reflects upon the poverty of our own nature, affords an evidence of God's glory, teaching us as it does, in the words of the apostle, that the only name naturally appropriate to God is to believe Him to be "above every name" [Phil 2:9]. That he transcends every effort of thought and is far beyond any circumscribing by a name, constitutes a proof for us of His ineffable majesty. {p. 309}

On the Holy Spirit, against Macedonius[6]

What is it we receive in holy baptism? Is it not participation in a life no longer subject to death? I think that no one who can in any way be reckoned amongst Christians will deny that statement. What then? Is the life-giving power in the water itself which is employed to convey the grace of baptism? Or is it not rather clear to everyone that this element is only employed as a means in the external ministry, and of itself contributes nothing towards the sanctification, unless it is first transformed itself by the sanctification, and that what gives life to the baptized is the Spirit, as our Lord himself says in respect to Him with His own lips, "It is the spirit that gives life" [John 6:63]? {p. 322}

On Virginity[7]

Let no one think that we depreciate marriage as an institution. We are well aware that it is not a stranger to God's blessing. But the common instincts of humankind can plead sufficiently for it. (ch. 8)

The habit of sinning entered as we have described [recounting the story of Adam and Eve], and with fatal quickness, into the life of humanity, and from that small beginning spread into this infinitude of evil. (ch. 12)

---

6 Excerpts taken from NPNF (2nd) 5:315–325.
7 Excerpts taken from NPNF (2nd) 5:343–371.

On the Soul and the Resurrection[8]

We make the Holy Scriptures the rule and the measure of every tenet; we necessarily fix our eyes upon that, and approve that alone which may be made to harmonize with the intention of those writings. {p. 439}

The true explanation of all these questions is still stored up in the hidden treasure-rooms of wisdom and will not come to light until that moment when we shall be taught the mystery of the resurrection by the reality of it. Then there will be no more need of phrases to explain the things which we now hope for. Just as many questions might be stated for debate amongst people sitting up at night as to the kind of thing that sunshine is, and then the simple appearing of it in all its beauty would render any verbal description superfluous, so every calculation that tries to arrive conjecturally at the future state will be reduced to nothingness by the object of our hopes when it comes upon us. {p. 464}

The Divine power, in the superabundance of omnipotence, not only restores you that body once dissolved, but makes great and splendid additions to it, by which the human being is furnished still more magnificently. "What is sown," he says, "is perishable, what is raised is imperishable. It is sown in dishonor, it is raised in glory. It is sown in weakness, it is raised in power. It is sown a physical body, it is raised a spiritual body" [1 Cor 15:42–44]. {p. 466}

On the Baptism of Christ[9]

Christ, then, was born as it were a few days ago—He whose generation was before all things, sensible and intellectual. Today He is baptized by John, so that He might cleanse him who was defiled, that He might bring the Spirit from above and exalt humanity to heaven, that he who had fallen might be raised up and he who had cast him down might be put to shame. {p. 518}

It is not the water that bestows these gifts (for in that case it would be something more exalted than all creation), but the command of God, and the visitation of the Spirit that comes sacramentally to set us free. But water serves to express the cleansing. {p. 519}

---

8   Excerpts taken from NPNF (2nd) 5:430–468.
9   Excerpts taken from NPNF (2nd) 5:518–524.

The bread, again, is at first common bread, but when the sacramental action consecrates it, it is called and becomes the body of Christ. {p. 519}

By a similar train of reasoning, water also, although it is nothing else than water, renews a person to spiritual regeneration when the grace from above hallows it. And if anyone answers me by raising a difficulty with his questions and doubts, asking repeatedly and inquiring how water and the sacramental act that is performed in it regenerate, I most justly reply to that person, "Show me the mode of that generation which is after the flesh, and I will explain to you the power of regeneration in the soul." {p. 520}

To speak concisely, everywhere the power of God and His operation are incomprehensible and incapable of being reduced to rule, easily producing whatever He wills, while concealing from us the minute knowledge of His operation. {p. 520}

The Lord's Prayer[10]

When the consciousness of God is firmly established in the heart, the devices of the devil remain sterile. (Sermon 1)

The person who makes prayer without being properly taught will not lift himself up to the height of the Giver, but will want the divine power to descend to the mean, earthly level of his own desires. (Sermon 1)

[On calling God "Our Father in heaven":] If we call our Father Him who is incorruptible and righteous and good, we must prove by our life that the kinship is real. (Sermon 2)

Of all good things the most important for me is that God's name should be glorified through my life. (Sermon 3)

We fell ill when we forsook the wholesome way of life in Paradise and filled ourselves with the poison of disobedience, through which our nature was conquered by this evil and deadly disease. Then there came the true Physician who cured the evil perfectly by its opposite, as is the law of medicine. (Sermon 4)

---

10 Excerpts taken from ACW 18:21–84.

[On the petition, "Forgive us our debts as we forgive our debtors":] You must be your own judge, your own lawgiver. By the disposition you show to the one who is under obligation to you you pronounce the judgment of heaven on yourself. (Sermon 5)

The Beatitudes[11]

The goal of the life of virtue is to become like God. (Sermon 1)

The same thing by which the devil had caused his own downfall to earth caused the miserable human race to fling itself down with him into a common ruin. There is no other evil so harmful to our nature as that which is caused by pride. (Sermon 1)

How can one best show the emptiness of pride? How, indeed, but by showing nature as it is? . . . Even if one would flatter our condition and greatly vaunt the human nobility, he will have to trace the pedigree of our nature to clay, and so the high dignity of the proud is related to bricks. (Sermon 1)

The Beatitudes are arranged in order like so many steps, so as to facilitate the ascent from one to the other. (Sermon 2)

The Word, who came down to us because we were unable to rise up to Him, adapts Himself to the lowliness of our understanding. Therefore He communicates the divine mysteries by words and names that are intelligible to us and uses such expressions as are within the range of human life and circumstances. (Sermon 2)

It was impossible that those good things that are above the sense experience and knowledge of human beings should be revealed to them by their proper names. (Sermon 2)

The inspired book teaches us in metaphors. (Sermon 2)

What human thought can search out the nature of what we seek? What names or expressions can we invent to produce in us a worthy conception of the light beyond? How shall I name the invisible, how describe the

---

11 Excerpts taken from ACW 18:85–175.

immaterial? How shall I show what cannot be seen, or comprehend what has neither size nor quantity, neither quality nor form? How can I grasp what is neither in place nor in time, which eludes all limitation and every form of definition? (Sermon 3)

It is impossible that such a thing should come within the scope of our comprehension. We have, however, gained one advantage from our examination: we have succeeded in forming an idea of the greatness of what we have sought by the very fact of having been unable to perceive it. (Sermon 3)

He who was ordained to rule has been enslaved. . . . He who lived in the delights of Paradise has migrated to this place of toil and sickness. . . . He who was once independent and self-determining is now ruled by so many tremendous evils that it is hard for us even to count our masters. . . . Each of our impulses, when it takes control, becomes the master and we the slave. (Sermon 3)

When desire goes beyond the limits of lawful need, what else is this than the counsel of the devil? (Sermon 4)

We need an unceasing desire for higher things, which is not content to acquiesce in past achievements; we ought to count it a loss if we fail to progress further. (Sermon 5)

To incline towards the good is one of the inherent characteristics of human nature. . . . If evil was presented to our life in its nakedness, unadorned with some semblance of good, mortals would surely not fly to it so easily. (Sermon 5)

The conception of the Divine is by nature inherent in all humans; but ignorance of the true God is responsible for the gross errors in regard to the object of worship. (Sermon 5)

The divine nature, whatever it may be in itself, surpasses every mental concept. It is altogether inaccessible to reasoning and conjecture, nor has there been found any human faculty capable of perceiving the incomprehensible; for we cannot devise a means of understanding inconceivable things. (Sermon 6)

Since such is He whose nature is above every nature, the invisible and incomprehensible is seen and apprehended in another manner. Many are the modes of such perception. For it is possible to see Him who has "made all things in wisdom" [Ps 104:24] by way of inference through the wisdom that appears in the universe. . . . When we look at the order of Creation, we form in our minds an image not of the essence, but of the wisdom of Him who has made all things wisely. . . . For He is invisible by nature, but becomes visible in His energies. (Sermon 6)

Somehow evil is mixed up with our nature through those who first succumbed to passion and by their transgression made a permanent place for the disease. (Sermon 6)

I have heard the divinely inspired Scriptures disclose marvelous things about the transcendent nature—yet what are they compared with that nature itself? For even if I were capable of grasping all that the Scripture says, yet that which is signified is more. (Sermon 7)

Human life lies between the boundaries of good and evil. (Sermon 8)

Let us not be sorrowful, then, if we are persecuted, but rather let us rejoice, because by being chased away from earthly honors, we are driven towards the heavenly good. For this He has promised, that those who have been persecuted for His sake shall be blessed, for theirs is the Kingdom of heaven, by the grace of our Lord Jesus Christ, to whom be glory and power forever and ever. (Sermon 8)

The Life of Moses[12]

In the case of virtue we have learned from the apostle that its one limit of perfection is the fact that it has no limit. (1:5)

To stop on the path of virtue is to begin on the path of evil. (1:6)

It may be that human perfection consists precisely in this constant growth in the good. (1:8)

---

12 Excerpts taken from Abraham J. Malherbe and Everett Ferguson, trans., *Gregory of Nyssa: The Life of Moses* (Mahwah, NJ: Paulist Press, 1978), pp. 27–137.

We should show great diligence not to fall away from the perfection which is attainable but to acquire as much as is possible: to that extent let us make progress within the realm of what we seek. For the perfection of human nature consists perhaps in its very growth in goodness. (1:10)

Human nature is divided into male and female, and the free choice of virtue or of evil is set before both equally. (1:12)

The one who is going to associate intimately with God must go beyond all that is visible and—lifting up his own mind, as to a mountaintop, to the invisible and incomprehensible—believe that the Divine is there where the understanding does not reach. (1:46)

Envy is the congenital malady in human nature. (1:61)

Profane education is truly barren; it is always in labor but never gives birth. (2:11)

If we should be involved with profane teachings during our education, we should not separate ourselves from the nourishment of the Church's milk. (2:12)

The victory of true religion is the death and destruction of idolatry. (2:15)

From this [the burning bush, which was not consumed] we learn also the mystery of the virgin: the light of Divinity which through birth shone from her into human life did not consume the burning bush, even as the flower of her virginity was not withered by giving birth. (2:21)

The foreign wife [Moses' Egyptian wife] will follow him, for there are certain things derived from profane education which should not be rejected when we propose to give birth to virtue . . . , provided that the offspring of this union introduce nothing of a foreign defilement. (2:37).

We have in ourselves, in our own nature and by our own choice, the causes of light or of darkness, since we place ourselves in whichever sphere we wish to be. (2:80)

[Regarding the Israelites' spoiling of the Egyptians as they left Egypt:] The loftier meaning is that those participating through virtue in the free life also should equip themselves with the wealth of pagan learning by which foreigners to the faith beautify themselves ... [and] receive such things as moral and natural philosophy, geometry, astronomy, dialectic, and whatever else is sought by those outside the Church, since these things will be useful when in time the divine sanctuary of mystery must be beautified with the riches of reason.

... It is possible to see this happening even now. For many bring to the Church of God their profane learning as a kind of gift. (2:115–116)

[Regarding the crossing of the Red Sea:] The water gives life to those who find refuge in it but destroys their pursuers.

This history teaches us what kind of people they should be who come through the water, bringing nothing of the opposing army along as they emerge from the water. . . . Those who pass through the mystical water in baptism must put to death in the water the whole phalanx of evil. (2:124–125)

The life of virtue becomes sweeter and more refreshing than all the sweetness that makes the senses tingle with pleasure, because it has been seasoned by our hope in the things to come. (2:132)

The knowledge of God is a mountain steep indeed and difficult to climb. (2:158)

[Regarding the darkness into which Moses entered on Mt. Sinai:] Religious knowledge comes at first to those who receive it as light. Therefore what is perceived to be contrary to religion is darkness, and the escape from darkness comes about when one participates in light. But as the mind progresses and, through an ever greater and more perfect diligence, comes to apprehend reality, as it approaches more nearly to contemplation, it sees more clearly what of the divine nature is uncontemplated.

For leaving behind everything that is observed, not only what sense comprehends but also what the intelligence thinks it sees, it keeps on penetrating deeper until by the intelligence's yearning for understanding it gains access to the invisible and the incomprehensible, and there it sees God. This is the true knowledge of what is sought; this is the seeing that consists in not seeing, because that which is sought transcends all knowledge, being separated on all sides by incomprehensibility as by a kind of darkness. (2:162–163)

Knowledge of the divine essence is unattainable not only by humans but also by every intelligent creature. (2:163)

[Regarding the first and second commandments:] The divine word at the beginning forbids that the Divine be likened to any of the things known by humans, since every concept which comes from some comprehensible image by an approximate understanding and by guessing at the divine nature constitutes an idol of God and does not proclaim God. (2:165)

We have received the authentic tradition of this mystery of our faith. (2:175)

But if we name such a God "tabernacle," the person who loves Christ should not be disturbed at all on the grounds that the suggestion involved in the phrase diminishes the magnificence of the nature of God. For neither is any other name worthy of the nature thus signified: all names equally fall short of accurate description, both those recognized as significant as well as those by which some great insight is indicated. (2:176)

Perfect virtue consists indeed of two things, having faith in God and living our lives according to our conscience. (2:192)

Hope always draws the soul from the beauty which is seen to what is beyond, always kindles the desire for the hidden through what is constantly perceived. (2:231)

The characteristic of the divine nature is to transcend all characteristics. (2:234)

The one who encloses the Divine by any boundary makes out that God is ruled over by an opposite. (2:238)

The true vision of God consists in this, that the soul that looks up to God never ceases to desire Him. (2:239)

Moses sought to see God, and this is the instruction he receives on how he is to see Him: seeing God means following Him wherever He might lead. (2:252)

Envy is the passion which causes evil, the father of death, the first entrance of sin, the root of wickedness.... For envy, it is not its own misfortune but another's good fortune that is unfortunate. (2:257–258)

The chief act of faith in the "mystery" is to look to Him who suffered the Passion for us. (2:273)

Overcoming one's pleasures does not mean being no longer liable to be seized by another kind of passion. (2:282)

It is in our power to remain unaffected by passion as long as we stay far away from the thing that enflames. (2:303)

This is true perfection: not to avoid a wicked life because like slaves we servilely fear punishment, nor to do good because we hope for rewards, as if cashing in on the virtuous life by some business-like and contractual arrangement. On the contrary, disregarding all those things for which we hope and which have been reserved by promise, we regard falling from God's friendship as the only thing dreadful and we consider becoming God's friend the only thing worthy of honor and desire. This, as I have said, is the perfection of life. (2:320)

Commentary on Ecclesiastes[13]

The life that bears a likeness to the divine is completely in accord with human nature. (Sermon 1) {p. 84}

He who ... transcends the universe must surely transcend speech. (Sermon 7) {p. 126}

The soul, slipping at every point from what cannot be grasped, becomes dizzy and perplexed and returns once again to what is connatural to it, content now to know merely this about the Transcendent, that it is completely different from the nature of the things that the soul knows. (Sermon 7) {p. 128}

In speaking of God, when there is question of His essence, then is the "time

---

13 Excerpted from Herbert Musurillo, S.J., trans. and ed., *From Glory to Glory: Texts from Gregory of Nyssa's Mystical Writings* (Crestwood, NY: St. Vladimir's Seminary Press, 1995), pp. 81–288.

to keep silence" [Eccl 3:7]. When, however, it is a question of His operation, a knowledge of which can come down even to us, that is the "time to speak" of His omnipotence by telling of His works and explaining His deeds, and to use words to this extent. (Sermon 7) {p. 128}

Commentary on the Canticles[14]

All human wisdom or the exercise of the imagination cannot at all be compared with the simple nourishment we derive from divine revelation. (Sermon 1) {p. 157}

What is superior in the wisdom of the world is far inferior to the child-like instruction we receive from the divine word. (Sermon 1) {p. 157}

Our greatest protection is self-knowledge. (Sermon 2) {p. 159}

Custom is no sure guarantee for the future. (Sermon 2) {p. 161}

Though He is so great that He can grasp all creation in His palm, you can wholly embrace Him; He dwells within you, nor is He cramped as He pervades your entire being. (Sermon 2) {pp. 162–163}

Jesus ... is not the same in everyone, but only according to the measure of those in whom He dwells, adapting Himself to the capacity of each one who receives Him. (Sermon 3) {p. 168}

It is a good wound and a sweet pain by which life penetrates the soul. (Sermon 4) {p. 179}

Those who look towards the true God receive within themselves the characteristics of the divine nature; so too, those who turn their minds to the vanity of idols are transformed into the objects which they look at. (Sermon 5) {p. 184}

It is not enough ... for you to rise up from sin. You must also advance in goodness. (Sermon 5) {p. 186}

---

14 *Ibid.*

We are thus taught never to set any bounds to the immensity of the Godhead; nor can any measure of human knowledge ever become a limit to our comprehension of our goal, so as to force us to stop in our ever forward progress toward heaven. Rather, the soul that is rising towards transcendent truth in the ways of higher understanding should be so disposed that every stage of perfection that is possible for human nature should be merely the beginning of a yearning for things more sublime. (Sermon 6) {p. 200}

I called Him by name—as though it were possible to find Him in a name when He cannot be named. No name would have a meaning that would reach Him Whom we seek. For how can He be discovered by a name when he is "beyond all names" [Phil 2:9]? (Sermon 6) {pp. 201–202}

When I gave up every finite mode of comprehension, then it was that I found my Beloved by faith. (Sermon 6) {p. 202}

It is sufficient if we are filled with the obvious sense of Scripture. . . . But if anyone desires the hidden marrow of the Word, he must seek it of Him Who reveals His mysteries to those who are worthy. In no case should we give the impression of letting the Scriptures pass without examination, negligent of the Lord's command to "search the Scriptures" [John 5:39]. (Sermon 6) {pp. 207–208}

The perfection we attain by our efforts is none other than that which was implanted in our nature at the beginning. (Sermon 6) {p. 210}

In our constant participation in the blessed nature of the Good, the graces that we receive at every point are indeed great, but the path that lies beyond our immediate grasp is infinite. This will constantly happen to those who thus share in the divine Goodness, and they will always enjoy a greater and greater participation in grace throughout all eternity.
 "The pure of heart will see God," according to the Lord's infallible word (Matt. 5:8), according to his capacity, receiving as much as his mind can sustain; yet the infinite and incomprehensible nature of the Godhead remains beyond all understanding. (Sermon 8) {pp. 211–212}

Though the new grace we may obtain is greater than what we had before, it does not put a limit on our final goal; rather, for those who are rising in perfection, the limit of the good that is attained becomes the beginning of the discovery of higher goods. . . . For the desire of those who thus rise never rests in what they can already understand; but by an ever greater and greater desire, the soul keeps rising constantly to another which lies ahead. (Sermon 8) {pp. 161, 212–213}

To those who have tasted and seen by experience "that the Lord is sweet" (Ps 33:9 [34:8]), this taste becomes a kind of invitation to further enjoyment. And thus the one who is rising towards God constantly experiences this continual incitement towards further progress. (Sermon 8) {p. 213}

Though we are changeable by nature, the Word wants us never to change for the worse; but by constant progress in perfection, we are to make our mutability an aid in our rise towards higher things, and so by the very changeability of our nature to establish it immovably in good. (Sermon 8) {p. 216}

The voice of the Word is ever a voice of power. At the creation, light shone forth at His command, and again at His order the firmament arose; and similarly all the rest of creation came into being at His creative Word. So too now, when the Word calls a soul that has advanced to come unto Him, it is immediately empowered at His command. (Sermon 8) {p. 217}

In her [the Church] they see more clearly that which is invisible. (Sermon 8) {p. 219}

The varied distribution of God's spiritual gifts is always in proportion to the efforts of those who seriously labor. (Sermon 9) {p. 225}

The divine message is so prepared that it does not answer the same needs in all who listen to it, but it is adapted to the capacities of the audience. (Sermon 9) {p. 225}

The aim of the life of virtue is to become like God. (Sermon 9) {p. 226}

The life of virtue is by no means everywhere the same and uniform. (Sermon 9) {p. 226}

For those who are ever advancing towards higher things there applies the saying of the Apostle: "If any man thinks that he knows anything, he has not yet known as he ought to know" (1 Cor 8:2). For up to this point, the soul is aware of only so much as she has understood. Yet what she still does not know is infinitely more than what she has comprehended. (Sermon 11) {p. 245}

It is the same with one who fixes his gaze on the infinite beauty of God. It is constantly being discovered anew, and it is always seen as something new and strange in comparison with what the mind has already understood. And as God continues to reveal Himself, man continues to wonder; and he never exhausts his desire to see more, since what he is waiting for is always more magnificent, more divine, than all that he has already seen. (Sermon 11) {p. 246}

Surely it is pleasure which precedes everything that is done out of wickedness, and we cannot find a sin that is not connected with pleasure. (Sermon 12) {p. 259}

Man by his death to the true life entered into this life of death. So too when he dies to this irrational life of death, he is restored to life eternal. (Sermon 12) {p. 259}

The only way of apprehending that Power which transcends all understanding is never to remain fixed in any single notion of Him, but ever to move forward and never to stop with what we have already perceived. (Sermon 12) {p. 260}

Neither the fact that he spoke with God as with a friend, nor that he had enjoyed intimate conversation with Him, prevented Moses from desiring more. (Sermon 12) {p. 262}

The soul that looks up towards God, and conceives that good desire for his eternal beauty, constantly experiences an ever new yearning for that which lies ahead, and her desire is never given its full satisfaction. Hence she never ceases "to stretch herself forth to those things that are before" [Phil 3:13], ever passing from her present stage to enter more deeply into the interior, into the stage which lies ahead. And so at each point she judges each great marvelous grace to be inferior to what is yet to come, because each newly won grace always seems to be more beautiful than those she has previously enjoyed. It was in this way that Paul died daily (1 Cor 15:13). For each moment that he participated more deeply in life he died to all that was past, forgetting those graces which he had already attained. (Sermon 12) {p. 268}

In Christ, that which is uncreated, eternal, existing before the ages, is completely inexpressible and incomprehensible to all created intellects. Yet that which was revealed in the flesh can to a certain extent be grasped by human understanding. It is towards this element in Christ that the Church, our teacher, looks, and of this does she speak, in as much as this can be made intelligible to those who listen to her. What I am chiefly referring to here is the mystery of salvation, by which God was revealed to us in the flesh. (Sermon 13) {p. 271}

Contemplation alone cannot perfect the soul without good works to support a morally good life; nor, on the other hand, is the active life completely sufficient without the guidance of true piety. (Sermon 13) {p. 274}

Letters[15]

Although the people of Mesopotamia had among them wealthy satraps, they preferred Thomas above them all as president of their church; the Cretans preferred Titus, the dwellers at Jerusalem James, and we Cappadocians the centurion who at the Cross acknowledged the Godhead of the Lord. (#13)

The lawgiver of our life has enjoined upon us one single hatred, that of the serpent. For no other purpose has He bidden us exercise this faculty of hatred, but as a resource against wickedness. (#17)

Sin is a miscarriage, not a quality, of human nature. Just as disease and deformity are not congenital to it in the first instance, but are its unnatural accretions, so activity in the direction of sin is to be viewed as a mutilation of the goodness innate in us. It is not itself a real thing; we see it only in the absence of that goodness. (#17)

---

15 Excerpts taken from NPNF (2nd) 5:527–548.

~ John Chrysostom

John (347–407) was an outstanding, eloquent preacher: his epithet, Chrysostom, means "golden-tongued." He served the churches in Antioch and Constantinople for several years, the latter as its bishop. He was a fearless spokesman for Christian faith and practice, respected by the common people and the leading families in Constantinople, but his bold denunciation of wayward morals in the imperial court earned him the hostility of the queen, who eventually secured his exile.

John produced many commentaries on Scripture via the sermons he preached. Other sermons amounted to extensive treatments of various topics as well. His *On the Priesthood* showed his keen understanding of the responsibilities and tensions involved in the life and service of the clergy.

Two Letters Exhorting Theodore after His Fall[1]

When the evil one perceives that we are oppressed by the consciousness of evil we have done, he steps in and lays upon us the additional burden, heavier than lead, of anxiety arising from despair. If we allow that, then we are immediately dragged down by the weight . . . and descend into the depths of misery. (1:2)

We should have good courage and trust in the power of repentance. (1:4)

In God's loving-kindness, He never turns His face away from a sincere

---
1 Excerpts taken from NPNF (1st) 9:91–116.

repentance. Even if someone has pushed on to extremes of wickedness but then chooses to return to the path of virtue, God accepts and welcomes and does everything to restore him to his former position. Beyond that, He does what is even more merciful, for even if that person does not manifest complete, but just a small and insignificant, repentance, He does not dismiss it, but assigns a great reward even to that. (1:6)

Repentance is judged not by quantity of time but by disposition of soul. (1:6)

To have fallen is not as grievous as to remain prostrate after falling and not to get up again, and—playing the coward and the sluggard—to conceal feebleness of moral purpose under claim of despair. (1:7)

Consider the transfiguration which is to take place in the whole creation. It will not continue to be like it is now, but will be far more brilliant and beautiful; and as gold glistens more brightly than lead, so the future state of the universe will be greater than the present. (1:11)

To prove that these words are no empty claim, let us journey in thought to the mountain where Christ was transfigured. . . . That the vision there was accommodated to human eyes and not an exact manifestation of the reality is plain from the words of the evangelist. . . . At that time on the mountain He disclosed to them [the disciples] as much as it was possible for them to see without injuring their sight; even so, they could not endure it, but fell on their faces. (1:11)

What language can describe to us the things that will follow [the day of resurrection]? The pleasure, the profit, the joy of being in the company of Christ! When the soul will have returned to its proper condition of nobility and is able from then on to behold its Master with much boldness, it is impossible to say what great pleasure it will derive from that, what great gain, rejoicing not only in the good actually in hand, but in the persuasion it will never come to an end. All that gladness then cannot be described in words or grasped by the mind. (1:13)

If God had made us in order to punish us, you might well despair and question the possibility of your salvation. But if He created us for no other reason than His own good will, and so that we might enjoy everlasting blessings, and if He does and works out everything for this purpose, from the first day to the present, what can ever cause you to doubt? . . . The evils we have committed do not provoke Him so much as our unwillingness to change in the future. To sin may be a human failing, but to continue in the same sin ceases to be human and becomes altogether devilish. (1:15)

He who is so concerned to be loved by us and does everything for that purpose, who did not spare even His only begotten Son because of His love for us, and who counts it desirable for us to be reconciled to Himself, how will He not welcome and love us when we repent? (1:15)

The only person who is free is the one who lives for Christ. (2:5)

It is not possible for one who has departed to the other world to repent. (2:5)

Letter to a Young Widow[2]

Death in this body is not so much death as it is a kind of emigration and translation from the worse to the better, from earth to heaven. (3)

This body, even if it reaches a very high standard of beauty, is nevertheless perishable; but the bodies of those who have been well pleasing to God will be invested with such glory as these eyes cannot even look upon. God has given us signs and obscure indications of these things in both the old and the new dispensations. In the former the face of Moses shone with such glory that it was intolerable to the eyes of the Israelites, and in the new the face of Christ shone far more brilliantly than his. (3)

Sermon on St. Ignatius of Antioch[3]

What should we speak of first? The teaching of the apostles which he gave proof of throughout, his indifference to this present life, or the strictness of his virtue, with which he administered his rule over the Church—which should take precedence, the martyr or the bishop or the apostle? (1)

---

2 Excerpts taken from NPNF (1st) 9:121–128.
3 Excerpts taken from NPNF (1st) 9:135–140.

Just as with a lyre the strings are different, but the harmony is one, so also in the band of the apostles, the persons are different, but the teaching is one, since the musician is one—I mean the Holy Spirit, who moves their souls. Paul shows this when he says, "Whether therefore they or I, so we preach." (1 Cor 15:11)

It is not at all the same thing for one to come and teach after many teachers as it is to be the first to sow the seed. For what has already been practiced and become the custom with many would be easily accepted, but what is heard for the first time agitates the minds of the hearers and so gives the teacher much to do. (3)

It is the greatest proof of the resurrection that the slain Christ should show forth such great power after death that He persuaded the living to despise country, home, friends, acquaintance, and life itself in order to confess Him, and to choose in place of present pleasures stripes, dangers, and death. This could be accomplished, not by any dead man or one who had remained in a tomb, but only by one risen from the dead and alive. (4)

This is why God allowed us to have the remains of the saints: He wished to lead us by them to emulate those saints and to offer us a kind of haven, a sure consolation against the evils which are always overtaking us. (5)

Sermon on St. Babylas the Martyr[4]

The bodies of the living who are full of evil are more polluting than those of the dead. (2)

For all these things let us give thanks to God, for He has granted us noble martyrs and pastors worthy of the martyrs to perfect the saints, to edify the body of Christ—with whom be glory, honor, and might to the Father, with the Holy and life-giving Spirit, now and always, and forever and ever. Amen. (3)

---

[4] Excerpts taken from NPNF (1st) 9:141–143.

Sermon on Humility (Philippians 1:8)[5]

For us, humility is the foundation of the love of wisdom. (2)

Do not tell me that this or that person is a runaway slave or robber or thief, that he is weighed down with innumerable faults, or that he is a beggar and hopeless. Instead, consider that Christ died for his sake—that suffices you as reason to care for him. Consider what sort of person he must be, whom Christ valued at so high a price that He did not spare even His own blood. (5)

Love casts out all inequality and knows no superiority or dignity. (7)

You need no mediators to win you an audience with God; you need no solicitors or others to fawn for you. Even if you are destitute, without anyone to speak for you, alone by yourself, if you call on God for help you will win your request. (11)

Sermons against the Power of Demons[6]

Man cast away all that he had—his right to speak freely, his communion with God, his home in Paradise, his unclouded life—and as if from a shipwreck went forth bare. But God received him and immediately clothed him and, taking him by the hand, gradually conducted him to heaven. Even so, the shipwreck was quite unpardonable: this tempest in all its enormity was due, not to the force of the winds but to the carelessness of the sailor.

And yet God did not look at this, but having compassion for the magnitude of the calamity and for him who had suffered shipwreck in harbor, He received him as lovingly as if he had undergone this in the midst of the open sea. (1:2)

God made the gain greater than the loss and brought our nature to the royal throne. That is why Paul cries out and says, "He raised us up with Him and made us to sit with Him on His right hand in the heavenly places, that in the ages to come He might show the exceeding riches of His grace towards us" [Eph 2:6, 7]. (1:2)

---

5 Excerpts taken from NPNF (1st) 9:147–155.
6 Excerpts taken from NPNF (1st) 9:178–197.

Just as slippery bodies, even if countless hands try to grasp them, escape our hold and slip through easily, so we are unable to get hold of the loving-kindness of God, no matter the ways we try to describe it, since its utter magnitude baffles our feeble utterances. (1:3)

If you would like to learn from the mother of this man [Cain] what a good result the expulsion from the life of Paradise had, compare what Eve was before this and what she afterwards became. Before, she considered that deceiving devil, the wicked demon, to be more worth believing than the commandments of God, and at the mere sight of the tree she trampled underfoot the law He had laid down. But when the expulsion from Paradise came, consider how much better and wiser she became. When she bore her son, she said, "I have gotten the man through the Lord" [Gen 4:1]. Immediately she flew to her master, she who before had despised him: she ascribed this birth neither to the laws of nature nor to the laws of marriage, but she recognized the Lord of nature and thanked Him for the birth of this little child. (1:3)

The woman suffered expulsion from Paradise, but through her ejection she was led to a knowledge of God, so she found something greater than she had lost. (1:3)

If a person is called wicked, his wickedness is not from his nature, but from his choice. (2:2)

The ways of repentance are many, various, and different, and all lead to heaven. (2:6)

Now that we have learned about the healing of our wounds, let us constantly apply these medicines, so that we may return to health and enjoy the sacred table with assurance, and with much glory reach Christ the king of glory and receive everlasting good by the grace, compassion, and loving-kindness of our Lord Jesus Christ, by whom and with whom be glory, power, and honor, to the Father, together with the all-holy, good, and life-giving Spirit, now and always and forever and ever. Amen. (2:6)

Sermon on Matthew 26:29[7]

The cross destroyed the enmity of God towards humanity, brought about reconciliation, made the earth heaven, associated human beings with angels, pulled down the citadel of death, hamstrung the force of the devil, extinguished the power of sin, delivered the world from error, brought back the truth, expelled the demons, destroyed temples, overturned altars, suppressed sacrificial offerings, implanted virtue, and founded the Church. (2)

The cross has broken our bond, it rendered the prison of death powerless, it demonstrated the love of God. (2)

The cross is the impregnable wall, the invulnerable shield, the safeguard of the rich, the resource of the poor, the defense of those exposed to snares, the armor of those who are attacked, the means of suppressing passion and acquiring virtue, the wonderful and marvelous sign. . . . The cross opened Paradise. (2)

The doctrine of the incarnation is very hard to receive . . . , that this God who surpasses all understanding and baffles all calculation, having passed by angels, archangels, and all the spiritual powers above, deigned to become human, and to take flesh formed of earth and clay, and enter the womb of a virgin and be borne there for nine months, be nourished with milk, and suffer all those things to which human beings are liable. (3)

Just as He hungered, as He slept, as He felt fatigue, as He ate and drank, so also did He pray for deliverance from death—in this He manifested His humanity and the weakness of that human nature which does not submit without pain to be torn from this present life. (4)

Sermon against Publishing Others' Errors and Uttering Curses on Enemies[8]

Earnest prayer is an unquenchable and perpetual light for the understanding and the soul. That is why the devil collects and pours into our minds countless rubbish-heaps of ideas and things we had never imagined, at the very moment we pray. (5)

---

7 Excerpts taken from NPNF (1st) 9:201–207.
8 Excerpts taken from NPNF (1st) 9:236–242.

[In making the annunciation to the Virgin:] Do not look to the ways of the earth; it is from the heavens that this will come. What will take place is by the grace of the Spirit, so do not inquire about nature and the laws of marriage. But since those words were too exalted for her, He gives another demonstration. Observe how the barren one leads her to believe all this. ... He brought down what He said to lower things also, leading her by the hand: "Behold, Elizabeth your kinswoman—she also has conceived a son in her old age; and this month is the sixth for her who was called barren." Do you see that the barren one was for the sake of the Virgin? (8)

[If someone angers you:] Make your mind contrite, humble your soul with the memory of the offenses you have committed, and you will not be enflamed with anger. (12)

The cause of our evils in this regard is that we scrutinize the sins of others with great exactitude, while we let our own pass with carelessness. (12)

Sermons on Marriage and Family Life[9]

Sins have become an art! We pursue them not by chance, but with studied earnestness, and finally the devil assumes control of his own troops. When drunkenness arrives, chastity departs. Where there is filthy talk, the devil is always eager to make his own contribution. ... You mock me when I rebuke you, and say I am too austere. This is only another proof of your perverted manner of life. Don't you remember St. Paul's words: "So, whether you eat or drink, or whatever you do, do all to the glory of God" [1 Cor 10:31]? (Sermon 12, on Colossians 4:18)

No teacher is so effective as a persuasive wife. (Sermon 19, on 1 Corinthians 7)

This love [eros] is deeply implanted within our inmost being. Unnoticed by us, it attracts the bodies of men and women to each other, because in the beginning woman came forth from man, and from man and woman other men and women proceed. Can you see now how close this union is, and how God providentially created it from a single nature? . . . He made

---

9 Excerpted from Catharine P. Roth and David Anderson, trans., *St John Chrysostom: On Marriage and Family Life* (Crestwood, NY: St. Vladimir's Seminary Press, 1986), pp. 25–114.

the one man Adam to be the origin of all mankind, both male and female, and made it impossible for men and women to be self-sufficient. (Sermon 20, on Ephesians 5:22–33)

The love of husband and wife is the force that welds society together. (Sermon 20, on Ephesians 5:22–33)

What kind of marriage can there be when the wife is afraid of her husband? (Sermon 20, on Ephesians 5:22–33)

How difficult it is to have harmony when husband and wife are not bound together by the power of love! Fear is no substitute for this. (Sermon 20, on Ephesians 5:22–33)

How foolish are those who belittle marriage! If marriage were something to be condemned, Paul would never call Christ a Bridegroom and the Church a bride. (Sermon 20, on Ephesians 5:22–33)

An intelligent, discreet, and pious young woman is worth more than all the money in the world. (Sermon 20, on Ephesians 5:22–33)

Remind one another that nothing in life is to be feared, except offending God. If your marriage is like this, your perfection will rival the holiest of monks. (Sermon 20, on Ephesians 5:22–33)

See what an admirable foundation St. Paul lays for a virtuous life: honor and respect for one's parents. This is the first good practice commanded us in the Scriptures, because before all others, except God, our parents are the authors of our life, and they deserve to be the first ones to receive the fruits of our good deeds. Only after we honor our parents can we do anything good for the rest of mankind. If a person does not honor his parents, he will never treat other people with kindness. (Sermon 21, on Ephesians 6:1–4)

It is necessary for everyone to know Scriptural teachings, and this is especially true for children. Even at their age they are exposed to all sorts of folly and bad examples from popular entertainments. Our children need remedies for all these things! We are so concerned with our children's schooling; if only we were equally zealous in bringing them up in the discipline and instruction of the Lord! (Sermon 21, on Ephesians 6:1–4)

Let everything take second place to our care for our children, our bringing them up in the discipline and instruction of the Lord. (Sermon 21, on Ephesians 6:1–4)

Don't worry about giving your child an influential reputation for worldly wisdom, but ponder deeply how you can teach him to think lightly of this life's passing glories; thus he will become truly renowned and glorious. Whether you are poor or rich, you can do this; these lessons are not learned from a skillful professor, but from divine revelation. (Sermon 21, on Ephesians 6:1–4)

Great will be the reward in store for us, for if artists who make statues and paint portraits of kings are held in high esteem, will not God bless ten thousand times more those who reveal and beautify his royal image (for man is the image of God)? (Sermon 21, on Ephesians 6:1–4)

We can't be saved through individual righteousness alone. (Sermon 21, on Ephesians 6:1–4)

God helps those who work, not those who are idle. (Sermon 21, on Ephesians 6:1–4)

I do not seek your favor but your benefit. I do not ask for the applause of praise, but the profit of wisdom. Let no one tell me that this is the custom. Where sin is boldly committed, forget about custom. If evil things are done, even if the custom is ancient, abolish them. (Sermon on Marriage)

These are the two purposes for which marriage was instituted: to make us chaste, and to make us parents. Of these two, the reason of chastity takes precedence. When desire began, then marriage also began. It sets a limit to desire by teaching us to keep to one wife. Marriage does not always lead to child-bearing, although there is the word of God which says, "Be fruitful and multiply, and fill the earth" [Gen 1:28]. We have as witnesses all those who are married but childless. So the purpose of chastity takes precedence, especially now, when the whole world is filled with our kind. At the beginning, the procreation of children was desirable, so that each person might leave a memorial of his life. Since there was not yet any hope of resurrection, but death held sway, and those who died thought that they would perish after this life, God gave the comfort of children, so as to leave living images of the departed and to preserve our species.... But now that the resurrection is at our gates, and we do not speak of death, but advance toward another life better than the present, the desire for posterity is superfluous. (Sermon on Marriage)

God will judge you at the last day not by the civil law but by His law. (How to Choose a Wife)

Just as the woman was fashioned while Adam slept, so also, when Christ had died, the Church was formed from His side. (How to Choose a Wife)

You must consider that marriage is not a business venture but a fellowship for life. (How to Choose a Wife)

When you are looking for a bridegroom or a bride, ask this first of all, whether your intended is loved by God and enjoys good will from above. If these blessings are present, everything else follows. If they are absent, even if the goods of this life are present in great abundance, they are of no benefit. (How to Choose a Wife)

A Comparison Between a King and a Monk[10]

He is a king who truly rules over anger and envy and pleasure, who commands all things under the laws of God, who keeps his mind free, and who does not allow the power of the pleasures to dominate his soul. (ch. 2)

Against the Opponents of the Monastic Life[11]

This is how the matter stands: a great recompense awaits those who do good works, but this reward is better and greater when those who do the good works have had to experience danger and great dishonor. (1:4)

---

10 Excerpts taken from David G. Hunter, trans. and with an introduction, *A Comparison Between a King and a Monk /Against the Opponents of the Monastic Life: Two Treatises by John Chrysostom,* Studies in the Bible and Early Christianity, vol. 13 (Lewiston/Queenston, Ontario: The Edwin Mellen Press, 1989), pp. 69–76.

11 Excerpted from Hunter, *A Comparison,* pp. 77–176.

What benefit is the faith, tell me, unless there is also a pure way of life? (1:6)

When God declares something, even if he speaks only once, what he says should be accepted as if it had been uttered many times. (1:6)

We will not change our mind, nor will we value the multitude more highly than the truth. (1:8)

To have many companions in sin does not acquit us of accusations and punishments. (1:8)

Others will listen more readily when the person who speaks about philosophy proves his words true by his actions. (2:8)

Virtue among Christians does not require many days, since it grows by divine grace. (2:10)

God did not create man to provide only for himself, but to provide for many others as well. (3:2)

The greatest sin of all and the absolute height of wickedness is to neglect one's children. (3:3)

"Why, then," you ask, "is not everyone punished in this life?" Because God has established the day on which he will judge the world, and this day has not yet come; if it were otherwise, our entire race already would have been destroyed and exterminated. (3:3)

If wickedness were in people by nature, then one would have the right to make excuses. . . . It is by free choice that we become either wicked or good. (3:4)

Habit is a terrible thing, terrible enough to capture and rule the soul, especially when it has pleasure acting in conjunction with it. (3:6)

To call vices by their bare and proper names helps to no small degree in avoiding them. (3:7)

True wisdom and true education is nothing other than fear of God. (3:12)

It would be a contradiction to be confident of salvation, even when one is enslaved to worldly business, and yet, when one is free of all this, to tremble and fear that an illustrious life is impossible without these things. (3:13)

You certainly deceive yourself and are greatly mistaken if you think that there is one set of requirements for the person in the world and another for the monk. (3:14)

The act of begetting does not a parent make. (3:16)

The best instruction consists, not in first allowing wickedness to gain the upper hand and later seeking how to eliminate it, but rather in doing and working in every way so that our nature becomes inaccessible to evil. (3:18)

Then do we most truly possess our children when we have entrusted them to the Master. (3:20).

Six Books on the Priesthood[12]

It is necessary to make a man better not by force but by persuasion.... For this reason a lot of tact is needed, so that the sick may be persuaded of their own accord to submit to the treatment. (ch. 4)

So the shepherd [pastor/priest] needs great wisdom and a thousand eyes, to examine the soul's condition from every angle.... There are plenty of people who are puffed up into arrogance and then fall into heedlessness of their own salvation because they cannot stand bitter medicines. (ch. 4)

If a man wanders away from the right faith, the shepherd needs a lot of concentration, perseverance, and patience. He cannot drag by force or constrain by fear, but must by persuasion lead him back to the true beginning from which he has fallen away. (ch. 4)

I am afraid that if I receive the flock from Christ plump and well-fed and then damage it through ineptitude I may provoke against me God who so loved it that he gave himself for its salvation and redemption. (ch. 5)

---

12 Excerpted from Graham Neville, trans. and introduction, *Saint John Chrysostom: Six Books on the Priesthood* (Crestwood, NY: St. Vladimir's Seminary Press, 1977), pp. 35–160.

We must not mind insulting human beings, if by respecting them we offend God. (ch. 6)

The work of the priesthood is done on earth, but it is ranked among heavenly ordinances. (ch. 7)

How great is the honor which the grace of the Spirit has bestowed on priests. (ch. 7)

Those who are lords on earth have indeed the power to bind, but only men's bodies. But this binding [Matt 18:18] touches the very soul and reaches through heaven. What priests do on earth, God ratifies above. The Master confirms the decisions of his slaves. Indeed he has given them nothing less than the whole authority of heaven. (ch. 7)

More billows toss the priest's soul than the gales which trouble the sea. (ch. 8)

It [the priestly office] is not itself the cause of the evils I have mentioned. It is we on our part who have smirched it with stain upon stain, by entrusting it to commonplace men. And they eagerly accept what is offered to them, without first examining their own souls or considering the gravity of the matter. And when they come to exercise this ministry, their eyes are blinded with inexperience. (ch. 8)

Tell me, where do you think all the disorders in the churches originate? I think their only origin is in the careless and random way in which the clergy are chosen and appointed. (ch. 8)

I think a man must rid his mind of this ambition [fame] with all possible care. . . . For if he does not want to achieve fame in this position of authority, he will not dread its loss either. (ch. 9)

Nothing muddies the purity of the mind and the perspicacity of the wits as much as an ungovernable temper that fluctuates violently. (ch. 9)

A blazing temper is a kind of pleasure, and it tyrannizes over the soul more harshly than pleasure, thoroughly upsetting all its healthy condition. (ch. 9)

The priest's shortcomings simply cannot be concealed. On the contrary, even the most trivial soon get known. (ch. 9)

The sins of ordinary people are committed in the dark, so to speak, and ruin only those who commit them. But when a man becomes famous and is known to many, his misdeeds inflict a common injury on all. (ch. 9)

Everyone measures sin, not by the size of the offense, but by the standing of the sinner. (ch. 9)

For as long as the priest's life is well regulated in every particular point, their intrigues cannot hurt him. But if he should overlook some small detail, as is likely for a human being on his journey across the devious ocean of this life, all the rest of his good deeds are of no avail to enable him to escape the words of his accusers. That small offense casts a shadow over all the rest of his life. Everyone wants to judge the priest, not as one clothed in flesh, not as one possessing a human nature, but as an angel, exempt from the frailty of others. (ch. 9)

The priest [is] assailed with as many accusations as there are persons under his rule. (ch. 10)

I myself, so far from thinking these are worthy grounds for approving priests, should not dare to select a man quickly, even if he showed great piety (though to me it is no small qualification for that office), unless he combined with piety considerable intelligence as well. (ch. 10)

They simply take commonplace men and put them in charge of those things for which the only-begotten Son of God did not disdain to empty himself of his own glory and to be made man and to receive the form of a servant and to be spitted upon and buffeted and to die the most shameful death. (ch. 10)

They not merely choose the unworthy; they reject those who are suitable. (ch. 10)

Yet all these evils are suffered and borne patiently by the one who "does not desire the death of a sinner, but rather that he should be converted and live" [Ezek 18:23]. How can we marvel enough at his love for humanity, or wonder at his mercy? Christians damage Christ's cause more than his enemies and foes. (ch. 10)

He [the priest] must be dignified yet modest, impressive yet kindly, masterful yet approachable, impartial yet courteous, humble but not servile, vehement yet gentle. (ch. 10)

The gift is doubled by the manner of giving. (ch. 10)

The subtle serpent knows very well how to spread his poison even by means of good deeds. (ch. 10)

If the bishop does not pay a more extensive round of daily visits than ordinary loungers, indescribable offense will be taken. Not only the sick, but the healthy want to be visited by the bishop, not so much because their piety prompts them, as because most of them lay claim to honor and distinction. (ch. 10)

But why mention favoritism and visiting? The mere way in which they [the clergy] address people is enough to incur such a load of criticism that they are often burdened and prostrated by despondency. Why, they have to render account for the merest glance! People subject their casual doings to a minute examination, assessing the strength of their voice, the expression of their face, and the frequency of their laugh. (ch. 10)

When a crowd is seated together, if he does not turn his eyes in every direction while conversing, the rest say his action is an insult. (ch. 10)

He must firmly refuse to be dismayed by these complaints. A man who is justly accused can easily bear with his accuser. For since there is no accuser more bitter than our own conscience, we have no difficulty in bearing the milder accusations of others, when we have first been convicted by that most severe accuser. But when someone whose conscience acquits him of evil is accused without a cause, he is quickly roused to anger and easily falls into desperation, unless he has trained himself already to bear the mischief of the mob. (ch. 10)

And how can one describe the grief bishops feel when anyone has to be excommunicated from the body of the Church? (ch. 10)

What punishment, then, must a man expect, when he not only has to render account for his own offenses but also stands in the utmost peril for the sins of others? (ch. 10)

All these excuses are feeble, and not only feeble but dangerous; and they rouse God's anger even more. For a man who has received an honor beyond his deserving should not use its greatness as a cloak for his faults. He ought rather to use God's abundant favor towards him as a stronger incentive to improvement. (ch. 11)

Do you see, then, that it is not only those who snatch at the office, but those who are led to it through the insistence of others, who have no excuse left when they stumble? (ch. 11)

Others call God to account for his judgments and struggle to measure the great deep. For the Psalmist says, "Thy judgments are a great deep" [Ps 36:6]. You will find that few are deeply concerned about faith and conduct, but the majority go in for elaborate theories and investigate questions to which there is no answer and whose very investigation rouses God's anger. (ch. 12)

Most of those who are under authority refuse to treat preachers as their instructors. They rise above the status of disciples and assume that of spectators sitting in judgment on secular speech-making. (ch. 13)

Most people usually listen to a preacher for pleasure, not profit, like adjudicators of a play or concert. (ch. 13)

The right course is neither to show disproportionate fear and anxiety over ill-directed abuse (for the president will have to put up with unfounded criticism), nor simply to ignore it. We should try to extinguish criticisms at once, even if they are false and are leveled at us by quite ordinary people. (ch. 13)

Despondency and constant anxieties have a terrible power to numb the soul and reduce it to utter impotence. (ch. 13)

No one ever takes it into consideration that a fit of depression, pain, anxiety, or in many cases anger, may cloud the clarity of his [the priest's] mind and prevent his productions from coming forth unalloyed; and that in short, being only a man, he cannot invariably reach the same standard or always be successful, but will naturally make many mistakes and obviously fall below the standard of his real ability. People are unwilling to allow for any of these factors. (ch. 13)

Men are so made that they overlook their neighbor's successes, however many or great; yet if a defect comes to light, however commonplace and however long since it last occurred, it is quickly noticed, fastened on at once, and never forgotten. (ch. 13)

When he has composed his sermons to please God (and let this alone be his rule and standard of good oratory in sermons, not applause or commendation), then if he should be approved by men too, let him not spurn their praise. But if his hearers do not accord it, let him neither seek it nor sorrow for it. It will be sufficient encouragement for his efforts, and one much better than anything else, if his conscience tells him that he is organizing and regulating his teaching to please God. (ch. 13)

If it is better for a man who offends just one other person, and him the least of all, that a millstone should be hanged about his neck and that he should be sunk in the depth of the sea [Matt 18:6]; and if all who wound the conscience of the brethren, sin against Christ himself [1 Cor 8:12]: what will be the fate and what the punishment of those who ruin, not one or two or three, but great multitudes? (ch. 14)

A priest must not only be blameless, as befits one chosen for so high a ministry, but also very discreet and widely experienced. He ought to be as much aware of mundane matters as any who live in the midst of them, and yet be more detached from them than the monks who have taken to the mountains. Since he must mix with people who have married and are bringing up children, keep servants, own great possessions, take part in public life, and hold high office, he must be many-sided. (ch. 14)

Making a list of all the difficulties involved is like trying to measure the ocean. (ch. 15)

I cannot myself believe it possible for anyone to be saved who never works for the salvation of his neighbor. (ch. 16)

No one can feel such implacable hatred for his worst enemies as the Evil One feels for the human race. (ch. 16)

He [Satan] takes more trouble to damn our souls than we take to save them. (ch. 16)

On the Incomprehensible Nature of God[13]

Christ said, "By this all will know that you are My disciples" [John 13:35]. By what? Tell me. Was it by raising the dead or by cleansing lepers or by driving out demons? No. Christ passed over all these signs and wonders when He said, "By this all will know that you are My disciples, if you have love for one another." (1:5)

Without it [love] nothing will be able to save a man even if he possess faith, understanding, knowledge of mysteries, martyrdom itself, or any other gift. (1:7)

I know many things but I do not know how to explain them. I know that God is everywhere and I know that He is everywhere in His whole being. But I do not know how He is everywhere. I know that He is eternal and has no beginning. But I do not know how. My reason fails to grasp how it is possible for an essence to exist when that essence has received its existence neither from itself nor from another. I know that He begot a Son. But I do not know how. I know that the Spirit is from Him. But I do not know how the Spirit is from Him. (1:19)

Not even in heaven does any created power know God in His essence. (1:34)

Nothing is more forceful and effective than treatment which is gentle and kind. (1:40)

When God reveals something, we must accept His words on faith; we must not be arrogant and busy ourselves making investigations into what He has said. (2:6)

---

13 Excerpts taken from FC 72:49–307.

Surely whenever God reveals something with which it is not our place to meddle, we must accept it on faith. When God makes such revelations, only an insolent and reckless soul is so meddlesome as to seek causes, as to call for an explanation and accounting, as to search out how God's revelations can be true. (2:8)

[Comparing the healing brought by the angel stirring the water (John 5:4) and the promise in baptism:] The servant [angel] cured by going down into the pool and stirring up the water. The master does not do this. It is enough merely to invoke His name over the waters and so to bestow on them the entire cause of their power to cure. The servant healed imperfections and mutilations of the body; the master cures the wickedness of the soul. (2:10)

It is an unpardonable thing to be so curious as to question how God's revelations can be true. Rather it is our duty to accept on faith whatever God says. (2:11)

Whenever God makes a revelation, there is no need to stir up the workings of one's reason nor to propose to oneself either a sequence of events, or a necessity rooted in nature, or any other such thing. (2:13)

We still find some people who surpass the devil himself with their boasting. (2:20)

God made all these powers with such ease that no words can explain it. The mere act of God's will was enough to make them all. An act of will does not make us tired. Neither did creating so many and such mighty powers weary God. The prophet revealed this when he said, "Whatever the Lord pleases He does, in heaven and in earth" [Ps 135:6]. (2:30)

[Commenting on Rom 4:20, 21] Do you see that the person who is fully persuaded by whatever God shall reveal gives glory to God? (2:36)

The distance between the essence of God and that of a human is so great that no words can express it, nor is the mind capable of measuring it. (2:37)

No one can do God harm by dishonoring Him, nor can anyone increase God's glory by blessing Him. God always abides in His own glory; to bless Him does not increase it, to curse Him does not make it less. Those who glorify God as He deserves or, rather—since no one can give Him such glory—those who glorify Him to the best of their ability reap the profit of the praise they give Him. (3:3)

Let us call upon Him, then, as the ineffable God who is beyond our intelligence, invisible, incomprehensible, who transcends the power of mortal words. Let us call on Him as the God who is inscrutable to the angels, unseen by the seraphim, inconceivable to the cherubim, invisible to the principalities, to the powers, and to the virtues, in fact, to all creatures without qualification, because He is known only by the Son and the Spirit. (3:5)

God condescends whenever He is not seen as He is, but in the way one incapable of beholding Him is able to look upon Him. In this way God reveals Himself by accommodating what He reveals to the weakness of vision of those who behold Him.

This is clear from Isaiah's very words that, in his case, he saw God by such condescension. For he said, "I saw the Lord sitting on a throne, high and lofty" [Is 6:1]. But God is not sitting. This is a posture for bodily beings. And Isaiah said, "On a throne." But God is not encompassed or enclosed by a throne; Divinity cannot be circumscribed by limits. (3:15–16)

The blind person does not know that the sun's rays are unapproachable as does one who can see. So we do not know the incomprehensibility of God in the same way as these powers [the seraphim of Is 6:2] do. (3:17)

[Reflecting on proper decorum in worship, in light of Heb 12:22–24] Think by whose side you are standing, think of those with whom you will call on God. It is with the cherubim. Think of those with whom you are joining to form this choir, and this will be enough to sober you. Although you wear a body around you, although you are entangled with flesh, reflect on the fact that you have been deemed worthy to join with the spiritual powers above to praise in song the common Master of all. But if anyone has allowed himself to lose his zeal and goodwill, let him not share in those sacred and mystic hymns. Let no one keep his thoughts on the affairs of daily life at that sacred time. Let him rid his mind of all earthly things, let him transfer himself entirely to heaven, and let him stand next to the very throne of glory and raise his all-holy hymn to the God of glory and majesty. (4:43)

The terms "Father" and "Son" characterize what is proper to the personal realities; the terms "God" and "Lord" show what is common. (5:12)

What we must say is that we know that the soul is in our bodies but that we do not know how it is there. (5:29)

All that we are required to know is that God exists; we are not asked to be busybodies and be inquisitive about His essence. (5:40)

Prayer is a mighty weapon, an unfailing treasure, a wealth which is never expended, a harbor that is always calm, a foundation for tranquility. Prayer is the root and source and mother of ten thousand blessings. It is more powerful than the empire itself. (5:44)

Nothing puts carelessness and negligence to flight the way grief and affliction do. They bring together our thoughts from every side and make our mind turn back to ponder itself. (5:47)

A large gathering of clouds at first makes the air murky. But after the clouds send down continuous showers and empty themselves of all their rain, they make the air calm and bright. In the same way, as long as distress and anguish stay cramped and compressed in our hearts, they darken our thinking. When they are emptied and evaporate through the words of our supplication and the tears which flow from our eyes as we pray, they bring a great brightness to the soul. Why? Because, like the rays of the sun, God's help has entered into the soul of the person who is praying. (5:48)

But what are the cold-hearted words offered by many people as an excuse for not praying? "I lack the confidence to speak freely to God," they say. "I am filled with shame and cannot open my mouth." Your pious caution was spawned by Satan. Your words are a cloak for your own careless indifference. It is the devil who wishes to lock the doors which give you access to God. (5:49)

Even if you carry the burden of ten thousand sins on your conscience, you will still find great freedom to approach and speak to God, as long as you are convinced that you are the least of all people. (5:50)

It is no humility to think that you are a sinner when you really are a sinner.

But whenever someone is conscious of having done many great deeds but does not imagine that he is something great in himself, that is true humility. (5:51)

In His ineffable loving-kindness, God welcomes and receives not only the humble-minded but also those who have the prudence to confess their sins. Because they are so disposed toward Him, He is gracious and kind to them. (5:51)

Therefore, I exhort, I entreat, and I beg you never to stop confessing your faults to God. I am not leading you onto a stage before your fellow servants, nor do I force you to reveal your sin to others. Open your conscience before God, show Him your wounds, and beg Him for medication to heal them. Do not point them out to someone who will reproach you but to One who will cure you. Even if you remain silent, God knows all things. Tell your sins to Him so that you may be the one who profits. (5:56)

If you tell others your personal misfortunes, if you describe to them in tragic tones the evils which have befallen you, you may find some consolation in your distress—that is, if you think that talking about your troubles will make them evaporate. But if you share with your Master the sufferings you feel in your soul, it is much surer that you will receive comfort and consolation in abundance. People often grow weary of one who comes to them with wailing and bitter laments. At times, they even push such a person from their path to get rid of him. But God does not act in this way. He lets the wailing person come to Him and even draws him to Himself. Even if it takes you all day to share your misfortunes with God, He will love you all the more and will grant your petitions. (5:59)

That He who is God was willing to become human, that He endured to accommodate Himself to our weakness and to come down to our level is too great for our minds to grasp. (6:25)

Surely, prayer is a harbor for those caught in a storm; it is an anchor for those tossed by the waves; it is a staff for those who stumble. Prayer is a treasure for the poor, security for the rich, a cure for the sick, a safeguard for those in good health. It keeps our blessings inviolable and quickly changes our ills to good. If temptation comes, it is easily repelled. If loss of possessions or any of the other things which cause grief to our souls befall us, prayer is quick to drive them all away. Prayer is a refuge from every sorrow, a basis for cheerfulness, a means for continual pleasure, a mother for our philosophy and way of life. (7:61)

[In trying to understand Scripture:] I warn you and advise you not to go merely to what is written but to search out the meaning of what is said. If a person should busy himself simply with the words, if he should search for nothing more than what has been written, he will fall into many errors. (8:4)

You must not think of giving alms to the poor as an expense but as a source of income. It is not an outlay of money, but it is a profitable business. For you get back more than you give. You give bread and get back eternal life. You give a coat and get back a garment of immortality. You give your house to be shared, and you get back a heavenly Kingdom. (8:10)

God does not demand a large contribution, but He does require a wealth of good intention. The spirit of almsgiving is not shown by the measure of what has been given but by the willingness of those who give. (8:12)

After one departs from this world, and the theater audience has dispersed, one cannot find a remedy for the things which have already happened. There is neither pardon nor defense but, for all future time, one must pay the penalty. (8:14)

He [Christ] erased the Curse, He triumphed over death, He opened Paradise. He struck down sin, He opened wide the vaults of the sky, He lifted our first fruits to heaven, He filled the whole world with godliness. He drove out error, He led back the truth, He made our first fruits mount to the royal throne. He accomplished so much good that neither I nor all people together could set it all before your minds in words. (8:46)

Christ taught by example, spending whole long nights in the desert praying. He did this to teach and admonish us that, whenever we are going to converse with God, we must flee from the noise, the confusion, and the crowds. Instead, we should go off to a place which is deserted and go at a time when our solitude will not be interrupted. A mountain does not offer the only solitude; a room where there is no clamor or uproar is just as much a place of solitude. (10:16)

As for ourselves, let us not think that faith alone is enough for our salvation. We must also feel concern for our own conduct and give an example of the most perfect life. In this way, we shall have made ready for ourselves a profitable benefit from two sources, from faith and from good works. (10:57)

[Commenting on John 5:8–10] The eyes of the envious see nothing whole and entire. . . . They closed their eyes to the miracle but denounced the breaking of the Sabbath. (12:34)

Make your way of life a robe which is woven together from good moral conduct and correct doctrine. (12:53)

Sickness withers physical beauty, length of years destroys it, old age drains it dry, death comes and takes it all away. But beauty of the soul cannot be marred by time, disease, old age, death, or any other such thing. It stays constantly in bloom. (12:58)

Cyril of Alexandria

Cyril (376–444) served as bishop of Alexandria. A vigorous church leader, he wrote some significant commentaries on Scripture. He was also the chief opponent of the heresy of Nestorius, who espoused a duality within Christ, such that a complete human person was related to the Second Person of the Trinity. As against this, Cyril urged the oneness of the incarnate Son of God as necessary for the accomplishment of salvation. With this oneness, Cyril urged, the Virgin Mary is appropriately called Theotokos—"bearer of God" or "mother of God"—since the Person within her was the Son of God taking humanity unto Himself in her womb. Cyril's teaching was endorsed at the Council of Ephesus in 431, at which he played a prominent role.

Commentary on Isaiah[1]

The word of the holy prophets is always obscure. It is filled with hidden meanings and is in travail with the predictions of divine mysteries. (Introduction)

It seems to me that the blessed prophet Isaiah has been rightly crowned [in Christian teaching], not only with the grace of prophecy, but also with the distinction of apostolicity. For he is at the same time both a prophet and an

---

1 Excerpts taken from Norman Russell, *Cyril of Alexandria* (New York: Routledge, 2000), pp. 70–95.

apostle, and in his writings there are discourses which do not fall short of the splendor of the Gospel proclamations. (Introduction)

We have become fellow heirs to the evils experienced by our first parent. In a similar way we shall be partakers of those things which have come through the second first-fruits of our race—that is to say, through Christ. (on Is 11:3)

"If I have told you earthly things and you do not believe, how can you believe if I tell you heavenly things?" [John 3:12]. It is therefore necessary to give way to what God says. He himself knows the way of his own works, and what he has fashioned is not to be curiously inquired into. It belongs to us to honor what transcends the human mind with an unquestioning faith. (Is 45:10)

Commentary on John[2]

The Word of God who transcends all things could make his own proper good—which is life—operative in the flesh. That, in my opinion, is the most probable reason why the holy evangelist, indicating the whole living being by the part affected, says that "the Word of God became flesh." It is so that we might see side by side the wound together with the remedy, the patient together with the physician, that which had sunk towards death together with him who raised it up towards life, that which had been overcome by corruption together with him who drove out corruption, that which had been mastered by death together with him who was superior to death, that which was bereft of life together with him who is the provider of life. He does not say that the Word "came into" flesh; he says that he "became" flesh in order to exclude any idea of a relative indwelling, as in the case of the prophets and the other saints. (on John 1:14a)

The holy body of Christ endows those who receive it with life and keeps us incorrupt when it is mingled with our bodies. For it is not the body of anyone else, but is the body of him who is life by nature, since it has within itself the entire power of the Word that is united with it, and is endowed with his qualities, or rather is filled with his energy, through which all things are given life and maintained in being. (on John 6:35)

---

2 Excerpted from Russell, *Cyril of Alexandria*, pp. 98–129.

Let us approach the divine and heavenly grace, and go up to the holy partaking of Christ [in the Eucharist]. For that is precisely the way in which we shall overcome the deceits of the devil, and "having become partakers of the divine nature" [2 Pet 1:4], shall ascend to life and incorruption. (on John 6:35)

Those who do not receive Jesus through the sacrament will continue to remain utterly bereft of any share in the life of holiness and blessedness and without any taste of it whatsoever. (on John 6:53)

If the flesh of the Savior became life-giving, seeing that it was united with that which is life by nature—i.e., the Word that is from God—when we taste of it we have that life within ourselves, since we too are united with the flesh of the Savior. (on John 6:53)

It [the Eucharist] will certainly transform those who partake of it and endow them with its own proper good—that is, eternal life.
　Do not be astonished at this, or ask yourself in a Jewish manner about the "how." Instead, reflect on the fact that water is cold by nature, but when it is poured into a kettle and put on the fire, it all but forgets its own nature and moves across to the energy of that which has dominated it. In the same way, although we are corruptible because of the nature of the flesh, we too through our mingling with life abandon our own weakness and are transformed into its property—life. (on John 6:53)

The Word was united with its own flesh in a transcendent manner that is beyond human understanding, and having, as it were, transferred the flesh wholly to himself by that energy by which it lies in his power to give life to those things that lack life, he drove corruption out of our nature and also rid it of that which through sin has prevailed from of old—namely, death. Therefore he who eats the holy flesh of Christ has eternal life, for the flesh contains the Word who is by nature life. That is why he says, "I will raise him up at the last day." Instead of saying, "My body shall raise him up"—that is, will raise up the person who eats it—he has put in the word "I," since he is not other than his own flesh. (on John 6:54)

It was surely impossible that he who is life by nature did not defeat corruption and overcome death absolutely. Therefore although death, which sprang upon us because of the Fall [1 Pet 5:8], forces the human body towards unavoidable decay, nevertheless if Christ comes to be in us through his own flesh, we shall certainly rise. (on John 6:54)

Now if we really yearn for eternal life, if we long to have the provider of immortality within ourselves, let us not abstain from the Eucharist like some of the more negligent, nor let us provide the devil in the depths of his cunning with a trap and a snare for us in the form of a pernicious kind of reverence. "Yes, indeed," someone might say, "But it is written, 'Any one who eats of the bread and drinks of the cup unworthily, eats and drinks judgment upon himself' [1 Cor 11:29]. I have examined myself and I see that I am not worthy." But then when will you be worthy? . . . Make up your mind, then, to lead a more devout life in conformity with the law, and so partake of the Eucharist in the conviction that it dispels not only death but even the diseases that are in us [1 Cor 11:30]. (on John 6:56)

In Christ as the first-fruits human nature was restored to newness of life. And in him we have gained also that which transcends nature. That is also why he was called a second Adam in the divine Scriptures [1 Cor 15:45]. (on John 12:27)

Against Nestorius[3]

Human nature, which fell sick through the disobedience of Adam, became glorious in Christ through his utter obedience. For it is written that "as by one man's disobedience many were made sinners, so by one man's obedience many will be made righteous" [Rom 5:19]. In Adam it suffered the penalty: "You are earth and to earth you shall return" [Gen 3:19]. In Christ it was enriched by being able to overcome the snares of death and, as it were, exult in triumph over decay, repeating the prophetic text, "O death, where is your victory? O Hades, where is your sting?" [Hos 13:14; 1 Cor 15:55]. (1:1)

Is not silence better than ignorant speech? (2:Introduction)

We believe in one God, the Father almighty, maker of all things both visible and invisible, and in one Lord Jesus Christ, and in the Holy Spirit; and following the professions of faith of the holy Fathers that supplement this,

---

3 Excerpts taken from Russell, *Cyril of Alexandria*, pp. 131–174.

we say that the Word begotten from the essence of God the Father became as we are and took flesh and became human—that is, he took for himself a body from the holy virgin and made it his own. (2:1)

We deny that the flesh of the Word became the Godhead, but we do say that it became divine in virtue of its being his own. (2:8)

The same subject who before the incarnation was Son and God and Word of the Father became after it a man like us endowed with flesh. (2:10)

"To all who received him he gave power to become children of God; who were born, not of blood nor of the will of the flesh, nor of the will of man, but of God" [John 1:12]. For the Word of God the Father was born according to the flesh in the same way as ourselves, so that we too might be enriched with a birth which is from God through the Spirit, no longer being called children of flesh but rather, having been transformed into something that transcends nature, being called children of God by grace. (3:2)

The body of the Word himself is life-giving, since he has made it his own by a real union transcending our understanding and power of expression. In a similar way, if we too come to participate in his holy flesh and blood, we are endowed with life completely and absolutely, because the Word dwells within us, both in a divine way through the Holy Spirit and in a human way through the holy flesh and the precious blood. (4:5)

The Word of God has become human and this faith is in harmony with the sacred and divine Scriptures, and the aim of the apostolic and evangelical tradition is entirely concentrated on this same goal. (4:6)

Is it not obvious to everybody that it is quite absurd to be determined to take up an offensive position against an enemy who is not in the least inclined to come out and fight, or to take as opposition that which no one has a mind to think or to say? (4:7)

Since the Word, being God, made the body born from a woman his own body without undergoing change or alteration in any way, why could he not say to us without any dissimulation, "Take, eat; this is my body" [Matt 26:26]? For being life in virtue of being God, he rendered the body life and life-giving. (4:7)

The Third Letter to Nestorius[4]

When seen as a babe and wrapped in swaddling clothes, even when still in the bosom of the virgin who bore Him, He filled all creation as God, and was enthroned with Him who begot Him. {p. 350}

We confess that He who was begotten from God the Father as Son and God only-begotten, although He was by His own nature impassible, suffered in the flesh for us, according to the Scriptures, and He was in the crucified flesh impassibly making His own the suffering of His own flesh. {p. 351}

Proclaiming the death in the flesh of the unique Son of God—that is, Jesus Christ—and confessing His return from the dead, and His reception into heaven, we celebrate the unbloody service in the churches. So we approach to the mystical gifts and are sanctified, becoming partakers of the holy flesh and the honorable blood of Christ the Savior of us all, not receiving it as ordinary flesh . . . , but as truly life-giving and the Word's own flesh. For being by nature, as God, Life, when He had become one with His own flesh, He made it life-giving. {p. 352}

Since the holy virgin gave birth after the flesh to God who was united by hypostasis ["person"] with the flesh, therefore we say that she is Theotokos, not as though the nature of the Word had the beginning or its existence from flesh. {pp. 352–353}

We have learned to hold these things from the holy apostles and evangelists and all the God-inspired Scripture, and by the true confession of the blessed Fathers. {p. 353}

An Explanation of the 12 Chapters[5]

Having become like us, even though he remained what he was, he will not repudiate what belongs to us, but instead accepts what is human along with the limitations that belong to the human condition, for the sake of the dispensation of the incarnation, without thereby compromising in any way his glory or his nature. For even in this state he is God and Lord of all. (§9)

---

4 Excerpts taken from Edward E. Hardy, trans., *Christology of the Later Fathers* (Louisville, KY: Westminster John Knox Press, 1954), pp. 349–354.
5 Excerpts taken from Russell, *Cyril of Alexandria*, pp. 176–189.

On the Unity of Christ[6]

The base material of their [the pagans'] poets is merely lies fashioned in rhythms and meters for grace and harmony, but for the truth they have little if any regard. {p. 49}

He [the Son of God] took what was ours to be his very own so that we might have all that was his. {p. 59}

The Word becoming flesh is the undoing and the abolition of all that fell upon human nature as our curse and punishment. {pp. 59–60}

The mystery of Christ runs the risk of being disbelieved precisely because it is so incredibly wonderful. For God was in humanity. He who was above all creation was in our human condition; the invisible one was made visible in the flesh; he who is from the heavens and from on high was in the likeness of earthly things; the immaterial one could be touched; he who is free in his own nature came in the form of a slave; he who blesses all creation became accursed; he who is all righteousness was numbered among transgressors; life itself came in the appearance of death. {p. 61}

Godhead is one thing, and manhood is another thing, considered in the perspective of their respective and intrinsic beings, but in the case of Christ they came together in a mysterious and incomprehensible union without confusion or change. The manner of this union is entirely beyond conception. {p. 77}

The Son can be truly understood to be one only if we confess that one and the same God the Word is divinely begotten from God, and mysteriously is man born of a woman according to the flesh. {p. 91}

He made our poverty his own, and we see in Christ the strange and rare paradox of Lordship in servant's form and divine glory in human abasement. That which was under the yoke in terms of the limitations of manhood was crowned with royal dignities, and that which was humble was raised to the most supreme excellence. The Only Begotten did not become man only to remain in the limits of the emptying. The point was that he

---

6 Excerpted from John A. McGuckin, trans., *St. Cyril of Alexandria: On the Unity of Christ* (Crestwood, NY: St. Vladimir's Seminary Press, 2000), pp. 49–133.

who was God by nature should, in the act of self-emptying, assume everything that went along with it. This was how he would be revealed as ennobling the nature of man in himself by making it participate in his own sacred and divine honors. {p. 101}

We had become accursed through Adam's transgression and had fallen into the trap of death, abandoned by God. Yet all things were made new in Christ (2 Cor 5:17) and our condition was restored to what it was in the beginning. It was entirely necessary that the Second Adam, who is from heaven (1 Cor 15:45) and superior to all sin, that is, Christ, the pure and immaculate first-fruits of our race, should free that nature of man from judgment, and once again call down upon it the heavenly graciousness of the Father. {p. 105}

The deity is invisible by nature, yet he who in his own nature is not visible, was seen by those on earth in our likeness, and God who is Lord appeared to us. {p. 111}

There was no other way to shake off the gloomy dominion of death, only by the incarnation of the Only Begotten. This was why he appeared as we are and made his own a body subject to corruption according to the inherent system of its nature. In so far as he himself is life, for he was born from the life of the Father, he intended to implant his own benefit within it [human nature], that is life itself. {p. 125}

He [the incarnate Son] came from Adam according to the flesh, as a second beginning for those on earth, to transform the nature of man in himself into a newness of life in holiness and incorruptibility through the resurrection from the dead. {p. 126}

There was no other way for the flesh to become life-giving [John 6:33], even though by its own nature it was subject to the necessity of corruption, except that it became the very flesh of the Word who gives life to all things. {p. 132}

Follow in the track of the faith of our holy Fathers. In this way we shall not be carried away from the right path, and will not abandon the royal road. {p. 133}

Hilary of Poitiers

Hilary (315–368) became bishop of Poitiers in 353 or 354. At the time, the Arian heresy was agitating the Western world, and Hilary was exiled for his opposition to it. While in exile, he wrote *The Trinity*, an extended confrontation with the Arians in which he valiantly upheld the full deity of the Son of God.

The Trinity[1]

By humbling Himself to take our flesh He did not lose His own proper nature, because as the Only Begotten of the Father he is "full of grace and truth" [John 1:14]; He is perfect in His own nature and true in ours. (1:11)

A firm faith rejects the captious and useless questions of philosophy, and truth does not become the victim of falsehood by yielding to the fallacies of human absurdities. It does not confine God within the terms of ordinary understanding, nor does it judge of Christ, in whom "the whole fullness of the deity dwells bodily" [Col 2:9], "according to the rudiments of the world" [Col 2:8]. (1:13)

By His death we are buried together in baptism so that we may return to eternal life, while death after life is our rebirth to life, and in dying to our vices we are born again to immortality. Renouncing His immortality, He died for us so that we might be raised from death to immortality with Him.

---

1 Excerpted from FC 25:1–543.

He received the flesh of sin, so that by assuming our flesh He might forgive our sin; but while He takes our flesh, He does not share in our sin. (1:13)

They [foolish people] measured the omnipotent nature of God by the weakness of their own nature—not by exalting themselves to the heights of infinity in their conjectures about infinite things, but by confining infinite things within the boundaries of their own power of comprehension. (1:15)

The best reader is the one who looks for the meaning of the words in the words themselves rather than reading his meaning into them, who carries away more than he brought, and who does not insist that the words signify what he presupposed before reading them. (1:18)

There is no comparison between earthly things and God, but the limitations of our knowledge force us to look for certain resemblances in inferior things as if they were manifestations of higher things, in order that, by our familiarity with ordinary things, we may be drawn away from the way we normally think and come to think in a fashion to which we are not accustomed. Every analogy, therefore, is to be considered as more useful to humans than as appropriate to God, because it hints at the meaning rather than explaining it fully. (1:19)

The guilt of the heretics and blasphemers compels us to undertake what is unlawful, to scale arduous heights, to speak of the ineffable, and to trespass upon forbidden places. . . . We are forced to raise our lowly words to subjects which cannot be described. By the guilt of another we are forced into guilt, so that what should have been restricted to the pious contemplation of our minds is now exposed to the dangers of human speech. (2:2)

Heresy does not come from Scripture, but from the way it is understood; the fault is in the mind, not in the words. (2:3)

I must undertake something that cannot be limited and venture upon something that cannot be comprehended, so that I may speak about God who cannot be accurately defined. (2:5)

Language will weary itself in speaking about Him, but He will not be encompassed. Reflect upon the periods of time; you will find that He always is, and when the numerals in your statement have finally come to an end, the eternal being of God does not come to an end. (2:6)

God is present everywhere and is present in his entirety wherever he is. Thus, He transcends the realm of understanding. (2:6)

I would rather think of these things about the Father than speak of them, for I am aware that all language is powerless to express what must be said. Moreover, in regard to what He is in Himself—that He is invisible, incomprehensible, and immortal—in these words there is admittedly an encomium of His majesty, an intimation of our thoughts, and a sort of definition of our meaning, but speech falls short of the nature and words do not portray the subject as it is. (2:7)

No matter what kind of language is used, it will be unable to speak of God as He is and what He is. The perfection of learning is to know God in such a manner that, although you realize He is not unknown, you perceive that He cannot be described. (2:7)

How shall we represent to ourselves the birth of the Only Begotten from the Unbegotten? . . . Can you not bear calmly our ignorance of the birth of the Creator, since you do not know the origin of the creature? (2:8–9)

We have touched upon these facts concerning the nature of the Divinity, not so as to assemble in one place the sum total of our knowledge, but in order to make us realize that what we are discussing cannot be comprehended. You declare that faith serves no purpose if there is nothing that can be comprehended. On the contrary, faith proclaims that this is its purpose: to know that it cannot comprehend that for which it is seeking. (2:11)

In solving these difficult questions that I have just mentioned I am aided by the poor fisherman who stands at my side. He is unknown, unlearned, a fishing net in his hands; his clothes are drenched; he is oblivious to the mud beneath his feet; he is in every respect a sailor. . . . Was it more wonderful to raise up the dead than to instruct an uneducated man in the knowledge of this doctrine? He said, "In the beginning was the Word" [John 1:1]. What is the meaning of the phrase, "in the beginning was"? The periods of time are passed by, the centuries are omitted, and the ages are laid aside. Think of any beginning that you please, you cannot contain Him in time, for at the beginning of the period of which you are thinking He already was. (2:13)

How shall we make a fitting recompense for so great a condescension? The Only Begotten God, born of God in an unutterable manner, is enclosed in the form of a tiny human body in the womb of the virgin and grows in size. He who contains all things and in whom and through whom all things come into existence is brought forth according to the law of human birth, and He at whose voice the archangels tremble and the heavens, earth, and all the elements of this world dissolve is heard in the cries of infancy. He who is invisible and incomprehensible and is not to be judged according to sight, feeling, and touch is covered up in a cradle. (2:25)

One thing is comprehended; another is seen; one thing is observed by the eyes; another, by the soul. The virgin begets; the birth comes from God. The infant weeps; the praise of the angel is heard. The swaddling-clothes are humiliating; God is adored. Thus the majesty of omnipotence is not lost when the lowliness of the flesh is assumed. (2:27)

Human language and comparisons cannot offer a satisfactory explanation for the things of God. That which is ineffable surpasses the limits and measure of any description, and that which is spiritual differs from the nature and analogy of human things. Our treatise is concerned with heavenly natures, but we will have to speak of those things which lie within the realm of spiritual concepts by employing an ordinary manner of speech—not, of course, because this is suitable to the dignity of God, but because it is necessary in view of the feebleness of our understanding. That is to say, we will have to speak about what we think and understand in accordance with our own environment and in our own words. (4:2)

The human mind, incapable of grasping the wisdom of God and foolish according to the standards of heavenly wisdom, passes judgment in harmony with its helplessness, and is wise in keeping with the weakness of its own nature. It should become foolish in its own estimation in order to be wise unto God; by admitting the poverty of its own reasoning and seeking after the wisdom of God, it may become wise, not in conformity with human wisdom, but in those things that lead to God, in order to pass from the knowledge of the folly of the world into the wisdom of God. (5:1)

We must not judge God according to our human sense of values. Our nature cannot lift itself up by its own power to the comprehension of heavenly things. We should learn from God what we are to think about God, because He is the only source of information about Himself. (5:21)

I know that it is difficult to bring about an improvement in the will when it has become rooted in its error, because many have approved of it and the weight of public opinion is in its favor. (6:1)

He who is the Way does not guide us to the wrong roads or to those that are impassable, nor does He who is the Truth deceive us by falsehoods, nor does He who is the Life leave us in the error of death. (7:33)

We must realize that God did not speak to Himself, but to us, and adapted the words of His discourse to our power of comprehension, so as to enable the weakness of our nature to grasp His meaning. (8:43)

If they are dazed who strain their power of sight by looking into the brightness of the sun, so that their sense of vision is extinguished by their curiosity as they seek more eagerly for the source of the blinding light, and as a result, in their endeavor to see more, they do not see at all, what are we to expect in the things of God and in the sun of righteousness? Will not they who wish to be too wise lapse into folly? Will not the dullness of a senseless stupidity take the place even of the keen light of knowledge? A lower nature will not grasp the principle of a higher nature, nor does heaven's plan of action come within the range of human comprehension. (10:53)

It is piety not to doubt; it is righteousness to believe; and it is salvation to confess. (10:70)

Faith is in simplicity, righteousness is in faith, and piety is in the confession. God does not call us to the blessed life via difficult questions, nor does He lure us on by the various categories of oratorical eloquence. Eternal happiness is obtained completely and solely by believing that God raised Jesus from the dead, by confessing that He is Lord [Rom 10:9]. (10:70)

It seems no less sacrilegious for me, whose only knowledge of God consists in my worship of Him, to refute these objections as it is to defend them, and to feel confident that I can express myself in words, which are even more limited than my thoughts, about the nature that surpasses the understanding of the human mind. (11:44)

An earthly intellect cannot fix any limits for God, nor can the faculties of a probing mind sound the depth of His wisdom, nor do skillful investigators grasp the judgment of His decrees, nor do the unsearchable ways of His knowledge yield to the endeavors of those who pursue them. (11:45)

We confess that the Only Begotten God was born, but born before the eternal ages. Our profession of faith must be kept within the limits that the words of the apostles and the prophets have determined, because the human mind does not grasp the idea of a timeless birth and because it is inconsistent with worldly natures to be born before time. (12:26)

Keep this piety of my faith undefiled, I beseech You, and let this be the utterance of my convictions even to the last breath of my spirit: that I may always hold fast to that which I professed in the creed of my regeneration when I was baptized in the Father, Son, and the Holy Spirit, so that I may adore You, our Father, and Your Son together with You, and that I may gain the favor of Your Holy Spirit who is from you through the Only Begotten. (12:57)

～ Ambrose

Ambrose (333–397) was a Roman imperial official who was elected bishop of Milan. He was a noted rhetorician, and his sermons attracted large crowds—among them the North African orator Augustine (later bishop of Hippo), who came to faith in Christ under Ambrose's preaching. Ambrose had close relationships with the imperial court, owing to his widely recognized leadership abilities, his remarkable preaching, and his episcopal position in the significant city of Milan; this led to frequent correspondence with the emperor and other members of the court.

Poems/Hymns[1]

✝ O splendor of God's glory bright,
    from light eternal bringing light,
O Light of Light, light's living spring,
    true day, all days illumining:

O come, true Sun of heaven's love,
    in lasting radiance from above,
and pour the Holy Spirit's ray
    on all we think or do today.

And now to You our prayers ascend,
    O Father glorious without end;

---

1 These hymns are in the public domain.

we plead with sovereign grace for power
> to conquer in temptation's hour.

Confirm our will to do the right,
> and keep our hearts from envy's blight;

let faith her eager fires renew,
> to hate the false, and love the true.

Let joyful be the passing day
> with thoughts as pure as morning's ray,
> with faith like noontide shining bright,
> our souls unshadowed by the night.

Dawn's glory gilds the earth and skies,
> let Him, our perfect morn, arise,
> the Word of God the Father one,
> the Father imaged in the Son.

✢ Savior of the nations, come,
> virgin's Son, make here Your home!

Marvel now, O heaven and earth,
> that the Lord chose such a birth.

Not of flesh and blood the Son,
> offspring of the Holy One;

born of Mary every blessed
> God in flesh is manifest.

Wondrous birth! O wondrous child
> of the virgin undefiled!

Though by all the world disowned,
> still to be in heaven enthroned.

From the Father forth He came
> and returns He to the same,
> captive leading death and hell—
> high the song of triumph swell!

You, the Father's only Son,
> over sin the victory won.
Boundless shall Your kingdom be;
> when shall we its glories see?

Praise to God the Father sing,
praise to God the Son, our King,
praise to God the Spirit be
> ever and eternally.

Hexaemeron (or, The Six Days of Creation)[2]

In the beginning of time, God created heaven and earth. Time proceeds from this world, not before the world. (1:20)

The earth is not suspended in the middle of the universe like a balance hung in equilibrium: the majesty of God holds it together by the law of His own will. (1:22)

Evil arose from us, and was not made by the Creator God. It is produced by the created thing; it does not have the dignity of a natural substance. It is a fault due to our mutability and is an error due to our fall. (1:30)

No thinking being can deny that evil exists in a world like this in which accident and death are so frequent. Yet from what we have already said, we can gather that evil is not a living substance, but is a deviation of mind and soul from the path of true virtue, a deviation which frequently steals upon the souls of the unaware. The greater danger is not, therefore, from what is external to us, but from our own selves. Our adversary is within us. (1:31)

Look closely at your intentions; explore the disposition of your mind; set up guards to watch over the thoughts of your mind and the cupidities of your heart. You yourself are the cause of your wickedness; you yourself are the leader of your own crimes and the instigator of your own misdeeds. Why do you summon an alien nature to furnish as excuse for your sins? (1:31)

---

2 Excerpts taken from FC 42:1–283.

Let us not search outside of ourselves or attribute to others the causes of that of which we ourselves are sole masters. Instead, we must recognize that these causes belong only to us. (1:31)

And God said, "Let there be a dome in the midst of the waters and let it separate the waters from the waters; . . . and it was so"[Gen 1:6]. Listen to the words of God: "Let there be," He said. This is the word of a commander, not of an adviser. He gives orders to nature and does not comply with its power. He does not regard its measurements, nor does He examine its weight. His will is the measure of things and His word is the completion of the work. (2:4)

But since His word is nature's birth, justly therefore does He who gave nature its origin presume to give nature its law. (2:4)

It [natural law] is not the result of some natural propensity, but issues from the will and operation of the most high God. The waters listen to the command of God and the voice of God is the efficient cause of nature. . . . The creature followed the injunction of its Creator and from the law proceeded custom; the law of its first constitution left its imprint for future ages. (3:8)

May God grant us our prayer: to sail on a swift ship under a favorable breeze and finally reach a haven of safety; that we may not be exposed to spiritual obstacles too great to overcome; that we may not meet with shipwreck to our faith. We pray also for a peace profound and, if there be anything that may arouse the storms of this world against us, that we may have as our ever-watchful pilot our Lord Jesus, who by His command can calm the tempest and restore once more the sea's tranquillity. To Him be honor and glory in perpetuity, both now and forever, and for all ages to come. Amen. (3:24)

The elegance of our life is entrenched and hedged about by certain cares, so that sadness is close neighbor to beauty. . . . Although you may shine with the splendor of nobility, or because of your superior power, or by the brilliance of your virtue, the thorn is ever close to you, the bramble is ever near you. (3:48)

Equality should be observed in the Church, so that no one of wealth and high position should exalt himself and that no one who is poor and lowly should despair. Liberty is one and the same for all members of the Church; all possess justice and favor in an impartial manner. (3:51)

"Let the earth bring forth," God said, and immediately the whole earth was filled with growing vegetation. And to humanity it was said, "Love the Lord your God"; yet the love of God is not instilled in the hearts of all. Deafer are human hearts than the hardest rock. (3:70)

The bramble preceded in time the light of the sun; the blade of grass is older than the moon. Therefore, do not believe that object to be a god to which the gifts of God are seen to be preferred. Three days [of creation] have passed. No one, meanwhile, has looked for the sun, yet the brilliance of light has been in evidence everywhere. (4:1)

[Regarding astrology:] Some people have attempted to set down the characteristics of birth days and the future state of each newborn child. Yet a prognostication of this sort is both vain and useless to those who seek it and is an impossibility for those who promise it. What is so inane as to suppose that everyone should be convinced that he is what his birth has made him? ... Why has the Lord laid down rewards for the good or punishment for the wicked if their habits are prescribed by fate and their social behavior depends on the course of the stars? (4:13)

How many do we see snatched from amid their vices and sins to be converted to a better life? It was certainly not because of their birth that the apostles were freed and called from the company of sinners. Rather, the coming of Christ sanctified them and the hour of His Passion redeemed them from death. The condemned thief who was crucified with our Lord passed over into everlasting Paradise, not because of a favorable nativity but because of his confession of faith. (4:13)

Where destiny decides, personal initiative is held in no esteem. (4:19)

"Let the waters bring forth swarms of living creatures" [Gen 1:20], said the Lord—a brief statement, but a significant one and one widely effective in endowing with their nature the smallest and the largest animals without distinction. The whale as well as the frog came into existence at the same time by the same creative power. (5:5)

Fish follow a divine law, whereas human beings contravene it. Fish duly comply with the celestial mandates, but humans make void the precepts of God. (5:29)

Moses saw that there was no place in the words of the Holy Spirit for the vanity of this perishable knowledge which deceives and deludes us in our attempt to explain the unexplainable. He believed that only those things should be recorded which tend to our salvation. (6:8)

The Word of God permeates every creature in the constitution of the world. (6:9)

The divine wisdom penetrates and fills all things. Far more conviction is gained from the observation of irrational creatures than from the arguments of rational beings. Of more value is the testimony given by nature than the proof presented by teaching. (6:21)

The Mysteries [a treatise on the sacraments][3]

God in his desire to repair what He had given caused the flood [Gen 5], and ordered Noah the righteous one to embark on the ark. When, as the flood subsided, he first sent forth a raven which did not return, he afterwards sent forth a dove, which is said to have returned with an olive twig. You see the water; you see the wood; you perceive the dove—and do you doubt the mystery? (§10)

Water without the preaching of the Cross of the Lord is of no advantage for future salvation; but when it has been consecrated by the mystery of the saving cross, then it is ordered for the use of the spiritual laver and the cup of salvation. (§14)

You should not trust only your physical eyes. What needs to be discerned here cannot be seen, for the one is temporal, the other eternal. Here, what is seen cannot be comprehended by the eyes; rather, it is discerned by the spirit and the mind. (§15)

You say, "I see waters which I see every day; are these able to cleanse me

---

3 Excerpts taken from FC 44:5–28.

from sin? I have often descended into water and never been cleansed that way." From this you should learn that water does not cleanse without the Spirit. (§19)

You say, "I see something else [i.e., bread]; how can you tell me that I receive the body of Christ?" This still remains to be demonstrated. For that, we use examples great enough to show that this is not what nature formed, but what benediction consecrated, and that the power of benediction is greater than that of nature, because even nature itself is changed by benediction. (§50)

That sacrament which you receive is effected by the words of Christ. But if the words of Elijah had such power as to call down fire from heaven, will not the words of Christ have power enough to change the nature of the elements? You have read about the creation of the world, that "He commanded and they were created" [Ps 148:5]. So, cannot the words of Christ, which were able to make what was not out of nothing, change things from what they were into things they previously were not? (§52)

By the mysteries of the Incarnation let us establish the truth of the mysteries [i.e., the sacraments]. Did the process of nature [for generation] precede when the Lord Jesus was born of Mary? If we seek the usual course, a woman conceives after intercourse with a man. It is clear then that the virgin conceived contrary to the course of nature. And this body made in the Eucharist is from the virgin. Why are you concerned to find the course of nature in the body of Christ, when the Lord Jesus Himself was born of the virgin contrary to nature? (§53)

What we eat, what we drink, the Holy Spirit expresses to you saying, "Taste and see that the Lord is good; happy are those who take refuge in him" [Ps 34:8]. Christ is in that sacrament, because the body is Christ's. So the food is not corporeal but spiritual. (§58)

If the Holy Spirit coming upon the virgin effected conception, and accomplished the work of generation, surely there must be no doubt that the Spirit, coming upon the font [of baptism], or upon those who obtain baptism, effects regeneration. (§59)

Letters[4]

No one is injured by having almighty God preferred to him. (#17:7)

Nothing is more important than religion, nothing is higher than faith. (#17:12)

I would rather fall somewhat short in my duty than in humility. (#51:5)

That one sins is no cause for surprise. What is blameworthy is failure to acknowledge one's error and humble oneself before God. (#51:9)

You are human, and temptation has come to you. Conquer it. Sin is only put away by tears and repentance. (#51:11)

Are not those who condemn their sin truer Christians than those who think to defend it? (#51:15)

It has never been my way to turn my mind away from Him, or to count anyone's favor of more value than the favor of Christ. I wrong no one when I prefer God to all. (#57:1)

The fear of God requires us to act with constancy. (#57:6)

---

[4] Excerpts taken from S. L. Greenslade, trans., *Early Latin Theology* (Louisville, KY: Westminster John Knox Press, 1954), pp. 182–278.

~ Rufinus

Rufinus (345–410) spent some years in a monastery in northern Italy. In due course, he became involved in translation work. However, his approach was too freewheeling for many of his contemporaries, for Rufinus readily shortened or modified what the original presented. Through his work, though, several works of the Greek Church Fathers became available to Latin Christian readers. One of his few original writings was his *Commentary on the Apostles' Creed,* an exposition of the basic creed in use in the church in Rome and in several other cities in Italy.

A Commentary on the Apostles' Creed[1]

I cannot forget the acute maxim of sensible men, "Speaking even the truth about God has its perils." (§1)

No one embarks on the sea, committing his life to the watery depths, without first believing in the possibility of his survival. No farmer buries his seeds under the upturned sods or scatters his fruits on the earth without the confident belief that, fostered by the rains and the cooperation of the sun's warmth, the soil will multiply the fruit and bear its crop, ripening it with favorable winds. In fact, there is nothing in life that can be transacted without a preliminary readiness to believe. Is it then at all surprising that, when we approach God, we first of all confess that we believe, seeing that without belief even the common routine of life cannot be accomplished?

---

1 Excerpts taken from ACW 20:28–87.

I have set these axioms down at the outset because pagans are in the habit of objecting that our religion lacks a rational basis, depending solely on the persuasion of belief.... But if no one undertakes enterprises like these without first believing that certain results will ensue, is it not understandable that belief should be the way to the knowledge of God? (§3)

He who is the originator of all things is Himself without origin. (§4)

I would rather, however, you did not discuss how God the Father generated the Son, and did not plunge too inquisitively into the depths of the mystery. There is a danger that, in prying too persistently into the brightness of inaccessible light, you may find yourself deprived of the tiny glimpse which is all the good God grants to mortals. (§4)

In the case of God, when we describe Him as One, we use the term in an absolute, not a numerical, sense. (§5)

Being incorporeal, His generation neither results in plurality nor involves division: He who is born is not separated from His begetter. (§6)

Nothing that is unique can admit of any comparison: He who is the maker of all things cannot bear any likeness in substance to the things He has made. (§8)

It is congruous that He who is only Son in heaven should be only Son on earth as well, and therefore should be born in a unique manner. (§9)

The Trinity... is everywhere concealed and yet is everywhere manifested. (§10)

You should not presuppose anything impossible in a transaction in which the power of the Most High was at work. (§13)

Whenever one indulges his lusts, he sells his soul for a price. (§15)

The death to which He [Jesus Christ] submits is going to result in the despoiling of death. (§16)

Christ's suffering in His flesh entailed no loss or injury to His deity. It was in order to accomplish salvation through the weakness of flesh that His divine nature went down to death in the flesh. The intention was not that He might be held fast by death according to the law governing mortals, but that, assured of rising again by His own power, He might open the gates of death. It was as if a king were to go to a dungeon. (§17)

It was because facts like these were bound to arouse incredulity when proclaimed by the apostles that the prophet, speaking in their person, exclaimed, "[Lord,] who has believed our report?" [Is 53:1]. For it passes belief that God, the Son of God, should, as Christian preachers affirm, have suffered such indignities. In order, therefore, to prevent doubts arising among prospective believers, these things were announced beforehand by the prophets. (§21)

A crown of thorns, it is written, was set upon Him. . . . If I may disclose to you, however, the heart of a mystery, it was appropriate that He who came to remove the sins of the world should at the same time release the earth from the curses inflicted on it when the first-formed man sinned, and it received the sentence of transgression in the Lord's words: "Cursed is the ground for your sake; . . . thorns and thistles it shall bring forth for you" [Gen 3:17, 18]. Jesus was therefore crowned with thorns in order that the primordial sentence of condemnation might be remitted. (§22)

He was led to the Cross, and the life of the whole world hung suspended from its wood. (§22)

It is He alone who has committed no sin, and who has taken away the sin of the world. For if by one man death could enter the world, how much more could life be restored by one man, who was God as well? (§25)

The glory of His Resurrection brought out in Christ the splendor of everything that previously seemed feeble and weak. (§29)

You should discern the Creator's goodness in His readiness to follow you down to the depths to which your sins have plunged you. (§29)

By His Passion He made perfect that human flesh which had been brought down to death by the first man's sin, and restored it by the power of His Resurrection; sitting at God's right hand, He placed it in the highest heavens.

In view of this the apostle says, "[God] raised us up together, and made us sit together in the heavenly places" [Eph 2:6]. (§29)

Since His entry through the gates of heaven struck its doorkeepers and princes as something novel, and they saw fleshly nature penetrating the secret recesses of heaven, they uttered to one another the words which David, under the Holy Spirit's influence, foretold: "Lift up your heads, O you gates! And be lifted up, you everlasting doors! And the King of glory shall come in. Who is this King of glory? The Lord strong and mighty, the Lord mighty in battle" [Ps 24:7–8]. (§31)

Hold fast to the holy Church, which proclaims its faith in God the Father almighty, and His only Son Jesus Christ our Lord, and the Holy Spirit, as existing in one harmonious and indivisible substance, and believes that the Son of God was born from the virgin, suffered for humanity's salvation, and rose from the dead in the identical flesh with which He was born. (§39)

He who has promised forgiveness is king of all things: He who assures us of it is Lord of heaven and earth. Are you reluctant for me to believe that He who made me a man out of mere clay can transform my guilt into innocence? (§40)

Why, I ask you, should you take such a restricted, feeble view of the divine power as to believe it is impossible for the dust out of which each individual's flesh is composed, once it is dispersed, to be collected together and restored to its original form? Are you not prepared to admit the possibility when you see the ingenuity of mere mortals discovering veins of metal buried deep in the earth, or the expert's eye noticing gold where the inexperienced man's assumes nothing but earth? Is there any reason why we should not allow such power to Him who made humankind, seeing the heights to which the creature made by Him can attain? (§42)

[In the resurrection:] Each soul has restored to it not a composite or alien body, but the actual one it formerly possessed. (§42)

Just as Christ, "having been raised from the dead, dies no more; death no longer has dominion over Him" [Rom 6:9], so those who will rise again in Christ will be no longer subject to either corruption or death not because they will have discarded their flesh, but because its status and character will have been altered. (§45)

It is my prayer that the Lord would vouchsafe to me and all my hearers that, having kept the faith we have embraced and having finished our course, we may await the crown of righteousness which has been laid up for us, and, being delivered from confusion and everlasting reproach, may be found among those who rise again to eternal life: through Christ our Lord, through whom to God the Father almighty, along with the Holy Spirit, be glory and dominion forever and ever. Amen. (§48)

~ Jerome

Jerome (345–420) lived a life of severe asceticism, mostly in the Christian East. Even so, he always counted himself a Roman, and his example and extensive correspondence helped to establish the ascetic life in the Western half of the Church. A gifted linguist, he learned Hebrew under the tutelage of a Jewish scholar; with that, plus his already extensive knowledge of Greek, he translated the Scriptures anew into Latin. The resultant version came to be known as the Vulgate; it became the version of the Bible used throughout the Western Church during the Middle Ages.

Letters[1]

For my part, I am like a sick sheep astray from the flock. Unless the Good Shepherd shall place me on His shoulders and carry me back to the fold, my steps will totter, and in the very effort of rising I shall find my feet give way. (#2)

As the Scripture says, "God resists the proud, but gives grace to the humble" [1 Pet 5:5]. Think what a sin it must be which has God for its opponent. In the gospel the Pharisee is rejected because of his pride, and the publican is accepted because of his humility. (#12)

You are mistaken if you suppose that there is ever a time when the Chris-

---

1 Excerpted from NPNF (2nd) 6:1–295.

tian does not suffer persecution. You are most dangerously under attack when you are not aware that you are under attack. (#14:4)

Not to aim at perfection is itself a sin. (#14:7)

There is one nature of God and one only; and this, and this alone, truly is. For absolute being is derived from no other source but is all its own. All things besides—that is, all things created—although they appear to be, are not. For there was a time when they were not, and that which once was not may again cease to be. (#15:4)

Do not wish to seem very devout nor more humble than need be, lest you seek glory by shunning it. (#22:27)

If there is anything of which you are ignorant, if you have any doubt about Scripture, ask one whose life commends him, whose age puts him above suspicion, whose reputation does not belie him. (#22:29)

No meal should be begun without prayer, and before leaving table thanks should be returned to the Creator. . . . In every act we do, in every step we take, let our hand trace the Lord's cross. (#22:37)

Some people take being dull-witted or coarsely ignorant for holiness, calling themselves the disciples of fishermen, as if we were made holy by knowing nothing. (#27:1)

The rude and simple brother must not suppose himself a saint just because he knows nothing; and he who is educated and eloquent must not measure his saintliness merely by his fluency. Of two imperfect things, holy rusticity is better than sinful eloquence. (#52:9)

He [Christ] it was who of old threatened you [death] in Hosea: "O Death, I will be your plagues! / O Grave, I will be your destruction!" [Hos 13:14]. By His death you are dead; by His death we live. You have swallowed up and you are swallowed up. When you were smitten with a longing for the body He had assumed and when your greedy jaws fancied it a prey, your inward parts were wounded with hooked fangs.
 To You, O Savior Christ, do we Your creatures offer thanks that, when You were slain, You slew our mighty adversary! (#60:2–3)

Apart from knowledge of his Creator anyone is nothing more than a brute. But now the voices and writings of all nations proclaim the Passion and the Resurrection of Christ. I say nothing of the Jews, the Greeks, and the Romans, peoples whom the Lord has dedicated to His faith by the title written on His Cross. The immortality of the soul and its continuance after the dissolution of the body—truths of which Pythagoras dreamed, which Democritus refused to believe, and which Socrates discussed in prison to console himself for the sentence passed upon him—are now the familiar themes of Indian and of Persian, of Goth and of Egyptian. The fierce Bessians [a Thracian tribe] and the throng of skin-clad savages who used to offer human sacrifices in honor of the dead have broken out of their harsh discord into the sweet music of the Cross, and Christ is the one cry of the whole world. (#60:4)

The mind that is given to Christ shows the same earnestness in things of small as of great importance, knowing that it must render an account of every idle word. (#60:12)

It is no small gain to know your own ignorance. (#61:3)

Time would fail me were I to try to lay before you in order all the passages in the Holy Scriptures which relate to the efficacy of baptism, or to explain the mysterious doctrine of that second birth which, though it is our second, is yet our first in Christ. (#69:7)

The best advice I can give you is this: church traditions, when they do not run counter to the faith, should be observed in the form in which previous generations have handed them down; and the usage of one church is not to be annulled because it is contrary to that of another. (#71:6)

To change one's disposition is a greater achievement than to change one's dress. It is harder for us to part with arrogance than with gold and gems. (#77:2)

[Regarding Matt 19:9:] Now a commandment which is given to men logically applies to women also. For it cannot be that, while an adulterous wife is to be put away, an incontinent husband is to be retained.... [In this regard,] the laws of Caesar are different, it is true, from the laws of Christ. ... But with us Christians what is unlawful for women is equally unlawful for men, and since both serve the same God, both are bound by the same obligations. (#77:3)

The poor wretch whom we despise, whom we cannot so much as look at, and the very sight of whom turns our stomachs, is human like ourselves, is made of the same clay as we are, is formed out of the same elements. All that he suffers we too may suffer. Let us then regard his wounds as though they were our own, and then all our insensibility to another's suffering will give way before our pity for ourselves. (#77:6)

No place is left for flattery with its sordid calculations. (#79:4)

If David the friend of God and Solomon who loved God were overcome like others, if their fall is meant to warn us and their repentance to lead us to salvation, who in this slippery life can be sure of not falling? (#79:7)

Suggestions of sin tickle all our minds, and the decision rests with our own hearts either to admit or to reject the thoughts which come. (#79:9)

We are all made of the same clay and formed of the same elements. Whether we wear silk or rags, we are all at the mercy of the same desire. It does not fear the royal purple; it does not disdain the squalor of the beggar. (#79:10)

Let us not lull ourselves with the delusion that we can always fall back on repentance. For this is at best but a remedy for misery. Let us shrink from incurring a wound which must be painful to cure. (#79:10)

The objects which we seek are either good or bad. If they are good, they need no help from another; and if they are bad, the fact that many sin together is no excuse. (#81:1)

Let us not imitate the faults of one whose virtues we cannot equal. (#84:8)

I would sooner risk my reputation than my faith. (#84:11)

We may not "serve the creature rather than the Creator, who is blessed forever" [Rom 1:25]. Even so, we honor the relics of the martyrs, so that we may adore Him whose martyrs they are. We honor the servants, so that their honor may be reflected upon their Lord who Himself says, "He who receives you receives Me" [Matt 10:40]. (#109:1)

Nothing makes God so angry as when people from despair of better things cleave to those which are worse; indeed, this despair in itself is a sign of unbelief. (#122:1)

Only by trampling youthful lusts underfoot can you hope to climb the heights of true maturity. For the path along which you walk is a slippery one and the glory of success is less than the shame of failure. (#125:1)

Sometimes the quicksands of vice suck us down as we sail at ease through the calm water, and the desert of this world is inhabited by venomous reptiles. (#125:2)

Let your fasts be moderate, since if they are carried to excess they weaken the stomach, and by making more food necessary to make up for it lead to indigestion, which is the parent of lust. A frugal, temperate diet is good for both body and soul. (#125:7)

You must not think yourself an old soldier while you are still a recruit, a master while you are still a pupil. (#125:8)

The first point with which I must deal is whether you ought to live alone or in a monastery with others. I would prefer you to have the society of holy people and not to be your own teacher. If you set out on a strange road without a guide you may easily at the start take a wrong turn and make a mistake, going too far or not far enough. . . . In solitude pride quickly creeps in, and when one has fasted for a little while and has seen no one, thinks oneself a person of some accomplishment. (#125:9)

Do not let your mind offer a lodging to disturbing thoughts, for if they once find a home in your breast they will become your masters and lead you into fatal sin. Engage in some occupation, so that the devil may always find you busy. (#125:11)

But now persons who profess religion are not ashamed to seek unjust profits, and the good name of Christianity is more often a cloak for fraud than a victim to it. (#125:16)

Godly habits will gradually grow on you, and finally you will do of your own accord what was at first a matter of compulsion. (#125:16)

In every rank and condition of life the very bad is mingled with the very good. (#125:17)

Do not be carried away by some caprice and rush into authorship. Learn long and carefully what you propose to teach. (#125:18)

Never speak evil of anyone or suppose that you make yourself better by assailing the reputations of others. (#125:18)

Well does one of our own writers [Tertullian, in *Against Hermogenes*] say, "The philosophers are the patriarchs of the heretics." With their perverse doctrine they have stained the spotlessness of the Church. (#133:2)

A nice return, truly, does one make to God when to assert the freedom of his will he rebels against God! For our part we gladly embrace this freedom, but we never forget to thank the giver, knowing that we are powerless unless He continually preserves in us His own gift. (#133:6)

You fancy that a wrong is inflicted on you and your freedom of choice is destroyed if you are forced to fall back on God as the moving cause of all your actions, if you are made dependent on His will. . . . And so you presume rashly to maintain that each individual is governed by his own choice. But if he is governed by his own choice, what becomes of God's help? (#133:7)

Despair is the one sin for which there is no remedy. By obstinate rejection of God's grace people turn His mercy into sternness and severity. (#147:3)

~ Augustine of Hippo

Augustine (354–430) served as bishop of Hippo in North Africa. The most profound of all the Latin Church Fathers, he has exercised more influence on the subsequent history of Christian thought in the West than any other figure.

Augustine had received an excellent education, become a professor of rhetoric, and moved to Italy to pursue his career. His mother, Monica, had prayed faithfully for her son. In due course, Augustine—who had been searching for truth—went to hear the sermons of Ambrose of Milan, one of the great orators of that day. For the first time, Augustine came under the impact of the Christian message in all its richness; not long afterward, he turned to Christianity.

He returned to North Africa, set up a monastic community, and was eventually chosen to be bishop in Hippo. His writings include sermons, letters, polemical treatises, expositions of doctrine, his spiritual autobiography (*Confessions*), and his magnum opus on the course of history, *The City of God*. He held and taught a strong view of predestination and divine sovereignty in the dispensation of grace; his views in this regard stimulated vigorous argument in Western Christianity, in his own day and in subsequent centuries.

Orthodox Christianity views Augustine with some suspicion. His greater confidence in human reason for penetrating the mysteries of the Christian faith, his views on the imputation of original sin, and his denial of the freedom of the human will after our first parents' sin have all been rejected within Orthodoxy. Excerpts in which Augustine presents such views are footnoted.

Against the Academics[1]

It may be that what is commonly called "fortune" is governed by a secret ordinance; and we call "chance" that element in things for which we can offer no cause or reason. (1:1)

We have real progress in philosophy when a disputant thinks little of victory as compared with the discovery of what is just and true. (1:3)

Is there any word of which nature has imprinted in our spirit a clearer notion than that word "wisdom"? I admit, however, that once the notion itself leaves, as it were, the harbor of our mind and spreads the sails of words, immediately it is menaced a thousand times with the shipwreck of misrepresentation. (1:15)

The true and inscrutable God, who is perhaps—but only rarely—perceived by intelligence,[2] is never perceived by any sense. (1:8)

If people, wrongly, think that they have already found truth, they do not seek it with diligence even if they seek it—indeed, they even acquire an aversion for such search. (2:1)

I am at this time doing nothing but purging myself of futile and harmful opinions. (2:9)

It is a disgrace for disputants to haggle about words, when no difference about the subject matter remains. (2:11)

On the Profit of Believing[3]

Nothing is easier than for one not only to say but also to think that one has found out the truth—but how difficult that is in reality! (§1)

---

1 Excerpted from ACW 12:35–151.
2 Augustine's confidence in human intelligence to penetrate God, even though he limits its possibility, still goes well beyond what other Church Fathers affirm. It is in that regard a novelty in teaching and is suspect from an Orthodox Christian vantage point.
3 Excerpts taken from NPNF (1st) 3:347–366.

The pathway of catholic teaching, which has flowed down from Christ Himself through the apostles to our day, will hereafter flow down to posterity. (§20)

If the providence of God does not preside over human affairs, we have no need to busy ourselves about religion. (§34)

The First Catechetical Instruction[4]

For my part, I am nearly always dissatisfied with my discourse. For I desire something better, which I often inwardly enjoy before I begin to unfold my thought in spoken words; but when I find that my powers of expression come short of my knowledge of the subject, I am sorely disappointed that my tongue has not been able to answer the demands of my mind. (§3)

But often the eagerness of those who desire to hear me shows me that my discourse is not as dull as it seems to me. From the enjoyment, too, which they manifest I gather that they receive some benefit from it. (§4)

People listen to us with much greater pleasure when we ourselves take pleasure in the work of instruction. The thread of our discourse is affected by the very joy that we ourselves experience, and as a consequence is delivered more easily and received more gratefully. (§4)

For no other reason were all the things that we read in the Holy Scriptures written before our Lord's coming than to announce His coming and to prefigure the Church to be—that is to say, the people of God throughout all nations, which is Christ's body, in which are included and numbered all the righteous who lived in this world even before His coming and who believed that He would come, as we believe that He has come. . . . They were not separated from Him by being His precursors, but rather were joined to Him by their obedience to His will. (§6)

Christ came chiefly for this reason, that human beings might learn how much God loves them, and might learn this so that they might begin to love Him by whom they were first loved, and so might love their neighbors at the bidding and after the example of Him who made Himself man's

---

4 Excerpted from ACW 2:13–87.

neighbor by loving him, when instead of being His neighbor he was wandering far from Him. If, moreover, all divine Scripture that was written before was written to foretell the coming of the Lord, and if whatever has since been committed to writing and established by divine authority tells of Christ and counsels love, then it is evident that on these two commandments of the love of God and the love of our neighbor depend not merely the whole Law and the Prophets (which, at the time when the Lord uttered these precepts, were as yet the only Holy Scripture), but also all the inspired books that have been written at a later period for our welfare and handed down to us. (§8)

In the Old Testament the New is concealed, and in the New the Old is revealed. (§8)

Nothing is more opposed to love than envy, and the mother of envy is pride. (§8)

Love must be built up out of the sternness of God, which makes a human heart quail with a most salutary fear, so that, rejoicing to find oneself loved by Him whom he fears, one makes bold to love Him in return, and at the same time may shrink from offending His love, even if one could do so with impunity. (§10)

Even those who have departed this life as catholics and have left to posterity some Christian literature, in certain passages of their works—either because they have not been understood, or else (as is the case with human infirmity) because they were not able by keenness of intellect to pierce the more hidden truths, and were led astray from the truth by a semblance of truth—have served as an occasion to presumptuous and rash men to devise and beget some heresy. (§12)

The only voice that reaches the ears of God is the emotion of the heart. (§13)

How can the mind that feeds on dissension and strife preserve the health that comes from peace? (§25)

Christ the Lord, made human, despised all the good things of earth, that He might show us that these things are to be despised; and endured all earthly ills that He taught must be endured; so that neither might happiness be sought in the former nor unhappiness be feared in the latter. For, since He was born of a mother who, although she conceived, was untouched by man and always remained untouched—a virgin in conception, a virgin in childbearing, a virgin in death—espoused to a mere workman, He put an end to all the inflated pride of carnal nobility. Since He was born, moreover, in the city of Bethlehem, which among all the cities of Judea was so insignificant that even today it is called a village, He did not want anyone to glory in the exaltation of an earthly city. Likewise, He became poor, He to whom all things belong and by whom all things were created, lest anyone believing in Him should dare to be unduly exalted because of earthly riches. He refused to be made a king by men, because He was showing the way of lowliness to those wretches whom their pride had separated from Him; and yet the whole creation bears witness to His everlasting kingdom. He hungered who feeds all, He thirsted by whom all drink is created—He who is spiritually both the bread of those who hunger and the wellspring of those who thirst; He was wearied with earthly journeying who has made Himself the way to heaven for us; He became, as it were, one dumb and deaf in the presence of His revilers, He through whom the dumb spoke and the deaf heard; He was bound who has freed humankind from the bonds of their infirmities; He was scourged who drove out from human bodies the scourges of all pains; He was crucified who put an end to our torments; He died who raised the dead to life. But He also rose again, nevermore to die, that none might learn from Him so to despise death as though destined never to live hereafter. (§40)

He shall come in the splendor of power who before condescended to come in the lowliness of human nature; and He shall separate all the holy from the unholy—not only from those who have altogether refused to believe in Him, but also from those who have believed in Him in vain and without fruit. (§45)

The devil speaks seductive words, bent as he is above all on making a mockery of our faith in the resurrection. But from your own self receive the assurance that, since you have been, so also you will be—since though before you were not, you see that you now are. For where was that mass of your body, and where that form and structure of your members a few years ago, before you were born, or even before you had been conceived in your mother's womb—where was this present mass and stature of your body? Did it not come forth into the light from the hidden recesses of this creation, secretly fashioned by the Lord God, and rise by a regular growth through various stages to its present size and shape? Is it, then, too difficult a thing for God, who even in a moment brings together from their hiding places the cloudbanks and overcasts the sky in the twinkling of an eye, to restore the substance of your body as it was before, since He was able to make it as before it was not? Believe, therefore, with a strong and unshaken conviction, that all things that seem to be withdrawn from the eyes of human beings, as it were, by decay, are safe and sound as regards the omnipotence of God, who shall restore them without any delay or difficulty. (§46)

[In the final state,] we will no longer shout the equality of the Father and of the Son and of the Holy Spirit, and the unity of the Trinity itself, and the manner in which these three are one God, in a profession of faith expressed in babble of words, but may absorb this by most pure and most fervent contemplation in the heavenly silence. (§47)

Whatever you hear from the canonical books that you cannot refer to the love of eternity, and truth, and holiness, and to the love of your neighbor, believe to have been said or done with a figurative meaning, and try to understand it as referring to that twofold love. (§50)

Once a flood took place over the whole earth that sinners might be destroyed. And yet those who escaped in the ark were a figure of the Church that was to be, which now floats upon the waves of the world and is saved from sinking by the wood of the Cross of Christ. (§53)

On Faith and the Creed[5]

By no other way was it possible for us who fell by pride to return but by humility. (§6)

Just as in that sepulcher no other dead person was buried, whether before or after Him, so neither in that womb, whether before or after, was anything mortal conceived. (§11)

---

5   Excerpted from NPNF (1st) 3:321–333.

Concerning Faith in Things Not Seen[6]

You will not doubt a virgin having a son, if you are willing to believe a God being born. (§5)

On Christian Doctrine[7]

The wisdom of God in healing humankind has applied Himself to its cure, being Himself both healer and medicine. Since humanity fell through pride, He restored it through humility. We were ensnared by the wisdom of the serpent; we are set free by the foolishness of God. ... We used our immortality so badly as to incur the penalty of death; Christ used His mortality so well as to restore us to life. The disease was brought in through a woman's corrupted soul; the remedy came through a woman's virgin body. (1:14)

Faith will totter if the authority of Scripture begins to shake. (1:37)

In regard to the canonical Scriptures, one must follow the judgment of the greater number of catholic churches; and among these, of course, a high place must be given to those which have been privileged to be the seat of an apostle and to receive apostolic letters. With this, among the canonical Scriptures one will judge according to the following standard: to prefer those that are received by all the catholic churches to those which some do not receive. Among those, again, which are not received by all, he will prefer those which have the sanction of the greater number and those of greater authority to those held by the smaller number and those of less authority. (2:8)

Two books, one called Wisdom and the other Ecclesiasticus, are ascribed to Solomon from a certain resemblance of style, but the most likely opinion is that they were written by Jesus the son of Sirach. Still they are to be reckoned among the prophetical books, since they have attained recognition as authoritative. (2:8)

Unless we walk by faith, we shall not attain to sight. (2:12)

---

6 Excerpts taken from NPNF (1st) 3:337–343.
7 Excerpts taken from NPNF (1st) 2:519–597.

Let every good and true Christian understand that wherever truth may be found, it belongs to his master; and while he recognizes and acknowledges the truth, even in their religious literature, let him reject the figments of superstition. (2:18)

The science of reasoning is of very great service in searching into and unraveling all sorts of questions that come up in Scripture; only in the use of it we must guard against the love of wrangling and the childish vanity of entrapping an adversary. (2:31)

If those who are called philosophers, and especially the Platonists, have said anything that is true and in harmony with our faith, we are not only not to shrink from it, but to claim it for our own use from those who have unlawful possession of it. (2:40)

[When one is uncertain about the meaning of a scriptural passage:] Let the reader consult the rule of faith gathered from the plainer passages of Scripture and from the authority of the Church. (3:2)

The proof of our liberty has shone forth so clearly in the Resurrection of our Lord. (3:9)

Our Lord Himself and apostolic practice have handed down to us a few rites in place of many, and these at once easy to perform, most majestic in their significance, and most sacred in the observance—the sacrament of baptism and the celebration of the body and blood of the Lord. (3:9)

Scripture commands nothing except love and condemns nothing but lust, and in that way fashions the lives of human beings. . . . By "love" I mean the affection of the mind which aims at the enjoyment of God for His own sake and the enjoyment of oneself and one's neighbor in subordination to God. By "lust" I mean that affection of the mind which aims at enjoying oneself and one's neighbor, and other corporeal things, without reference to God. What lust, when unsubdued, does towards corrupting one's soul and body is called "vice"; but what it does to injure another is called "crime". . . . In the same way, what love does with a view to one's own advantage is "prudence," but what it does with a view to a neighbor's advantage is called "benevolence." (3:10)

There is no difficulty in abstaining except when there is lust in enjoying. (3:18)

What more liberal and more fruitful provision could God have made in regard to the sacred Scriptures than that the same words might be understood in several senses, all of which are sanctioned by the concurring testimony of other passages equally divine? (3:27)

The Septuagint translators, being themselves under the guidance of the Holy Spirit in their translation, seem to have altered some passages [in the Hebrew text] with the view of directing the reader's attention more particularly to the investigation of the spiritual sense. (4:7)

On the Creed: A Sermon to Catechumens[8]

Through sin in our first parents we fell and have all come into the inheritance of death. We were brought low, became mortal, were filled with fears and errors, all through this sin. With this inheritance and this guilt everyone is born.[9] (§2)

[Commenting on "Conceived by the Holy Spirit and born of the Virgin Mary":] He was born lowly, that He might thereby heal the proud. Man exalted himself and fell; God humbled Himself and raised him up. (§6)

A virgin conceived, a virgin bore, and after the birth was a virgin still. (§6)

He showed us in the Cross what we should have had to endure; He showed us in the Resurrection what we have to hope. (§9)

What will I lack if I have God? And what is the good of all else to me, if I have not God? (§10)

When you have been baptized, hold fast a good life in the commandments of God, that you may guard your baptism even unto the end. (§15)

[Commenting on "Forgive us our debts, as we forgive our debtors":] Once

---
8 Excerpts taken from NPNF (1st) 3:369–375.
9 Orthodox Christianity rejects the teaching, first articulated by Augustine, that the guilt of Adam and Eve's sin is imputed to their descendants.

for all we have washing in baptism; every day we have washing in prayer. (§16)

The Lord's Sermon on the Mount[10]

There are certain grades in sins and in the liability to punishment, but how these are shown invisibly by the punishments of souls, who can say? (1:24)

If it is not lawful to be angry with one's brother without cause or to say "Raca" or to say "You fool" [Matt 5:22], much less is it lawful to retain in mind anything that may turn anger into hatred. (1:26)

Who agrees with divine Scripture except the one who religiously reads or hears it, according it the highest authority, such that what he learns there does not make him hate it because it thwarts his sinning? Rather, it makes him love what corrects him and makes him rejoice that his diseases receive attention until they are cured; and if he finds anything obscure or what appears to him absurd, he does not forthwith start a contest of contradicting it, but he prays for further knowledge and bears in mind the reverence and good disposition of soul that is to be shown to so commanding an authority. (1:32)

For there are three steps in the commission of sin: suggestion, pleasure, and consent. Suggestion comes about either through memory or a sense perception—as when we see, hear, smell, taste, or touch anything. If to enjoy any of these sensations brings pleasure, the pleasure, if forbidden, must be checked. . . . Were we to yield consent to it, we would commit sin surely, a sin in the heart known to God, though actually it may remain unknown to other human beings. (1:34)

As, therefore, one comes to sin by three steps—suggestion, pleasure, consent—so there are three varieties of sin itself: in the heart, in the act, in the habit. (1:35)

The lower morality of the Pharisees is not to exceed due measure in revenge, not to pay back more than you have received. Actually, this is a high level, for you do not easily find a person content to return only blow for blow or

---

10 Excerpted from ACW 5:11–174.

make only one reply to the work of the one scoffing at him, and that just enough to match him. But he usually is less moderate in avenging himself, whether perturbed by his anger or because he deems it only just that one who comes with insult should receive more of the same than he who was not the insulter to begin with. This latter frame of mind the Law in great part restrained, in which it was written, "Eye for eye, tooth for tooth" [Ex 21:24]. By these words moderation is indicated: revenge is not to exceed the wrong done. And this is the beginning of peace; but perfect peace is to have no desire at all for such revenge. (1:56)

The person who pays back no more than he has received has already forgiven something, for the one who wrongs another does not deserve merely what his victim has endured innocently. (1:57)

Many know how to turn the other cheek, but do not know how to love the person who strikes them. (1:58)

No Christian ought to possess a slave as he might a horse or money. (1:59)

Wrongdoing can better be punished in a spirit of love than be left unpunished; the one who punishes does not wish the one punished to be unhappy by the punishment but happy through the correction he receives. (1:63)

Since God gives back to the merciful more than they give, everyone who confers a kindness lends at interest. (1:68)

Many there are who are quick enough to say that they have sinned and who are so angry with themselves that they vehemently wish they had not sinned; yet they do not give up their pride so as to have a humble and contrite heart and to ask forgiveness. (1:74)

What need is there for prayer at all if God already knows what we need? None, except that the very effort we make in praying calms the heart, makes it clean, and renders it more capable of receiving the divine gifts which are poured upon us in a spiritual manner. For God does not hear us because He seeks the favor of our prayers: He is always ready to give us His light—not that which strikes the eye, but that of the intellect and spirit. But we are not always prepared to receive, attracted as we are to other things and benighted by our desire for temporal things. Hence there takes place in prayer a turning of the heart to Him who is ever ready to give if we will but accept what He gives. (2:14)

We almost take for granted that we are going to obtain what we are about to ask for, because before we make any request we have already received so great a gift as to be permitted to call God "Our Father." Indeed, what would He not give His children asking Him, when He has already given them this great thing in advance, that they should be His children! (2:16)

Just as light that is present is absent to the blind or to those who shut their eyes, so the Kingdom of God, though it never departs from the earth, yet is absent to those who know nothing about it. To none, however, will ignorance of God's Kingdom be permitted when His only begotten Son comes again from heaven, not merely so that He is recognizable by the intellect, but visibly as the Man of the Lord, to judge the living and the dead. (2:20)

It is incumbent on us to forgive all sins which are committed against us if we wish our Father to forgive those that we commit. (2:29)

God does not fill place or space by any mass of body and thus exist in one place while being absent in another, or at least have some part here and another elsewhere. Through the greatness of His being He is everywhere present, not divided into parts but everywhere complete. (2:32)

No one is broken down by the coming of adversity who does not succumb to the lure of prosperity. (2:34)

There can be ostentation, not only amid the splendor and pomp of material things, but also in the drab of sackcloth itself; and the latter is all the more dangerous, since it sometimes masquerades in the guise of service to God. (2:41)

"Judge not, that you be not judged. For with what judgment you judge, you will be judged; and with the measure you use, it will be measured back to you" [Matt 7:1–2]. I think this text enjoins on us this one thing: that in the case of those actions whose motivation is in doubt, we are to put the better construction on them. (2:59)

We must be scrupulously careful to see to it that when the situation makes it incumbent on us to chide or rebuke someone, we first reflect whether the fault is one that we have never had or one from which we are now free. And if we have never had it, let us reflect that we are only human and might have had it. But if we have had it and no longer have it, let it be impressed upon the memory that here is a weakness we share, so that not hatred but pity will go out in advance of our chiding or upbraiding. (2:64)

The sheep must not hate their own clothing because wolves often use it to conceal themselves. (2:80)

Temptation is twofold: it is present either in the hope of gaining some temporal advantage or in the fear of losing it. (2:82)

The Enchiridion (also known as On Faith, Hope, and Love)[11]

For humanity true wisdom consists in piety. (§2)

There is no love without hope, no hope without love, and neither hope nor love without faith. (§8)

For the Christian it is enough to believe that the cause of all created things in heaven and on earth, visible or invisible, is none other than the goodness of the Creator, who is the one and true God; that there is no being whatsoever but God Himself or what comes from Him; that God is a Trinity, that is to say, the Father, the Son begotten of the Father, and the Holy Spirit proceeding from the same Father, but one and the same Spirit of the Father and the Son.
    By this Trinity, supremely and equally and unchangeably good, all things were made; but they were not made supremely and equally and unchangeably good. Nevertheless, they are all good, even taken individually; and then taken as a whole, they are very good, since it is their totality that constitutes the marvelous beauty of the universe. (§9–10)

Every sin harms the one who commits it more than the one against whom it is committed. (§17)

---

11 Excerpts taken from ACW 3:11–112.

Every lie is truly a sin, although it makes a great difference with what intention and in what matter one lies. For the sin of the one who lies in order to give help is not the same as that of one who lies in order to do harm. (§18)

Everyone who lies says the opposite of what is in his mind, and that in order to deceive. Surely, language was appointed, not that by it humans should deceive each other, but that through it one might make known one's thoughts to another. Hence, to use language for the purpose of deception and not for what it was appointed is sin.
    And we must not think that because we can on occasion help others by lying, some lies are for that reason not sinful. (§22)

The goodness of the Creator does not indeed cease to administer even to the bad angels life and vitality, without which they would cease to exist. (§27)

God deemed it better to bring good out of evil than not to permit any evil to exist at all. (§27)

Assuming it to have been God's will that there should be absolutely no rehabilitation in the case of humanity, as there was none on the part of the wicked angels: would it not have been just if the being that had deserted God, that abusing its endowment had trampled underfoot and transgressed the law of its Creator when it could so very easily have kept it, that had obstinately turned away from His light, defiling the image of the Maker which it bore, and had maliciously and deliberately broken with the wholesome subjection of legislation—would it not have been just if such a being had been abandoned by God in its entirety and unto eternity and made to undergo everlasting punishment, as it deserved? Certainly God would have done this, were He only just and not also merciful, and had He not chosen to give proof far more striking of His unmerited mercy by setting free those who were undeserving of it. (§27)

But can these members of the human race to whom God promised deliverance and a place in the eternal kingdom be saved by the merits of their works? That is out of the question. For what good work can one do who is ruined, unless he has been delivered from his ruin? Can he do so by the free determination of his will? That, too, is out of the question. For it was by the evil use of free will that humans destroyed both themselves and their free will. (§30)

When by free will sin was committed, sin being the conqueror, free will was lost; "by whom a person is overcome, by him also he is brought into bondage" [2 Pet 2:19].

This is certainly the mind of the Apostle Peter. And since this is true, what sort of liberty, I ask you, can the bondslave possess except the liberty to sin?[12] (§30)

This is what constitutes true liberty—the joy experienced in doing what is right. (§31)

It follows that the saying "It is not of him who wills, nor of him who runs, but of God who shows mercy" [Rom 9:16] is rightly understood to mean that the entire work is to be credited to God, who both readies the will to accept assistance, and assists the will once it has been made ready. (§32)

To say of this Mediator all the great things that would be fitting would take entirely too long: in fact, no one could do justice to the subject. For example, who could explain in adequate terms this single statement that "the Word became flesh and dwelt among us" [John 1:14]? (§34)

Even in that one sin that "through one man ... entered the world" [Rom 5:12] and passed on to all humankind, and because of which even infants are baptized, a plurality of sins can be discovered if we break it down, so to speak, into its component parts. For in it there is pride, since man chose to be under his own dominion, rather than under God's; also blasphemy, since man refused to believe God; and murder, for he rushed headlong into death; and spiritual fornication, since the innocence of the human soul was corrupted by the seduction of the serpent; and theft, since man appropriated to himself forbidden food; and avarice, since he craved for more than sufficed for his needs; and whatever else may be found by diligent reflection to have been involved in the commission of this one sin. (§45)

Still, that one sin, committed in a place and a state of such great happiness, a sin of such enormity that through one man the whole human race was originally and, I might say, radically condemned, is absolved and blotted

---

12 Orthodox Christianity denies this Augustinian affirmation. Following common patristic teaching, Orthodox affirm that the human will is not in bondage but remains free, even after our first parents' fall, to turn toward God and respond positively to what He enjoins.

out only through "one God and one Mediator between God and men, the Man Christ Jesus" [1 Tim 2:5], who alone could be so born as not to need to be reborn. (§48)

Death found nothing in Him [Christ] that needed to be punished. Hence, it was by strict justice and not by a mere imposition of force that the devil was crushed and conquered, for, as he had most unjustly caused Him to be slain who was free from all guilt of sin, most justly should he lose through Him those whom he held in subjection because of the guilt of sin. (§49)

Outside the Church there is no remission of sins. (§65)

By forming a correct judgment concerning our own misery and by loving God with the love that He Himself bestowed, it is possible for us to lead holy and upright lives. (§76)

Which sins are light and which are grave is a matter to be weighed not by human but by divine judgment. (§78)

Because of these sins and others like them, and of others again perhaps of even lesser moment and consisting of offenses in words and thoughts, and because, as the Apostle James confesses, "we all stumble in many things" [James 3:2], we should pray to the Lord daily, saying often, "Forgive us our debts"; and let us not be lying in what follows: "as we forgive our debtors" [Matt 6:12]. (§78)

Sins, however grave and detestable they may be, once they become habit, are regarded [by those who commit them] as small sins or no sins at all. (§80)

Woe to the sins of mortals, that we should shrink from them only when we are not accustomed to them! But once we become inured to them, even though the Son of God shed His blood to wash them away and though they be so great as to shut off completely the Kingdom of God from them, yet, seeing them so often, we are led to tolerate them all, and tolerating them so often to commit many of them ourselves. (§80)

We commit sin because of one of two reasons: either we do not as yet see what we ought to do, or we do not do what we know ought to be done. (§81)

We are also transgressors of the law in that we do not do what we know beforehand ought to be done, or do what we know ought not to be done. Wherefore, not only should we pray for pardon when we have sinned, saying, "Forgive us our debts, as we forgive our debtors" [Matt 6:12]; but we should also pray for guidance that we may be kept from sinning, saying, "do not lead us into temptation" [Matt 6:13]. (§81)

But the one who does not believe that sins are forgiven in the Church, and therefore scorns this great largesse of divine bounty and ends his days in such obstinacy of heart, is guilty of the unpardonable sin against the Holy Spirit, through whom Christ forgives sins. (§83)

There is no true life unless there is happy living. (§92)

No one is redeemed except through unmerited mercy, and no one is condemned except through merited judgment. (§94)

He says to Moses, "I will be gracious to whom I will be gracious, and I will have compassion on whom I will have compassion" [Ex 33:19]. For who but a fool would consider God to be unfair either in inflicting penal justice upon the deserving or in showing mercy to the undeserving? (§98)

In a wondrous, indescribable way, even what is done against His will is not done without His will. It simply could not be done if He did not permit it, and of course He permits it not against His will, but with it; nor would He in His goodness permit evil unless in His omnipotence He could bring good even out of evil. (§100)

As a matter of fact, God brings about some of His purposes, which are of course good, through the evil designs of bad people; for example, it was by the good will of the Father working through the malevolence of the Jews that Christ was slain for us. And the result was so great a good that when the Apostle Peter protested that this should not take place, he was called Satan by Him who had come to be slain. (§101)

In the afterlife we will be so constituted as not to be able to desire evil. But this does not mean that we will lack free will. In fact, our will shall be much more free because it will be utterly impossible for us to serve sin. And certainly neither should fault be found with a will, nor does it cease to be will, nor should its freedom be denied, by which we so desire to be happy that not only do we not wish to be unhappy, but find it utterly impossible to have such a desire at all. (§105)

The devil was conquered by that same nature which he rejoiced to have deceived, without any mere human, however, taking glory in himself, lest pride spring up anew. (§108)

Among the former [those received into eternal life] some will outrank others in bliss, and among the latter [condemned to eternal death] some will have a more bearable portion of misery than others. (§111)

It is in vain that some, indeed, very many, out of mere human sentiment deplore the eternal punishment and the unceasing and everlasting torments of the damned, and do not believe that such things will be.... Governed by their feelings, they tone down everything that seems harsh and give a milder turn to the meaning of what they try to believe was said more to terrify than to express literal truth. (§112)

One who has no love believes in vain, even though what he believes may be the truth. (§117)

Confessions[13]

You made us for Yourself, and our hearts are restless until they rest in You. (1:1)

Let me not tire, O Lord, of thanking You for Your mercy in rescuing me from all my wicked ways, so that You may be sweeter to me than all the joys which used to tempt me; so that I may love You most intensely and clasp Your hand with all the power of my devotion; so that You may save me from all temptation until the end of my days. (1:15)

The path that leads us away from You and brings us back again is not measured by footsteps or milestones. (1:18)

---

13 Excerpts taken from R. S. Pine-Coffin, trans., *St. Augustine: Confessions* (New York: Dorset Press, 1961), pp. 21–347.

O Lord my God, be patient, as You always are, with the people of this world as You watch them and see how strictly they obey the rules of grammar which have been handed down to them, and yet ignore the eternal rules of everlasting salvation which they have received from You. (1:18)

You were always present, angry and merciful at once, strewing the pangs of bitterness over all my lawless pleasures to lead me on to look for others unalloyed with pain. You meant me to find them nowhere but in Yourself, O Lord, for You teach us by inflicting pain, You smite so that You may heal, and You kill us so that we may not die away from You. (2:2)

No one can part You from the things that You love, and safety is assured nowhere but in You. (2:6)

I had no liking for the safe path without pitfalls, for although my real need was for You, my God, who are the food of the soul, I was not aware of this hunger. I felt no need for the food that does not perish, not because I had had my fill of it, but because the more I was starved of it the less palatable it seemed. (3:1)

My God, my God of mercy, how good You were to me, for You mixed much bitterness in that cup of pleasure! (3:1)

How infinite is Your mercy, my God! You are my refuge from the terrible dangers amongst which I wandered, head on high, intent upon withdrawing still further from You. I loved my own way, not Yours, but it was a truant's freedom that I loved. (3:3)

Your goodness is almighty; You take good care of each of us as if You had no others in Your care, and You look after all as You look after each. (3:11)

Without You I am my own guide to the brink of perdition. (4:1)

No one can lose You, my God, unless he forsakes You. And if he forsakes You, where is he to go? If he abandons Your love, his only refuge is Your wrath. (4:9)

Wherever one's soul may turn, unless it turns to You, it clasps sorrow to itself. (4:10)

Let my soul praise You for these things, O God, Creator of them all; but the love of them, which we feel through the senses of the body, must not be like glue to bind my soul to them. (4:10)

If the things of this world delight you, praise God for them but turn your love away from them and give it to their Maker, so that in the things that please you, you may not displease Him. (4:12)

Wisdom and folly are like different kinds of food. Some are wholesome and others are not, but both can be served equally well on the finest china dish or the meanest earthenware. (5:6)

By Your promises You deign to become a debtor to those whom You release from every debt. (5:9)

And so, since we are too weak to discover the truth by reason alone and for this reason need the authority of sacred books, I began to believe that you would never have invested the Bible with such conspicuous authority in every land unless you had intended it to be the means by which we should look for You and believe in You. (6:5)

Its [the Bible's] plain language and simple style make it accessible to everyone, and yet it absorbs the attention of the learned. (6:5)

The less You allowed me to find pleasure in anything that was not Yourself, the greater, I know, was Your goodness to me. (6:6)

It was by my own doing that habit had become so potent an enemy, because it was by my own will that I had reached the state in which I no longer wished to stay. Who can justly complain when just punishment overtakes the sinner? (8:5)

The rule of sin is the force of habit, by which the mind is swept along and held fast even against its will, yet deservedly, because it fell into the habit of its own accord. (8:5)

But You, O Lord, are good. You are merciful. You saw how deep I was sunk in death, and it was Your power that drained dry the well of corruption in the depths of my heart. And all that You asked of me was to deny my own will and accept Yours. (9:1)

O most merciful Lord, did You not forgive this sin and remit its guilt, as well as all my other horrible and deadly sins, in the holy water of baptism? (9:2)

O God, unseen by us You plant Your gifts like seeds in the hearts of Your faithful, and they grow to bear wonderful fruits. (9:11)

However praiseworthy someone's life may be, it will go hard with that person if You lay aside Your mercy when You come to examine it. But You do not search out our faults ruthlessly, and because of this we hope and believe that one day we shall find a place with You. Yet if anyone makes a list of his deserts, what would it be but a list of Your gifts? (9:13)

O Lord, the depths of a person's conscience lie bare before Your eyes. Could anything of mine remain hidden from You, even if I refused to confess it? I should only be shielding my eyes from seeing You, not hiding myself from You. (10:2)

So, O Lord, all that I am is laid bare before You. I have declared how it profits me to confess to You, and I make my confession, not in words and sounds made by the tongue alone, but with the voice of my soul and in my thoughts which cry aloud to You. Your ear can hear them. For when I am sinful, if I am displeased with myself, this is a confession that I make to You; and when I am good, if I do not claim the merit for myself, this too is confession. (10:2)

You have forgiven my past sins and drawn a veil over them, and in this way You have given me happiness in Yourself, changing my life by faith and Your sacrament. (10:3)

It is You, O Lord, who judge me. For "what man knows the things of a man except the spirit of the man which is in him?" [1 Cor 2:11]. But there are some things in us which even our own spirits within us do not know. But You, O Lord, know all there is to know of us, because You made us. (10:5)

My love of You, O Lord, is not some vague feeling: it is positive and certain. Your Word struck into my heart and from that moment I loved You.

Besides this, all about me, heaven and earth and all that they contain, proclaim that I should love You, and their message never ceases to sound in the ears of all humankind, so that there is no excuse for any not to love You. But, more than all this, You will show pity on those whom You pity; You will show mercy where You are merciful; for if it were not for Your mercy, heaven and earth would cry Your praises to deaf ears. (10:6)

True happiness is to rejoice in the truth, for to rejoice in the truth is to rejoice in You, O God, who are the Truth—You, my God, my true Light, to whom I look for salvation. This is the happiness that all desire. (10:23)

People love the truth when it bathes them in its light; they hate it when it proves them wrong. (10:23)

The one who serves You best is the one who is less intent on hearing from You what he wants to hear than on shaping his will according to what he hears from You. (10:26)

You called me; You cried aloud to me; You broke my barrier of deafness. You shone upon me; Your radiance enveloped me; You put my blindness to flight. You shed Your fragrance about me; I drew breath, and now I gasp for Your sweet fragrance. I tasted You, and now I hunger and thirst for You. You touched me, and I am inflamed with love of Your peace. (10:27)

Give grace to do what You command, and command what You will! (10:29)

One loves You so much the less if, besides You, he also loves something else which he does not love for Your sake. (10:29)

You grant us many gifts when we pray for them. And even before we pray for them, all the good things that we have ever received have come from You. And that we should later recognize that they came from You is also Your gift. (10:31)

When Your commands are obeyed, it is from You that we receive the power to obey them. (10:31)

During this life, which may be called a perpetual trial, no one should be confident that although he has been able to pass from a worse state to a better, he may not also pass from a better state to a worse. Our only hope, our only confidence, the only firm promise we have is Your mercy. (10:32)

I raise the eyes of my spirit to You, so that You may "pluck my feet out of the net" [Ps 25:15]. Time and again You save them, for I fail to escape the trap. You never cease to free me, although again and again I find myself caught in the snares that are laid all about me. (10:34)

My life is full of faults, and my only hope is in Your boundless mercy. For when our hearts become repositories piled high with such worthless stock as this, it is the cause of interruption and distraction from our prayers. And although, in Your presence, the voices of our hearts are raised to Your ear, all kinds of trivial thoughts break in and cut us off from the great act of prayer. (10:35)

It happens, too, not that praise is given to the one who is proud of his wicked end achieved or that the evildoer wins applause, but that one is praised for some gift which You have given him. And if he takes greater joy in the praise which he receives than in the possession of the gift for which others praise him, then the price he pays for their applause is the loss of Your favor and he, the receiver of praise, is worse off than the giver. For the one finds pleasure in God's gift in another, while the other finds less pleasure in God's gift than the gift of others. (10:36)

I cannot easily deduce how far I am cured of this disease, and I have great fear of offending You unawares by sins to which I am blind, though to Your eyes they are manifest. (10:37)

I wish that words of praise from others did not increase the joy I feel for any good qualities that I may have. Yet I confess that it does increase my joy. What is more, their censure detracts from it. (10:37)

You have walked everywhere at my side, O Truth, teaching me what to seek and what to avoid, whenever I laid before You the things that I was able to see in this world below and asked You to counsel me. (10:40)

A mediator between God and humankind [1 Tim 2:5] must have something in common with God and something in common with humanity. (10:42)

Like men, He [Jesus Christ] was mortal: like God, He was just. And because the reward of the just is life and peace, He came so that by His own justness, which is His in union with God, He might make null the death of the wicked whom He justified, by choosing to share their death. (10:43)

He who alone was free among the dead—for He was free to lay down His life and free to take it up again—was for us both victor and victim in Your sight, and it was because He was the victim that He was also the victor. In Your sight He was for us both priest and sacrifice, and it was because He was the sacrifice that He was also the priest. By being Your Son, yet serving You, He freed us from servitude and made us Your children. (10:43)

The price of my redemption is always in my thoughts. (10:43)

Your today is eternity. And this is how the Son, to whom You said, "Today I have begotten You" [Ps 2:7], was begotten coeternal with Yourself. You made all time; You are before all time; and the "time," if such we may call it, when there was no time was not time at all. (11:13)

To whom am I to put my questions? To whom can I confess my ignorance with greater profit than to You? For my burning desire to study Your Scriptures is not displeasing to You. Grant me what I love, for it was Your gift that I should love You. (11:22)

How wonderful are Your Scriptures! How profound! We see their surface and it attracts us like children. And yet, O my God, their depth is stupendous. We shudder to peer deep into them, for they inspire in us both the awe of reverence and the thrill of love. (12:14)

But the truths which those words contain appear to different inquirers in a different light, and of all the meanings that they can bear, which of us can lay his finger upon one and say that it is what Moses had in mind and what he meant us to understand by his words? (12:24)

The arbitrary assurance with which they insist upon it [their interpretation] springs from presumption, not from knowledge. It is the child of arrogance, not of true vision. (12:25)

When so many meanings, all of them acceptable as true, can be extracted from the words that Moses wrote, do you not see how foolish it is to make a bold assertion that one in particular is the one he had in mind? Do you not see how foolish it is to enter into mischievous arguments which are an offense against that very love for the sake of which he wrote every one of the words that we are trying to explain? (12:25)

It is only rarely and with great difficulty that one can discern Your eternity,[14] O Lord, creating things that are subject to change yet never suffering change itself and thereby being prior to them all. (12:29)

For all the differences between them, there is truth in each of these opinions. May this truth give birth to harmony, and may the Lord our God have pity on us so that we may apply the law legitimately, that is, to the end prescribed in the commandment, which is love undefiled. (12:30)

As for the rest of us, who all, as I admit, see true meanings in those words and explain them accordingly, let us love one another, and if our thirst is not for vanity but for the truth, let us likewise love You, our God, who are the source from which it flows. (12:30)

I call upon You, O God, my Mercy, who made me and did not forget me when I forgot You. I call You to come into my soul, for by inspiring it to long for You, You prepare it to receive You. Now, as I call upon You, do not desert me, for You came to my aid even before I called upon You. (13:1)

Since, then, Your good is in Yourself, what would have been lacking to that good, if the creature which You made had not even existed or had remained in its formless state? You created, not because You had need, but out of the abundance of Your own goodness. You molded Your Creation and gave it form, but not because You would find Your own happiness increased by it. (13:4)

All that I know is this, that unless You are with me, and not only beside me but in my very self, for me there is nothing but evil, and whatever riches I have, unless they are my God, they are only poverty. (13:8)

---

14 Even with the qualification Augustine includes, this is out of keeping with the other Church Fathers, who show no confidence in human reason to penetrate such divine mysteries. Orthodoxy rejects the confidence Augustine allows in this teaching.

Who can understand the omnipotent Trinity? We all speak of it, though we may not speak of it as it truly is, for rarely does a soul know what it is saying when it speaks of the Trinity.[15]... This is a mystery that none can explain, and which of us would presume to assert that he can? (13:11)

O Lord, You create happiness and give it to us to ease our lives. (13:18)

Your Church, by reason of the grace which You have given it, has the power of spiritual judgment, which is given both to those who have spiritual charge of others and to those who are in their spiritual care. For You created humankind male and female, but in Your spiritual grace they are as one. Your grace no more discriminates between them according to their sex than it draws distinction between Jew and Greek or slave and free [Gal 3:28]. (13:23)

When it is because of You that things please us, it is You who please us in them; and when it is by Your Spirit that they please us, they please You in us. (13:31)

The City of God[16]

To reform an abuse of long standing is an enterprise full of peril. (3:24)

To confess that God exists, and at the same time to deny that He has foreknowledge of future things, is manifest folly. (5:9)

The reason we pay such honors to their [the martyrs'] memory is that by so doing we may both give thanks to the true God for their victories and, by recalling them afresh to remembrance, may stir ourselves up to imitate them by seeking to obtain similar crowns and palms, calling to our help the same God on whom they called. So whatever honors the religious may pay in the places of the martyrs, they are only honors rendered to their memory, not sacred rites or sacrifices offered to the dead as if they were gods. (8:27)

---

15 This is another evidence of Augustine's confidence in human reason, here to deal with what must remain utterly beyond us, to penetrate God's being! This is definitely out of step with other Church Fathers and is rejected by Orthodoxy.
16 Excerpts taken from Marcus Dods, trans., *St. Augustine: The City of God* (New York: The Modern Library, 1993), pp. 3–867.

As the Creator Himself is hidden and incomprehensible to human beings, so also is the manner of Creation. (10:12)

He is both the Priest who offers and the sacrifice offered. And He designed that there should be a daily sign of this in the sacrifice of the Church, which, being His body, learns to offer herself through Him. (10:20)

In order that He might heal the whole human being from the plague of sin, He took without sin the whole human nature. (10:27)

Since change and motion were also created when the world was created, then time was also made simultaneously with the world, as seems evident from the order of the first six or seven days. . . . What kind of days these were it is extremely difficult, probably impossible, for us to conceive, and how much more to say! (11:6)

God "spoke, and it was done" [Ps 33:9]—spoke by the spiritual and eternal, not audible and transitory word. (11:8)

Who can be sure that he will persevere to the end in the exercise and increase of grace, unless he has been certified by some revelation from Him who, in His just and secret judgment, while He deceives none, informs few regarding this matter? (11:12)

It is not as if God's knowledge were of various kinds, knowing in different ways things which are not yet, things which are, and things which have been. He does not look as we do to what is future, or at what is present, or back upon what is past; He thinks in a manner quite different and far and profoundly remote from our way of thinking. . . . He beholds all things with absolute unchangeableness; so that of those things which emerge in time, the future, indeed, are not yet, and the present are now, and the past no longer are; but all of these are comprehended by Him in His steady and eternal presence. . . . His present knowledge does not differ from what it ever was or shall be, for those variations of time—past, present, and future—although they alter our knowledge, do not affect His, "with whom there is no variation or shadow of turning" [James 1:17]. Neither is there any growth from thought to thought in His conceptions; in His spiritual vision all things are embraced at once. (11:21)

Even those natures which are vitiated by an evil will, in so far as they are vitiated, are evil, but in so far as they are natures they are good. (12:3)

From the fact that the woman was made for him [Adam] from his side, it was plainly meant that we should learn how dear the bond between husband and wife should be. (12:27)

Knowing that the cause of this burdensomeness [of "the flesh"] is not the nature and substance of the body, but its corruption, we do not desire to be deprived of the body, but to be clothed with its immortality. (14:3)

The corruption of the body, which weighs down the soul, is not the cause but the punishment of the first sin; and it was not the corruptible flesh that made the soul sinful, but the sinful soul that made the flesh corruptible. (14:3)

No one is evil by nature; whoever is evil is evil by vice. (14:6)

This is already sin, to desire the things which the law of God forbids but to abstain from them through fear of punishment, not through love of righteousness. (14:10)

Evil cannot exist without good, because the natures in which evil exists, in so far as they are natures, are good. (14:11)

Two cities have been formed by two loves: the earthly by the love of self, even to the contempt of God; the heavenly by the love of God, even to the contempt of self. The former glories in itself, the latter in the Lord. (14:28)

This [the ark built by Noah] is certainly a figure of the city of God sojourning in this world—that is to say, of the Church, which is rescued by the wood on which hung the "Mediator between God and men, the Man Christ Jesus" [1 Tim 2:5]. (15:26)

While the hot restlessness of heretics stirs questions about many articles of the catholic faith, the necessity of defending them forces us to investigate them more accurately, to understand them more clearly, and to proclaim them more earnestly; thus, the question mooted by an adversary becomes the occasion of instruction. (16:2)

Since we find nothing else in the Scriptures than what the Spirit of God has spoken through men, if anything is in the Hebrew copies [of the Old Testament] and is not in the version of the Seventy [the Septuagint], the Spirit of God did not choose to say it through them [the seventy translators], but only through the prophets. But whatever is in the Septuagint and not in the Hebrew copies, the same Spirit chose rather to say through the latter, thus showing that both were prophets. . . . As the one Spirit of peace was in the former when they spoke true and concordant words, so the selfsame one Spirit has appeared in the latter, when, without mutual conference, they still interpreted everything as if they had only one mouth. (18:43)

It is not incongruous to believe that even in other nations there may have been people to whom this mystery [of salvation by divine mercy] was revealed, and who were also impelled to proclaim it. . . . Indeed, there was no other people [than the Israelites] who were specially called the people of God; but they cannot deny that there have been certain people even of other nations [like Job, mentioned in the context as an example] who belonged, not by earthly but heavenly fellowship, to the true Israelites, the citizens of the country that is above. (18:47)

The gospel of Christ was preached in the whole world, not only by those who had seen and heard Him before His Passion and after His Resurrection, but also after their death by their successors, amid horrible persecutions, manifold torments, and deaths of the martyrs, God also bearing them witness with signs and wonders, and diverse miracles and gifts of the Holy Spirit, so that the people of the nations, believing in Him who was crucified for their redemption, might venerate with Christian love the blood of the martyrs which they had poured forth with devilish fury, and the very kings by whose laws the Church had been laid waste might become profitably subject to that Name which they had cruelly sought to take away from the earth. (18:50)

In vain do we attempt to compute definitely the years that may remain to this world, when we hear from the mouth of the Truth that it is not for us to know this. (18:53)

In this, then, consists one's righteousness, that he submit himself to God, his body to his soul, and his vices, even when they rebel, to his reason, which either defeats or at least resists them; and also that he beg from God grace to do his duty, and the pardon of his sins, and that he render to God thanks for all the blessings he receives. (19:27)

Prophetic diction delights in mingling figurative and real language, and thus in some sort veiling the sense. (20:16)

No doubt, though this book [Revelation] is called the Apocalypse ["the unveiling"], there are in it many obscure passages to exercise the mind of the reader, and there are few passages so plain that they assist us in the interpretation of the others, even though we take pains; and this difficulty is increased by the repetition of the same things, in forms so different, that the things referred to seem to be different, although in fact they are only differently stated. (20:17)

The words, "And now you know what is restraining"—i.e., you know what hindrance or cause of delay there is—"that he may be revealed in his own time" [2 Thess 2:6], show that he [St. Paul] did not make an explicit statement, since he said that they knew. But we who do not have their knowledge wish, but are unable even with great effort, to understand what the apostle referred to, especially since his meaning is made still more obscure by what he adds. For what does he mean when he says, "The mystery of lawlessness is already at work; only He who now restrains will do so until He is taken out of the way. And then the lawless one will be revealed" [2 Thess 2:7–8]? I frankly confess I do not know what he means. (20:19)

The way in which this [the resurrection at the last day] shall take place we can now only feebly conjecture; we shall understand it only when it comes to pass. We must believe that there shall be a bodily resurrection of the dead when Christ comes to judge the living and the dead, if we want to be Christians. But although we are unable to comprehend the way in which it shall take place, our faith is not on this account vain. (20:20)

Who could have hoped that the nations would hope in the name of Christ, when He was arrested, bound, scourged, mocked, crucified, when even the disciples themselves had lost the hope which they had begun to have in Him? The hope which was then entertained scarcely by the one thief on the cross is now cherished by nations everywhere on the earth, who are marked with the sign of the Cross on which He [Jesus Christ] died that they may not die eternally. (20:30)

In proportion as one loves what Christ disapproves does that person abandon Christ. (21:27)

And now we have three incredibles, all of which have nevertheless come to pass. It is incredible that Jesus Christ should have risen in the flesh and ascended with flesh into heaven; it is incredible that the world should have believed so incredible a thing; it is incredible that a very few men, of insignificant birth, the lowest rank, and no education, should have been able so effectually to persuade the world, and even the learned, of so incredible a thing. (22:5)

The leading truth they [the martyrs] professed is that Christ rose from the dead. (22:10)

At the beginning of the human race the woman was made of a rib taken from the side of the man while he slept, for it seemed fit that even then Christ and His Church should be foreshadowed in this event. That sleep of the man was the death of Christ, whose side, as He hung lifeless on the Cross, was pierced with a spear, and from it flowed blood and water; these we know to be the sacraments by which the Church is built up. (22:17)

As the first immortality which Adam lost by sinning consisted in his being able not to die, while the last shall consist in his not being able to die, so the first free will consisted in his being able not to sin, but the last shall consist in his not being able to sin. (22:30)

~ John Cassian

John Cassian (c. 360–435) traveled among the monks of Egypt for several years to learn about and experience monasticism. In due course, he sat under the ministry of John Chrysostom and was ordained by him into the clergy. In 415, Cassian journeyed to the West and established a monastery in what is now southern France. He encouraged both men and women to enter monastic life. Much of his writing—including his *Conferences*—dealt with monastic life and how to practice it humbly and wisely.

Conferences[1]

For those who travel without a marked road there is the toil of the journey and no arrival at a destination. (1:4)

What we really want to learn is the extent to which the spirit can actually be at one with the invisible, ungraspable God. (1:12)

Despite ourselves, indeed without our even knowing it, useless thoughts slip into us, subtly and without our knowing it. (1:16)

The devil drags a monk headlong to death by way of no other sin than that of submission to private judgment and the neglect of the advice of our elders. (2:11)

---

1 Excerpts taken from Colm Luibheid, trans., *John Cassian: Conferences* (Mahwah, NJ: Paulist Press, 1985), pp. 37–201.

The rule handed on by the Fathers is that whoever is guided solely by his own judgment and decision will never climb up to the summit of perfection and will fall victim to the devil's ruinous power to delude. (2:24)

Nothing is ours except what is in our hearts, what belongs to our souls, what cannot be taken away by anyone. (3:10)

Of this much we must be sure. Never by our sole diligence or zeal nor by our most tireless efforts can we reach perfection. Human zeal is not enough to win the sublime rewards of blessedness. The Lord must be there to help us and to guide our hearts toward what is good. (3:12)

The introduction to salvation, made available to us by God's gifts and grace, is not itself sufficient. It has to be brought to perfection by God's mercy and His everyday assistance. (3:15)

It is right for us to believe, with unshaken faith, that nothing is done in this world without God. It must be admitted that everything happens either by His will or with His permission. (3:20)

The whole purpose of the monk and indeed the perfection of his heart amount to this—total and uninterrupted dedication to prayer. He strives for undistracted calm of mind. (9:2)

Because of the workings of memory, whatever has preoccupied our mind before the time for prayer must of necessity intrude on our actual prayers. Therefore in advance of prayer we must strive to dispose ourselves as we would wish to be during prayer. The praying spirit is shaped by its own earlier condition. . . . Therefore, before we pray we must hasten to drive from our heart's sanctuary anything we would not wish to intrude on our prayers. (9:3)

Prayer changes at every moment in proportion to the degree of purity in the soul and in accordance with the extent to which the soul is moved either by outside influence or of itself. Certainly the same kind of prayers cannot be uttered continuously by any one person. A lively person prays one way. Someone brought down by the weight of gloom or despair prays another. A person prays one way when the life of the spirit is flourishing, and another way when pushed down by the mass of temptation. (9:8)

But one thing is certain. Anyone who prays and who doubts that he will be heard will not be listened to at all [James 1:5–7]. (9:34)

One is very close to knowledge when one clearly recognizes the questions to be asked. One is not far from true awareness when one begins to understand one's ignorance. (10:9)

Before the time of prayer we must put ourselves in the state of mind we would wish to have in us when we actually pray. (10:14)

There is a great difference between the one who extinguishes the fires of sin out of fear of hell or hope of future reward and the one who, moved by love of God, turns in horror from evil and uncleanliness. (11:8)

A clear proof that a soul has not yet cut loose from the corruption of sin is when it feels no sympathizing pity for the wrongdoing of others but holds instead to the strict censoriousness of a judge. (11:10)

Never dare to teach someone what you have not practiced yourself. (14:9)

It is impossible for the unclean of heart to acquire the gift of spiritual knowledge. (14:10)

I feel that a particular obstacle to my salvation is the very slight knowledge I have of literature. (14:12)

The hungry mind is unable to be empty of all thought. . . . No matter how often there is talk that has to do with holy subjects, a soul thirsting for true knowledge will never have too much of it and never grow tired of it. (14:13)

Purity is corrupted more speedily than corruption is made pure. So it goes with the container which is our heart. (14:14)

The greater miracle is to root out the tinder of luxury from one's flesh, rather than to drive unclean spirits from the bodies of others. A more resplendent wonder is the restraint exercised over the wild stirrings of anger by the virtue of patience, rather than the capacity to hold sway over the creatures of the air. (15:8)

The one who teaches himself by engaging in arguments will never reach the truth. The enemy will note that he relies more on his own judgment than upon that of the Fathers and he will easily bring him to the point where he considers even the most useful and saving matters to be unnecessary or dangerous. The master of deceit will take advantage of his presumptuousness and that person will hold so stubbornly to his unreasonable opinions that he will reach the stage of being convinced that the only thing that is holy is that which his own blind obstinacy deems to be right and just. (18:3)

No one fights against me more than my own heart. (18:16)

~ Vincent of Lérins

Vincent (?–c. 450) was a monk on Lérins (an island off the southern coast of France). During his time, the western half of the Roman Empire endured repeated assaults from barbarian tribes, and the Church struggled with various heresies. Beyond that, Vincent had become suspicious of Augustine's teachings about predestination and grace: Vincent saw these views as beyond what had been accepted and could be defended from the perspective of the historic faith of the Church. In his work *Commonitories* (written c. 435–440), Vincent tried to show how one could stand fast in the historic Christian faith, the catholic (i.e., "according to the whole" or "complete") faith passed down faithfully within the Church in that tradition stemming from Christ and the apostles and transmitted by the Fathers—the teachers, bishops, and ecumenical councils.

Commonitories[1]

Since time snatches away all things human, we ought to snatch from it something which may profit us unto life eternal. (ch. 1)

Perhaps someone may ask, "Since the canon of the Scripture is complete and more than sufficient in itself, why is it necessary to add to it the authority of ecclesiastical interpretation?" Because Holy Scripture, given its depth, is not universally accepted in one and the same sense. The same text is interpreted differently by different people, so that one may almost gain the

---

1 Excerpted from FC 7:267–332.

impression that it can yield as many different meanings as there are people who speak about it. . . . Thus, because of the great distortions caused by various errors, it is, indeed, necessary that the trend of the interpretation of the prophetic and apostolic writings be directed in accordance with the rule of the ecclesiastical and catholic meaning. (ch. 2)

In the Catholic Church itself, every care should be taken to hold fast to what has been believed everywhere, always, and by all [*quod ubique, semper, et ab omnibus creditum est*]. . . . In regard to universality [i.e., "everywhere"] . . . , we confess that faith alone to be true which the entire Church confesses all over the world. In regard to antiquity [i.e., "always"], we do not deviate from those interpretations which our ancestors and Fathers have manifestly proclaimed as inviolable. In regard to consent [i.e., "by all"] . . . , in this antiquity, we adopt the declarations and propositions of all, or almost all, the bishops and teachers. (ch. 2)

What, therefore, will the catholic Christian do if some members of the Church have broken away from the communion of universal faith? What else, but prefer the sanity of the body universal to the pestilence of the corrupt member? (ch. 3)

[A genuine Christian] must believe without hesitation whatever not only one or two but all equally and with one and the same consent, openly, frequently, and persistently have held, written, and taught. (ch. 3)

The disaster of that perilous period [the struggles with Donatism and Arianism in the fourth century] demonstrates abundantly what calamity is brought about by teaching a novel dogma. (ch. 4)

[Regarding the martyrs and confessors:] They preferred to surrender themselves rather than the faith universally held from the beginning. (ch. 5)

Profane novelty, with all its boastful display of errors, is to be crushed . . . by the authority of sacred tradition. This method, to be sure, is not at all new: it has been an established custom in the Church that the more devout a person is, the more prompt he is to oppose innovations. (ch. 6)

The principle of piety admits of only one attitude: namely, that everything be transferred to the sons in the same spirit of faith in which it was accepted by the Fathers; that religion should not lead us wherever we want to go, but that we must follow wherever it leads.... Christian modesty and earnestness do not transfer to posterity one's own ideas, but preserve those received from one's ancestors. (ch. 6)

[Referring to Gal 1:6, 7 and similar warnings:] We should dread with a great fear the sacrilege of changing faith and profaning religion. We should be deterred from such a sin not only by the discipline of ecclesiastical rule, but also by the censure of apostolic authority. (ch . 7)

It was ever necessary, is everywhere necessary, and will ever be necessary that those who proclaim a doctrine other than that which was received once and for all be anathema. (ch. 9)

In God there is one substance, but three Persons; in Christ, two substances, but one Person. In the Trinity there is distinction of Persons, but not of substance. In our Savior there is distinction of substances, but not of Person. (ch. 13)

There are two substances in one and the same Christ: the one is Divine, the other human; one is from God the Father, the other from the virgin mother; one co-eternal and co-equal with the Father, the other temporal and less than the Father; one consubstantial with the Father, the other consubstantial with the mother; yet one and the same Christ in either substance. (ch. 13)

But one and the same Christ is God and man; one and the same uncreated and created; one and the same unchangeable and impassible, yet also transformed and having suffered; one and the same co-equal with and less than the Father; one and the same begotten of the Father before time and born from a mother in time—perfect God and perfect man; as God, highest divinity, and as man, fullest humanity. (ch. 13)

The catholic faith affirms that the Word of God was made human in such a way that He assumed our nature, not fallaciously and unreally, but in truth and reality; that He did not imitate human nature as if it were something different, but rather as being His very own. (ch. 14)

This unity of the Person in Christ was formed and completed, not after the birth from the virgin, but in the very womb of the virgin. (ch. 15)

God forbid that anyone should attempt to defraud holy Mary of her privileges of divine grace and of her special glory. For by a unique favor of our Lord and God she is to be confessed to be the most true and most blessed Mother of God (Theotokos). (ch. 15)

This unity of the Person [in Christ] has such power that, because of it, by a wonderful and ineffable mystery, divine action can be ascribed to man and human action to God. (ch. 16)

Almost each word of his [Tertullian's] is a thought, and each sentence a victory. (ch. 18)

I cannot help wondering about such madness in certain people, the dreadful impiety of their blinded minds, their insatiable lust for error that they are not content with the traditional rule of faith as once and for all received from antiquity, but are driven to seek novelties. (ch. 21)

"Keep that which is committed to you" [1 Tim 6:20]—what is "committed"? It is that which has been entrusted to you, not that which you have invented; what you have received, not what you have devised; not a matter of ingenuity, but of doctrine; not of private acquisition, but of public tradition; a matter brought to you, not created by you; a matter you are not the author of, but the keeper of; not the teacher, but the learner; not the leader, but the follower. This deposit, he says, guard. (ch. 22)

At this point, the question may be asked, "If this is right, then is no progress of religion possible within the Church of Christ?" To be sure, there has to be progress, even exceedingly great progress. . . . But it must be progress in the proper sense of the word, and not a change in faith. Progress means that each thing grows within itself, whereas change implies that one thing is transformed into another. (ch. 23)

They [Christian doctrines] may take on more evidence, clarity, and distinctness, but it is absolutely necessary that they retain their plenitude, integrity, and basic character. (ch. 23)

The Church of Christ, zealous and cautious guardian of the dogmas deposited with it, never changes any element of them. It does not diminish them or add to them; it neither trims what seems necessary nor grafts things superfluous; it neither gives up its own nor usurps what does not belong to it. But it devotes all its diligence to one aim: to treat tradition faithfully and wisely; to nurse and polish what from old times may have remained unshaped and unfinished; to consolidate and to strengthen what already was clear and plain; and to guard what already was confirmed and defined. What the [ecumenical] councils have brought forth in their decrees assured that what before was believed plainly and simply might from now on be believed more diligently. (ch. 23)

Aroused by the novelties of the heretics, again and again the Catholic Church has, by the authoritative decrees of its [ecumenical] councils, handed down to posterity what it earlier received from our forefathers by tradition alone, condensing weighty matters in a few words and, particularly for the enlightenment of the mind, presenting in new words the old interpretation of the faith. (ch. 23)

One might ask, do the heretics also make use of the testimonies of Holy Scripture? Indeed, they do—and to a great degree. . . . They utter almost nothing of their own that they do not try to support with passages from the Scripture. . . . There is no easier way to deceive people with wicked errors than by fraudulently claiming the authority of the Bible. (ch. 25)

How shall they [genuine Christians] discern truth from falsehood in what claims to be taught from Holy Scripture? By reference to what holy and scholarly men have handed down to us. Christians must devote all their care and attention to interpreting the divine canon [of Scripture] according to the traditions of the universal Church and the rules of catholic dogma; within the Catholic and Apostolic Church they must follow the principles of universality, antiquity, and consent. If, at any time, a part is in rebellion against the whole, or some novelty against tradition, or if there is a dissension of one or a few involved in error against the consent of all or the vast majority of catholics, then they should prefer the integrity of the whole to the corruption of a part. With regard to universality, they should place the ancient faith before profane novelty. With regard to tradition, before the inconsiderate attitude of a very few they should place, first, the general decrees (if there are any) of a universal council, and secondly, they should follow the concordant opinions of great and outstanding teachers. (ch. 27)

The older abominable schisms and heresies cannot be overcome except by refuting them on the authority of Holy Scripture alone, or by avoiding them if they have already been refuted and condemned by universal councils of the catholic bishops. (ch. 28)

Only those opinions of the Fathers are to be held without question which were expressed by those who lived, taught, and persevered in the holy catholic faith and communion. . . . Those men are to be believed, moreover, in accordance with the following rule: only that is to be held as certain, valid, and beyond doubt, which either all or most of them have confirmed in one and the same sense—manifestly, frequently, and persistently, as though in a council of masters, all agreeing—and which they have accepted, kept, and handed on. On the other hand, what some saint, learned man, bishop, confessor, or martyr has individually thought outside of, or even contrary to, the general opinion must be considered his personal, particular, and quite private opinion. (ch. 28)

Everyone who disregards these men [i.e., the Fathers] whom God has given to his Church in all times and in all places, who disregards them when they agree in Christ about the interpretation of catholic dogma, does not disregard man, but God Himself. (ch. 28)

As we said in earlier sections, it always was and is today the usual practice of catholics to test the true faith by two methods: first by the authority of the divine canon, and then by the tradition of the Catholic Church. Not that the canon is insufficient in itself in each case, but because most false interpreters of the Divine Word make use of their own arbitrary judgment and thus fall into various opinions and errors, the understanding of Holy Scripture must conform to the single rule of catholic teaching—and this especially in regard to those questions upon which the foundations of all catholic dogma are laid. (ch. 29)

Further, with regard to the tradition of the Church, we have said that two precautions have to be rigorously and thoroughly observed, adhered to by everyone who does not wish to become a heretic: first, it must be ascertained whether there exists from ancient times a decree established by all the bishops of the catholic Church with the authority of a universal council; second, should a new question arise for which no such decree can be found, one must revert to the opinions of the Holy Fathers—to be more precise, of those Fathers who remained in their own times and places in the unity of communion and of faith and who taught doctrine faithfully. If we can discover what they held in full agreement and consent, then we can conclude without hesitation that this is the true and catholic doctrine of the Church. (ch. 29)

∾ *Prosper of Aquitaine*

Prosper of Aquitaine (c. 390–c. 463) lived several years as a monk in southern France. He accompanied Leo to Rome when the latter was elected bishop there and served him as secretary. In his *The Call of All Nations,* Prosper sought to defend Augustine's views on predestination and grace against the criticism brought by John Cassian and Vincent of Lérins; in the course of the controversy, Prosper somewhat modified Augustine's teachings on the points at issue.

The Call of All Nations[1]

Human nature, vitiated in the first man's sin, is always inclined, even when surrounded with God's mercies, with His precepts and aids, towards a degenerate will, to surrender to which is sin. This will is . . . more desirous of glory than of virtue, more solicitous of a good reputation than of a good conscience. (1:6)

Even when one's action is morally good, one's life remains bad if one does not live for God's glory. For this is the chief characteristic of the devout, that they glory in the Lord and do not love themselves except in God. (1:6)

God loves in us what He Himself has wrought in us, and He hates what is not His work. (1:6)

---

[1] Excerpts taken from ACW 14:26–153.

All of us have been created in the first man without any blemish and we have all lost the integrity of our nature through the sin of the same first man. (1:7)

Although some, guided by their natural reason, tried to resist vices, the life of decency they led here on earth was sterile. They did not acquire true virtues and attain eternal happiness. Without worship of the true God even what has the appearance of virtue is sin. (1:7)

Neither the learned nor the illiterate of whatever race or rank come to God led by human reason; but everyone who is converted to God is first stirred by God's grace. (1:8)

With the pen of the Holy Spirit the truth mercifully rewrites on the pages of their souls all that the devil enviously falsified. (1:8)

It is in our own best interest to hold that all good things, especially those conducive to eternal life, are obtained through God's favor, increased through God's favor, and preserved through God's favor. (1:9)

This is a condition we must keep—that we do not permit what is inaccessible to our knowledge to render obscure what we clearly know, and that we do not, while wantonly insisting on knowing what we cannot know, lose sight of what we are able to know. (1:9)

We always need to preserve our reverence for God's justice even when we do not understand its course. (1:9)

For the universal Church this [God's desire that all be saved, as stated in 1 Tim 2:4, just cited] constitutes a fundamental norm of the apostle's teaching. Let us, then, seek the mind of the universal Church about it in order not to understand it amiss by relying on our own judgment. (1:12)

The Church pleads before God everywhere, not only for the saints and those regenerated in Christ, but also for all infidels and all enemies of the Cross of Christ, for all worshipers of idols, for all who persecute Christ in His members, for the Jews whose blindness does not see the light of the gospel, for heretics and schismatics who are alien to the unity of faith and love.

But what does she beg for them, if not that they leave their errors and be converted to God, that they accept the faith, accept love, that they be freed from the shadows of ignorance and come to the knowledge of the truth? (1:12)

In the divine economy, the reasons of many things actually remain hidden and only the facts become known. (1:14)

I do not know, for example, why this person was created a Greek and that one a barbarian, why this one was born in wealth and another in destitution; why the strength and beauty of a stately body exalts this one, while the withered thinness of feeble limbs deforms that person; why one is born of catholic stock and nourished in the cradle of the faith, while another is a child of heretics and drinks the poison of error with its mother's milk.

A thousand other differences in the conditions of the bodies and the qualities of the minds, in the circumstances of time and the customs of countries, I cannot account for. But I do not for that reason fail to know that God is the Creator and Ruler of all these things. (1:14)

These works of God would not be withdrawn from our human understanding were there any need for us to know them. It would be revealed why each particular event takes place were it not sufficient to know that it happens. (1:14)

But who is so learned as to understand, or who is so wise as to discover why God did not have mercy on the former, but was merciful towards the latter? The reason of this discrimination escapes us; the difference itself we see. We do not understand God's judgment, but we see His work. Shall we accuse His justice which is hidden, when we must give thanks for His mercy which is manifest? No, let us praise and reverence God's action, while there is no risk in not knowing what He keeps veiled. (1:15)

There are no crimes so hateful that can prevent the gift of grace, just as there can be no good works so excellent that can claim as their just reward what God gives gratuitously. (1:17)

Suppose that justification, which is the work of grace, were due to previous merits; suppose it were like the pay of a laborer rather than the gift of a donor: would not our redemption in the blood of Christ then be debased, and the initiative claimed by human works refuse to yield to God's mercy? (1:17)

We must not scrutinize what God wants to be hidden, but we may not disregard what He has made manifest, else we may be wrongly inquisitive about the former and deserve blame for not gratefully receiving the latter. (1:21)

Could there be a fuller or more evident proof that the faith of the believers is a gift of God than those thanks given to God precisely because they who heard the word of God in man's preaching did not disbelieve in it as coming from a man's mouth, but believed in God speaking through men and producing in their hearts this very faith? (1:23)

The authority of sacred Scripture confirms that a divine gift and a divine help is necessary for one to make progress in faith and good works and to persevere in them till the end. (1:24)

Although it lies in one's power to reject what is good, yet unless it is given him, he is unable by himself to choose this good. The power to do the former was contracted by our nature with original sin; but nature has to receive the ability to do the latter from grace. (1:25)

He condemns no one without guilt and saves no one for his merits. (2:1)

We must not profane with our human dialectics the texts quoted from the divine Scriptures. (2:2)

What the promulgation of the Law and the preaching of the Prophets did for Israel, that the testimony of the whole creation with all the wonders of God's goodness wrought at all times for all nations. (2:4)

When the Apostle Paul stopped in his knowledge and discussion of this problem [God's sovereign distribution of grace] and gave way to utter astonishment, who would be so presumptuous as to believe that he could try to explain it rather than admiring it in silence? (2:9)

The human will is by itself able to sin, but cannot by itself perform good works. (2:12)

The ark of astounding capacity, which sheltered as many animals of all species as would be needed for the restoration of their kind, is the figure of the Church which is to assemble into herself the whole of humankind. In the wood and the water we see disclosed the redemption through the Cross of Christ and the laver of regeneration. Those who were saved from the worldwide destruction symbolize the chosen fullness of all nations . . . , and a many-colored rainbow is the symbol of God's multiform grace. (2:14)

Heaven gave so great a steadfastness in the faith, so great a trust in hope, so great a fortitude in endurance, that the fire of love kindled in the hearts of the faithful by the Holy Spirit could in no way be extinguished by their persecutors . . . , and frequently their persecutors themselves were caught by the flame they were fighting. (2:15)

We believe that God's providence had willed the expansion of the Roman Empire as a preparation for His design over the nations, who were to be called into the unity of the Body of Christ: He first gathered them under the authority of one empire.

But the grace of Christianity is not content with the boundaries that are Rome's. Grace has now submitted to the scepter of the Cross of Christ many peoples whom Rome could not subject with her arms, though Rome by her primacy of the apostolic priesthood has become greater as the citadel of religion than as the seat of power. (2:16)

If we are humble of heart we shall not be disturbed by the unfathomable depth of this discrimination of God. We must only believe with firm and steadfast faith that all of God's judgments are just, and not wish to know what He wanted to remain secret. Where we cannot possibly investigate the reason of His judgment, we should rest content with knowing who He is that judges. (2:21)

Once mortality invaded our nature through sin, every day of our life was forfeited to it. . . . The beginning of life is the commencement of death. (2:21)

Grace, in all the variety of remedy or help which it provides, first operates to prepare the will of the recipient of its call to accept and follow up its gift. (2:26)

It is love that leads to Him all those who come to Him. He loved them first and they returned His love. (2:27)

God's protection gives the strength of final perseverance to His countless saints, yet He does not free any of them from the resistance which their efforts encounter in their own nature. (2:28)

Rightly, therefore, do not only beginners but advanced saints as well beseech the Lord in the same manner and say, "Do not lead us into temptation, but deliver us from the evil one" [Matt 6:13]. For to all who persevere in faith and love it is He who grants the strength not to be overcome in temptation. (2:28)

Many people are in love with their own darkness and do not accept the splendor of the truth. (2:29)

In God there is neither sudden impulse, nor new will, nor temporary design. His thought does not alter with the alternations of changeable things: He comprehends with His eternal and immoveable glance all times and things of time alike. (2:33)

God's knowledge—which embraces the past, the present, and the future—is not encompassed by time, and future events are as present to Him as are current or past ones. (2:34)

Of no one can the verdict be given before his death that he will share in the glory of the elect; rather, a salutary fear should make him persevere in humility. "Therefore let him who thinks he stands take heed lest he fall" [1 Cor 10:12]; and if he should happen to fall, overcome by a temptation, let him not be consumed by sadness, nor despair of the mercy of Him who "upholds all who fall, and raises up all who are bowed down" [Ps 145:14]. For as long as we live in our bodies we must not neglect to correct anyone, nor despair of anyone's conversion. (2:37)

⌒ Leo the Great

Leo (?–461) served as bishop of Rome and thus leader of the Western Church from 440–461. A stalwart champion of the historic Christian faith and a defender of the ecclesiastical practices that had been endorsed by ecumenical councils, Leo nevertheless showed remarkable magnanimity in dealing with the complex issues brought before him. At the Council of Chalcedon, one of his lengthy letters—known as *The Tome of Leo*—received endorsement as a statement of the catholic faith, as against the heresies spawned by both Nestorius and Eutyches.

Leo's extant works consist of sermons and a large collection of letters. Due to the significance of his *Tome* (Letter 28) and a subsequent letter offering a basic presentation of the same arguments (Letter 165, sometimes called *The Minor Tome*), excerpts from these two letters will appear separately from extracts from the rest of his letters below.

The Tome (Letter 28)[1]

What is more iniquitous than to hold blasphemous opinions and not yield to persons wiser and more learned? Those fall into this foolishness who, when they are kept from learning the truth by some lack of understanding, have recourse, not to the voice of prophecy, not to the letters of the apostles, not to the authority of the Scriptures, but to themselves. Hence, they become teachers of error because they were not pupils of the truth. (§1)

---

1 Excerpts taken from FC 34:92–105.

The common and uniform profession of faith which all the faithful make is that they believe in one God, the Father Almighty, and in Jesus Christ, His only Son, our Lord, who was born of the Holy Spirit and the Virgin Mary. It is by these three ideas that the machinations of almost all heretics are destroyed. For when there is belief in God and the omnipotent Father, then the Son is shown to be coeternal with Him, in no way differing from the Father, because He was born God from God, the Omnipotent from the Omnipotent, the Coeternal from the Eternal, not coming later in time or inferior in power, not of unequal glory, not separate in essence. This same only begotten Son of the eternal Father was truly born eternal of the Holy Spirit and the Virgin Mary. This birth in time in no way minimized his divine and eternal birth, nor did it add to it. He sacrificed His entire self in order to redeem humankind (which had been deceived), to overcome death, and by His power to destroy the devil, who held sway over death. We could not overcome the author of sin and death, had not Christ taken on our nature and made it His; sin could not defile Him nor death hold Him in bondage. He was truly conceived of the Holy Spirit within the womb of His virgin mother, who bore Him while preserving her virginity just as, preserving her virginity, she conceived Him. (§2)

Fecundity was given to the virgin by the Holy Spirit, but the reality of the body was taken from her body. (§3)

Accordingly, while the distinctness of both natures and substances is preserved, both being united in one Person, lowliness was taken on by majesty, weakness by strength, mortality by eternity; and in order to pay the debt of our fallen state, the inviolable nature has been united to one capable of suffering, so that, as the appropriate remedy for our ills, one and the same "mediator between God and humankind, Christ Jesus, himself human" [1 Tim 2:5], could die in the one nature and not die in the other. In the whole and perfect nature of true man, then, true God was born, complete in His own nature, complete in ours. But by "ours" we mean that which the Creator formed in us at the beginning and which He took upon Himself, to redeem it. That part which the deceiver added and humankind, deceived, accepted [i.e., sin] left no traces in the Savior. He did not share in our sins just because he undertook to share in our weaknesses. (§3)

That "emptying of himself" [Phil 2:7] whereby the invisible made Himself visible, and the Creator and Lord of all things willed to be one among mortals, was a stooping down of compassion, not a failure of power. (§3)

He who in His own nature is invisible became visible in ours; incomprehensible, He desired to be comprehended; enduring before time began, He began to exist in time; the Lord of the universe allowed His infinite majesty to be overshadowed, and took upon Him the form of a servant. God, incapable of suffering, deigned to become a man who could suffer and, though immortal, to become subject to the laws of death. . . . From the mother the Lord took His nature, but no fault; and the Lord Jesus Christ, born from a virgin's womb, does not have a nature different from ours just because his birth was an unusual one. He who is true God is also true man; there is no illusion in this union, in which the lowliness of humanity and the greatness of Divinity are mutually united. (§4)

To deny His true flesh is also to deny His bodily sufferings. (§5)

Then indeed is true faith defended with the best results, when a false opinion is condemned even by those who have followed it. (§6)

The Minor Tome (Letter 165)[2]

The outpouring of Christ's blood for sinners was so rich in value that, if all the enslaved believed in their Redeemer, none of them would be held by the chains of the devil. {p. 266}

Since those born under the sentence of original sin have received the power of rebirth unto justification, the gift of freedom became stronger than the debt of slavery. {p. 266}

Although the death of many holy people was precious in the sight of the Lord [Ps 116:15], the redemption of the world was not effected by the killing of any of these guiltless persons. These righteous ones received, but did not give, crowns; and from the courage of the faithful came examples of patience, but not the gift of justification. Indeed, their deaths affected each of them, but none gave his life to pay another's debt. For among all humanity only one stood out, our Lord Jesus Christ, who was truly the spotless Lamb, in whose Person all were crucified, all died, all were buried,

---

2 Excerpts taken from FC 34:262–288.

all were even raised from the dead. {p. 267}

True faith can freely boast, through God's grace, of the power of Him who in the lowliness of our flesh attacked the enemy of the human race and who turned over His victory to those in whose body He triumphed. {p. 267}

It is true, therefore, that there is one Lord Jesus Christ, the true Son of God and man, one Person of the Word and the flesh; without separation and division they perform their acts in common. Still, we must understand the character of the acts themselves and must note, by the contemplation of pure faith, to which acts the lowliness of the flesh is elevated and to which the height of Divinity bends down; what the flesh does not perform apart from the Word, what the Word apart from the flesh does not effect. {pp. 267–268}

The bonds of captivity with which we are born could not be loosed unless one of our species and our nature existed who was not bound by any previous conviction for sin and who by His stainless blood would blot out the decree of death against us. {p. 272}

Letters[3]

Some heretics hold that the grace of God is given only according to the merits of the recipients. But, of course, if grace is not a free gift, it is not grace at all, but rather a reward. (#1)

No one is to be blamed more for the faults of others than their leaders, who often nourish a great plague while delaying to administer a rather harsh medicine. (#1)

[On the significance of Sunday as the Lord's Day:] It is a day which has been hallowed by such great mysteries in the divine plan of events that whatever of major importance the Lord decided on was carried out on this honored day. On this day the world had its origin. On this day, through Christ's Resurrection, death came to an end and life had its beginning. On this day the apostles received from the Lord the trumpet of the gospel to be preached to all nations and also received the sacrament of regeneration to

---

[3] Excerpted from FC 34:19–301.

be carried to the entire world. On this day, as blessed John the Evangelist testifies, the apostles being assembled in one place and the doors being shut, when the Lord entered into their midst, he said, "Receive the Holy Spirit. If you forgive the sins of any, they are forgiven them; if you retain the sins of any, they are retained" [John 20:22, 23]. Finally, on this day came the Holy Spirit promised by the Lord to the apostles. (#9)

Our Lord Jesus Christ, Savior of the human race, desired to have the observance of divine religion shine out through God's grace unto all nations and races. He established it in such a way that truth, previously contained only in the proclamations of the Law and the Prophets, might proceed from the apostles' trumpet for the salvation of all, as it is written: "Their voice goes out through all the earth, and their words to the end of the world" [Ps 19:4]. (#10)

It is difficult to bring to a good conclusion affairs that began with a false start. (#12)

Forgiveness of sin does not give permission to commit sin. (#12)

In the rite of baptism, death comes from the slaying of sin, and the triple immersion imitates the three days of burial, and the rising out of the water is like His rising from the tomb. (#16)

The grace of rebirth began with His Resurrection. (#16)

What the venerable Fathers have decided, divinely sanctioned and is part of the solid foundation of the faith, is not to be changed by anyone's unprincipled interpretation. (#23)

Why should it seem incongruous and impossible for the Word, on the one hand, and the flesh and the soul, on the other, to be one Jesus Christ and at the same time Son of God and of man, if flesh and soul (which are unlike in nature) unite to make one person, even when there is no connection with the Incarnation of the Word? For it is much easier for the power of God to effect this union of Himself with man than for the weakness of man alone to effect the union of its own two elements. (#35)

He is not one Person from the Father and another from the mother, but he is the same Person derived in one way from the Father before anything began and in another from the mother in the fullness of time, so that he might be the "mediator between God and humankind, Christ Jesus, himself human" [1 Tim 2:5]. (#35)

Let the preservation of the integrity of the catholic faith be the first consideration. And since the way which leads to life is everywhere narrow and arduous [Matt 7:14], let there by no deviation from this path, either to the left or to the right. (#85)

We could not speak of an Incarnation if the flesh were not taken on by the Word. This "taking on" is a union so great and of such a nature that there must be no belief in a separation between the Divinity and the animated flesh, either when the blessed virgin gave birth or even in the act of conception. For Divinity and humanity came together into a unity of Person, both in the conception and in the child-bearing of the virgin. (#88)

If there is no real and perfect human nature in Him, there is no taking on of our nature, and all that we believe and teach then becomes mere deceit and lies. But since the truth does not lie and Divinity cannot suffer, both natures remain in God the Word in one Person; and the Church in speaking of its Savior professes that He is incapable of suffering in his Divinity but can suffer in the flesh. As the apostle says, "For he was crucified in weakness, but lives by the power of God" [2 Cor 13:4]. (#88)

We have learned the catholic faith from the blessed apostles through the Holy Fathers under the guidance of the Spirit of God. (#89)

Let nobody be permitted to defend what nobody is permitted to believe. (#93)

The first slip from self-restraint is pride, the beginning of transgression and the origin of sin. (#106)

The Savior Himself constantly takes part in this [pastoral] work and is never absent from those affairs which He has entrusted to His ministers to carry out. (#108)

The insidious tempter inflicts no wounds on human hearts with more joy than when he infects unwary minds with those errors that are in conflict with evangelical truth. (#129)

Doctrine has flowed down to us from the blessed apostles and Holy Fathers. (#129)

Exhort all to make progress in the faith, in such a way as to show that you are teaching nothing new but are instilling into the hearts of all what the Fathers of venerated memory were in accord in teaching. (#129)

Almost all the heresies which have existed at different times have departed from the gospel in their understanding of the mystery of the bodily birth, the Passion, and the Resurrection of Christ. (#130)

Peace is not preserved except by having a single profession of faith. (#130)

This practice must be observed in all churches: once the washing [of baptism] has been performed, it may not be violated by any repetition. . . . The washing of baptism must not be contaminated by any repetition. (#159)

Persecution is to be reckoned not only as that which is done against Christian piety by the sword or fire or by torments, for the ravages of persecution are also inflicted by differences of character, the perversity of the disobedient, and the barbs of slanderous tongues. All the members of the Church are constantly buffeted by these afflictions, and no section of the faithful is free from trial. (#167)

Justice must be constantly observed, and clemency must be lovingly extended. Sin, not people, must be hated. (#167)

It is difficult to avoid sin in the business dealings of buyers and sellers. (#167)

The one who is eager to be involved in worldly warfare is not free from the snares of the devil. (#167)

⁓ *Julianus Pomerius*

Little is known about the life of Julianus Pomerius. He was born in North Africa sometime in the last half of the fifth century, moved to France and was teaching by 497, and died sometime in the sixth century. He wrote four works, but the only one extant is his *The Contemplative Life,* in which he urges Christians to contemplation and to an active lifestyle.

The Contemplative Life[1]

Let the one who pursues the contemplative life approach his Creator to be enlightened in heart; let that person watchfully serve Him by contemplating Him and untiringly enjoying Him; let that person desire Him continually; for love of Him let that person flee all that could turn him away; let him rest all his thoughts and all his hope on His pleasure. Let him take time for holy meditations on the sacred Scriptures; let him, being divinely illuminated, delight in them. There let him consider his whole being as in some gleaming mirror; let him correct what he sees disordered; let him hold to what is right; reform what is deformed; cultivate what is beautiful; preserve what is sound; and by careful reading strengthen what is weak. (1:8,1)

I told you that by praying you could accomplish what you could not effect by teaching; that faithful catholics usually profit more by good example than by brilliant words; and that the best and perfect teaching is that which

---
1 Excerpts taken from ACW 4:13–169.

a spiritual way of life exemplifies, not that which empty speech utters; and that on Judgment Day we shall be asked not for words but for deeds. (1:17)

Faith does not come from reason; reason comes from faith. (1:19)

Held captive by the sweetness of the present life, we have no desire to consider what everlasting punishment awaits our negligence. (1:21,1)

A priest's doctrine should be none other than his life. . . . A teacher of the Church should not parade an elaborate style, lest he seem not to want to edify the Church of God but to reveal what great learning he possesses. Not in the glitter of his words, then, but in the virtue of his deeds let him place all his confidence in preaching. Let him delight not in the shouts of the people who acclaim him but in their tears. Let him be zealous to desire not applause from the people but their sighs. (1:23)

The tears which he desires his listeners to shed let him first weep himself and so inflame them by the contrition of his own heart. Such should be the simplicity and straightforwardness of the bishop's language. (1:23)

Truth . . . does not first become great when great men teach it; no, truth itself makes great those who have the capacity of teaching it or learning it. (2:Foreword,2)

Since people sin in so many and such different ways, who does not understand that those whose maladies are so varied certainly cannot be cured by one and the same method? (2:1,2)

These are the people who, content to have renounced the world in word only, not in deed, live in a worldly manner and hide their faults under the empty profession of a better life and, cloaked by the name of pretended religion, assume a reputation for virtue instead of true virtue. . . . Displeased with what they do in secret, they are eager to seem great, not to become great. (2:4,2)

It is a fact that one is ignorant of his own sins, which he ought to acknowledge and mourn, even while he pries and probes into those of others. But if, turning to himself, he looks to his own morals, he will seek not what he may especially blame in others but what he may grieve for in himself. (2:6)

Sins themselves are so hidden—those of others from us and our own from them—that very often a saint is concealed among sinners, and a sinner attains the reputation of a saint. (2:7,1)

It is an abomination for people of means to be fed with the alms of the poor. (2:12)

Let the one whom the pomp of possession entices instead seek with a disengaged heart to possess God. Then that one will possess all that God has created, and in Him that one will have whatever he desires, in a holy fashion, to have. But because no one possesses God except the one who is possessed by God, let him first be the possession of God, and God will become his possessor and portion. (2:16,2)

What further does one seek whose Maker becomes his all? Or what will suffice that person whom God does not suffice? (2:16,2)

Health becomes more precious when pain tortures, and the bitterness of illness lends appreciation of health that is lost. (2:19,2)

Adam took Paradise from us; Christ gave us heaven. (2:20)

What is it to die to sin except not to live at all to works that condemn one to punishment? (2:21,2)

The holy apostle fixed a sure rule: "Do not be drunk with wine, in which is dissipation" [Eph 5:18], as though he were to say, "An excessive use of wine, not its nature, causes and fosters dissipation. Therefore I do not forbid you to use wine, but I forbid you to become intoxicated." (2:22,2)

A soul is doubly guilty if it not only fails to do good, by which it might live spiritually, but makes a pretense of good, under which it may live badly and hide. The proud person wishes himself to be thought steadfast; the prodigal, liberal; the avaricious, frugal; the rash, brave; the inhuman, humane; the gluttonous, refined; the slothful, retiring; the cowardly, circumspect. Boldness claims the name of confidence, insolence alleges the title of liberty, loquacity imagines itself eloquent, and the evil of inquisitiveness skulks behind the appearance of spiritual zeal. (3:1,2)

Without God's gift, virtues can be neither sought nor possessed, nor can their imitations, made to resemble virtues, be avoided. (3:1,2)

If one who lives religiously, temperately, soberly, and compassionately gives the credit to God, by whose gift he is assisted to live well, he lives according to God—spiritually. If, however, he ascribes to his own strength all that he does well, as though he were sufficient to himself, even without God's help, for doing good, he lives according to man—carnally. (3:1,2)

Not only is pride itself a sin: no sin in the past, present, or future could be committed without it. For all sin is nothing but contempt of God, by which His precepts are trodden underfoot; and that which prompts people to this contempt of God is pride alone. (3:2,1)

We who sinned in the sin of the first man, not in our present individual life but in his nature in which we existed, contracted corruption from his disease of corrupt pride as if from a root; and in this our corruption we have all the causes of sins. We do not become corrupt because we sin; but because we are corrupt, we commit every sin from this corruption of ours. (3:2,3)

Where our nature, weakened by sin, has not as yet been restored but is still being healed by grace, our pious efforts are opposed by that base concupiscence which is not according to nature, but which has been imposed and engrafted on our nature as a punishment—a concupiscence which was caused by sin and which causes sin if it conquers. Although we have this concupiscence as long as we live as mortals, nevertheless let us not support it with the desire of our will, and we shall conquer; for not by feeling it in us but by consenting to it do we sin; nor does it conquer us the moment it assails us, but only if—may that not happen!—it casts our mind down from the sublimity of its resolve into consent to sin. (3:2,3)

If pride is the beginning of every sin and concupiscence is the punishment of sin, evil concupiscence cannot be overcome unless pride is first guarded against by the virtue of humility, which is its enemy. (3:3,1)

Humility renders human beings like the holy angels. (3:3,1)

Vices only depart if they are firmly cast out and made to give place to virtues. Otherwise, if virtues have not taken the places of the vices which have been expelled, these bide their time and return. (3:3,1)

Out of pride are born heresies, schisms, detractions, envy, talkativeness, boasting, strife, enmity, ambition, haughtiness, presumption, vanity, irritability, lying, perjury, and other such vices. (3:4,1)

The envious one by envy makes the good of another his own punishment. (3:5)

Sordid thought does not make a mind sordid, but from a sordid mind arise sordid thoughts. If this is so, the forms of beautiful bodies, stealing in through the eyes, do not trouble an incorrupt soul; and when they do excite a soul corruptly, they do not corrupt a healthy soul but reveal one corrupt by its own choice. (3:6,2)

The one who is chaste by compulsion is impure in will. (3:7)

While the soul in this life never ceases to have to combat vices, the very frequency of its victories supports it and leads it on and, to the extent this is possible in the present life, perfects it. (3:7)

The envious through envy make the achievements of those who live holy lives their own sins. (3:9,1)

Who will be able to help the person who through envy sets himself up as his own tormentor? (3:9,2)

Vanity is greedy to gain honors and at the same time ignorant as to how to acquire them. It is flushed by the fever of pretended superiority—hollow, morbid, moody. It dominates the light-minded, charms all the shiftless. (3:10,1)

Nothing so keeps us immune from every sin as the fear of punishment and the love of God. (3:10,4)

Let a soul before it sins look to the penalty that is due to sin. Let it weigh against carnal enticements the torture and anguish that usually pursue the sinner, and no sin will please it nor will any carnal delight tempt it to sin. In fact, we yield to our temptations and passions not because we cannot resist them, but because we promise ourselves security in hiding our sin. (3:11)

When we come to the Last Judgment to be sentenced by that Judge whom we can neither deceive by the concealment of crimes nor corrupt by the offer of any gift to promise impunity; when the secrets of all begin to be revealed, and not only our deeds and words but even our very thoughts begin to be shown: what shall we do before the majesty of so great a Judge? (3:12,1)

"Though," he says, "I speak with the tongues of men and angels, but have not love, I have become sounding brass or a clanging cymbal" [1 Cor 13:1]. By "tongues of men and angels" we ought to understand him to mean the empty oratory of certain people who speak whatever they wish, correctly, it may be, and eloquently; but, however excellent the style and the content of their speech, nevertheless, if they undertake the office of teaching from vanity of pleasing more than from love of counseling; not to teach others, but to show that they are learned; not to seek the advancement of their audience, but to strive for their applause; if with evil wit they transfer all their conscience's concern to their tongue and aspire more earnestly to improve their eloquence than their way of life; if in the conceit of their empty loquacity they desire their words to be praised rather than to be acted upon; if they are solicitous not for the holiness of their labor but for the elegance of a polished style: are not such men rightly compared to "sounding brass or a clanging cymbal"? (3:14,1)

One sins in that part in which one loves God less. (3:15,1)

What is it to love God, except to be occupied with Him in our soul, to conceive the desire of enjoying the sight of Him, to have hatred of sin and contempt of the world, to love one's neighbor also (whom He decreed should be loved in Himself)? (3:15,1)

As to our neighbors, we love them as ourselves when we love them not for any advantage to ourselves, not for benefits expected or received, not for affinity or blood relationship, but for this reason alone, that they share our nature; for we do not love them as ourselves when we love them for the reasons stated above. (3:15,2)

We should think of all people as our neighbors since they are sharers in our nature. (3:15,2)

We love all our neighbors as ourselves when, in regard to morality and to gaining eternal life, we have concern for their salvation as for our own; when we imagine ourselves in their sins and dangers; and when, just as we wish them to help us, so we come to their aid according to our strength, or if we have not the means to help them, have the will to do so. (3:15,3)

These [who genuinely love God] are they who sincerely believe that He gave them the power to accomplish all the good they have been able to do. Whatever evil they have committed they ascribe to the fault of their own will; whatever good they have not been able to accomplish they continually ask Him that they may be able to do; when they have been able, they thank Him. They charitably wish that His blessings, which they have attained, may be granted to others also; and, extending the breadth of their love even to their enemies, they wish all to be what they are. (3:15,4)

When anyone, won by the convincing fairness of virtue, has broken to some extent with his former way of life, immediately another temptation against which he must struggle confronts him. Vanity of the world will attack the one whom carnal passion has abandoned in defeat, an example of which we have in those who deny themselves the enjoyment of lustful passion and allow their will the license of windy vanity. They have no intercourse with shame, but give in to ambition. (3:17,1)

The Lord becomes our praise when we wish others not to praise us because of God's gifts, but to praise His gifts in us. Those whose salvation the Lord has become cannot boast of their own virtue. (3:20,2)

Whether we despair of God's gift by which we are strengthened, or boast of our own ability, we are not equal to the task of resisting vices. (3:20,3)

Faith, which is the foundation of righteousness, which no good works precede and from which they all proceed, cleanses us from all sins, enlightens our minds, reconciles us to God, and unites us with all who share our nature. (3:21)

We who are human should think nothing human alien to us. (3:22)

We should prefer to incur the enmity of those who are unwilling to be corrected rather than to risk offending God by humoring sinners. (3:23,2)

It will profit us nothing to have learned what we should do unless we strive to carry out what we have learned. (3:27)

Virtue differs from vice precisely in this: the latter corrupts sound things; the former heals what the attack of vice has corrupted. (3:29,3)

Not by having emotions, but by using them badly, do we transgress. For the nature of human emotions indicates the Creator of humankind; their quality shows one's good or bad will. (3:31,2)

~ *Gregory the Great*

Gregory (c. 540–604) served as bishop of Rome from 590 to 604. Born into an illustrious Roman senatorial family, Gregory sold all his possessions, established a monastery, and entered it as a monk. In due course, the Roman bishop utilized Gregory's noted administrative abilities, and Gregory, much to his chagrin, received public notice. When the pope died, the people of Rome by acclamation demanded Gregory as his successor. Reluctant to accept the office because he recognized it would entail much that would distract him from the contemplative lifestyle he had chosen and by which he wanted to continue to serve God, Gregory nonetheless eventually accepted this summons to serve the well-being of the church in Rome and, because of the stature of its bishop and the additional duties expected of the pope, the rest of the Church in the West.

Gregory was the last of the Latin Church Fathers; he has also been called the first of the medieval popes. As bishop of Rome, he conducted an extensive correspondence; he also sent out missionaries to far-flung areas of Western Europe. He wrote numerous practical works to guide the Church; his *Pastoral Care* taught clergy how to lead their lives and conduct their responsibilities faithfully.

Hymn[1]

O Christ, our King, Creator, Lord,
    Savior of all who trust Your Word,

---

1 This is in the public domain.

to those who seek You ever near,
now to our praises bend Your ear.

In Your dear Cross a grace is found—
    it flows from every streaming wound—
its power our inbred sin controls,
    breaks the firm bond, and frees our souls.

You did create the stars of night;
yet You have veiled in flesh Your Light,
    have deigned a mortal form to wear,
    a mortal's painful lot to bear.

And when You hanged upon the tree,
    the quaking earth acknowledged You;
when You yielded up Your breath,
    the world grew dark as shades of death.

Now in the Father's glory high,
    great conqueror, nevermore to die,
    us by Your mighty power defend,
    and reign through ages without end.

Pastoral Care[2]

The government of souls is the art of arts. (1:1)

Although those who have no knowledge of the powers of drugs shrink from giving themselves out as physicians of the flesh, people who are utterly ignorant of spiritual precepts are often not afraid of professing themselves to be physicians of the heart. (1:1)

There are some who investigate spiritual precepts with shrewd diligence, but in the life they live trample on what they have penetrated by their understanding. They hasten to teach what they have learned, not by practice, but by study, and belie in their conduct what they teach by words. (1:2)

---

2 Excerpts taken from ACW 11:20–237.

In the school of adversity the heart is forced to discipline itself. (1:3)

We would have no one who is not fully qualified for it venture to snatch at supreme rule, just as we would not have those who stumble on plain ground try to set their feet on a precipice. (1:4)

What disposition of mind is revealed in the one who could perform conspicuous public benefit on coming to his task, but prefers his own privacy to the benefit of others, seeing that the Only Begotten of the Supreme Father came forth from the bosom of His Father into our midst, so that He might benefit many? (1:5)

One is quite incapable of learning humility in a position of superiority, if he did not refrain from acting proudly when he was in a position of subjection. (1:9)

Pleasure not repressed in thought gains mastery in act. (1:11)

A pastor must be pure in thought, exemplary in conduct, discreet in keeping silence, profitable in speech, in sympathy a near neighbor to everyone, in contemplation exalted above all others, a humble companion to those who lead good lives, erect in his zeal for righteousness against the vices of sinners. He must not be remiss in his care for the inner life by preoccupation with the external; nor must he, in his solicitude for what is internal, fail to give attention to the external. (2:1)

The ruler should ever be pure in thought. No impurity should stain one who has undertaken the duty of cleansing the stains of defilement from the hearts of others as well as from his own. (2:2)

His voice penetrates the hearts of his hearers the more readily, if his way of life commends what he says. (2:3)

Rulers must also see to it with careful concern that not only should nothing evil proceed from their lips, but that not even what is proper be said in excess or in a slovenly manner. Often the force of what is said is wasted when it is enfeebled in the hearts of hearers by a careless and offensive torrent of words. Indeed, this sort of loquacity defiles the speaker himself, since it takes no notice of the practical needs of the audience. (2:4)

It is in vain that an army, seeking contact with the enemy, hurries behind its leader, if he has lost the way. (2:7)

Doctrine taught does not penetrate the minds of the needy, if a compassionate heart does not commend it to the hearts of hearers; but the seed of the Word germinates promptly when the kindness of a preacher waters it in the hearer's heart. (2:7)

That one is an enemy to his Redeemer who on the strength of the good works he performs desires to be loved by the Church, rather than by Him. Indeed, a servant is guilty of adulterous thought, if he craves to please the eyes of the Bride when the Bridegroom sends gifts to her by him. (2:8)

It is also to be observed that good rulers should wish to please people, but so as to draw their neighbors to the love of truth by the fair esteem they have of their rulers—not that these long to be loved themselves, but wish that this love should be a road, as it were, whereby they lead the hearts of the hearers to the love of the Creator. It is difficult for one who is not loved, however well he preaches, to find a sympathetic hearing. (2:8)

Rulers should understand that vices commonly masquerade as virtues. (2:9)

When sin is committed not through malice, but through sheer ignorance or frailty, it is necessary to temper reproof of the sin with great forbearance. For, in truth, all of us are subject to the frailties of our corrupt nature so long as we remain in this mortal flesh. (2:10)

When the strict Judge comes, He who has made Himself one of us by sharing our nature, He undoubtedly does not bring a charge of guilt against one who is screened by faith, hope, and love under the shelter of His forgiveness. (2:10)

As long before us Gregory Nazianzen of revered memory has taught, one and the same exhortation is not suited to all, because they are not compassed by the same quality of character. (3:Prologue)

The discourse of a teacher should be adapted to the character of the hearers, so as to be suited to the individual in his or her respective needs, and yet never deviate from the art of general edification. (3:Prologue)

Every teacher, in order to edify all in the one virtue of love, must touch the hearts of his hearers by using one and the same doctrine, but not by giving to all one and the same exhortation. (3:Prologue)

The words of a preacher should be quickly adapted to the life led by his hearer. (3:2)

We should aim at making them more wisely foolish, to make them abandon their foolish wisdom, and to make them learn the wise foolishness of God. (3:6)

The impudent are better corrected by direct reproof, but in the case of the timid it is more profitable if what is reprehended in them is touched upon, as it were, incidentally. (3:7)

Patience is the guardian of our estate. (3:9)

The patient must, therefore, be told to aim diligently at loving those whom they have to put up with, lest, if love does not wait on patience, the virtue that appears outwardly may be turned into a worse fault of hatred. (3:9)

It is in vain that indignation, clamor, and blasphemy are put away outwardly, if interior malice, which is the mother of vices, reigns. In vain is wickedness cut away from the outward branches, if it is retained in the root within, to shoot up in more ways than ever before. (3:9)

Among people, it is virtuous to put up with enemies; but before God it is virtue to love them. God accepts only that sacrifice which, in His eyes, is enkindled by the flame of love on the altar of good works. (3:9)

We sin greatly if we do not regard with affection the good deeds of others. (3:10)

Falsehood always harms the one who utters it. (3:11)

Nothing is more safely defended than sincerity, nothing easier to speak than the truth. But when one is forced to defend his deceit, his heart is wearied with the toilsome labor of doing so. . . . They who could have been the friends of truth without effort, labor to sin, and as they decline to live in sincerity, they are at pains to perish laboriously. (3:11)

They are to be admonished that if they are unwilling to please God when they can, they may not be able to please Him when, too late, they decide to do so. (3:12)

The sick are to be admonished to consider what great health of the heart is bestowed by bodily affliction, for it recalls the mind to a knowledge of itself and renews the memory of our infirmity, which health commonly disregards. (3:12)

To preserve the virtue of patience, the sick are to be admonished ever to bear in mind how great were the evils endured constantly by our Redeemer at the hands of those whom He had created, how many horrible insults of reproaches He endured, how many blows in the face He received at the hands of scoffers, while He was daily snatching the souls of captives from the power of the ancient enemy; that while cleansing us with the water of salvation, He did not screen His face from the spitting of perfidious men; that He silently endured the scourging to free us by His mediation from eternal torments; that He endured buffeting to give us everlasting honors among the choirs of angels; that while saving us from being pierced by our sins, He did not shrink from offering His head to thorns; that He took bitter gall in His thirst in order to inebriate us with everlasting sweetness; that when mockingly adored, He held His peace and adored in our behalf the Father, though equal to Him in the Godhead; and that He who was the Life passed to death that He might prepare life for those who were dead. Why, then, is it considered hard that one should endure stripes from God for his evil-doing, if God endured so great evil in requital for His own good deeds? (3:12)

The mind that is under the slavery of fear does not know the grace of liberty. Good should be loved for its own sake, not pursued under the compulsion of established penalties. The person who acts well from fear of torments wishes that what he fears did not exist, so that he might boldly commit sin. (3:13)

One represses the tongue but lifts up his mind and, without any regard to his own bad qualities, he accuses others within his own heart the more freely, as does so the more secretly. (3:14)

There is nothing in us more fugitive than the heart which deserts us as often as it slips away in evil thoughts. (3:14)

By our neglect to guard against idle words, we come to utter harmful ones. (3:14)

One who does not curb his tongue routs concord. (3:14)

When vice is thought to be virtue, guilt accumulates without apprehension. (3:16)

The pride of the devil became the occasion of our perdition, and the humility of God proved to be the pledge of our redemption. For our enemy, created like all other things, wished to appear superior to all, but our Redeemer, remaining great above all things, deigned to become little among all. Let the humble, therefore, be told that in abasing themselves, they rise to the likeness of God. Let the haughty be told that in exalting themselves, they debase themselves to the likeness of the rebel angel. (3:17)

There is no virtue in subduing the flesh, if the spirit is overcome by anger. (3:19)

When we administer necessities to the needy, we give them what is their own, not what is ours; we pay a debt of justice, rather than do a work of mercy. . . . It surely is a matter of justice that they who receive what is bestowed by the Lord of all should use it for the common good. (3:21)

The quarrelsome are to be admonished to know for certain that however great the virtues which they have, they cannot become spiritual at all if they disregard union in concord with their neighbors, for it is written, "The fruit of the Spirit is love, joy, peace" [Gal 5:22]. Therefore, the one who does not endeavor to preserve peace refuses to bring forth the fruit of the Spirit. (3:22)

Those who wrangle are to be admonished to bear in mind that they offer God no sacrifice of a good work so long as they are in disaccord with the love of neighbors. For Scripture states, "If you bring your gift to the altar, and there remember that your brother has something against you, leave your gift there before the altar, and go your way. First be reconciled to your brother, and then come and offer your gift" [Matt 5:23–24]. (3:22)

If we consider the case well, irrational nature shows by its concord how great is the evil committed by rational nature by discord, when it has lost, though exercising reason, what irrational nature retains by natural instinct. (3:22)

The peaceable are also to be admonished not to desire human peace too much and so fail entirely to reprove the evil conduct of people. (3:22)

What is transitory peace but the footprint, so to speak, of the peace that is eternal? (3:22)

If those who make peace are called the children of God, surely those who disturb it are the children of Satan. (3:23)

Since nothing is more esteemed by God than the virtue of love, nothing is more desired by the devil than its extinction. (3:23)

That one is a poor and unskilled physician who aims at healing others, but is ignorant of his own ailment. (3:24)

The one who goes out and dispenses blessings by his preaching receives the fullness of interior increase; and while he unceasingly inebriates the souls of his hearers with the wine of eloquence, he is himself increasingly inebriated with the draught of multiplied grace. (3:25)

The married are . . . also to be admonished to consider not so much what each has to endure from the other, as what the other is made to endure. (3:27)

Admonish people to rely confidently on the mercy they ask for, lest they perish through the violence of immoderate affliction. . . . On the other hand, admonish them to have only such a degree of confidence in hope, that they will not grow remiss in the sense of a false security. For often when the crafty enemy observes the soul afflicted because of its fall, he seduces it with blandishments of a baneful reassurance, in order to trip it up in sin. (3:29)

We have learned in the case of our first parent that a sin is committed in three stages—namely, the suggestion of it, the pleasure experienced, and the consent. The first is the act of the enemy, the second that of the flesh, the third that of the spirit. (3:29)

As for those who lament their sins but do not give them up, they are to be admonished to realize and observe carefully that, though bewailing their sins, their attempts to cleanse themselves are vain if they continue defiling themselves with evil in their way of life. (3:30)

Those who transgress in small matters only, but do so frequently, are to be admonished to consider not what kind of sins they commit, but how many. (3:33)

It commonly happens that the mind, by becoming used to slight sins, does not dread even great ones; and, being emboldened in sinning, it comes to a kind of justification of evil, and disdains fear in the case of the greater sins, in proportion as it has learned to sin without fear in the case of lesser sins. (3:33)

Those who do evil secretly and good openly are to be admonished to consider how swiftly human judgments pass away, but how permanent and lasting divine judgments are. (3:35)

Those greatly misjudge their good deeds who think that human approval is a sufficient reward. Actually, when transitory praise is sought for a good deed, then what is worthy of an eternal reward is sold for a trifling price. (3:35)

Whereas in exhorting individuals great exertion is required to be of service to each individual's particular needs, and whereas it is very laborious to instruct each one in what applies to him in particular by urging appropriate considerations, the task is a far more laborious one when on one and the same occasion one has to deal with a numerous audience subject to different passions. In this case the address must be formulated with such skill that, notwithstanding the diversity of failings in the audience as a whole, it carries a proper message to each individual, without involving itself in self-contradictions. (3:36)

Every preacher should make himself heard rather by deeds than by words, and by his righteous way of life should imprint footsteps for people to tread in, rather than show them by word the way to go. (3:40)

Often when a sermon is delivered with due propriety and with a fruitful message, the mind of the speaker is exalted by joy all his own over his performance. If so, he must be careful to torment himself with painful misgivings: in restoring others to health by healing their wounds, he must not disregard his own health and develop tumors of pride. (4:1)

∽ *Pseudo-Dionysius*

At some point in time, at the latest by the early sixth century, a Greek-speaking Christian had penned several works under the pseudonym Dionysius the Areopagite (a convert under St. Paul's preaching in Athens [Acts 17:34]). In short order, these works were accepted as the works of the Athenian convert and accorded significant status. Doubts about the quasi-apostolic authorship surfaced periodically throughout the history of the Church, and by the sixteenth century those doubts had become widespread. Who the original author may have been is still a subject of scholarly controversy.

The works of Pseudo-Dionysius have exercised considerable influence on Christian spirituality. He offers a vigorous, challenging presentation of the ineffability of God and builds a distinctive spirituality around that emphasis.

The Divine Names[1]

We must not dare to resort to words or conceptions concerning that hidden Divinity which transcends being, apart from what the sacred Scriptures have divinely revealed. (1:1)

The inscrutable One is out of the reach of every rational process. (1:1)

---

1 Excerpts taken from Colm Luibheid, trans., *Pseudo-Dionysius: The Complete Works* (Mahwah, NJ: Paulist Press, 1987), pp. 49–131.

Mind beyond mind, word beyond speech, It is gathered up by no discourse, by no intuition, by no name. It is, and It is as no other being is. Cause of all existence, and therefore Itself transcending existence, It alone could give an authoritative account of what It really is. (1:1)

To sum up: It is the Life of the living, the Being of beings, It is the Source and the Cause of all life and of all being, for out of Its goodness It commands all things to be and It keeps them going. (1:3)

If all knowledge is of that which is and is limited to the realm of the existent, then whatever transcends being must also transcend knowledge. (1:4)

If we watch over the Scriptures we ourselves will be watched over by them, guarding them and being guarded. (2:2)

The sacred Incarnation of Jesus for our sakes is something which cannot be enclosed in words nor grasped by any mind. (2:9)

The Trinity is not in any one location in such a manner as to be "away from" one place or moving "from one spot to another." Even to speak of It as "present in everything" is inaccurate, since this does not convey the fact that It infinitely transcends everything and yet gathers everything within It. (3:1)

We must begin with a prayer before everything we do, but especially when we are about to talk of God. (3:1)

The divine Mind, therefore, takes in all things in a total knowledge which is transcendent. Because It is the Cause of all things, It has foreknowledge of everything. (7:2)

The divine Mind does not acquire the knowledge of things from things. (7:2)

We cannot know God in His nature, since this is unknowable and is beyond the reach of mind or of reason. But we know Him from the arrangement of everything. (7:3)

It seems to me that anyone reared on Scripture cannot be unaware of the fact that the Godhead transcends and surpasses every real and every conceivable power. (8:1)

His greatness takes in all space, surpasses all number, moves far beyond infinity in Its abundance, in the overflowing of Its great works and in the gifts welling up from It. (9:2)

The Mystical Theology[2]

What actually has to be said about the Cause of everything is this: since It is the Cause of all beings, we should posit and ascribe to It all the affirmations we make in regard to beings, and, more appropriately, we should negate all these affirmations, since It surpasses all being. Now we should not conclude that the negations are simply the opposites of the affirmations, but rather that the Cause of all is considerably prior to this—beyond privations, beyond every denial, beyond every assertion. (1:2)

The Celestial Hierarchy[3]

Let us, then, call upon Jesus, the Light of the Father, the true Light enlightening everyone coming into the world [John 1:4], "through whom also we have access" [Rom 5:2] to the Father, the Light which is the source of all light. (1:2)

The Word of God makes use of poetic imagery . . . not for the sake of art, but as a concession to the nature of our minds. (2:1)

The Deity is far beyond every manifestation of being and life; no reference to light can characterize It; every reason or intelligence falls short of similarity to It.

Then there is the scriptural device of praising the Deity by presenting It in utterly dissimilar revelations. He is described as invisible, infinite, ungraspable, and other things which show not what He is, but what in fact He is not. This second way of talking about Him seems to me much more appropriate, for, as the secret and sacred tradition has instructed, God is in no way like the things that have being, and we have no knowledge at all of

---
2 Excerpted from Luibheid, *Pseudo-Dionysius*, pp. 135–141.
3 *Op. cit.*, pp. 145–191.

His incomprehensible and ineffable transcendence and invisibility.

Since the way of negation appears to be more suitable to the realm of the divine, and since positive affirmations are always unfitting to the hiddenness of the inexpressible, a manifestation through dissimilarities is more correctly to be applied to the invisible. (2:3)

It was to avoid this kind of misunderstanding among those incapable of rising above visible beauty that the pious theologians so wisely and upliftingly stooped to incongruous dissimilarities, for by doing this they took account of our inherent tendency toward the material and our willingness to be lazily satisfied by base images. (2:3)

One truth must be affirmed above all else. It is that the transcendent Deity has out of goodness established the existence of everything and brought it into being. It is characteristic of the universal Cause, of this goodness beyond all, to summon everything to communion with Him to the extent that this is possible. (4:1)

Of course, God has appeared to certain pious people in ways which were in keeping with His Divinity. He has come in certain sacred visions fashioned to suit the beholders. (4:3)

The Ecclesiastical Hierarchy[4]

Divinization consists of being as much as possible like and in union with God. (1:3)

The sacred chanting of the Scriptures and the readings teach the rules of virtuous living. Above all, it teaches the need for the total purification of the self from destructive evil. The shared, peaceful, and most divine distribution of the one bread and of the one cup lays down as a norm that, having been nourished by the same food, their lives must be joined in full sharing of inspired food. It also sacredly reminds them of the most divine Supper, which is the original symbol of all the rites. The Author Himself of all these symbols very rightly excluded from that sacred feast the one not devoted to Himself. (3:1)

---

4 Excerpts taken from Luibheid, *Pseudo-Dionysius,* pp. 195–259.

When we had lost the divine gifts because of our own folly, God took the trouble to recall us to our original condition through additional gifts: He gave us a most perfect share of His nature by completely taking on our own, and in this way He made it possible for us to enter into communion with Himself and with divine reality. (3:7)

We are enticed and encouraged to follow their example and to adopt a mode of living which will guarantee us greater happiness, that happiness which comes from conformity to God. For this proclamation announces them as alive, as those who have not died but, as the Word of God teaches us, who have passed from death to a more perfectly divine life. (3:9)

From the very beginning human nature has stupidly glided away from those good things bestowed on it by God. It turned to the life of the most varied desires and came at the end to the catastrophe of death. There followed the destructive rejection of what was really good, a trampling over the sacred law laid down in Paradise for humanity. Having evaded the yoke which gave them life, humankind rebelled against the blessings of God and were left to their own devices, to the temptation and the evil assaults of the devil. And in exchange for eternity they pitiably opted for mortality. Born of corruption, it was only right that they should leave the world as they entered it. They freely turned away from the divine and uplifting life and were dragged instead as far as possible in the opposite direction and were plunged into the utter mess of passion. Wandering far from the right path, ensnared by destructive and evil crowds, the human race turned away from the true God and witlessly served neither gods nor friends but its enemies who, out of their innate lack of pity, took the cruelest advantage of its weakness and dragged it down to the deplorable peril of destruction and dissolution of being.

Yet the goodness of the Deity has endless love for humanity and never ceased from benignly pouring out on us Its providential gifts. It took upon Itself in a most authentic way all the characteristics of our nature, except sin. It became one with us in our lowliness, losing nothing of Its own real condition, suffering no change or loss. It allowed us, as those of equal birth, to enter into communion with It and to acquire a share of Its own true beauty. Thus, as our hidden tradition teaches, It made it possible for us to escape from the domain of the rebellious, and It did this not through overwhelming force, but, as Scripture mysteriously tells us, by an act of judgment and in all righteousness. Beneficently It wrought a complete change in our nature. It filled our shadowed and unshaped minds with a kindly, divine light and adorned them with a loveliness suitable to their divinized state. It saved our nature from almost complete wreckage and delivered the dwelling place of our soul from the most accursed passion and from destructive defilement. Finally, It showed us a supramundane uplifting and an inspired way of life in shaping ourselves to It as fully as lay in our power. (3:11)

This imitation of God, how else are we to achieve it if not by endlessly reminding ourselves of God's sacred works and doing so by way of the sacred hymns and the sacred acts established by the hierarchy? We do this, as the Scriptures say, in remembrance of Him. (3:12)

If our longing is for communion with Him, then we must give our full attention to His divine life in the flesh. His sacred sinlessness must be our model, so that we may aspire to a godlike and unblemished condition. This is how, in a way that suits us, He will grant us communion with His likeness. (3:12)

Whoever wrongfully dares to teach holiness to others before he has regularly practiced it himself is unholy and is a stranger to sacred norms. (3:14)

The sign of the cross indicates the renunciation of all the desires of the flesh. It points to a life given over to the imitation of God and unswervingly directed toward the divine life of the incarnate Jesus, who was divinely sinless and yet lowered Himself to the Cross and to death and who, with the sign of the cross, that image of His own sinlessness, marks all those imitating Him. (5:4)

The Scriptures which God Himself handed down . . . reveal to us all that we can know of God, all His works and words and manifestations, every sacred word and work—everything, in short, which the Divinity has so generously wished to pass on to the human hierarchy, every sacred thing done and said by God. (5:7)

And scriptural truth has passed on to us the fact that the prayers of the righteous are of use only to those who are worthy of them, and only in this life, not after death. (7:6)

You might say, however, that what could really earn the ridicule of the impious is the fact that infants, despite their inability to understand the divine things, are nevertheless admitted to that sacrament of sacred divine-birth and to the sacred symbol of the divine communion. (7:11)

Our knowledge is far from being commensurate with the divine mysteries, many of which remain beyond our grasp and with a meaning outside our power to understand. (7:11)

Letters[5]

He exists beyond being and He is known beyond the mind. (#1)

Out of His very great love for humanity, He became quite truly human, both superhuman and among humans; and, though Himself beyond being, He took upon Himself the being of humans. Yet His is not less overflowing with transcendence. He is the ever-transcendent, and super-abundantly so. (#4)

Being above human beings, He yet truly became human. Furthermore, it was not by virtue of being God that He did divine things, not by virtue of being human that He did what was human, but rather, by the fact of being God-made-man He accomplished something new in our midst—the activity of the God-man. (#4)

It is in this sense that one says of the divine Paul that he knew God, for he knew that God is beyond every act of mind and every way of knowing. He says too that "unsearchable are His judgments and His ways past finding out" [Rom 11:33], that His gifts are indescribable [2 Cor 9:15], and that His peace "surpasses all understanding" [Phil 4:7]. (#5)

But you say that the sophist Apollophanes reviles me, that he is calling me a parricide, that he charges me with making unholy use of things Greek to attack the Greeks. It would be more correct to say to him in reply that it is the Greeks who make unholy use of godly things to attack God. (#7)

The word of God calls "good" all those people who neither planned nor did

---

5 Excerpts taken from Luibheid, *Pseudo-Dionysius*, pp. 263–289.

evil things, whose goodness stood up against the evil of others, people who lived in conformity with God. They did good to those wronging them and extended to them their own abundant goodness so as to bring them gently around to behaving like them. (#8:1)

Does not God support His accusers and plead on their behalf? He even promises to be concerned for them and when they are far away from Him, they have only to make a backward turn and there He is, hastening to meet them. (#8:1)

Even if disorder and confusion should undermine the most divine ordinances and regulations, that still gives no right, even on God's behalf, to overturn the order which God Himself has established. God is not divided against Himself. (#8:1)

The Word of God commands us "to pursue just things justly" [Deut 16:20, LXX], and justice is pursued when each wishes to give everyone his due. (#8:3)

Let the hierarchs bow to the apostles and to the successors of the apostles. (#8:4)

Those who do not know must be taught, not punished. We do not hit the blind. We lead them by the hand. (#8:5)

Theological tradition has a dual aspect, the ineffable and mysterious on the one hand, the open and more evident on the other. The one resorts to symbolism and involves initiation. The other is philosophic and employs the method of demonstration. (Further, the inexpressible is bound up with what can be articulated.) The one uses persuasion and imposes the truthfulness of what is asserted. The other acts and, by means of a mystery which cannot be taught, puts souls firmly in the presence of God. (#9)

In the times to come it is not God who will rightly separate Himself from the wicked; rather, it is the wicked who will separate themselves completely from God. (#10)

~ Maximus the Confessor

Maximus (580–662) lived as a monk. He served the Church by brilliant doctrinal teaching based on the heritage of the faith received from the preceding Church Fathers, and by the insightful spiritual advice he offered—also based on the experience of the godly before him. In both regards, he exercised profound influence on the subsequent teaching and spirituality of the Church, for while he passed on what he had received, he also coordinated it and offered clarification that has shaped subsequent doctrinal teaching and spirituality. Maximus also spoke and wrote against a heresy espoused by the Byzantine emperors toward the end of his lifetime. For his opposition, he was mutilated by having his tongue cut out and his right hand amputated (thus earning the epithet Confessor).

The record of his first trial before the imperial court has been preserved and gives clear evidence of Maximus's fidelity to the faith that had been proclaimed and defended by the Church up to his time. The other works are all directed to fellow monks, setting forth basic perspectives on the faith and describing the life they and—from Maximus's viewpoint—any Christian should live.

The Trial of Maximus[1]

God incarnate both wills and works in both His divinity and in His humanity. For He is lacking in nothing of those things by which He is known as

---

1 Excerpts taken from George C. Berthold, trans., *Maximus Confessor: Selected Writings* (Mahwah, NJ: Paulist Press, 1985), pp. 17–28.

God and of those things by which He is known as human by nature except sin. If He is complete according to each nature, since nothing is lacking to either, it is obvious that one is corrupting the whole mystery unless one confesses that He is what He is with the natural properties which belong to Him according to each nature in which and which He is. (§9)

Commentary on the Our Father[2]

The mystery of salvation belongs to those who desire it, not to those who are forced to submit to it. (§2)

Christ conquers the flesh which had been overcome in Adam by brandishing it as an instrument against evil. Thus He shows how the flesh, which had been bruised first by death, captures its captor and destroys its life by natural death. (§2)

The same God is truly Unity and Trinity: Unity according to the principle of essence and Trinity according to the mode of existence. The same reality is wholly Unity without being divided by the Persons, and wholly Trinity without being confused in unity. (§4)

In the Christian life we make life a preparation for death. (§4)

Let us prove that we eat to live and let us not be convicted of living to eat. (§4)

Questions and Doubts[3]

Whoever calls his brother of the same faith "ungodly" and "idolater" or "heretic" and "unfaithful," this person says "fool" [Matt 5:22], and, rightly, he becomes liable to Gehenna. (Question 40)

Prayer is higher than theology. For the one theologizes about the divine based on past events, whereas prayer joins the soul, in an unknowable and ineffable way, to God Himself. (Question 46)

---

2 Excerpted from Berthold, *Maximus Confessor*, pp. 101–119.
3 Excerpts taken from Despina D. Prassas, trans., *St. Maximus the Confessor's Questions and Doubts* (DeKalb, IL: Northern Illinois University Press, 2010), pp. 143–157.

He [St. Paul] . . . says that it is necessary for those who have believed and have been justified, in order to guard the justification which is by faith and grace, to adhere ardently to the virtues. (Question 114)

Chapters on Knowledge[4]

Faith is a true knowledge from undemonstrated principles, since it is the substance of realities which are beyond intelligence and reason. (1:9)

In freeing us from the bitter bondage of tyrannical demons, God has given us the loving yoke of holy piety, which is humility. (1:15)

The soul would never be able to reach out toward the knowledge of God if God did not allow Himself to be touched by it through condescension and by raising it up to Him. (1:31)

The mystery of the incarnation of the Word bears the power of all the hidden meanings and figures of Scripture as well as the knowledge of visible and intelligible creatures. The one who knows the mystery of the Cross and the Tomb knows the principles of these creatures. And the one who has been initiated into the ineffable power of the Resurrection knows the purpose for which God originally made all things. (1:66)

Just as a transgression of the commandments is a concomitant of disobedience and a separation from the one who enjoined them, so the keeping of the commandments and union with the one who gave them follow obedience. (2:7)

The fear of hell trains beginners to flee from evil, and the desire for the reward of good things gives to the advanced the eagerness for the practice of virtues. But the mystery of love removes the mind from all created things, causing it to be blind to all that is less than God. (2:9)

It is possible for the Lord not to appear in the same form to all those who meet Him, but to some in one way and to others in another way. (2:13)

The Bread of Life, because He loves humankind, gives Himself to all who

---

4 Excerpted from Berthold, *Maximus Confessor,* pp. 129–170.

ask, but not to all in the same way. (2:56)

It is necessary that the one who seeks after God in a religious way never hold fast to the letter, lest that one mistakenly understand things said about God for God Himself. (2:73)

Ambigua ("Difficulties")[5]

And what could be more amazing than the fact that, being God by nature, and seeing fit to become man by nature, he did not defy the limits of either one of the natures in relation to the other, but instead remained wholly God while becoming wholly human? . . . Given that the natural difference between the two essential parts admitted no mixing, he was not divided, and in view of the supreme unity of his person, he knew no confusion. (§42)

In the beginning humanity was created in the image of God (Gen 1:26, 27) in order to be perpetually born by the Spirit in the exercise of free choice, and to acquire the additional gift of assimilation to God by keeping the divine commandment, such that man, as fashioned from God by nature, might become son of God and divine by grace through the Spirit. (§42)

Ad Thalassium ("To Thalassius")[6]

The immobility of virtue is the beginning of vice. (§17)

God became a man and provided another beginning, a second nativity, for human nature, which, through the vehicle of suffering, ends in the pleasure of the life to come. (§61)

None of the persons, places, times, or other things recorded in Scripture—animate and inanimate, sensible and intelligible—has its concurrent literal or spiritual meanings rendered always according to the same interpretive mode. (§64)

---

5 Excerpts taken from Paul M. Blowers and Robert L. Wilken, trans., *On the Cosmic Mystery of Jesus Christ: Selected Writings from St. Maximus the Confessor* (Crestwood, NY: St. Vladimir's Seminary Press, 2003), pp. 45–95.
6 Excerpted from Blowers and Wilken, *On the Cosmic Mystery,* pp. 97–171.

The Lord mounted his flesh on the fish-hook of his divinity as bait for the Devil's deceit, so that, as that insatiable spiritual serpent, the Devil would take his flesh into his mouth (since its nature is easily overcome) and quiver convulsively on the hook of the Lord's divinity, and, by virtue of the sacred flesh of the Logos, completely vomit the Lord's human nature once he had swallowed it. As a result, just as the Devil formerly baited man with the hope of divinity, and swallowed him, so too the Devil himself would be baited precisely with humanity's fleshly garb; and afterward he would vomit up man, who had been deceived by the expectation of becoming divine, the Devil himself having been deceived. . . . The transcendence of God's power would then manifest itself through the weakness of our inferior human nature, which would vanquish the strength of its conqueror. As well, it would be shown that it is God who, by using the flesh as bait, conquers the Devil, rather than the Devil conquering man by promising a divine nature. (§64)

The law of grace teaches those who follow it directly to imitate God himself, who, if I may rightly say so, loves us, his virtual enemies because of sin, more than himself, such that, even though he himself transcends every essence and nature, he consented to enter our human essence without undergoing change, and, while retaining his transcendence, to become a man and willingly to interact as one among men. He did not refuse to take our condemnation on himself, and indeed, the more he himself became a man by nature in his incarnation, the more he deified us by grace, so that we would not only learn naturally to care for one another, and spiritually to love others as ourselves, but also like God to be concerned for others more than for ourselves, even to the point of proving that love to others by being ready to die voluntarily and virtuously for others. For as the Lord says, "There is no greater love than this, that a man lay down his life for his friend" [John 15:13]. (§64)

The Ascetic Life[7]

The Lord joined to right faith the keeping of all the commandments for this reason: He knew that one, apart from the other, was not able to save us. (§2)

---

7 Excerpted from ACW 21:103–135.

Our Lord Jesus Christ, being God by nature and, because of His kindness, deigning also to become human, was born of a woman and made under the law, as the divine apostle says, so that by observing the commandment as man He might overturn the ancient curse on Adam. (§10)

After securing complete victory over the devil, Jesus Christ crowned Himself with the Resurrection for our sake. Thus the new Adam renewed the old. (§12)

By being conquered deliberately, He conquered him who hoped to conquer and snatched the world from his dominion. (§13)

Out of my carelessness the demons always take occasion against me. (§18)

The foolish person often asks God to be merciful, but when the mercy comes does not accept it, since it did not come as he desired, but as the Physician of souls thought fitting. (§22)

Unceasing prayer is to keep the mind in great reverence and attached to God by desire, and to cling always to Him in hope, to be of good courage in Him in all things, both in our activity and in all that happens to us. (§25)

How can we be called Christians, who have nothing at all of Christ in us? (§33)

Any ascetic life or practice that is without love is a stranger to God. (§36)

We find the forgiveness of our trespasses in forgiving our brothers and sisters, and the mercy of God is hidden in mercifulness toward our neighbor. (§42)

The Four Centuries [or Four Hundred Chapters] on Love[8]

What follows is not the fruit of my own meditation. Instead, I went through the writings of the Holy Fathers and selected from them whatever had reference to my subject, summarizing many things in a few words so that they

---

8 Excerpted from Berthold, *Maximus Confessor,* pp. 35–87.

can be seen at a glance to be easily memorized. (Prologue)

If someone reads this (or any other book whatever) not for the sake of spiritual profit but to hunt for phrases to reproach the author so that he might then set himself up in his own opinion as wiser than the author, such a person will never receive any profit of any kind. (Prologue)

The one who loves God prefers knowledge of Him to all things made by Him. (1:4)

The one who loves God cannot help loving also every person as himself, even though he is displeased by the passions of those who are not yet purified. (1:13)

Blessed is the one who has learned to love all people equally. (1:17)

The one who imitates God by giving alms knows no difference between evil and good or just and unjust in regard to the needs of the body, but distributes to all without distinction according to their need, even if he prefers the virtuous person over the wicked because of his good intention. (1:24)

As the memory of fire does not warm the body, so faith without love does not bring about the illumination of knowledge in the soul. (1:31)

Do not say, "Mere faith in our Lord Jesus Christ can save me." For this is impossible unless you acquire love for Him through works. (1:39)

The work of love is the deliberate doing of good to one's neighbor, as well as long-suffering and patience and the use of all things in the proper way. (1:40)

The one who fears the Lord always has humility as his companion and through its promptings is led to divine love and thanksgiving. (1:48)

Do not lend your ear to the slanderer's tongue nor your tongue to the fault-finder's ear by readily speaking or listening to anything against your neighbor. Otherwise you will fall away from divine love and be found excluded from eternal life. (1:58)

Silence the one who is slandering in your hearing, lest you commit a double sin with him—by accustoming yourself to this deadly vice and by not restraining him from foolish talk against his neighbor. (1:60)

The battle against memories is more difficult than the battle against deeds, as sinning in thought is easier than sinning in deed. (1:63)

First the memory brings up a simple thought to the mind, and when it lingers about it arouses passion. When it is not removed it sways the mind to consent, and when this happens the actual sinning finally takes place. (1:84)

The demons' battle against us through thoughts is more severe than that through deeds. (1:91)

Through the working out of the commandments the mind puts off the passions. Through the spiritual contemplation of visible realities it puts off impassioned thoughts of things. Through the knowledge of invisible realities it puts off contemplation of visible things. And finally this it puts off though the knowledge of the Holy Trinity. (1:94)

We do not know God from His being, but from His magnificent works and His providence for beings. Through these as through mirrors we perceive His infinite goodness and wisdom and power. (1:96)

When the passions hold sway over a mind they bind it together with material things and, separating it from God, make it to be all-engrossed in them. But when love of God is in control, it releases the mind from the bonds and persuades it to think beyond not only things of sense but even this transient life of ours. (2:3)

The one who loves God cultivates pure prayer and throws off every hindering passion. (2:7)

If you hate some people and some you neither love nor hate, while others you love only moderately and still others you love very much, know from this inequality that you are far from perfect love, which lays down that you must love everyone equally. (2:10)

In applying itself to visible things, the mind knows them in accordance with nature through the medium of the senses, so that neither is the mind evil, nor is natural knowledge, nor the things, nor the senses, for these are all works of God. (2:15)

When you intend to know God, do not seek the reasons about His being, for the human mind and that of any other being after God cannot discover this. (2:27)

From the passions embedded in the soul the demons take their starting base to stir up passionate thoughts in us. Then by making war on the mind through them, they force it to go along and consent to sin. When it is overcome, they lead it on to a sin of thought, and when this is accomplished, they finally bring it as a prisoner to the deed. (2:31)

There are three things that move us to the good: natural tendencies, the holy angels, and a good will. . . . Likewise there are three things that move us to evil: passion, the demons, and a bad will. (2:32–33)

The one who does not envy or is not angry, or who does not bear grudges against the one who has offended him, does not yet have love for that person. For it is possible for one who does not yet love not to return evil for evil, because of the commandment. But love returns good for evil spontaneously. (2:49)

It is the impure demons who strengthen the passions and arouse them, taking advantage of our carelessness. (2:69)

As much as it is easier to sin in thought than in deed, so is a war with thoughts more exacting than one with things. (2:72)

Nothing created and given existence by God is evil. (3:3)

If you want to prevail over your thoughts, take care of your passions and you will easily drive them from your mind. (3:13)

Every human being is made to the image of God, but only those who are good and wise are made to His likeness [Gen 1:26]. (3:25)

God who is beyond fullness did not bring creatures into being out of any need in Him, but so that He might enjoy their proportionate participation in Him, and that He might delight in His works, seeing them delighted and ever insatiably satisfied with the One who is inexhaustible. (3:46)

When we wish to do something good, let us not have human applause in view but rather God, so that always looking to Him we might do everything on His account; otherwise we shall undergo the labor and still lose the reward. (3:48)

When you see that your mind is giving itself over to sins in thought and you do not resist, know that it will not be long before your body falls in with those sins. (3:52)

Ascribing our right actions to God removes pride. (3:62)

A person who has been honored with the knowledge of God and is abundantly enjoying the pleasure it provides disdains all the pleasures begotten from lust. (3:63)

God created the invisible world and the visible world, and naturally He made the soul and the body, as well. Now if this visible world is so beautiful, what sort of world will the invisible be? If it is better than the former, how much better than both is the One who created them? If then the Maker of everything that is beautiful is better than all creatures, for what reason does the mind leave the best of all to be engrossed in the worst of all, by which I mean the passions of the flesh? (3:72)

There is not just one reason why sinners commit the same sin, but several. (3:74)

If you bear a grudge against anyone, pray for that person and you will stop the passion in its tracks. . . . On the other hand, if someone else bears you a grudge, be generous and humble with him, treat him fairly, and you will deliver him from the passion. (3:90)

The perfect mind is the one that through genuine faith supremely knows in supreme ignorance the supremely Unknowable, and in gazing on the universe of His handiwork has received from God comprehensive knowledge of His providence and judgment in it, as far as allowable to humans. (3:99)

The inscrutable wisdom of the infinite nature is not subject to human knowledge. (4:3)

Evil is not to be regarded as in the substance of creatures, but in their mistaken and irrational movement. (4:14)

Bless when being reviled, keep silent when spoken ill of, and remain friendly when being conspired against. This is the way of Christ's wisdom, and the one who will not take it is not in His company. (4:30)

Scripture takes away none of the things given by God for our use, but it restrains immoderation and corrects unreasonableness. For example, it does not forbid eating or begetting children or having money or managing it, but it does forbid gluttony, fornication, and so forth. Nor does it even forbid us to think of these things, for they were made to be thought of; what it forbids is thinking of them with passions. (4:66)

Purify your mind of anger, resentment, and shameful thoughts, and then you will be able to know the indwelling of Christ. (4:76)

Be as eager as you can to love everyone, but if you cannot do this yet, at least do not hate anyone. (4:82)

Only God is good by nature, and only the one who imitates God is good by will. (4:90)

When the underlying passions of the soul are aroused, they blind the understanding and do not allow it to look at the rays of truth or to discern the better from the worse. (4:92)

The Church's Mystagogy[9]

God can in no way be associated by nature with any being and thus because of His superbeing is more fittingly referred to as nonbeing. For since it is necessary that we understand correctly the difference between God

---

9 Excerpts taken from Berthold, *Maximus Confessor,* pp. 183–241.

and creatures, then the affirmation of superbeing must be the negation of beings, and the affirmation of beings must be the negation of superbeing. (Introduction)

Maintaining about Himself as cause, beginning, and end all beings which are by nature distant from each other, He makes them converge in each other by the singular force of their relationship to Him as origin. (ch. 1)

Numerous and of almost infinite number are the men, women, and children who are distinct from one another and vastly different by birth and appearance, by nationality and language, by customs and age, by opinions and skills, by manners and habits, by pursuits and studies, and still again by reputation, fortune, characteristics, and connections: all are born into the Church and through it are reborn and recreated in the Spirit. (ch. 1)

The whole spiritual world seems mystically imprinted on the whole sensible world in symbolic forms, for those who are capable of seeing this. (ch. 2)

By the first appearance in the flesh of Jesus Christ the Son of God and our Savior in this world, He freed human nature which had been enslaved by corruption, betrayed through its own fault to death because of sin, tyrannically dominated by the devil. He redeemed all its debt as if He were liable even though He was not liable but sinless, and brought us back again to the original grace of His kingdom by giving Himself as a ransom for us. And in exchange for our destructive passions He gives us His life-giving Passion as a salutary cure which saves the whole world. (ch. 8)

The end will appear in the second coming of our great God and Savior Jesus Christ from the heavens in glory [Titus 2:13; Matt 24:30]. The divine apostle says that the Lord Himself will come down from heaven at the archangel's voice and the Lord's trumpet [1 Thess 4:16]. And He will wreak vengeance on His enemies and through the holy angels will separate the faithful from the unfaithful, the righteous from the unrighteous, the saints from the accursed and, in short, those who have walked uprightly in the Spirit of God from those who follow after the flesh; and for infinite and endless ages, as the truth of God's declarations affirm, He will render to each the just reward of the life that one has led. (ch. 14)

God is the same reality, sometimes to be thought of in one way, sometimes in the other. For the Holy Trinity of Persons is an unconfused Unity in essence and in its simple nature; and the holy Unity is a Trinity of persons in its mode of existence. We are to think of both of these distinctly, first one way, then the other: one, single, undivided, unconfused, simple, undiminished, and unchangeable Divinity, completely one in essence and completely three in Persons, and sole ray shining in the single form of one triple-splendored Light. (ch. 23)

Those who are saved can be classed as slaves, mercenaries, or children. The slaves are the faithful who execute the Lord's commandments out of fear of threats and who willingly work for those who are obeyed. Mercenaries are those who out of a desire for promised benefits bear with patience "the burden of the day and the scorching heat" [Matt 20:12]—that is, the affliction innate in and yoked to the present life from the condemnation of our first parents, and the temptations from it on behalf of virtue, and who by free choice of will wisely exchange life for life, the present one for the future. Finally, children are the ones who out of neither fear of threats nor desire of promised things but rather out of character and habit of the voluntary inclination and disposition of the soul toward the good never become separated from God. (ch. 24)

The grace of adoption was given through holy baptism in the Holy Spirit and makes us perfect in Christ. (ch. 24)

Therefore, let us to the best of our ability not be careless in obeying God who calls us to eternal life and to a blessed end through the observance of His divine and saving commandments to "receive mercy and find grace to help in time of need" [Heb 4:16]. "For grace," says the divine apostle, is "with all who have an undying love for our Lord Jesus Christ" [Eph 6:24]. (ch. 24)

God is pleased with anything which is genuinely offered from the soul to the best of its ability, even if this seems small in comparison with great things. (Conclusion)

～ John of Damascus

John of Damascus (c. 675–749) is commonly recognized as the last of the Church Fathers. He lived in the capital of the Muslim state and, like his father, served in its treasury department. In due course, he obtained permission to enter the monastic life near Jerusalem. A faithful student of the Church Fathers before him, he synthesized their doctrinal teachings in *On the Orthodox Faith,* which stood for more than a millennium as the best comprehensive exposition of the faith of the Eastern Church. As a controversialist, he was the chief spokesman for the defenders of icons during the first phase of the iconoclastic controversy. In addition, he penned hymns that have endeared him to Christians through the ages in Western and Eastern Christianity alike.

Philosophical Chapters[1]

Philosophy is a love of wisdom. But true wisdom is God. Therefore, the love of God is the true philosophy. (ch. 3)

On Heresies[2]

We venerate the Cross of Christ, by which the power of the demons and the deceit of the devil were destroyed. (§101)

---

1 Excerpted from FC 37:3–110.
2 Excerpts taken from FC 37:111–163.

We believe in Father and Son and Holy Spirit; one Godhead in three hypostases; one will, one operation, alike in three Persons; wisdom incorporeal, uncreated, immortal, incomprehensible, without beginning, unmoved, unaffected, without quantity, without quality, ineffable, immutable, unchangeable, uncontained, equal in glory, equal in power, equal in majesty, equal in might, equal in nature, exceedingly substantial, exceedingly good, thrice radiant, thrice bright, thrice brilliant. Light is the Father, Light the Son, Light the Holy Spirit; Wisdom the Father, Wisdom the Son, Wisdom the Holy Spirit; one God and not three Gods; one Lord the Holy Trinity discovered in three hypostases. Father is the Father, and unbegotten; Son is the Son, begotten and not unbegotten, for He is from the Father; Holy Spirit, not begotten but proceeding, for He is from the Father. There is nothing created, nothing of the first and second order, nothing of lord and servant; but there is Unity and Trinity—there was, there is, and there shall be forever. This is perceived and adored by faith—by faith, not by inquiry, nor by searching out, nor by visible manifestation: for the more He is sought out, the more He is unknown, and the more He is investigated, the more He is hidden. And so, let the faithful adore God with a mind that is not over-curious. And believe that He is God in three hypostases, although the manner in which He is so is beyond manner. For God is incomprehensible. Do not ask how the Trinity is Trinity, for the Trinity is inscrutable. But, if you are curious about God, first tell me of yourself and the things that pertain to you. How does your soul have existence? How is your mind set in motion? How do you produce your mental concepts? How is it that you are both mortal and immortal? But if you are ignorant of these things which are within you, then why do you not shudder at the thought of investigating the sublime things of heaven? (§103)

The Holy Trinity transcends by far every similitude and figure. (§103)

The Orthodox Faith[3]

The Godhead is ineffable and incomprehensible. . . . No one has even known God unless God Himself revealed it to him. (1:1)

God has not gone so far as to leave us in complete ignorance. . . . He has given us knowledge of Himself in accordance with our capacity. (1:1)

---

3 Excerpts taken from FC 37:165–406.

He has revealed to us what it was expedient for us to know, but what we were unable to bear He has withheld. (1:2)

[In talking about God:] We are obliged to express in human terms things which transcend the human order. (1:2)

What the substance of God is, or how it is in all things, or how the only begotten Son, who was God, emptied Himself out and became human from a virgin's blood, being formed by another law that transcended nature, or how He walked dry-shod upon the waters, we neither understand nor can say. (1:2)

All things are either created or uncreated. (1:3)

The very harmony of creation, its preservation and governing, teach us that there is a God who has put all this together and keeps it together, ever maintaining it and providing for it. (1:3)

It is clear that God exists, but what He is in essence and nature is unknown and beyond all understanding. (1:4)

The fact of His being unbegotten, without beginning, immutable, and incorruptible, or any of those other things which are affirmed of God or about Him—these do not show what He is, but rather what He is not. (1:4)

He does not belong to the number of beings, not because He does not exist, but because He transcends all beings and being itself. (1:4)

The Divinity, then, is limitless and incomprehensible, and this His limitlessness and incomprehensibility is all that can be understood about Him. (1:4)

All that we state affirmatively about God does not show His nature, but only what relates to His nature. (1:4)

We believe in one God, . . . maker of all things both visible and invisible, holding together all things and conserving them, provider for all, governing and dominating and ruling over all in unending and immortal reign; without contradiction, filling all things, contained by nothing, but Himself containing all things, being their conserver and first possessor; pervading all substances without being defiled, removed far beyond all things and every substance as being supersubstantial and surpassing all, supereminently divine and good and replete; . . . above essence and life and speech and concept; . . . the very source of being for all things that are . . . ; known in three perfect Persons and adored with one adoration, believed in and worshiped by every rational creature, united without confusion and distinct without separation, which is beyond understanding. We believe in Father and Son and Holy Spirit in whom we have been baptized. (1:8)

It is impossible to find in creation any image which exactly portrays the manner of the Holy Trinity in itself. (1:8)

One should not suppose that any of these things which are affirmed of God is indicative of what He is in essence. Rather, they show either what He is not, or some relation to some one of those things that are contrasted with Him, or something of those things which are consequential to His nature or operation. (1:9)

Since we are human beings clothed in this gross flesh, we are unable to think or speak of the divine, lofty, and immaterial operations of the Godhead unless we have recourse to images, types, and symbols that correspond to our own nature. (1:11)

Since the Divinity is incomprehensible, He must remain absolutely nameless. Accordingly, since we do not know His essence, let us not look for a name for His essence, for names are indicative of what things are. . . . So, in His ineffable goodness He sees fit to be named from things which are on the level of our nature, that we may not be entirely bereft of knowledge of Him but may have at least some dim understanding. (1:12)

He is the Spirit of the Son, not as being from Him, but as proceeding through Him from that Father—for the Father alone is Cause. (1:12)

He alone is incomprehensible, undefinable, and known by no one; and He alone has a clear vision of Himself. (1:13)

God, although invisible by nature, becomes visible through His operations we know from the arrangement of the world and from its governing. (1:13)

It is His nature that communicates all good to His own creatures in accordance with the capacity of each. (1:14)

Toward Him all things tend, and in Him they have their existence, and to all things He communicates their being in accordance with the nature of each. (1:14)

He who exists before the ages made the ages. (2:1)

Now, because the good and transcendentally good God was not content to contemplate Himself, but by a superabundance of goodness saw fit that there should be some things to benefit by and participate in His goodness, He brings all things from nothing into being and creates them, both visible and invisible, and humanity, made up of both. By thinking He creates, and, with the Word fulfilling and the Spirit perfecting, the object of His thought subsists. (2:2)

[Upon reviewing various views about how creation came to be:] Whichever way it may be, all things have been made and established by the command of God and have their foundation in the divine will and desire. (2:6)

With his own hands he created humankind after his own image and likeness from the visible and invisible natures. . . . He made them a sort of miniature world within the larger one. . . . A human being is a microcosm. (2:12)

We maintain that transformation and change are inherent in created beings. For everything that is created is also changeable, because whatever has originated in a change must needs be subject to change. (2:27)

Providence, then, is the solicitude which God has for existing things. And again, providence is that will of God by which all existing things receive suitable guidance through to their end. (2:29)

One should note that, while the choice of things that may be done rests with us, the accomplishment of the good ones is due to the cooperation of God, who in accordance with His foreknowledge justly cooperates with those who in right conscience choose the good. (2:29)

John of Damascus

One should furthermore bear in mind that the ways of God's providence are many, and that they can neither be explained in words nor grasped by the mind. (2:29)

Repentance is a return through discipline and toil from that which is against nature to that which is according to it, from the devil to God. (2:30)

And so it was that man was overcome by the envy of the devil. For that envious and hateful demon, having himself been brought low by his conceit, would not suffer us to attain the higher things. [WSol 2:23, 24]. So the liar tempted that wretched man with the very hope of divinity, and, having raised him up to his own heights of conceit, dragged him down to the same abyss of ruin. (2:30)

Man succumbed to the assault of the demon, the author of evil; he failed to keep the Creator's commandment and was stripped of grace and deprived of that familiarity which he had enjoyed with God. . . . He was excluded from Paradise by the just judgment of God, condemned to death, and made subject to corruption. (3:1)

Since it was by sin that death had come into the world like some wild and savage beast to destroy the life of humanity, it was necessary for the one who was to effect a redemption to be sinless and not liable to the death which is due to sin. And it was further necessary for human nature to be strengthened and renewed, to be taught by experience and to learn the way of virtue which turns back from destruction and leads to eternal life. (3:1)

And since the enemy had caught humanity with the bait of the hope of divinity, he himself was taken with the bait of the barrier of the flesh. (3:1)

He did not have another conquer the tyrant, nor did He snatch humanity away from death by force, but He, the good and just, made him victor against death whom death had once enslaved through sin. (3:1)

He, while being perfect God, became perfect man and accomplished the newest of all new things, the only new thing under the sun [Eccl 1:9]. (3:1)

We recognize both the miracles and the sufferings as His [Christ's], even though it was in one nature that He worked miracles and in another that He endured suffering. (3:3)

[Regarding the completeness and purpose of the Incarnation:] He in his entirety assumed me in my entirety and was wholly united to the whole, so that He might bestow the grace of salvation upon the whole. For that which has not been assumed cannot be healed. (3:6)

We venerate His two begettings—one from the Father before the ages and surpassing cause and reason and time and nature, and one in later times for our sake, after our own manner, and surpassing us. For our sake, because it was for the sake of our salvation; after our own manner, because He was made man from a woman and with a period of gestation; and surpassing us, because, surpassing the law of conception, He was not from seed but from the Holy Spirit and the holy Virgin Mary. (3:7)

By saying "perfect God and perfect man" we show the fullness and completeness of the natures, while by saying "God entire and man entire" we point out the individuality and the indivisibility of the Person. (3:7)

The Word was made flesh without giving up His own immateriality, and He was wholly made flesh while remaining wholly uncircumscribed. (3:7)

Christ, then, who is perfect God and perfect man, is one. Him do we adore with the Father and the Spirit together with His immaculate body in one adoration. And we do not say that His body is not to be adored, because it is adored in the one Person of the Word who became Person to it. Yet we do not worship the creature, because we do not adore it as a mere body, but as being one with the Divinity, because His two natures belong to the one Person and the one subsistence of the Word of God. (3:8)

The whole choir of inspired Fathers bear witness to the fact that the thrice-holy hymn [Is 6:3] is not addressed to the Son alone, but to the Holy Trinity, saying that by the threefold sanctification the holy seraphim are intimating to us the three Persons of the supersubstantial Godhead. (3:10)

And we proclaim the holy virgin to be properly and truly Mother of God [Theotokos]. For, as He who was born of her is true God, so is she truly mother of God who gave birth to the true God who took His flesh from her. Now, we do not say that God was born of her in the sense that the Divinity of the Word has its beginnings of being from her, but in the sense that God the Word Himself, who was timelessly begotten of the Father before the ages and exists without beginning and eternally with the Father and the Holy Spirit, did in the last days come for our salvation to dwell in her womb and of her was, without undergoing change, made flesh and born. For the holy virgin did not give birth to a mere man but to true God, and not to God simply, but to God made flesh. And He did not bring His body down from heaven and come through her as through a channel, but assumed from her a body consubstantial with us and subsisting in Himself. (3:12)

God the Word was made human for this reason: so that the very nature which had sinned, fallen, and become corrupt should conquer the tyrant who had deceived it. (3:12)

In so far as He was made human, He was born corporeally and did not come to inhabit a previously formed man, as a prophet, but Himself substantially and truly became human—that is, He made flesh animated by a rational and intellectual soul subsist in His Person and Himself became the Person to it. (3:12)

We rightly and truly call holy Mary the mother of God, for this name expresses the entire mystery of the Incarnation. (3:12)

Christ's humanity was not first made like us and then made to surpass us. On the contrary, it was always both from its first beginning of being, because from the first instant of conception it had its existence in the Word himself. (3:12)

Since we confess our Lord Jesus Christ to be at once both perfect God and perfect man, we declare that this same one has all things that the Father has, except the being unbegotten, and, with the sole exception of sin, all that the first Adam has—namely, a body and a rational and intellectual soul. We furthermore declare that corresponding to His two natures He has the twofold set of natural properties belonging to the two natures—two natural wills, the divine and the human; two natural operations, a divine and a human; two natural freedoms, a divine and a human; and wisdom and knowledge, both divine and human. For, since He is consubstantial with God the Father, He freely wills and acts as God. And since He is also consubstantial with us, the same one freely wills and acts as man. Thus, the miracles are His, and so are the sufferings. (3:13)

Because of the Fall, we went from what is according to nature to what is against it. But the Lord brought us back from what is against nature to what is according to it. (3:14)

He became human in order that what had been conquered might conquer. Now, it was not impossible for Him who can do all things to deliver humanity from the tyrant by His almighty power and might; but had the tyrant after having conquered humanity been prevailed over by God, he would have had grounds for complaint. For this reason the compassionate and loving God wished to make the victor him who had fallen, and so He became man and restored like by like. (3:18)

That which has not been assumed has not been healed. And so, He assumes the whole man, who had fallen through weakness, and his most noble part, in order that He might grace the whole with salvation. (3:18)

Consequently, while He had naturally the power of willing both as God and as man, the human will followed after and was subordinated to His will, not being motivated by its own opinion, but willing what His divine will willed. (3:18)

We do not say that the operations are separated and that the natures act separately, but we say that they act conjointly, with each nature doing in communion with the other that which it has proper to itself. (3:19)

Moreover, we confess that He assumed all the natural and blameless passions of humanity. This is because He assumed the whole man and everything that is his, except sin. (3:20)

He assumed all that He might sanctify all. He was put to the test and He conquered that He might gain for us the victory and give to our nature the power to conquer the adversary, so that through the very assaults by which the nature had been conquered of old it might conquer its former victor. (3:20)

Examples do not have to be absolutely and unfailingly exact, for, just because it is an example, one must find in it that which is like and that which is unlike. For likeness in everything would be identity and not an example, which is especially true with divine things. So, in the matter of theology and the Incarnation, it is impossible to find an absolutely perfect example. (3:26)

[Regarding the saving efficacy of Christ's death:] Death approaches, gulps down the bait of the body, and is pierced by the hook of the Divinity. Then, having tasted of the sinless and life-giving body, it is destroyed and gives up all those whom it had swallowed down of old. (3:27)

What we call the right hand of the Father is the glory and honor of the Godhead in which the Son of God existed as God and consubstantial with the Father before the ages and in which, having in the last days become incarnate, He sits corporeally with His flesh glorified together with Him, for He and His flesh are adored together with one adoration by all creation. (4:2)

Creation has been sanctified with the divine blood. (4:4)

O Christ, all things are Yours and You ask nothing of us but that we be saved. Even this You have given us, and by Your ineffable goodness You are grateful to those who accept it. (4:4)

We were made children of God through Him by being adopted through baptism. (4:8)

We confess one baptism unto remission of sins and life everlasting. . . . Therefore, just as the death of the Lord happened but once, so it is necessary to be baptized but once. (4:9)

He made a fountain of forgiveness gush out for us from His sacred and immaculate side. (4:9)

All the things of God are above the natural order and beyond speech and understanding. (4:11)

Faith is an assent devoid of all curiosity. (4:11)

By the Cross all things have been set right. (4:11)

We also adore the likeness of the honorable and life-giving Cross, even though it be made of another material [than wood], not that we honor the material—God forbid!—but the likeness as a symbol of Christ. (4:11)

Since we are composed of a visible and an invisible nature—one both intellectual and sensitive, that is—we also offer a twofold worship to the Creator. (4:12)

Everything beautiful should be dedicated to God, from whom everything that is good receives its goodness. (4:12)

"Through him are all things" [Rom 11:36], not only because He has brought them from nothing into being, but because it is by His operation that all things He made are kept in existence and held together. (4:13)

By His own birth, or incarnation, and by His baptism and Passion and Resurrection, He freed our nature from the sin of our first parent, from death and corruption. And He became the first-fruit of the resurrection and set Himself to be a way, a model, and an example, so that we too might follow in His footsteps and become by adoption, as He is by nature, children and heirs of God and joint heirs together with Him. Thus, He gave us a second birth, so that, as we had been born of Adam and had been likened to him and had become heir to his Curse and corruption, we might by being born anew of Him be likened to Him and become heir to His incorruption and blessing and glory. (4:13)

And now you ask how the bread becomes the body of Christ and the wine and water the blood of Christ. And I tell you that the Holy Spirit comes down and works these things which are beyond description and understanding. (4:13)

The very bread and wine are changed into the body and blood of God. However, should you inquire as to the manner in which this is done, let it suffice for you to hear that it is done through the Holy Spirit, just as it was through the Holy Spirit that the Lord made flesh subsist for Himself and in Himself from the blessed mother of God. And more than this we do not know, except that the Word of God is true and effective and omnipotent, but the manner in which it is so is impossible to find out. (4:13)

As Eve was formed from Adam without carnal conjunction, so did this one [Mary] bring forth the new Adam in accordance with the law of gestation but surpassing the nature of generation. Thus, He who is without a mother begotten of a Father was without a father born of a woman. (4:14)

Let us faithful do honor to the saints, through whom most especially honor is rendered to God. . . . Let us carefully observe their manner of life and emulate their faith, love, hope, zeal, life, patience under suffering, and perseverance unto death, so that we may also share their crowns of glory. (4:15)

We are disposed to virtuous action and untroubled contemplation by the sacred Scriptures. In them we find exhortation to every virtue and dissuasion from every vice. (4:17)

[Regarding reading Scripture:] Should we read once and then a second time and still not understand what we are reading, let us not be discouraged. Rather, let us persist, let us meditate and inquire. (4:17)

Let us revel in them [the Scriptures], let us revel greedily in them to satiety, for they contain the grace which cannot be exhausted. Should we, however, be able to get some profit from other sources, this is not forbidden. (4:17)

The true celebration of the Sabbath is the desisting from sin. (4:23)

Circumcision was a sign by which Israel was set apart from the Gentiles among whom they lived. Now, this was a figure of baptism, for just as circumcision cuts off from the body a part which is not useful, but a useless superfluity, so by holy baptism are we circumcised of sin. (4:25)

If there is no resurrection, there is no God and no providence, and all things are being driven and carried along by mere chance. For just consider how many righteous people we see in need and suffering injury, yet getting no recompense in this present life, whereas we see sinners and the wicked possessing wealth and every luxury in abundance. Who in his right mind would understand this to be the work of righteous judgment or wise providence? Therefore, there will be, there certainly will be, a resurrection. For God is just and He rewards those who await Him in patience. Now, if the soul had engaged alone in the contest for virtue, then it would also be crowned alone; and if it alone had indulged in sinful pleasures, then it alone could be justly punished. However, since the soul followed neither virtue nor vice without the body, it will be just for them to receive their recompense together. (4:27)

And so, with our souls again united to our bodies, which will have become incorrupt and put off corruption, we shall rise again and stand before the terrible judgment seat of Christ. And the devil and his demons, and his man—which is to say, the Antichrist—and the impious and sinners will be given over to everlasting fire, which will not be a material fire such as we are accustomed to, but a fire such as God might know. And those who have done good will shine like the sun together with the angels unto eternal life with our Lord Jesus Christ, ever seeing Him and being seen, enjoying the unending bliss which is from Him, and praising Him together with the Father and the Holy Spirit unto the endless ages of ages. Amen. (4:27)

Against the Attackers of the Holy Images[4]

A small thing is not small when it leads to something great; and it is no small matter to forsake the ancient tradition of the Church which was upheld by all those who were called before us, whose conduct we should observe, and whose faith we should imitate. (1:2)

I do not adore the creation rather than the Creator, but I adore the one who became a creature, who was formed as I was, who clothed Himself in creation without weakening or departing from His divinity, that He might raise our nature in glory and make us partakers of His divine nature. (1:4)

Fleshly nature was not lost when it became part of the Godhead, but just as the Word made flesh remained the Word, so also flesh became the Word, yet remained flesh, being united to the person of the Word. Therefore I boldly draw an image of the invisible God, not as invisible, but as having become visible for our sakes by partaking of flesh and blood. I do not draw an image of the immortal Godhead, but I paint the image of God who became visible in the flesh. (1:4)

---

4 Excerpts taken from David Anderson, trans., *St. John of Damascus, On the Divine Images: Three Apologies Against Those Who Attack the Divine Images* (Crestwood, NY: St. Vladimir's Seminary Press, 1980), pp. 13–107.

John of Damascus

It is obvious that when you contemplate God becoming man, then you may depict Him clothed in human form. When the invisible One becomes visible to flesh, you may then draw His likeness. When He who is bodiless and without form, immeasurable in the boundlessness of His own nature, existing in the form of God, empties Himself and takes the form of a servant in substance and in stature and is found in a body of flesh, then you may draw His image and show it to anyone willing to gaze upon it. (1:8)

Anyone would say that our inability immediately to direct our thoughts to contemplation of higher things makes it necessary that familiar everyday media be utilized to give suitable form to what is formless, and make visible what cannot be depicted, so that we are able to construct understandable analogies. If, therefore, the Word of God, in providing for our every need, always presents to us what is intangible by clothing it with form, does it not accomplish this by making an image using what is common to nature and so brings within our reach that for which we long but are unable to see? A certain perception takes place in the brain, prompted by the bodily senses, which is then transmitted to the faculties of discernment, and adds to the treasury of knowledge something that was not there before. (1:11)

Again, things which have already taken place are remembered by means of images.... These images are of two kinds: either they are words written in books, as when God had the law engraved on tablets and desired the lives of holy men to be recorded, or else they are material images, such as the jar of manna, or Aaron's staff, which were to be kept in the ark as a memorial. (1:13)

In former times God, who is without form or body, could never be depicted. But now when God is seen in the flesh conversing with men, I make an image of the God whom I see. I do not worship matter; I worship the Creator of matter who became matter for my sake, who willed to take His abode in matter; who worked out my salvation through matter. (1:16)

Do not despise matter, for it is not despicable. God has made nothing despicable. To think such things is Manichaeism. Only that which does not have its source in God is despicable—that which is our own invention, our willful choice to disregard the law of God—namely, sin. (1:16)

If we attempted to make an image of the invisible God, this would be sinful indeed. It is impossible to portray one who is without body: invisible, uncircumscribed, and without form. Again, if we made images of men and believed them to be gods, and adored them as if they were so, we would be truly impious. We do neither of these things. But we are not mistaken if we make the image of God incarnate, who was seen on earth in the flesh. (2:5)

Though the mind wear itself out with the effort, it can never cast away its bodily nature. (2:5)

It is good to search the Scriptures, but we must attend to them with a discerning mind. Beloved, it is impossible that God should prove false. (2:7)

Since divine nature has assumed our nature, we have been given a life-bearing and saving remedy, which has glorified our nature and led it to incorruption. (2:11)

If you speak of pagan abuses, these abuses do not make our veneration of images loathsome.... Pagans make images into demons, and Israel made images into gods, for they said, "These are your gods, O Israel, who brought you up out of the land of Egypt" [Ex 32:4]. But we have set up images of the true God, who became incarnate. (2:17)

God Himself first made an image, and presented images to our sight, for "God created man in his own image" [Gen 1:27]. (2:20)

Since we are fashioned of both soul and body, and our souls are not naked spirits, but are covered, as it were, with a fleshly veil, it is impossible for us to think without using physical images. Just as we physically listen to perceptible words in order to understand spiritual things, so also by using bodily sight we reach spiritual contemplation. (3:12)

No one [of the Old Testament worthies] saw the divine nature, but only the image and figure of what was yet to come. For the invisible Son and Word of God was to become truly man, that He might be united to our nature, and be seen on earth.... Shall I not make an image of Him who was seen in the nature of flesh for me? Shall I not worship and honor Him, through the honor and veneration of His image? (3:26)

May Christ fill you, His priestly flock, the Christian people, the holy nation, the body of the Church, with the joy of His Resurrection, and make us worthy to follow in the footsteps of the saints, the shepherds and teachers of the Church, leading us to enjoy His glory in the radiance of the saints. May you attain His love and glorify Him forever, with the unoriginate Father, to whom be glory unto ages of ages. Amen. (3:42)

Hymns of the Resurrection[5]

☩   The day of Resurrection! Earth, tell it out abroad,
     the Passover of gladness, the Passover of God.
From death to life eternal, from sin's dominion free,
     our Christ has brought us over with hymns of victory.

Let hearts be purged of evil that we may see aright
     the Lord in rays eternal of Resurrection light,
     and, listening to His accents, may hear so calm and plain
     His own "All hail!" and, hearing, may raise the victor strain.

Now let the heavens be joyful, let earth its song begin,
     let all the world keep triumph and all that is therein.
Let all things, seen and unseen, their notes of gladness blend;
     for Christ the Lord has risen, our joy that has no end.

☩   Come, you faithful, raise the strain of triumphant gladness;
God has brought His people forth into joy from sadness.
Now rejoice, Jerusalem, and with true affection
     welcome in unwearied strains Jesus' Resurrection.

'Tis the spring of life today! Christ has burst His prison,
     and from three days' sleep in death like the sun has risen.
All the winter of our sins, long and dark, is flying;
     welcome now the light of Christ, give Him praise undying.

"Alleluia!" now we cry to our King immortal,
     who, triumphant, burst the bars of the tomb's dark portal;
"Alleluia!" with the Son, God the Father praising;
"Alleluia!" yet again to the Spirit raising.

---

5 These are in the public domain.

~ Permissions

Works in the Public Domain

I hereby acknowledge my use of the following translations of patristic works. Since they are all in the public domain, I have sometimes revised the translations to bring them to contemporary English usage, for the sake of greater readability. These revisions included simplifying sentence structures and punctuation and, where appropriate, use of gender-inclusive language (for human beings).

BAKER BOOK HOUSE

The Ecclesiastical History of Eusebius Pamphilius. Translated by Isaac Boyle. 1850. Reprint, Grand Rapids, MI, 1969.

Holmes, Michael W., ed. *The Apostolic Fathers: Greek Texts and English Translations of Their Writings.* 2nd ed. Translated by J. B. Lightfoot and J. R. Harmer. Grand Rapids, MI, 1992.

BURT FRANKLIN

The Paradise or Garden of the Holy Fathers, Being Histories of the Anchorites, Recluses, Monks, Coenobites, and Ascetic Fathers of the Deserts of Egypt Between A.D. 250 and A.D. 400: Compiled By Athanasius, Archbishop of Alexandria; Palladius, Bishop of Helenopolis; Saint Jerome, and Others.

2 vols. Translated and edited by Ernest A. Wallis. 1907. Reprint, New York, 1972.

DORSET PRESS

St. Augustine: Confessions. Translated by R. S. Pine-Coffin. New York, 1961.

MODERN LIBRARY

St. Augustine: The City of God. Translated by Marcus Dods. New York, 1993.

WILLIAM B. EERDMANS PUBLISHING

Alexander Roberts and James Donaldson, eds. Ante-Nicene Fathers. 10 vols. 1885–1896. Reprint, Peabody, MA: Hendrickson Publishers, 2004.

————. Nicene and Post-Nicene Fathers, First Series. 14 vols. 1886–1900. Reprint, Peabody, MA: Hendrickson Publishers, 2004.

————. Nicene and Post-Nicene Fathers, Second Series. 14 vols. 1886–1900. Reprint, Peabody, MA: Hendrickson Publishers, 2004.

Copyright Permissions

It is a privilege to express gratitude to the following publishing houses and authors for permissions to reproduce excerpts from their published works, granted with the privilege of altering or editing the excerpts for the purposes of bringing them into conformity with Conciliar Press practices, simplifying sentence structures and punctuation, and, where appropriate, using gender-inclusive language.

CATHOLIC UNIVERSITY OF AMERICA PRESS, FROM THE SERIES FATHERS OF THE CHURCH (FC)

Vincent of Lérins: Commonitories. Translated by Rudolph E. Morris. FC 7. Washington, DC, 1949.

Clement of Alexandria: Christ the Educator. Translated by Simon P. Wood. FC 23. Washington, DC, 1954.

Saint Hilary of Poitiers: The Trinity. Translated by Stephen McKenna. FC 25. Washington, DC, 1954.

St. Leo the Great: Letters. Translated by Edmund Hunt, C.S.C. FC 34. Washington, DC, 1957.

Saint John of Damascus: Writings. Translated by Frederic H. Chase, Jr. FC 37. Washington, DC, 1958.

Saint Ambrose: Hexaemeron, Paradise, and Cain and Abel. Translated by John J. Savage. FC 42. Washington, DC, 1961.

Saint Ambrose: Theological and Dogmatic Works. Translated by Roy J. Deferrari. FC 44. Washington, DC, 1963.

Lactantius: The Divine Institutes. Translated by Sr. Mary Francis McDonald. FC 49. Washington, DC, 1964.

Lactantius: The Minor Works. Translated by Sr. Mary Francis McDonald. FC 54. Washington, DC, 1965.

The Works of Saint Cyril of Jerusalem. 2 vols. Translated by Leo P. McCauley, S.J., and Anthony A. Stephenson. FC 61 and 64. Washington, DC, 1969, 1970.

St. John Chrysostom: On the Incomprehensible Nature of God. Translated by Paul W. Harkins. FC 72. Washington, DC, 1982.

PAULIST PRESS, FROM THE SERIES CLASSICS OF WESTERN SPIRITUALITY

Gregory of Nyssa: The Life of Moses. Translated by Abraham J. Malherbe and Everett Ferguson. Mahwah, NJ, 1978.

Origen: An Exhortation to Martyrdom; Prayer; First Principles: Book IV; Prologue to the Commentary on The Song of Songs; Homily XXVII on Numbers. Translated by Rowan A. Greer. Mahwah, NJ, 1979.

Athanasius: The Life of Antony and the Letter to Marcellinus. Translated by Robert C. Gregg. Mahwah, NJ, 1980.

John Cassian: Conferences. Translated by Colm Luibheid. Mahwah, NJ, 1985.

Maximus Confessor: Selected Writings. Translated by George C. Berthold. Mahwah, NJ, 1985.

Pseudo-Dionysius: The Complete Works. Translated by Colm Luibheid. Mahwah, NJ, 1987.

Pseudo-Macarius: The Fifty Spiritual Homilies and the Great Letter. Translated by George A. Maloney. Mahwah, NJ, 1992.

PAULIST PRESS, FROM THE SERIES ANCIENT CHRISTIAN WRITERS: THE WORKS OF THE FATHERS IN TRANSLATION (ACW [ORIGINALLY PUBLISHED BY NEWMAN PRESS])

St. Augustine: The First Catechetical Instruction. Translated by Joseph P. Christopher. ACW 2. Westminster, MD, 1946.

St. Augustine: Faith, Hope, and Charity. Translated by Louis A. Arand. ACW 3. Westminster, MD, 1947.

Julianus Pomerius: The Contemplative Life. Translated by Sr. Mary Josephine Suelzer. ACW 4. Westminster, MD, 1947.

St. Augustine: The Lord's Sermon on the Mount. Translated by John J. Jepson. Edited by Johannes Quasten and Joseph Plumpe. ACW 5. Westminster, MD, 1948.

St. Gregory the Great: Pastoral Care. Translated by Henry Davis, S.J. ACW 11. Westminster, MD, 1950.

St. Augustine: Against the Academics. Translated by John J. O'Meara. ACW 12. Westminster, MD, 1950.

Tertullian: Treatises on Marriage and Remarriage. Translated by William P. Le Saint, S.J. ACW 13. Westminster, MD, 1951.

St. Prosper of Aquitaine: The Call of All Nations. Translated by P. De Letter, S.J. ACW 14. Westminster, MD, 1952.

St. Irenaeus: Proof of the Apostolic Preaching. Translated by Joseph P. Smith. ACW 16. Westminster, MD, 1952.

St. Gregory of Nyssa: The Lord's Prayer; The Beatitudes. Translated by Hilda C. Graef. ACW 18. Westminster, MD, 1954.

Rufinus: A Commentary on the Apostles' Creed. Translated and annotated by J. N. D. Kelly. ACW 20. Westminster, MD, 1955.

St. Maximus the Confessor: The Ascetic Life; The Four Centuries on Charity. Translated by Polycarp Sherwood, O.S.B. ACW 21. Westminster, MD, 1955.

Tertullian: The Treatise against Hermogenes. Translated by J. H. Waszink. Edited by Johannes Quasten and Joseph C. Plumpe. ACW 24. Westminster, MD, 1956.

St. Cyprian: The Lapsed; The Unity of the Catholic Church. Translated by Maurice Bevenot, S.J. ACW 25. Westminster, MD, 1957.

Tertullian: On Penitence and On Purity. Translated by William P. Le Saint, S.J. ACW 28. Westminster, MD, 1959.

The Octavius of Marcus Minucius Felix. Translated by G. W. Clarke. ACW 39. Westminster, MD, 1974.

PICKWICK PUBLICATIONS

Irenaeus on the Christian Faith: A Condensation of "Against Heresies." Revised, edited, and with an introduction by James R. Payton, Jr. Eugene, OR, 2011.

SISTERS OF THE LOVE OF GOD PRESS AND REV. DR. JOHN A. MCGUCKIN

Saint Gregory Nazianzen: Selected Poems. Translated by John A. McGuckin. Fairacres, Oxford, England, 1986.

WESTMINSTER JOHN KNOX PRESS, FROM THE SERIES LIBRARY OF CHRISTIAN CLASSICS

Christology of the Later Fathers. Translated by Edward E. Hardy. Louisville, KY, 1954.

Early Latin Theology: Selections from Tertullian, Cyprian, Ambrose, and Jerome. Translated by S. L. Greenslade. Louisville, KY, 1956.

I am also pleased to express gratitude to the following publishing houses and authors for permissions to reproduce excerpts from their published works, which appear in the precise form in which they were originally published.

CLARENDON PRESS AND REV. PROF. STUART G. HALL

Melito of Sardis: On Pascha and Fragments. Translated and edited by Stuart George Hall. Oxford, 1979. (A new edition is planned, date uncertain.)

CONSTABLE & ROBINSON AND M. L. ALLEN, COPYRIGHT OWNER OF HELEN WADDELL'S ESTATE

The Desert Fathers. Translated and edited by Helen Waddell. London, 1936.

EDWIN MELLEN PRESS

A Comparison between a King and a Monk /Against the Opponents of the Monastic Life: Two Treatises by John Chrysostom. Translated and with an introduction by David G. Hunter. Studies in the Bible and Early Christianity 13. Lewiston/Queenston, Ontario, 1989.

NORTHERN ILLINOIS UNIVERSITY PRESS

St. Maximus the Confessor's Questions and Doubts. Translated by Despina D. Prassas. DeKalb, IL, 2010.

ST. VLADIMIR'S SEMINARY PRESS

St John Chrysostom: Six Books on the Priesthood. Translated and introduction by Graham Neville. Crestwood, NY, 1977.

St John Chrysostom: On Marriage and Family Life. Translated by Catharine P. Roth and David Anderson. Crestwood, NY, 1986.

St John of Damascus: On the Divine Images; Three Apologies against Those Who Attack the Divine Images. Translated by David Anderson. Crestwood, NY, 1980.

From Glory to Glory: Texts from Gregory of Nyssa's Mystical Writings. Translated and edited by Herbert Musurillo, S.J. Crestwood, NY, 1995.

St Cyril of Alexandria: On the Unity of Christ. Translated by John A. McGuckin. Crestwood, NY, 2000.

On God and Man: The Theological Poetry of St Gregory of Nazianzus. Translated by Peter Gilbert. Crestwood, NY, 2001.

On the Cosmic Mystery of Jesus Christ: Selected Writings from St Maximus the Confessor. Translated by Paul M. Blowers and Robert L. Wilken. Crestwood, NY, 2003.

ST. VLADIMIR'S SEMINARY PRESS
AND ALISTAIR STEWART

Hippolytus: On the Apostolic Tradition. Translated by Alistair Stewart. Crestwood, NY, 2001.

TAYLOR & FRANCIS BOOKS UK

Cyril of Alexandria. Translated and edited by Norman Russell. The Early Church Fathers. London and New York: Routledge, 2000.

About the Editor

James R. Payton, Jr., is Professor of History at Redeemer University College (Ancaster, Ontario), where he teaches Eastern European history, Orthodoxy, and Patristics. He taught a course on Orthodoxy in Osijek, Croatia, and gave presentations on Orthodoxy and its role in the 21st century in Ukraine, Russia, England, and North America; several of these presentations have appeared as articles in scholarly journals or chapters in books. Dr. Payton taught a patristics course in Zagreb, Croatia, and presented conference papers on Maximus Confessor and John of Damascus (both published in scholarly journals). He also published articles on Gregory of Nyssa and Irenaeus. He authored *Light from the Christian East: An Introduction to the Orthodox Tradition* (2007) and *Irenaeus on the Christian Faith* (2011).

~ Suggested Reading

Traveling Companions: Walking with the Saints of the Church
by Christopher Moorey
Do you long to establish a relationship with the saints, but find them—or the volumes written about them—a little intimidating? The saints started out as ordinary Christians, just like us, and they are waiting to accompany us on our journey to heaven if we will only reach out our hands. *Traveling Companions* is a manageable volume that briefly introduces saints from a variety of times, places, and walks of life, all in language that brings them close to contemporary readers' lives. You're sure to find companions here that you will be happy to walk with all the way to the Kingdom.
• Paperback, 296 pages, ISBN 978-1-936270-47-7

Words for Our Time: The Spiritual Words of Matthew the Poor
translated by James Helmy
The twentieth-century elder Abba Matta of Egypt, known in the West as Matthew the Poor, is widely regarded as the greatest Egyptian elder since St. Antony the Great. He produced a huge and varied body of work in Arabic, only a little of which has been translated into English. In addition, a great many of his informal talks to monks and visitors were recorded. This volume is the first appearance in English of a small selection of these talks.

Abba Matta had a marvelous ability to communicate the deepest spiritual truths in the simplest and most practical language, making them accessible and actionable to laypeople as well as monastics. He speaks to the heart rather than the head, gently exhorting the reader to pursue a deeper life in Christ. To read these talks is to sit at the feet of one of the greatest spiritual teachers of our age.

• Paperback, 208 pages, ISBN 978-1-936270-45-3

The Christian Old Testament: Looking at the Hebrew Scriptures through Christian Eyes
by Lawrence R. Farley

Many Christians see the Old Testament as "the other Testament": a source of exciting stories to tell the kids, but not very relevant to the Christian life. *The Christian Old Testament* reveals the Hebrew Scriptures as the essential context of Christianity, as well as a many-layered revelation of Christ Himself. Follow along as Fr. Lawrence Farley explores the Christian significance of every book of the Old Testament.

• Paperback, 160 pages, ISBN 978-1-936270-53-8

Orthodoxy and Heterodoxy: Finding the Way to Christ in a Complicated Religious Landscape (2017 edition)
by Andrew Stephen Damick

This new edition of the bestselling *Orthodoxy & Heterodoxy* is fully revised and significantly expanded. Major new features include a full chapter on Pentecostalism and the Charismatic movements and two new appendices (Relations with the Non-Orthodox and How and Why I Became an Orthodox Christian). More detail and more religions and movements have been included, and the book is now addressed broadly to both Orthodox and non-Orthodox, making it even more sharable than before.

Are you an Orthodox Christian who wonders how to explain to your Baptist grandmother, your Buddhist neighbor, or the Jehovah's Witness at your door how your faith differs from theirs? Or are you a member of another faith who is curious what Orthodoxy is all about? Look no further. In *Orthodoxy & Heterodoxy,* Fr. Andrew Stephen Damick covers the gamut of ancient heresies, modern Christian denominations, fringe groups, and major world religions, highlighting the main points of each faith. This book is an invaluable reference for anyone who wants to understand the faiths of those they come in contact with—as well as their own.

• Paperback, 416 pages, ISBN 978-1-944967-17-8

To obtain complete ordering information, visit our website:
store.ancientfaith.com

Ancient Faith Publishing hopes you have enjoyed and benefited from this book. The proceeds from the sales of our books only partially cover the costs of operating our nonprofit ministry—which includes both the work of **Ancient Faith Publishing** and the work of **Ancient Faith Radio**. Your financial support makes it possible to continue this ministry both in print and online. Donations are tax-deductible and can be made at **www.ancientfaith.com.**

To view our other publications,
please visit our website: **store.ancientfaith.com**

Bringing you Orthodox Christian music, readings,
prayers, teaching, and podcasts 24 hours a day since 2004 at
ancientfaith.com

www.ingramcontent.com/pod-product-compliance
Lightning Source LLC
Chambersburg PA
CBHW021426080526
44588CB00009B/445